KT-555-804

...onal Christmas Day Speech with this fantastic...

...begun to look a little stale. Just imagine how much more exciting this year's Queen's Speech would be if it was delivered by Long John Silver, Elvis Presley or Adolf Hitler!

Well now you don't have to imagine any more. Because, thanks to this fantastic free gift, you can Pimp the Queen on your television set on December 25th.

INSTRUCTIONS

Simply cut out the fab disguises along the dotted lines, decide who *YOU* want to deliver the speech and stick the appropriate pieces to your TV screen with Blu-tak or double-sided sticky tape.

Then sit back and enjoy the most exciting Queen's speech of the last 53 years!

We've even included a form, so you can ask her Royal Highness to tailor her performance to your chosen character.

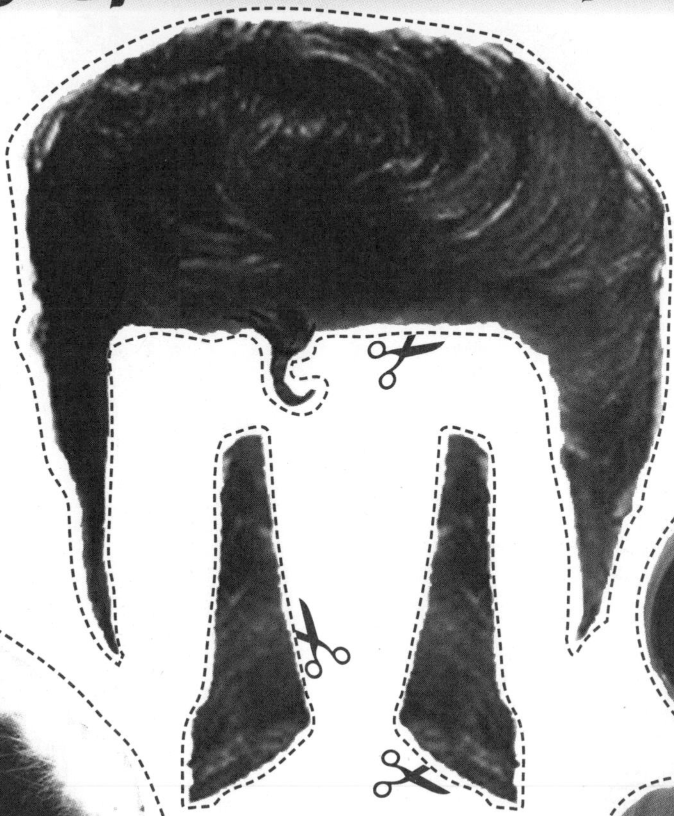
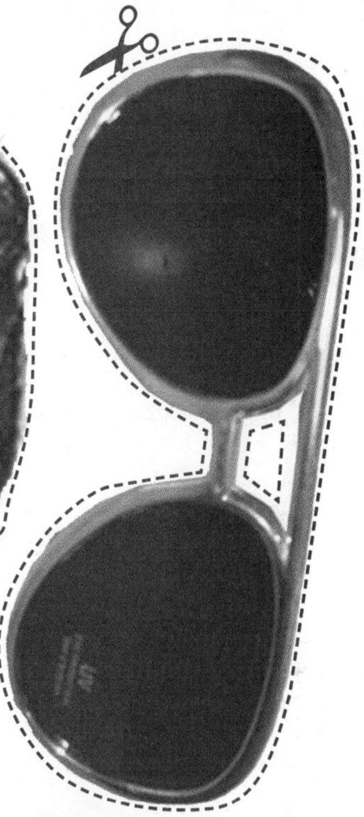
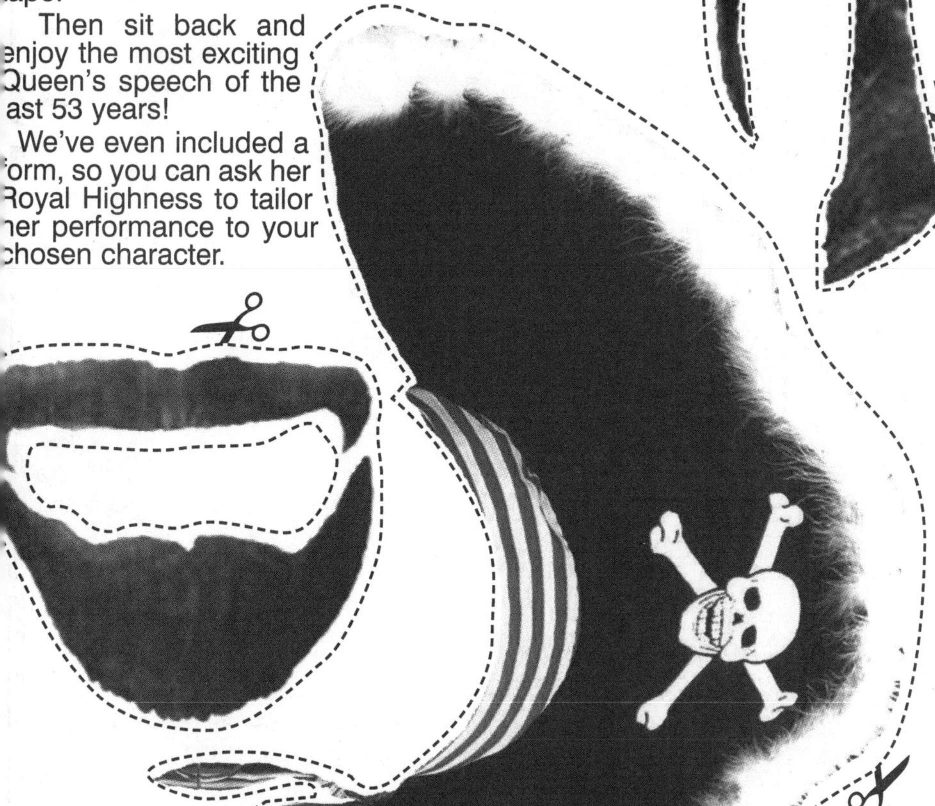

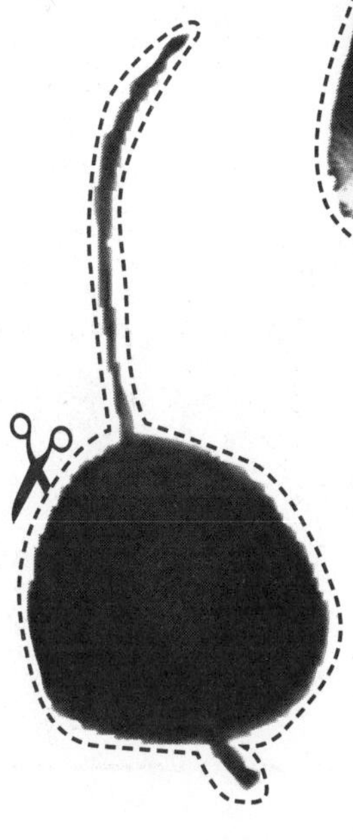

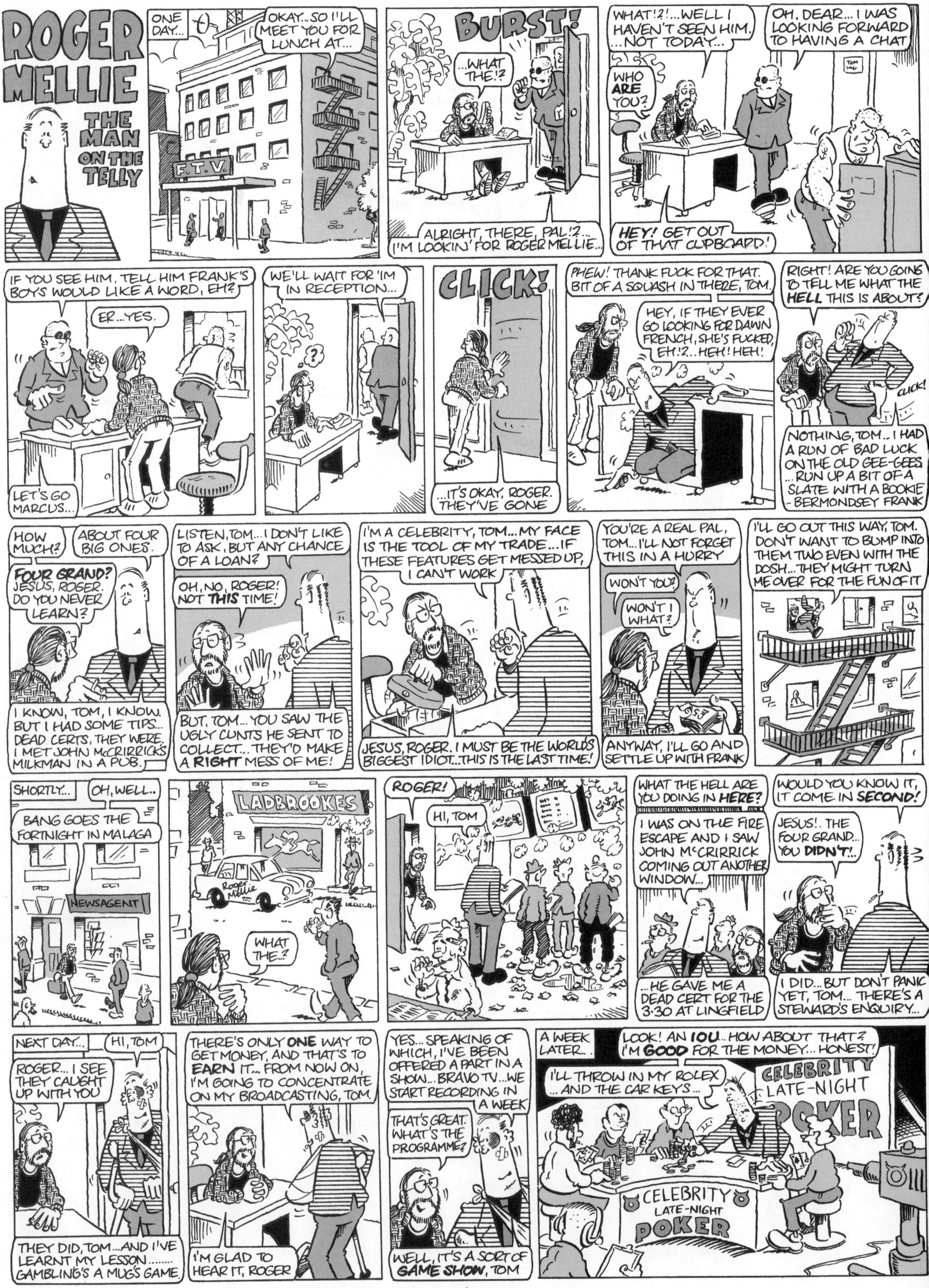
ROGER MELLIE
THE MAN ON THE TELLY
ONE DAY...
OKAY... SO I'LL MEET YOU FOR LUNCH AT...
F.T.V.
BURST!
...WHAT THE!?
ALRIGHT, THERE, PAL!?... I'M LOOKIN' FOR ROGER MELLIE...
WHAT!?!... WELL I HAVEN'T SEEN HIM. ...NOT TODAY...
OH, DEAR... I WAS LOOKING FORWARD TO HAVING A CHAT
WHO ARE YOU?
HEY! GET OUT OF THAT CUPBOARD!
IF YOU SEE HIM, TELL HIM FRANK'S BOYS WOULD LIKE A WORD, EH?
ER...YES.
LET'S GO MARCUS...
WE'LL WAIT FOR 'IM IN RECEPTION...
CLICK!
...IT'S OKAY, ROGER. THEY'VE GONE
PHEW! THANK FUCK FOR THAT. BIT OF A SQUASH IN THERE, TOM.
HEY, IF THEY EVER GO LOOKING FOR DAWN FRENCH, SHE'S FUCKED, EH!?...HEH! HEH!
RIGHT! ARE YOU GOING TO TELL ME WHAT THE HELL THIS IS ABOUT?
CLICK!
NOTHING, TOM... I HAD A RUN OF BAD LUCK ON THE OLD GEE-GEES ...RUN UP A BIT OF A SLATE WITH A BOOKIE - BERMONDSEY FRANK
HOW MUCH?
ABOUT FOUR BIG ONES.
FOUR GRAND? JESUS, ROGER. DO YOU NEVER LEARN?
I KNOW, TOM, I KNOW. BUT I HAD SOME TIPS... DEAD CERTS, THEY WERE. I MET JOHN McCRIRRICK'S MILKMAN IN A PUB.
LISTEN, TOM... I DON'T LIKE TO ASK, BUT ANY CHANCE OF A LOAN?
OH, NO, ROGER! NOT THIS TIME!
BUT, TOM... YOU SAW THE UGLY CUNTS HE SENT TO COLLECT... THEY'D MAKE A RIGHT MESS OF ME!
I'M A CELEBRITY, TOM... MY FACE IS THE TOOL OF MY TRADE... IF THESE FEATURES GET MESSED UP, I CAN'T WORK
JESUS, ROGER. I MUST BE THE WORLD'S BIGGEST IDIOT... THIS IS THE LAST TIME!
YOU'RE A REAL PAL, TOM... I'LL NOT FORGET THIS IN A HURRY
WON'T YOU?
WON'T I WHAT?
ANYWAY, I'LL GO AND SETTLE UP WITH FRANK
I'LL GO OUT THIS WAY, TOM. DON'T WANT TO BUMP INTO THEM TWO EVEN WITH THE DOSH... THEY MIGHT TURN ME OVER FOR THE FUN OF IT
SHORTLY...
OH, WELL..
BANG GOES THE FORTNIGHT IN MALAGA
NEWSAGENT
LADBROOKES
Roger Mellie
WHAT THE..?
ROGER!
HI, TOM
WHAT THE HELL ARE YOU DOING IN HERE?
I WAS ON THE FIRE ESCAPE AND I SAW JOHN McCRIRRICK COMING OUT ANOTHER WINDOW...
...HE GAVE ME A DEAD CERT FOR THE 3·30 AT LINGFIELD
WOULD YOU KNOW IT, IT COME IN SECOND!
JESUS!.. THE FOUR GRAND... YOU DIDN'T!..
I DID... BUT DON'T PANIC YET, TOM... THERE'S A STEWARD'S ENQUIRY...
NEXT DAY...
HI, TOM
ROGER... I SEE THEY CAUGHT UP WITH YOU
THEY DID, TOM... AND I'VE LEARNT MY LESSON........ GAMBLING'S A MUG'S GAME.
THERE'S ONLY ONE WAY TO GET MONEY, AND THAT'S TO EARN IT... FROM NOW ON, I'M GOING TO CONCENTRATE ON MY BROADCASTING, TOM.
I'M GLAD TO HEAR IT, ROGER
YES... SPEAKING OF WHICH, I'VE BEEN OFFERED A PART IN A SHOW... BRAVO TV... WE START RECORDING IN A WEEK
THAT'S GREAT. WHAT'S THE PROGRAMME?
WELL, IT'S A SORT OF GAME SHOW, TOM
A WEEK LATER...
LOOK! AN IOU.. HOW ABOUT THAT? I'M GOOD FOR THE MONEY... HONEST!
I'LL THROW IN MY ROLEX ... AND THE CAR KEYS...
CELEBRITY LATE-NIGHT POKER
CELEBRITY LATE-NIGHT POKER

Stand and Deliver! It's

VIZ

The Pearl Necklace

A heaving chest splattered with the rib-tickling cream of issues 142 - 151

Dandy Highwaymen:
Graham Dury, Wayne Gamble, Stevie Glover, Davey Jones, & Simon Thorp,

Cutpurses & Pickpockets:
Alex Collier, Simon Ecob, Robin Halstead, Jason Hazeley, Aidan Kelly, Alex Morris, Joel Morris, Paul Palmer, Lew Stringer, Cat Sullivan, Nick Tolson & Brian Walker.

Vagabond & Ruffian:
Richard "Dick Turpin" Downey

Swinging from the Gibbet:
Will "Turnip Dick" Watt

Published by Dennis Moore Publishing Ltd., 30 Yourmoneyoryourlife Street, London W1T 4JD

ISBN 0-9548577-7-1

First Printing Autumn 2007

© Fulchester Industries/Dennis Publishing Ltd. All rights reserved. No part of these valuables may be dropped into a small felt bag hung from a belt and/or galloped away with on the back of a swift, jet-black steed without prior written permission from Fulchester Industries and/or Dennis Publishing Ltd.

Printed in Ye Olde Englande

Subscribe online at:
www.viz.co.uk

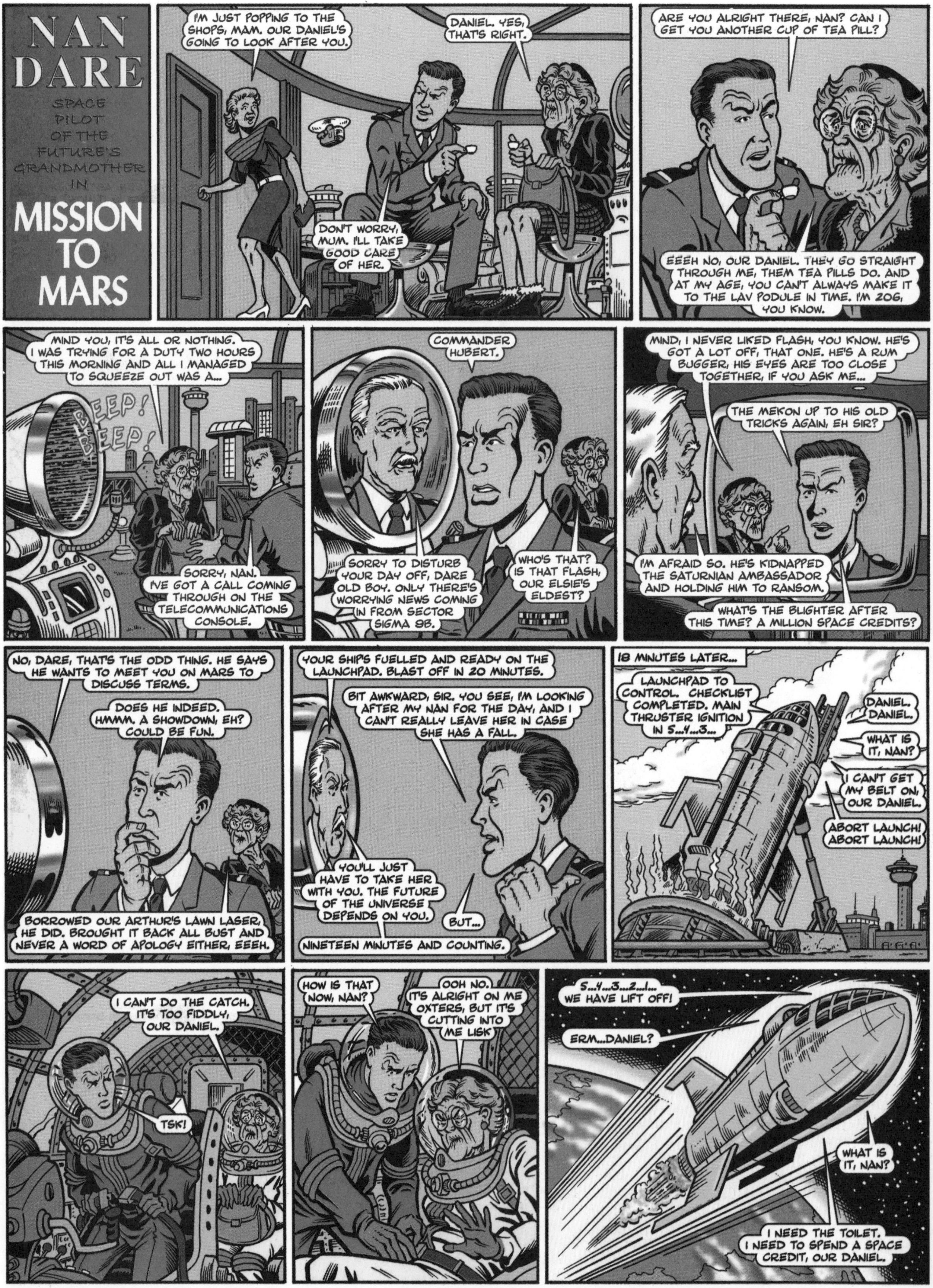
NAN DARE
SPACE PILOT OF THE FUTURE'S GRANDMOTHER IN
MISSION TO MARS
I'M JUST POPPING TO THE SHOPS, MAM. OUR DANIEL'S GOING TO LOOK AFTER YOU.
DANIEL. YES, THAT'S RIGHT.
DON'T WORRY, MUM. I'LL TAKE GOOD CARE OF HER.
ARE YOU ALRIGHT THERE, NAN? CAN I GET YOU ANOTHER CUP OF TEA PILL?
EEEH NO, OUR DANIEL. THEY GO STRAIGHT THROUGH ME, THEM TEA PILLS DO. AND AT MY AGE, YOU CAN'T ALWAYS MAKE IT TO THE LAV PODULE IN TIME. I'M 206, YOU KNOW.
MIND YOU, IT'S ALL OR NOTHING. I WAS TRYING FOR A DUTY TWO HOURS THIS MORNING AND ALL I MANAGED TO SQUEEZE OUT WAS A...
BEEP! BEEP!
SORRY, NAN. I'VE GOT A CALL COMING THROUGH ON THE TELECOMMUNICATIONS CONSOLE.
COMMANDER HUBERT.
SORRY TO DISTURB YOUR DAY OFF, DARE OLD BOY. ONLY THERE'S WORRYING NEWS COMING IN FROM SECTOR SIGMA 9B.
WHO'S THAT? IS THAT FLASH, OUR ELSIE'S ELDEST?
MIND, I NEVER LIKED FLASH, YOU KNOW. HE'S GOT A LOT OFF, THAT ONE. HE'S A RUM BUGGER, HIS EYES ARE TOO CLOSE TOGETHER, IF YOU ASK ME...
THE MEKON UP TO HIS OLD TRICKS AGAIN, EH SIR?
I'M AFRAID SO. HE'S KIDNAPPED THE SATURNIAN AMBASSADOR AND HOLDING HIM TO RANSOM.
WHAT'S THE BLIGHTER AFTER THIS TIME? A MILLION SPACE CREDITS?
NO, DARE, THAT'S THE ODD THING. HE SAYS HE WANTS TO MEET YOU ON MARS TO DISCUSS TERMS.
DOES HE INDEED. HMMM. A SHOWDOWN, EH? COULD BE FUN.
BORROWED OUR ARTHUR'S LAWN LASER, HE DID. BROUGHT IT BACK ALL BUST AND NEVER A WORD OF APOLOGY EITHER, EEEH.
YOUR SHIP'S FUELLED AND READY ON THE LAUNCHPAD. BLAST OFF IN 20 MINUTES.
BIT AWKWARD, SIR. YOU SEE, I'M LOOKING AFTER MY NAN FOR THE DAY, AND I CAN'T REALLY LEAVE HER IN CASE SHE HAS A FALL.
YOU'LL JUST HAVE TO TAKE HER WITH YOU. THE FUTURE OF THE UNIVERSE DEPENDS ON YOU.
BUT...
NINETEEN MINUTES AND COUNTING.
18 MINUTES LATER...
LAUNCHPAD TO CONTROL. CHECKLIST COMPLETED. MAIN THRUSTER IGNITION IN 5...4...3...
DANIEL. DANIEL.
WHAT IS IT, NAN?
I CAN'T GET MY BELT ON, OUR DANIEL.
ABORT LAUNCH! ABORT LAUNCH!
I CAN'T DO THE CATCH. IT'S TOO FIDDLY, OUR DANIEL.
TSK!
HOW IS THAT NOW, NAN?
OOH NO. IT'S ALRIGHT ON ME OXTERS, BUT IT'S CUTTING INTO ME LISK
5...4...3...2...1... WE HAVE LIFT OFF!
ERM...DANIEL?
WHAT IS IT, NAN?
I NEED THE TOILET. I NEED TO SPEND A SPACE CREDIT, OUR DANIEL.

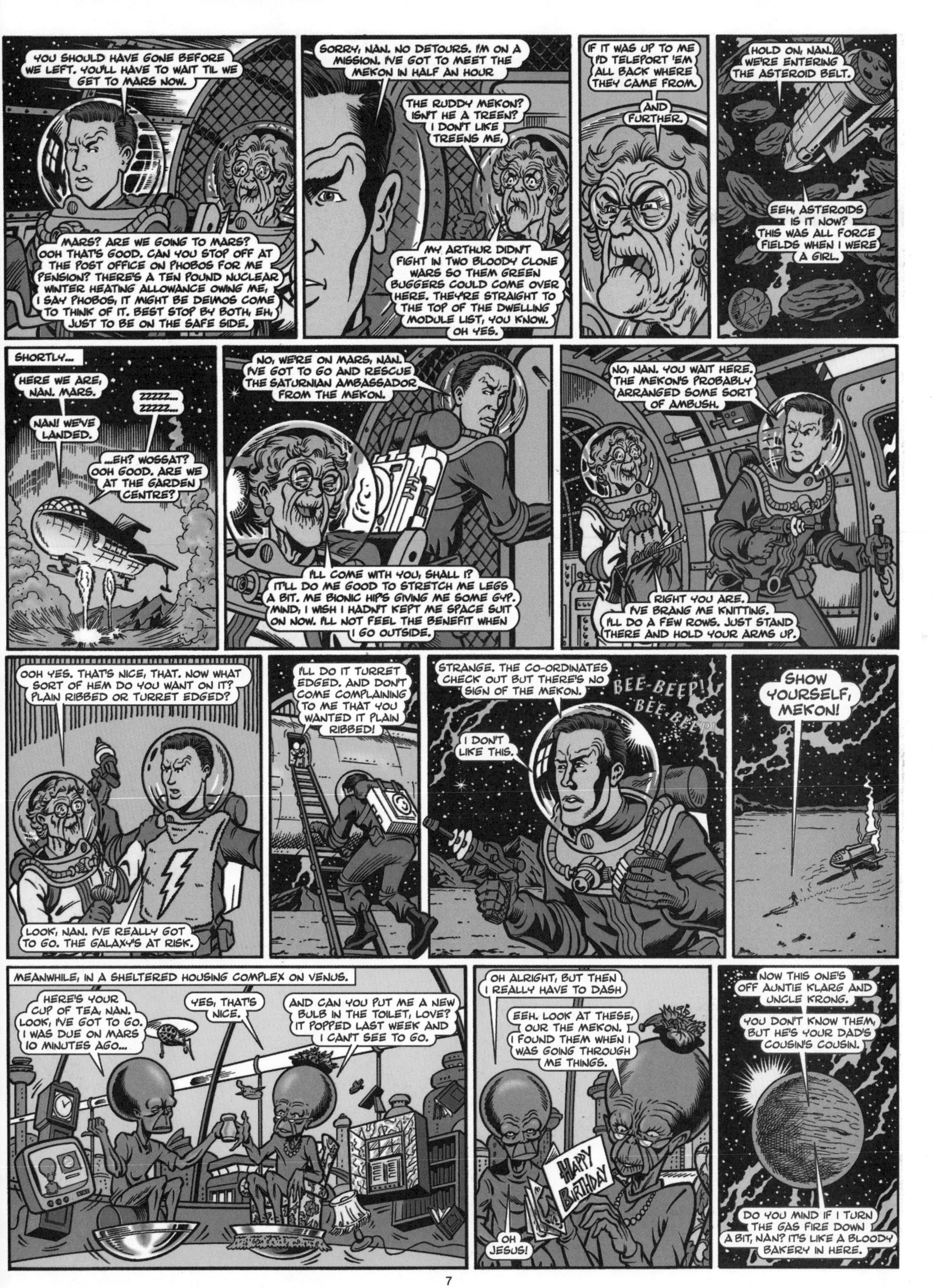

YOU SHOULD HAVE GONE BEFORE WE LEFT. YOU'LL HAVE TO WAIT TIL WE GET TO MARS NOW.
MARS? ARE WE GOING TO MARS? OOH THAT'S GOOD. CAN YOU STOP OFF AT THE POST OFFICE ON PHOBOS FOR ME PENSION? THERE'S A TEN POUND NUCLEAR WINTER HEATING ALLOWANCE OWING ME, I SAY PHOBOS, IT MIGHT BE DEIMOS COME TO THINK OF IT. BEST STOP BY BOTH, EH, JUST TO BE ON THE SAFE SIDE.
SORRY, NAN. NO DETOURS. I'M ON A MISSION. I'VE GOT TO MEET THE MEKON IN HALF AN HOUR
THE RUDDY MEKON? ISN'T HE A TREEN? I DON'T LIKE TREENS ME.
MY ARTHUR DIDN'T FIGHT IN TWO BLOODY CLONE WARS SO THEM GREEN BUGGERS COULD COME OVER HERE. THEY'RE STRAIGHT TO THE TOP OF THE DWELLING MODULE LIST, YOU KNOW. OH YES.
IF IT WAS UP TO ME I'D TELEPORT 'EM ALL BACK WHERE THEY CAME FROM.
AND FURTHER.
HOLD ON, NAN. WE'RE ENTERING THE ASTEROID BELT.
EEH, ASTEROIDS IS IT NOW? THIS WAS ALL FORCE FIELDS WHEN I WERE A GIRL.
SHORTLY...
HERE WE ARE, NAN. MARS.
ZZZZZ... ZZZZZ...
NAN! WE'VE LANDED.
...EH? WOSSAT? OOH GOOD. ARE WE AT THE GARDEN CENTRE?
NO, WE'RE ON MARS, NAN. I'VE GOT TO GO AND RESCUE THE SATURNIAN AMBASSADOR FROM THE MEKON.
I'LL COME WITH YOU, SHALL I? IT'LL DO ME GOOD TO STRETCH ME LEGS A BIT. ME BIONIC HIP'S GIVING ME SOME GYP. MIND, I WISH I HADN'T KEPT ME SPACE SUIT ON NOW. I'LL NOT FEEL THE BENEFIT WHEN I GO OUTSIDE.
NO, NAN. YOU WAIT HERE. THE MEKON'S PROBABLY ARRANGED SOME SORT OF AMBUSH.
RIGHT YOU ARE. I'VE BRANG ME KNITTING. I'LL DO A FEW ROWS. JUST STAND THERE AND HOLD YOUR ARMS UP.
OOH YES. THAT'S NICE, THAT. NOW WHAT SORT OF HEM DO YOU WANT ON IT? PLAIN RIBBED OR TURRET EDGED?
LOOK, NAN. I'VE REALLY GOT TO GO. THE GALAXY'S AT RISK.
I'LL DO IT TURRET EDGED. AND DON'T COME COMPLAINING TO ME THAT YOU WANTED IT PLAIN RIBBED!
STRANGE. THE CO-ORDINATES CHECK OUT BUT THERE'S NO SIGN OF THE MEKON.
BEE-BEEP! BEE-BEEP!
I DON'T LIKE THIS.
SHOW YOURSELF, MEKON!
MEANWHILE, IN A SHELTERED HOUSING COMPLEX ON VENUS.
HERE'S YOUR CUP OF TEA, NAN. LOOK, I'VE GOT TO GO. I WAS DUE ON MARS 10 MINUTES AGO...
YES, THAT'S NICE.
AND CAN YOU PUT ME A NEW BULB IN THE TOILET, LOVE? IT POPPED LAST WEEK AND I CAN'T SEE TO GO.
OH ALRIGHT, BUT THEN I REALLY HAVE TO DASH
EEH. LOOK AT THESE, OUR THE MEKON. I FOUND THEM WHEN I WAS GOING THROUGH ME THINGS.
HAPPY BIRTHDAY
OH JESUS!
NOW THIS ONE'S OFF AUNTIE KLARG AND UNCLE KRONG.
YOU DON'T KNOW THEM, BUT HE'S YOUR DAD'S COUSIN'S COUSIN.
DO YOU MIND IF I TURN THE GAS FIRE DOWN A BIT, NAN? IT'S LIKE A BLOODY BAKERY IN HERE.

Letterbocks

Letterbocks, Viz Comic, PO Box 656, North Shields, NE29 1BT Email: letters@viz.co.uk

STAR LETTER

Everywhere I go I see signs saying 'Post no bills', yet every day in the post I receive bills from the the gas board, electricity board and telephone company. It's just another example of one rule for multinational utilities and another for the rest of us.

Perry, e-mail

■ Bob Geldof, Midge Ure and Bono should all delve into their trillions and 'feed the world' their bloody selves instead of asking us poor fuckers on the dole to feed it. I get £52 a week and can't even feed myself after I've bought my Special Brews, snout and porn.

Keith
Caversham

■ Last night, whilst queuing to pay for petrol in the BP Express, I was behind a man who bought three cans of Tennant's Super, a can of HP All Day Breakfast, a loaf of medium sliced white bread and a copy of Club magazine. Has any other reader seen a more tragic shopping basket?

Lorna Bagpipe-Smart
Wood Green

■ 'An apple a day keeps the doctor away' according to the old maxim. Well, I'm married to a GP and no matter how many apples I eat the bastard keeps coming home.

M Bunford
e-mail

■ If David Blunkett was forced to fight a duel with his ex-lover's husband then we'd

find out if he really is blind or just putting it on in order to get a free dog.

TC Rusling
Cottingham

■ I have been a strict vegetarian for moral reasons for the past 20 years. However I have recently got the munchies for chicken. Would it be ethical for me to eat a chicken leg if, for instance, a chicken had lost one in a chicken fight or through natural causes? What do other readers think?

Confused,
Urmston

■ In their TV adverts, Burger King proclaim 'You're the boss'. Bearing this in mind, I visited one of their establishments in Newcastle and demanded a Whopper, fries and a Pepsi FREE as given to all members of staff. When my employees laughed at me, I immediately sacked the lot of them.

Graham Flintoft
Gateshead

■ I was arrested last year for watching through binoculars whilst the woman who lives across the road was getting changed. Yet two weeks ago, when I turned round after having a piss outside Lloyds bank I caught a policeman watching me... and I got arrested! It's just another example of one rule for people in positions of authority and another rule for the rest of us.

J Hill
House

■ A mate of mine recently went to the Bahamas and spent two weeks at a Holiday Inn. Imagine how pissed off he was when he got back and I told him there was one just down the road from us.

Geoff Barker,
e-mail

■ My missus recently shrank her own hat in the washer and then started crying. Does anyone else live with a daft mare?

G Sporran
e-mail

■ In *Charlie and the Chocolate Factory*, was nobody even a little bit suspicious that, after 20 years in bed, Grandpa Joe jumped to his feet and danced about like Fred Astaire when he got offered a free meal ticket? Lazy fuck.

Graeme Patterson
Email

■ What a tragedy it was to hear that little Jeanette Krankie had fallen off a beanstalk during a performance of her pantomine. But what I want to know is, when the ambulance arrived at the hospital, was she taken to the geriatric ward or the children's ward?

M Tailpipe
Musselborough

■ I was in the pantomine audience when Jimmy Krankie fell from the beanstalk and broke her collar-bone. The performance had been fairly average until that point and I had been planning to ask for a refund. Thankfully. Mrs Krankie's death-defying stunt rescued the show and I left more than satisfied with my £8 concessional ticket. If only other so-called celebrities showed such professional commitment.

Steve Kerr
e-mail

■ I dissagree with the writer of the above letter. An old lady falling some considerable distance is no laughing matter. However, had she been performing in Germany, she would have been taken to the hospital in a Krankenwagon, which would have been mildly amusing.

Frank Marino
e-mail

■ 'You never close your eyes any more when I kiss your lips...' wrote the Righteous Brothers in their 1964 hit. Well, to be fair, in order to see that your bird's not closing her eyes when you're copping off with her you would have to have your eyes open as well. It sounds to me like they've both 'lost that lovin' feeling.' I reckon the relationship is dead in the water and they should end it now before they both get hurt.

Mason
Rumpunter

■ I recently posted a letter to the same address that I live at to see if there were two houses with the same address. I included a photo of myself, along with my likes and dislikes. I received a prompt reply from a chap who not only looks like me, but who shares all my own tastes. How about that for a coincidence? I sent another letter suggesting we meet up and he agrees.

J Barrance,
e-mail

■ Why are huntsmen getting so upset about the ban on hunting foxes? If it comes into force, they could just paint one of their dogs ginger and hunt that instead.

Barry Fox
Chester le Street

■ I was devastated recently when my elderly father died. But the funeral directors sorted everything out which was terrific as I was

SUE-DO-KU

No. 3671

If you have finished every job that you need to do, read every book that has ever been written and watched every freshly painted wall dry, then why not do our fantastic *Sue-do-ku* puzzle, the craze that's sweeping the nation?

Inside the grid are the faces of Sue Pollard, Sue Lawley, Sue Barker, Susan Stranks, Susan Sarandon, Siouxsie Sioux, Suzanne Dando, Soo out of Sooty and Sweep and Supergirl. Can you complete the grid so that each Sue appears once in every row, column and block of nine? The answer is on page 149.

ONCE again, the New Year's Honours List has sparked controversy and debate up and down the land. And Viz readers have been writing in in their tens to let us know what they think. Here's a selection of the best we received...

Going! Going! GONG!

...The government proudly told us that this year's New Year's Honours were distributed fairly, as half of them were given to ordinary members of the public, the other half being awarded to celebrities in various field of entertainment and sport. Well, I'm no statistician, but if 50% is a fair reflection of our society, we must have about 31 million famous people in this country.

T Petty, Birmingham

...I read with dismay that half of this year's awards were given to ordinary men and women in the street. Well, what a ridiculous selection system. Absolutely anybody could have been walking past while they were giving them out, murderers, rapists, the lot. Even Nasty Nick off Big Brother.

Gladys Whalebone, Corsett

...Kelly Holmes is made a dame for winning a couple of races at the Olympics, and quite rightly so. But let us spare a thought for poor Paula Radcliffe. She trained as hard as Dame Kelly for the games, but because she was unfortunate enough to suffer a knicker-shitting mishap towards the end of the marathon, she was passed over for the honour . Had she been able to keep control of her bowels, she would have almost certainly have won the race and been awarded a damehood.

J Geils, Band

...With reference to the above letter. Predictably, the moaning minnies are out in force complaining that Paula Radcliffe was not made a Dame when Kelly Holmes was. Well perhaps she should have thought of that before she pappered her running trollies on live TV. I believe that Dames of the British Empire should have perfect control over their bowels. What kind of country would it be if the likes of Dames Judi Dench, Margot Fontayne and Diana Rigg went around shitting themselves in public?

Antony Music, Sexpeople

...I am a tramp, and unfortunately I shit myself on a regular basis. I have often wondered why I have never been made a Knight of the Realm. Thanks to Paula Radcliffe, it has now become clear.

Harold Ramp, Trafalgar Square

...Making Kelly Holmes a dame is an absolute disgrace. Let's not forget that she brought home two gold medals from the Athens Olympics. If the only way the government can reward this accomplishment is to give her a comedy part in a pantomime, it's a poor tale.

B Tee, Emgees

...I think the New Year's Honours is a farce. I was awarded an MBE last year, and when I went to collect it my trousers fell down. I tripped and grabbed hold of the Queen's dress which tore off, leaving her standing there in stockings and suspenders. Just at that moment, Prince Philip came in early from work, so Her Majesty bundled me into a wardrobe.

B Rix, Whitehall

in no state to do anything. Imagine my disgust a couple of weeks later when they sent me a bill! I later found out that they regularly send bills to the relatives of people they bury. These ghouls should be ashamed of themselves, making money out of people's grief. They are worse than vultures.

T Smith, London

■ They say that 'men are from Mars', and this is certainly true in my case. My husband leaves for work at 9 am every morning in a flying saucer and gets back home for his tea 18 months later.

Janice Butterfield Shropshire

■ Can you confirm that the chef at my old workplace was the stupidest fucker on the planet? Not only did she claim to have invented the word 'ting' (as in the patois for 'thing'), but she also claims that 1. the English Channel has a 'different type of water in it', 2. that 'nobody ever learnt anything from books' and 3. 'religion never hurt anybody.' Can your other reader beat this?

Andy Fairhurst e-mail

Top Tips

FELLAS. Pretend that you are TV's Anthony McPartlin out of Ant and Dec, by looking at yourself in the back of a spoon.

Mark Hudson, Email

DON'T waste money this Valentine's day buying your wife or girlfriend expensive underwear or chocolates. Simply buy her a pair of edible knickers from Anne Summers and kill two birds with one stone.

Duncan Brown, e-mail

EMPLOYERS. Avoid hiring unlucky people by immediately tossing half the CVs into the bin.

Johnny the E, Email

PARENTS of identical twins. Save money on school photographs by simply having one of your children snapped, then photocopying the resultant print. Repeatedly remark to visitors how incredibly similar your children are in order to disguise your deception.

Stewart Cowley, Email

BREAKFAST LOVERS. Make the 'toast always lands butter side down' myth wrong by dropping your toast, then quickly buttering it before someone sees.

LJB, Email

GIVE SPIDERS the nailbiting experience of a real life Indiana Jones adventure by tipping them down a cardboard tube whilst slowly closing the lower end with a playing card. For added excitement roll a Ferrero rocher down the tube and have a friend insert cocktail sticks through the side at regular intervals.

John Bottom, Email

IF YOU find yourself nervous at the prospect of addressing a group of senior lapdancers, try to imagine them all fully-clothed.

Graham Elvis Winning, Email

SCRABBLE PLAYERS. If you have a Q and a U, try to use the Q for words like 'Qi' or 'Qat'. This will free up the U for words like 'Bum', 'Mum' etc.

Stu, Email

GUN JUMPERS. Avoid premature ejaculation during intercourse by offloading during foreplay.

Yl Never, Email

DISCARDED PALLETS make ideal 'designer futons' for style-conscious tramps.

Jamaal, Email

Tell Me, Do

Dr Johannes Do, professor of Miscellany at the Hamburg Institute of Facts and Things, answers your queries.

IS THE actress Susan Hampshire related to the cricket team Hampshire?

Mrs Etherington, Hull

• *Hampshire cricket team play at the Rose Bowl ground in Southampton, and won the County Championship three times in the 1970s. The dyslexic actress Susan Hampshire starred as Fleur in 'the Forsyte Saga'. It is not known whether they are related, although they share the same surname.*

I RECENTLY bought a pair of trousers, but when I got them home they had three legs and no gusset. Am I entitled to my money back?

George Hermitage, Epsom

• *Ever since they were invented by the French Duc de Pantalon in 1654, trousers have usually been made with two legs and one gusset. If you take them back and swap them for another pair, make sure to count the number of legs and gussets before you leave the shop.*

I RECENTLY saw a crab singing in a cartoon. This got me thinking, can crabs really sing?

Dr J Miller, Cambridge

• *Crabs are sea-dwelling crustaceans with ten legs. The largest one on record was a Japanese spider crab with a legspan of over eleven feet. Crabs have lungs and gills, although scientists are undecided whether they have a mouth or can sing.*

WHILST ON holiday on the Isle of Man I received some fluff in my change. Is this legal tender on the UK mainland?

E George, Harwich

• *The capital of the Isle of Man is Douglas, which is 75 miles west of Liverpool. Famous people who live on the island include Nigel Mansell, David Icke and Norman Wisdom. Coins which are legal tender on the UK mainland include the 50p, the 10p and the 2p. The largest in size is the £2 coin, which is also the largest in money.*

COCKNEY WANKER
ORWIGHT, DARLIN'?
TICKETS! BOUGHT AN' SOLD! PRODUCERS... MAMA MIA... CHITTY BAING BAING!...ALL SEATS, ALL SHOW...
DOMINION
WE WILL ROCK YOU
SAY, BUDDY...
YES, CHIEF... WOTCHOO ARFTAH, THEN, EH?
COULD YOU DIRECT US TO YOUR HOUSES OF PAR-LIAY-MENT?
DIRECTCHAH?
AR CAN DO BETTER THAN THAT, MY OLD SEPTIC
SEE THESE?... TWO TICKETS FOR THE STATE OPENIN'... FRANT ROW, THESE... YOU'LL BE SAT RIGHT BETWEEN THE QUEEN AN TONY BLAYAH!
GEE!
'ANDRED KNICKAH AN' THEY'RE YAWS, MY SAN!
WELL,...I... DON'T KNOW
TWO FAASAND YEARS O' PAGEANTRY... STARTS IN ARF AN OUR!
I'M NOT SURE!
'SCUSE ME, CHIEF... MY DOG'S RINGIN'...
...IT'S ON SILENT MODE, INNIT!
YEAH?... WOT'S THAT? TWO TICKETS FOR THE STATE OPENIN' OF...? YEAH, AR FINK ARV GOT A PAIR LEFT... OLD ON A MO...
LOOK! D'YOU WANT THE TICKETS OR NOT? ONLY I GOT A COUPLE OF IRAQIS ON THE BLOWER WANT T'GIVE ME A MONKEY FOR 'EM
EYE-RAQIS? GODDAMIT!..GIVE ME THOSE TICKETS, BUB!
THERE Y'GO... TELL YOU WOT, I'LL FRO IN A VOUCHER TO TRY ON THE CROWN JEWELS
THANKS!
NO BOVVAH!
YOU GIVE THAT TO THE QUEEN PAL... SHE'LL SORT YOU AHT!
TICKETS! BOUGHT AN' SOLD. BILLY ELLIOT... ROCK YOU... WIMBLEDON... OLYMPICS TWO FAASAN' TWELVE... 'ANDRED METRES FINAL... RIGHT ON THE FINISH LINE...
ILL ROCK YOU
EXCUSE ME... I'VE GOT THESE TWO TICKETS FOR BILLY ELLIOT, BUT SOMETHING'S COME UP AND I CAN'T GO... HOW MUCH WILL YOU GIVE ME FOR THEM?
BILLY ELLIOT, EH? LET'S 'AVE A BUTCHERS
NAH! NOT WORF NAFFINK, THESE, GAL... NAH, SORRY.
BUT I PAID £50 EACH
YOU WAS RIPPED OFF MY LAV.
RIGHT AT THE BLEEDIN' BACK, THESE SEATS.
BUT IT SAYS ROW 'C'
NAH! NOT 'C'...
...IT'S ROW 'U' LOOK!... TELL Y' WOT, I'LL GIVE YOU FREE QUID FOR 'EM. AN' I'M CATTIN' ME OWN FROAT!
THREE QUID?
I'LL NEVER SHIFT 'EM... CHARITY, THIS IS, LAV, CHARITY!...'ERE'S YER TWO QUID
YOU SAID THREE!
PAAHND BOOKIN' FEE!
ILL ROCK YOU
TICKETS! BOUGHT AN' SOLD... LADY IN BLACK... F.A. CAP FINAL...
BIRRY ERRIOT. TWO TICKETS, PLEASE
GAW! YOU'RE IN LACK!
I JAST GOT THESE IN, LOOK... FRANT ROW OF THE ROYAL BOX, IN'T THEY?...RIGHT BETWEEN THE QUEEN AN' TONY BLAYAH!
WOW!
MIND YOU, THEY DON'T CAM CHEAP, TICKETS LIKE THESE... BAG OF SAND THE PAIR, ME OLD CHINA... AN' I'M JAST BREAKIN' EVEN
SHORTLY...
SORTED!
THERE HE IS, OFFICER... THAT'S THE GUY!
HUNH!?
HE TOOK A HUNDRED ENGLISH POUNDS OFF ME... GAVE ME WHAT HE SAID WERE TICKETS TO THE OPENING OF PAR-LIAY-MENT
I SO WANTED TO MEET YOUR QUEEN
WHY, I OUGHTA BUST HIS GODDAM ASS
THANK YOU, SIR... I'LL DEAL WITH THIS FROM HERE!
ORWIGHT, WANKER... UP TO YOUR OLD TRICKS, EH?... YOU BUYIN' AN' SELLIN' AGAIN, ARE YOU?
WOT IF I AM?
WELL... 'OW MUCH WILL YOU GIVE ME F' THESE...
...BRIAN TILSLEY RAPE TRIAL. OLD BAILEY... COURT NUMBER ONE, PUBLIC GALLERY...?
LET'S 'AVE A BUTCHERS...
...ROW 'D'... NOT A VERY GOOD VIEW OF THE DOCK, MY SAN. ...TELL YOU WOT, I'LL GIVE YOU A PONY FOR THE PAIR.
ROCK YOU

No Triple XXX Please, We're British

Cabinet Plans Extreme Porn Clampdown

The government recently announced plans to crack down on extreme pornography. It sounds a simple enough task at first glance, but as usual the legislation could prove to be a minefield of hot potatoes. What is the definition of extreme pornography? Erotic images that would make Anne Widdecombe vomit buckets may fail to provoke even a twitch in Peter Stringfellow's penis. And, assuming we could ever come to an agreement about what it is, how should we go about banning it? We went on the street to find out what YOU the public think.

"The government wants to ban images of bestiality, but where will it all end? Will they arrest the curator of the National Gallery for displaying Leonardo da Vinci's painting of the ancient Greek legend of Leda, in which a nude woman is seduced by a swan? Probably not, come to think of it, because you can't see it going in."

Brian Turpentine, Art Dealer

"I buy a lot of erotic mags and DVDs, so I reckon I have a pretty good idea of what constitutes extreme porn. Generally speaking, it's anything over about £20."

Spud, Van Driver

"All sorts of pornography turns my stomach, but extreme pornography does so even more. Any perverts caught looking at this sort of material should be dragged into the town square, stripped naked and tied to a post. Then members of the public should be allowed to whip them until their buttocks and genitals are a mass of bleeding scars. Their punishment should be videoed and shown in schools, where their weeping welts would serve as a warning to children of the dangers of looking at such disgusting material."

Ena Dailymail, Housewife

"My husband used to like me to dress up in sexy underwear like the models wore in Razzle magazine, which he used to buy each month. I didn't mind that, but recently he's been travelling to Amsterdam and buying more extreme pornography. These days I often find myself having to get dressed up as a pig, a great dane or an oven ready chicken."

Mrs Boldmoney, Primary School Teacher

"Extreme pornography to me means any pictures where the women have pubes. That's because when I was a lad in the fifties, all the ladies in mucky books had their pubic hair airbrushed out. It was very frustrating. Whilst doing National Service, I banged my head in a tank and fell into a coma for half a century. When I finally regained consciousness last week, I decided to treat myself to an Adult Channel subscription, but was disappointed to find that all the models now shave their bushes off. I've slept through pubes."

Reg Sneezewort, Milkman

"According to survey after survey, pornography has no effect on a man's behaviour. What a load of rot. It causes my husband to briskly rub his penis whilst making strange grunting noises for about a minute and a half."

Mrs Edna Cloudberry, Charity Shop Worker

"The spoilsport feminists tried to ban page three because they said it degraded women. Now they want to stop us looking at extreme pornography. Well, enough is enough. I like extreme pornography. A nice mpeg of a pretty girl who's been drugged and lashed to a kitchen chair whilst two men goad a rottweiler into anally raping her certainly brightens my morning, I can tell you."

Tommy Dodder, Scoutmaster

"Surely there is no need to ban it, since one's exposure to this sort of material is self-regulating. It is an established medical fact that the more extreme the pornography one looks at, the quicker one goes blind or mental."

Dr M Bader-Meinhoff, Haltwhistle

"The Home Office say they will ban any pornography that depicts pain, either real or simulated. If that's the case, then surely all the bongo videos in the world would be illegal. Because in every one I've seen, when the leading man goes for a pop shot he pulls a face like he's just shut his knackers in the car door."

Rex Whistler, Carpenter

"Surely, until you can adequately define extreme pornography, then you have no chance of framing legislation to make it illegal. And everyone's standards will be different. For example, me and my grandmother will have widely different views of what constitutes extreme pornography. To me, it might be a film of a woman performing oral sex on a donkey, whereas to my grandmother it might be a ladyboy defecating between the breasts of a woman tied to a snooker table, whilst twenty Japanese men in gimp masks stand around them masturbating, shooting pints of sticky ejaculate into their hair."

Clive Shipton, Grocer

MATALORD
The Millionare's Discount Store
EVERYTHING A MILLIONAIRE NEEDS - AT KNOCKDOWN PRICES
JUST LOOK AT OUR SUMMER SPECIALS
TOP HATS
3 for £1
MONOCLES
only £1
BARGAIN BIN!
MANORIAL LORDSHIPS
Latest titles available
Huge discounts
STRING QUARTETS
WOW!
HALF PRICE
WITH EVERY
GAZEBO
HIRED
Our string quartets are impeccably trained to play a selection of Millionaire's Music, such as Mozart's Eine Kleine Nachtmuzik and the theme from 'Arthur', 24 hours a day in a gazebo in your garden
ROLLS ROYCES
BUY ONE
GET ONE
FREE
Sharon "Ozzie" Osbourne says:
"I'm occasionally paid to look like I'm shopping in supermarkets such as this one or the other one"
MATALORD
MILLIONAIRE DISCOUNT STORES
"Will that be all, sir?" ©

FRU T. BUNN the MASTER BAKER & HIS GINGERBREAD SEX DOLLS
AW, LOOK AT TIDDLES CHASING HIS TAIL, FRUBERT. ISN'T IT CUTE!
H-RRUMPH
MIAAOW! MIAAOW! MIAAOW!
I'M GOING TO SEND THIS TAPE INTO 'YOU'VE BEEN FILMED'. THEY PAY £100 FOR HOME MOVIES, YOU KNOW.
TCHOH
FLOUR
I'M OFF TO THE SHOPS TO GET AN ENVELOPE AND SOME STAMPS, FRU. I'LL BE ABOUT AN HOUR.
TSK
...HEH-HEH! WHILE SHE'S OUT, I'M GOING TO MAKE SOME HOME MOVIES OF MY OWN... AND IT'S GOING TO BE A DIFFERENT SORT OF TAIL I'M CHASING ON MY TAPE..!
... GINGERBREAD TAIL! HEH-HEH! SLURP!
SLOT
SHORTLY...
RIGHT-INTO THE OVEN GOES MY CO-STAR...20 MINUTES AT GAS MARK 6...
JUST TIME TO GET THE TITLES IN THE CAN.
KWOOAR! I'M GETTING INTO CHARACTER ALREADY! I'M AS STIFF AS A BOWL OF DUNDEE CAKE MIXTURE MADE WITH 3 EXTRA EGGS.
DEEP PASTRY THROAT
STARRING & DIRECTED BY FRU T. BUNN
TING!
A-HA!
SHE'S READY!
...AND SHE'S WELL HORNY. I'VE JUST GOT TO PIPE HER MOUTH ON AND WE'LL BE READY TO START SHOOTING!
GAW! LOOK AT THAT! SHE'S GOT NO GAG REFLEX!
...THE FILTHY BISCUIT BITCH.
RIGHT. YOU KNEEL HERE WHILE I GET THE CAMERA ROLLING.
SNAP!
SILENCE ON SET! SCENE ONE...TAKE ONE...
...AND...
...ACTION!
...CUE FRUBERT!
HEY BABY - SUCK MY BIG DICK... THAT'S IT, BABY...SUCK ON MY BIG BAKER'S DICK... THAT FEELS SO GOOD...
...UH! UH! UH! OOH, YEAH!
UH! UH! UH! UH!
...UH! UH! UH!...UH-UH-UH-UUUUUUUUUH!
PANT...PANT...PANT
...AND CUT!
PHOOOAAR! I CAN'T WAIT TO SEE THIS TAPE..!
IT'S RED-HOT CLOSE-UP ORAL HARDCORE FROM START TO FINISH..!
DROOL
HMM...ON SECOND THOUGHTS I THINK I'LL WATCH IT IN THE FLAT ABOVE THE SHOP...
THAT WAY I WON'T GET DISTURBED WHILST I'M PLEASURING MYSELF.
AH, FRU! I GOT THE STAMPS AND A JIFFY BAG TO SEND OFF MY...
SCOOT!
RYMANS
BANG!
OOF!
OOYAH!
BLOODY HELL FIRE! WHY CAN'T YOU LOOK WHERE YOU'RE GOING!?
OOH...SORRY LOVE...

BUT WHERE ARE YOU OFF TO IN SUCH A HURRY, ANYWAY?
ERM...NOWHERE... ER... I'M JUST OFF TO THE BAKERY...
ERM... THERE'S BEEN A PROBLEM WITH A CROISSANT.
HEH-HEH I'M HOME AND FREE!
BUNN THE BAKERS
SHE DIDN'T SUSPECT A THING!
SHORTLY...
NOW TO PLAY MY BIT OF HOME-MADE GRUMBLE...
CLICK
BAKER SIZE TISSUES
SLAVER FOAM FROTH
PRESS
PLAY
BAKER SIZE TISSUES
MIAAOW! MIAAOW! MIAAOW!
BAKER SIZE TISSUES
BAKER SIZE TISSUES
1 WEEK LATER...
OOH, LOOK FRUBERT LOVE. IT'S ABOUT TO START! I'M SO EXCITED!
HELLO AND WELCOME TO ANOTHER FUN-PACKED EDITION OF YOU'VE BEEN FILMED!
I'VE TOLD EVERYONE WE KNOW TO TUNE IN. ALL OUR NEIGHBOURS AND RELATIVES ARE WATCHING...
WELL... IN TODAY'S SHOW WE'VE GOT LOADS OF FOOTAGE OF GRANNIES FALLING OVER AT WEDDING RECEPTIONS!
...NOT TO MENTION EVERYONE AT CHURCH AND ALL THE MUMS FROM CHELSEA'S PLAYGROUP.
...BUT OUR FIRST CLIP REALLY TAKES THE BISCUIT.... QUITE LITERALLY!
...A MRS. BUNN OF FULCHESTER SENT US IN THIS HOME VIDEO OF A BAKER EJACULATING ALL OVER THE FACE OF A GINGERBREAD SEX DOLL.
YOU'VE BEEN FILMED!
HEY BABY-SUCK MY BIG DICK... THAT'S IT, BABY... SUCK ON MY BIG BAKER'S DICK... THAT FEELS SO GOOD...UH! UH! UH! OOH, YEAH! UH! UH! UH! UH!
...UH! UH! UH!....UH-UH-UH-
UUUUUUUUUUUUUUUUH!!
PANT...PANT...PANT
SKY+ FROM £10*
0%
BUY NOW PAY NOTHING TILL 2006
FAST TEXT
REMOTE CONTROL
ULTRA FLAT TUBE!
12
NICAM STEREO!
BUDGET PORTABLE
WIDE SCREEN!
OPEN

TONY  PARSEHOLE

How I wish it was **me** who had died instead of Pope JP II

WHEN I heard that Pope John Paul II was dead I cried and cried and cried. I cried and cried and cried more than I have ever cried and cried and cried in my whole life.

I cried for all the children as yet unborn who would grow up in a world without ever knowing his smile. I cried for all the old people who must face the Autumn of their lives without his love to guide them. And I cried for all the people whose ages fall somewhere in bet-ween them other two ages who find themselves lost in an ocean of sadness. His was a life of astonishing compassion, courage and humanity. A life of compassion. A life of courage. A life of humanity.

But what really marked this wonderful, wonderful, wonderful, wonderful man out from the rest of us was not how he lived. It was how he died.

Most of us will meet our maker fighting for breath like drowning rats, desperately clinging on to life like the spineless cowards we are. Pope John Paul set us an example it will be hard to follow. If, when my time comes, I depart this life with the tiniest, tiniest, tiniest fraction of the dignity, tranquility and panache this marvellous, marvellous, marvellous, marvellous man showed then my time on this earth will not have been in vain.

And I should know. Because I was there in the room when the Pope slipped serenely away into his eternal sleep. I was sitting there on the bed next to him holding his hand. And it wasn't the hand of a frail old man. It was a strong hand. A dignified hand. A hand with proud nails and knuckles. But those knuckles were humble. They were placid and graceful. They were the knuckles of a true man of the people.

Most of us have knuckles. But in this Godless and secular age it was a revelation to behold a set of knuckles that embodied all that was best about Christianity. Knuckles that seemed ready to be gathered up into the arms of there that's 350 words.

Invoice enc.

● ● ● ● ● ● ● ● ● ● ● ●

Next Week - *Why I liked the Style Council more than the Jam.*

Billy the FISH
DESPITE BEING BORN HALF MAN-HALF FISH, YOUNG BILLY THOMSON HAD MADE THE 'KEEPER'S JERSEY AT FULCHESTER UNITED F.C. HIS OWN.
IT'S THE DAY OF THE FA CUP FINAL AND, AS USUAL, FULCHESTER UNITED TAKE THE FIELD TO FACE THEIR ARCH RIVALS GRIMTHORPE CITY...
ON THE FULCHESTER BENCH...
WELL ONE THING'S FOR CERTAIN, SYD. IT'S GOING TO BE A GAME OF TWO HALVES.
YES BOSS.
LET'S HOPE OUR LADS HAVE GOT STRENGTH IN DEPTH.
♪PHEEP!♪
GREAT! THE MATCH IS STARTING, TOMMY!
NOT QUITE, SYD. THAT WHISTLE WAS FOR THE START OF A MINUTE'S SILENCE IN MEMORY OF THE LATE POPE, JOHN PAUL II.
OH.
COUGH.
1 MINUTE LATER...
♪PHEEP!♪
HOORAY! NOW WE CAN START!
NOT YET, SYD. IT'S ANOTHER MINUTE'S SILENCE. THIS ONE'S FOR RECENTLY DECEASED EX-PRIME MINISTER JAMES CALLAGHAN...
AH.
...THEN AFTER THAT THERE'S ANOTHER ONE FOR PRINCE RAINIER OF MONACO.
COUGH.
SHH!
82 MINUTES LATER...
WHO'S THIS SILENCE FOR, TOMMY?
MAURICE GIBB OUT OF THE BEE GEES.
I SEE.
IT'S LOOKING LIKE EXTRA TIME, ISN'T IT, BOSS?
I THINK SO, SYD. WE'VE STILL GOT CAPTAIN SCOTT AND ALL FIVE OF JACK THE RIPPER'S VICTIMS FROM 1888 TO GO...
...NOT TO MENTION RAY LANGTON.

What a RIP-off!

Pope's death leaves Ernie out of pocket

THE RECENT DEATH of Pope John Paul II was a great loss to the world, but one north-east man has lost even more than most. For the pontiff's tragic death has left him £35 out of pocket, after the Vatican pulled out of a deal to buy his second-hand pressure washer.

By our Religeous Affairs Correspondent
Mr C. out of The Shamen

Ernie Loffgren of Morpeth placed an advert in the 'For Sale' section of his local yellow Free-Ads paper, offering his used Karcher 1200 pressure-washer at the bargain price of £35. The same day the paper came out, Ernie got a phonecall from a prospective purchaser.

He told us: "It was the Pope. He said he'd seen my ad and the pressure-washer was just what he wanted to get the moss off the cobbles at St Peter's Square. When I told him I'd throw in half a bottle of cleaning fluid and an attachment for getting pigeon mess off the Popemobile, he agreed to buy it sight unseen."

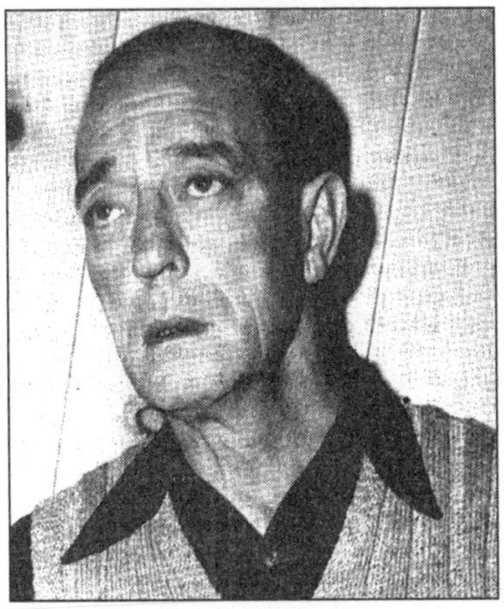

cash

The Pope assured Ernie that he'd be round with the cash within the week, so the 52 year-old gas fitter packaged the pressure-washer up and placed it in the hall awaiting the pontiff's knock at the door. "That was on the Monday," continued Mr Loffgren. "But by the Friday his holiness still hadn't turned up."

During the week Ernie received four other enquiries from prospective buyers. "Two of them even turned up at the door with the cash in their hands," he told us. "But I had to turn them away. I'd already promised the pressure-washer to the Pope, and I wasn't going to go back on my word."

sharpe

However when Ernie watched the news on Saturday, the reason for John Paul II's no-show in Morpeth became clear.

The Pope waves to people before facing his maker, whilst Ernie (left) faces placing another advert in the FreeAds paper. Below right, the original advert that caught the Pontif's eye.

lovely flowers . £6 ono. Tel. (0191) 253[redacted]

PLAY SHED Child's play house, wood, in need of painting. £40. Tel. (0191) 252[redacted]

PRESSURE WASHER Karcher 1200, used once, as new. £35. Tel. (01670) 223[redacted]

SHED 7' x 5', felt roof with base, buyer to dismantle. £90. Tel. (0191) 241[redacted]

TOP QUALITY TURF in rolls, 2 grades. Can deliver. £1 per roll.

"I couldn't believe my rotten luck when I heard the Pope had died," he told us. "I tried ringing the Vatican to see if they were going to send someone else round to pick up the pressure washer, but they were engaged. I wouldn't be surprised if they'd deliberately left the phone off the hook," he added.

Now Ernie is faced with the task of re-advertising the washer in next week's Free-Ads paper. He told us: "I'm going to say it's being re-offered due to timewasters, and if the new Pope rings up to buy it I'm going to tell him it's already sold."

The VIZ Solicitor, *Mr Ingledew Botteril* writes...

MR Loffgren's situation is not unusual. Many people make a contract, whether verbal or written, only to die before the terms of that contract are fulfilled. In law, the unfulfilled contract becomes one of the deceased's effects, and is treated as a chattel under the terms of his last will and testament.

Mr Loffgren should write to the Vatican demanding the name and address of the executor of the Pope's will. He should then write to the executor requesting settlement of the outstanding amount at their earliest convenience. However, if the bequests have already been disbursed he should contact each of the beneficiaries, eg wives or children, individually requesting payment of an amount equivalent to their share of the £35 which is owing to him to be paid in a proportion equivalent to that of the deceased's estate which they were bequeathed and of which they are already in receipt.

The beneficiaries should then be given a set period, usually 14 days, in which to call at Mr Loffgren's house and pick up the pressure washer. How it is disbursed amongst the individual assignees is a matter for the Pope's executor.

Legal Questions? The Viz Solicitor Ingledew Botteril is here to help. Send your queries along with a cheque for 400 guineas to:
Ingledew Botteril, PO Box 656, North Shields, NE29 1BT

Joan Collins turns 23 again

72-YEAR-OLD DYNASTY DIVA Joan Collins is changing her age by deed poll.

The veteran actress, who made her debut aged 19 in *'Ding! Dong! Daddio!'* (1951) is applying for the change through the usual channels, and will be 23 again next May.

SIREN

The geriatric siren, who was last 23 in 1956, says she can't wait to have never felt younger for the second time.

"I'm going to play lots of tennis, go to lots of parties and maybe, in about ten years' time, settle down and have a family again."

The unexploded sex doodlebug also confirmed she will be returning her free bus pass, to which she will no longer be entitled.

IT'S THE BACONS
BIFFA
MUTHA
FATHA
HOO, BIFFA. COME INTO THE KITCHEN A MINNIT, SON
FUCKIN' 'ELL!
WOT IS IT, MUTHA?.. I'M TRYIN' T' SIT AN' WATCH THE FRIGGIN' BOX
SLAM!
FUCKIN' 'ELL, SON, ARE YUZ AALLREET? Y' JUST WAALKED REET INTO THAT DOOR. DID YUZ NOT FUCKIN' SEE THE FUCKER?
NAH!.. I THOUGHT IT WAS URPEN
COME ON, BIFFA, YEE 'AVE A NICE BIT SIT DOON, AN' I'LL MEK A CUP O' TEA
AYE.. THAT'LL BE CHAMPION
SWING!
BUMP!
OOOF!
FRIGGIN' 'ELL, BIFFA... DID YUZ NOT SEE THERE WAS NEE FRIGGIN' CHAIR THERE, SON?
NAH, I DIDN'T
OOH, ME FUCKIN' ARSE
HOO! WHAT THE FUCK'S AALL THIS RACKET, FATHA?
EH!? WOT THE FUCK ARE YEE DEEIN' IN MUTHA'S DRESS, FATHA?
FATHA? I'M NOT FATHA...
I'M MUTHA, AREN'T I FATHA?
HE'S REET, BIFFA... THAT'S MUTHA, AN I'M FATHA
LOOKS LIKE THIS 'UN NEEDS 'IS EYES TESTIN, MUTHA...
...I MEAN FATHA
SHORTLY...
REET, SON... PUT Y'HAND AWA YER REET EYE...
...NOO, READ AALL THE LETTAZ ON THIS BIT CARDBOARD
FUCKIN' EASY THAT, FATHA... U.. R.. A.. E.. M.. S.. X
!
U R A EMSX
DID YUZ HEAR THIS 'UN, FATHA? HE JUST SAID THAT YEE IS A FUCKIN' HEEMASEX!
WHAAT!?
?
NEEBODY CALLS ME A FRIGGIN' HEEMASEX!
SMACK!
OOF!
Y' FUCKIN' BASTAAD
AALLREET, AALLREET, LESS IT FATHA... HE'S LORNT HIS LESSON
FLAIL!
SWING!
F' FUCK'S SAKE, SON, WUZ'RE DEEIN' THIS F' YOUR AAN GOOD. NOO SIT DOON AN' READ THE LETTAZ ON THIS CARD... REET?
AALLREET! GET ON WIRRIT
U... R... L... S... B... N
!
U R L SBN
I DIVVEN'T FUCKIN' BELIEVE THIS 'UN! FORST HE CAALLS ME A HEEMASEX, NOO HE'S CAALLIN' YEE A FRIGGIN' LEZZA!
AYE! I HORD THE BASTAAD, FATHA!
BOOT!
TEK THAT!
OOF!
GERROFF, FATHA! I'M GANNA FINISH THE LIRRLE CUNT
CALM DOON, MUTHA, CALM DOON... HE'S LORNT HIS LESSON

REET... LET'S TRY THIS AGAIN, EH, LIKE FUCKIN' CIVILISED PEOPLE, EH, SON? NEE FRIGGIN' INSULTS.
U
2RA
COUPLE
OF BIG CUNTS
ER...
30 SECONDS LATER...
THUMP!
OOF!
BASH!
OOYAH!
BIFF!
SHORTLY...
REET, SON, I'M AFRAID YUZ NEED A PAIR O'GLASSES. WUZ'LL GAN DOON THE POOND SHOP AN' GET YUZ A PAIR
GROAN!
SO...
POUND PLANET
HOO BIFFA! THEM'S PORFECT, THEM'S
AYE! THEY LOOK WELL MENTAL THEY DEE, SON
GEPS-£1
LOOKERS
READERS
AW, MUTHA... I DIVVEN'T WANT T' WEAR GLASSES. AALL THE KIDS AT SCHOOL WILL LAUGH AT US AN CAALL US FUCKIN' SPECKY FAWA-EYES.
YEE TEK NEE NURTICE OF EM, BIFFA
AYE. ANYHOO, WHO'S GANNA PICK ON YEE BIFFA, SON?
NEE FUCKER, THAT'S WHO
...YUZ'RE THE ROCKEST KID IN THE FUCKIN' CLASS, MAN
AYE! HE IS AN' AALL
WELL THERE Y' GAN! IF ANYBODY CAALLS YUZ NAMES, YUZ 'AVE A FUCKIN' POP AT 'EM
I FUCKIN' WILL!
NEXT DAY...
GOOD MORNING, CLASS
GOOD MORNING MR. NETTLESHIP!
NOW, FIRSTLY, I SEE THAT BIFFA IS WEARING HIS NEW SPECTACLES AND I THINK YOU'LL ALL AGREE THAT JOLLY SPLENDID THEY LOOK
AND SECONDLY, WE HAVE TWO NEW CHILDREN JOINING US TODAY WHO I'D LIKE YOU TO MAKE WELCOME...
BOYS AND GIRLS, SAY HELLO TO BASHA AND VERMINTRUDE
HELLO, BASHA... HELLO VERMINTRUDE...
HOO, YE.. JUR FUCKIN' NINETY
WUZ'RE GANNA GET YE AT PLAYTIME, YER FUCKIN' SPECKY FAWA-EYED CUNT!
CLASS 4B
A TEAM

Sexterminate!

TV'S FAVOURITE TIME LORD Dr Who is back on our screens at last, and most of us are once again getting used to watching the action from behind our sofas. But for one woman who worked on the series back in its 70s heyday, all the action took place ON the sofa!

EXCLUSIVE!

Tea lady Iris (above left) and some of her extraterrestrial lovers, yesterday

And now former BBC tealady Iris Poldark is set to blow the lid on the steamy behind-the-scenes goings on which went on behind the scenes of the popular sci-fi series.

In this exclusive extract from her new shockingly badly-written memoir *'Who Were You With in the Moonlight?'* (Beans on Toast Books, £1.99), Iris spills the beans on her sextra-terrestrial romps with a series of terrifying space aliens.

space

Iris began working at the BBC Television Centre straight from school in 1940. Starting as a lowly tea girl she quickly worked her way up, and by the 1960's she was a fully-fledged tea lady. In 1963, as one of the corporation's longest-serving catering staff members, she was given the important job of providing refreshments for the cast and crew of a brand new space adventure series - Doctor Who.

"William Hartnell was the Doctor in those days, and he was a perfect gentleman. However I can't say the same for his arch enemy. During a break in filming the Master came over to my trolley for a cuppa and a gypsy cream.

naked

We started chatting, one thing led to another and before I knew what was happening we were both naked inside his four-dimensional grandfather clock Tardis. One thing's for sure - it was certainly bigger on the inside, and I'm not talking about his time machine! I'm talking about his *cock*.

We made love for what seemed like hours but when we came out of the clock I noticed only a minute and a half had passed. He may have come away second best in all his battles with the Doctor, but let me tell you, the Master certainly lived up to his name between the sheets."

"...his sink plunger began to creep round until it was stroking my breast"

William Hartnell hung up his sonic screwdriver in 1966 when Patrick Troughton took over the title role. While the Doctor was having his first run in with the giant spiders on Metabilis 3, Iris was back on earth enjoying a sexy threesome with a couple of hunky Daleks.

"We'd been filming all day and it was getting quite hot under the studio lights. A couple of Daleks came over and asked me if I fancied a walk in the Blue Peter garden to cool off. I was pretty hot too, after standing next to my urn all afternoon, so I agreed. Little did I suspect that once they'd got me alone outside, things were set to get even hotter!

As we walked by the statue of Petra, one of the Daleks asked me what it was. I started explaining that it was an earth dog but I soon realised he wasn't listening to me. His sink plunger, which had been on my shoulder, began to creep round until it was stroking my breast.

drawers

Then the other one began to lift up my skirt and pull down my drawers. I realised resistance would be futile - and anyway, if truth be told I was enjoying myself too much by then to care - and it wasn't long before I found myself as the filling in a Dalek sandwich.

I pleasured one with my mouth whilst the other took me roughly from behind, taking me to new heights of ectasy with his egg-whisk. Their monotonous cries of electronic passion were soon echoing off the walls of the Blue Peter garden. If Percy Thrower was in his greenhouse, I'm sure he would have wondered what the heck was going on. I'm sure he'd never guess in a million years it was a BBC tealady being spit-roasted by two robotic denizens of the planet Skaro!"

Iris wasn't found out that time, but on another occasion she came pretty close.

"According to my contract, I wasn't allowed to have sexual relationships with Doctor Who baddies. If I'd been discovered making love to an alien monster I would have been sacked on the spot. However, the temptations were often too great, and sometimes I simply couldn't help myself.

lunch

I remember this one time we were on location filming a Doctor Who episode on a beach with John Pertwee. One of the Sea Devils started chatting me up over lunch, and before I knew it I found myself agreeing to go skinny dipping with him that night.

Later on, when the rest of

Sexterminate!

"I dropped my trolleys for Dr Who Monsters" says tea lady

the cast and crew had gone to bed, we sneaked out of the hotel and met up on the sand. As I slipped out of my blue-checked apron, he peeled off his seaweed-encrusted string vest and soon we were standing before each other stark naked.

There was no need for words, which is just as well as Sea Devils can't talk, and soon we were in the surf exploring every inch of each other's bodies.

chef

Despite his evil, reptiloid reputation, he was a tender and considerate lover and he knew exactly how to pleasure a human. Soon my cries of passion were mingling with his asthmatic hisses and the sound of the crashing surf at Frinton.

However, we never knew how close we had come to being discovered. Unbeknownst to us, the director had decided to have a walk along the beach and must have passed within feet of where we were having it off. If he'd spotted us, I'd have been fired and my Sea Devil romeo would have been banished back to the other side of the galaxy.

More of Iris's intergalactic lovers. The Master (left) ~ lived up to his name between the sheets and a sea Devil (right) ~ made love in the surf at Frinton-on-sea.

However, it would have been worth it for some of the best sex I ever had."

On another occasion Iris came even closer to being found out than the last time. She wasn't caught this time either, although it was close.

"There was this cyberman who I'd always fancied. I used to flirt with him during tea breaks, giving him an extra biscuit or three sugars instead of two in his cuppa. However, he seemed shy and it was difficult to strike up a conversation with him.

"...he peeled off his seaweed-encrusted string vest and soon we were standing before each other stark naked"

Eventually I cornered him and he confessed that he was feeling homesick for his native planet of Telos.

tongue

This seemed to open up the floodgates of emotion and he began to cry. I looked deep into his eyeholes and gently stroked the handles on the sides of his head. Our lips met and all thoughts of his home planet were soon forgotten as his aluminium tongue began probing the inner recesses of my mouth.

haslet

Our passions aroused to bursting point, we made our way into the empty *Animal Magic* studio to give free rein to our mutual longings. Pretty soon we were locked together in an embrace of intergalactic lust, our bodies becoming as one. I could tell things were getting hot as steam began to squirt out of a vent in the top of his head. Before long, his breathing began to quicken and seconds later, we both came to a shuddering climax.

Afterwards, I sparked up a post-coital Senior Service but when I offered him the packet he politely declined, explaining that as a silicon-based life-form, the carbon in the cigarette smoke would be fatal. Later on we discovered that a microphone had been left switched on in the studio and the sounds of our lovemaking had been caught on tape. Luckily, the evidence was never traced back to us. The powers-that-be assumed it was Johnny Morris masturbating and docked him a week's wages."

Next week: In a second exclusive extract from her dreadful book, Iris reveals all about the time Davros asked her to put on a show with a lesbian Zygon.

Cyberman ~ A shy alien, but Iris brought him out of his shell in the Animal magic studio.

IRIS POLDARK
WHO WERE YOU WITH IN THE MOONLIGHT?

SPOILT BASTARD
NOW, TIMMY... MRS. WILLIS IS A FULLY QUALIFIED CHILDMINDER... SHE'S GOING TO BE LOOKING AFTER YOU TODAY.
YOU SHOULD BE LOOKING AFTER ME, NOT SWANNING OFF ENJOYING YOURSELF
I WOULDN'T SAY PULLING THE GUTS OUT OF CHICKENS IS ENJOYABLE, MY POPPET! I'VE HAD TO TAKE THIS EXTRA JOB DURING THE DAY SO AS I CAN AFFORD THAT QUAD BIKE FOR YOUR BIRTHDAY
TWO QUAD BIKES... TWO!
AH, MRS. TIMPSON... AND YOU MUST BE TIMMY.
YES!
WOULD YOU LIKE TO COME IN, TIMMY?
WELL I DON'T WANT TO STAND HERE ALL DAY.
YOU'RE JUST IN TIME. WE'RE GOING TO MAKE SOME CHOCOLATE RICE CRISPY CAKES
I'M FIRST! GET BACK
I DO HOPE HE'LL BE ALRIGHT. HE'S... HE'S VERY SPECIAL
OUCH! THAT HURT, TIMMY
IT WAS MEANT TO!
OH, DON'T WORRY MRS. TIMPSON. I'VE BEEN CHILD MINDING FOR 30 YEARS... HE'LL GET ON FINE. I'LL SEE YOU AT FIVE-THIRTY.
6000 GUTTED CHICKENS LATER...
PUNT!
TIMMY!!
SMACK!
IF YOU BRING THAT LITTLE SHIT ANYWHERE NEAR ME, MY HOUSE OR MY CHILDREN EVER AGAIN, I'LL CALL THE POLICE
ERM...
CHRIST, IF I'D BROUGHT UP A KID LIKE THAT I'D OPEN MY WRISTS WITH A KNIFE
SLAM!!!
OH, TIMMY, LOVE! WHAT HAPPENED?
IT'S NOT MY FAULT... EVERYBODY ELSE STARTED IT. SHE'S A FILTHY LIAR!
YES. SHE IS
MIND YOU...
SHE IS RIGHT ABOUT ONE THING
OH... WHAT'S THAT?
THAT IT'S YOUR FAULT!
EH!?... WHAT... WHAT IS?
OH, BE HONEST, WOMAN, YOU HAVEN'T GOT A CLUE HOW TO BRING UP CHILDREN!
I MEAN LOOK AT ME! I'M OUT OF CONTROL... I'M A TINY TERROR, A TODDLER FROM HELL!
OH, NO. I WOULDN'T SAY THAT, TIMMY, MY LOVE. I THINK YOU'RE LOVELY
YES, I KNOW I AM... AS I SAY, THE PROBLEM IS WITH YOU! YOUR PARENTING SKILLS ARE PRACTICALLY NON-EXISTANT, WOMAN. YOU'VE LET ME GET AWAY WITH TOO MUCH FOR FAR TOO LONG. IN FACT...
COME ON!
THERE'S ONLY ONE THING FOR IT...
NEXT DAY...
HELLO, MRS. TIMPSON. I'M SUPERNANNY.
... AND YOU MUST BE THE LITTLE BOY WHO CALLED ME
Supernanny Film Crew
CHANNEL 4
SHORTLY... NOW, WHAT I PROPOSE IS THAT WE SET OUT SOME SIMPLE RULES...
...AND WE DESIGNATE THE CUPBOARD UNDER THE STAIRS AS A 'NAUGHTY ROOM' FOR WHEN THE RULES ARE BROKEN... DO YOU UNDERSTAND THAT, TIMMY?
RULES
OH, YES, SUPERNANNY

NOW, MRS. TIMPSON, YOUR JOB IS TO LET TIMMY KNOW WHEN HIS BEHAVIOUR IS UNASSEPTABLE
RIGHT! I SEE
HE'S GOT TO HAVE A SET OF BOUNDARIES AND HE MUSTN'T BE ALLOWED TO STEP OVER THEM
BOUNDARIES. YES
OKAY, THEN... IT'S BEDTIME... SHOW ME HOW YOU WOULD NORMALLY SEND TIMMY OFF TO BED
RIGHT... ER... OKAY...
ERM... I... I... I THINK IT'S TIME FOR... YOUR... BEDDY BYES, TIMMY
OH, DO YOU?... HOW INTERESTING...
I DON'T KNOW WHAT YOU KNOW ABOUT MY BEDTIME. I ALWAYS GO AFTER YOU
IF YOU WANT TO GO TO BED AT MIDNIGHT, THAT'S UP TO YOU, BUT I'M TRYING TO GET TO LEVEL 100 ON RUNESCAPE, THANK YOU VERY MUCH!
SO STICK THAT UP YOUR SMELLY OLD BOTTOM AND SMOKE IT
ERM... THAT... THAT'S HOW I... ER USUALLY DO IT
HMM!
WELL, YOUR APPROACH IS COMPLETELY WRONG, MRS TIMPSON. WATCH HOW I WOULD DO IT.
OKAY, TIMMY... TIME FOR BED.
NO IT ISN'T
AH, AH! REMEMBER THE RULES
...OFF TO BED NOW, OR I'LL PUT YOU IN THE NAUGHTY ROOM
OH, YES... I'M SORRY SUPERNANNY... I'LL GO AND GET MY JIMJAMS
NIGHT NIGHT
WHA... WHA... WHAT HAPPENED?
MRS. TIMPSON... TIMMY IS A LOVELY BOY.
YOU SIMPLY HAVE TO ESTABLISH WHO IS IN CHARGE, AND BE CONSISTANT IN THE PUNISHMENT TO MAINTAIN THAT HEIRARCHY
OKAY.. WE'LL COME BACK IN TWO WEEKS TO SEE HOW YOU'RE GETTING ON
YES! YES!
THANK YOU, SUPERNANNY
NOW THEN, BACK TO BED YOUNG MAN OR... AHEM... IT'S THE NAUGHTY ROOM FOR YOU
BUT MUMMY. I CAN'T SLEEP
CAN I JUST STAY UP FOR TWENTY MINUTES... PLEASE...
...PLEASE!.. PRETTY PRETTY PLEASE... LOOK, MUMMY, I'M DOING MY PUPPY EYES
AAH! HOW SWEET... OKAY
BUT JUST TWENTY MINUTES
GOD! YOU'RE USELESS! WHAT'S THE POINT IN HAVING THOSE RULES IF YOU'RE GOING TO BUCKLE THE FIRST TIME I DO PUPPY EYES?
HOW ON EARTH AM I SUPPOSED TO JUDGE WHERE THE RUDDY BOUNDARIES ARE?.. YOU'VE BROKEN THE RULES, WOMAN...
I'M SORRY, TIMMY. I DIDN'T MEAN...
TUT! TUT! COME ON, NOW, INTO THE NAUGHTY ROOM WITH YOU
SLAM!
THERE!
AND YOU CAN'T COME OUT 'TILL YOU LEARN TO TAKE CONTROL!
TIMMY!... TIMMY!...
TIMMY!..
TIMMY!...
2 WEEKS LATER...
BEEP! BEEP! BEEP! BEEP! BIDDIP! BIDDIP! BEEP!
DING! DONG!
HELLO, TIMMY. IS YOUR MUMMY IN?
YES
MRS. TIMPSON?.. HELLO!? ...MRS. TIMPSON?...
ERM... WHERE IS SHE, TIMMY?
OH, SHE'S IN THE NAUGHTY ROOM
BZZZZZ!!
OH, JESUS!
...w...w...water!...

Letterbocks

Letterbocks, Viz Comic, PO Box 656, North Shields NE29 1BT Email: letters@viz.co.uk

STAR LETTER

WHAT'S all this nonsense about that 66-year-old Romanian woman being the world's oldest mum? My mum's 77. Beat that.

Thomas J, e-mail

❑ I deplore racism in all its forms, but it is important to remember that it is a two way thing. As a young white man, I have lost count of the number of times me and my friends have been stopped on the street by black policemen and told to 'turn out your pockets, honky'.

H. Wellfield
Manchester

❑ Why is it that people travelling in hot air balloons feel the need to wave down at the people below? Do these caviar-eating, moneybag bastards need to rub it in any more?

Nick Davies
Herts

❑ So Prince Harry dressed up as a Nazi, did he? Well, good for him, I say! It's about time the Royals acknowledged their German roots.

Steve Ireland
Manchester

❑ I cannot understand what all the fuss is about Prince Harry wearing a Nazi uniform. I was watching the TV the other night and Clint Eastwood and Richard Burton were both dressed up as Nazis. It never did either of them any harm, and I don't think any the less of them for it.

Neville Snipe
e-mail

❑ 'It's too cold to snow', my grandmother said one day last winter. She was wrong. And if she's have said 'it's too cold to die of hypothermia', she'd have been wrong on that score as well.

Steven Barnfather
e-mail

❑ I have never had much time for Sir Mark Thatcher in the past, but after the recent events in South Africa he has gone up in my estimation. It must have taken a lot of courage to admit to his part in the attempted coup. And he acted with honour and integrity in identifying and testifying against the others involved. His mother should be very proud of him.

J French
Leeds

❑ Sir Mark Thatcher told a court in South Africa that he lent his helicopter to a group of mercenaries because he thought it would be used as an air ambulance. What I would like to know is, who is the bigger cunt? Him for saying it, or the court for pretending to believe him?

Edward Banana
London

❑ My mother used to say that 'life's too short to argue'. Bollocks! This morning I had a massive row with the wife, a set-to with a customer at work and a big barney with the boss... all before dinner time. And I still had time for my usual tea break.

M Short
Durham

❑ Tony Blair was very quick to announce that yachtswoman Ellen MacArthur was to be made a Dame for being the fastest person to sail round the world. I hope he is as quick to take it back off her should someone break her record.

J Geils
Band

❑ The news that round the world yachtswoman Ellen MacArthur is to be made a Dame of the British Empire is a slap in the face. She should be made a saint by the Pope, or at least beatified like Mother Teresa was. I know that normally one has to be dead to be given this honour, but in Ellen McArthur's case, I think the Vatican should make an exception.

T Holding
Falmouth

❑ Ellen MacArthur sailing round the world in a boat is the single most spectacular act of bravery I have ever seen. My grandfather fought the entire 6 years of the second world war, was captured and escaped twice and helped an entire village

escape the hands of the Nazis. But alongside MacArthur's achievements it almost seems like cowardice.

Frank Hubert
London

❑ What's the big deal about Ellen MacArthur sailing round the world in a boat? The wind was blowing her all the time, for heaven's sake. If she went round the other way, with the wind in her face, now that would be something to make a song and dance about.

T Lucklaw, Wales

❑ I wonder if any of your readers know if Rohypnol works on sheep. Erm, I have a friend who wants to know.

Toby Virgo,
e-mail

❑ Having decided to send you a letter about the funny things that kids say, I asked my 5-year-old son to come up with an amusing comment. When he failed, I sent him up to his room with no dinner and told him not to come down until he had something

TOP TIPS

CINEMA goers. Please have consideration for pirate DVD viewers by having a piss before the film starts.

Paul Collins, e-mail

BURGLARS. When fleeing from police, run with your right arm sticking out at 90°, wrapped in a baby mattress in case they set one of their dogs on you.

P Frampton, Chichester

DETER organ thieves from stealing your innards by swallowing several mousetraps minutes before your death.

Dean Rigg, e-mail

BARE patches on your lawn? Simply stop mowing a patch at the side and let it grow to a significant length. Then, with a rake, sweep it over the bare patch like Sir Bobby Charlton and TV's Robert Robinson do, to create a realistic look of healthy growth.

Tycho Andrews, Fulham

LEPRECHAUNS. Protect your finances by investing in a tracker fund, rather than relying on an ailing currency and leaving a 300foot technicolour arrow in the sky pointing to where you have hidden it.

David Goodall, e-mail

TEENAGE boys. Stop being mistaken for girls by not having such long hair. Eee! I don't know.

Ethel Levitt, London

FELLAS. Stand outside an Ann Summers shop dressed in a security guard's uniform with a smoke detector in your pocket. When a fit bird walks out, simply press the smoke alarm test button and voila! A free grope!

D Clegg, Cirencester

HOMEOWNERS. Put an ancient Egyptian type curse on all your property. then, if you are burgled and the police don't catch the culprit, you can rest assured they will die of a plague of boils or something.

P Nevitt, Springwell

SMOKERS. 'Every cigarette you smoke takes 10 seconds off your life', health experts say. To combat this, at the end of every day work out how many seconds you have 'lost', and simply go to bed that much later, or wake up that much earlier the next morning. Hey presto! your lost time is returned.

James Powell-Brett, e-mail

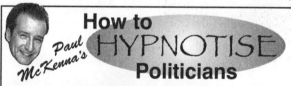

Paul McKenna's How to HYPNOTISE Politicians

No. 312 ~ Sir Cyril Smith MP

amusing to say. After six hours, the best he could manage was "Dad, I'm hungry." Kids these days, eh?

Paul Darren
e-mail

❑ With regards to Mr Darren's letter *(above)*. I sympathise wholeheartedly. Kids today have it too easy. I have four children under the age of ten who never say anything in the least bit amusing, ever. When I was their age, I was up at five thirty every morning, and I'd said at least half a dozen charmingly innocent comments beore I went to school.

P Gough
London

❑ Has anyone actually seen any of these so-called celebrities do any work? All they seem to do is galavant around on TV or swan off to Buckingham Palace to collect their OBEs. Pathetic.

Denzil Ferrari
St Ives

❑ I often receive bills saying 'final demand'. But it never is. If anything they start asking me for more money.

Ian Sertname
Brighton le Sands

❑ Could I advise Midge Ure that if Vienna means nothing to you, simply don't go there you fool. Good tune, though.

U Wumba
e-mail

❑ I found this in a graveyard the other day. Do I win a tenner?

Tom Koerner, Newcastle

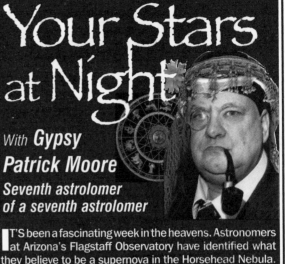

In
Loving Memory
HARRY FIDLER
1890 — 1929.
FANNY

❑ I don't think there is anything wrong with identical twins having sex with each other because, on a genetic level, it's just the same as having sex with yourself, so is therefore only as bad as having a wank. This argument should be made forcefully to the lesbian community. But only the good looking ones.

Matt Neave
e-mail

❑ I am sick and tired of my taxes going to waste on schools. I have three children and they all go to Eton, so I don't see why I should fork out for state schools. Quite frankly, in my opinion, if you can't afford to send your kids to Eton, then you shouldn't have children.

J Lemmington-Spa
Oxford

❑ The new airbus 380 is so big that it can fit 70 cars on each wing. Why don't the lazy sods just get a taxi to the airport and hire a car when they get to their destination?

Granville Canty
Hebden Bridge

❑ In 1964 Nelson Mandela was sentenced to life imprisonment. Twenty seven years later, not only was he released but he also became president of South Africa. Time was once that life meant life. Once again, there is one rule for wrongfully imprisoned political leaders and another rule for everybody else.

R Silk
e-mail

❑ They say that you shouldn't mix your drinks. So what are these cocktail bars all about then?

Garrod Hutchison
Ispswitch

❑ I onced banged a girl who looked like Princess Fiona from Shrek, all be it the ogre version. Has anyone else had such a brush with fame?

David
e-mail

❑ My wife is going to the bingo with her sister-in-law on March 18th. Do any *Viz* readers know the management for 'Girls Aloud', as I thought it would be an ideal opportunity for them to come round and take it in turns to suck my cock? They must be gone by eleven though, as the missus would do her bollocks if she found them here when she got back.

A Jessop
Wigan

❑ According to the news, more money is spent on boob jobs and viagra than on research into Alzheimer's disease. So by 2040, the elderly will all have perky tits and stiff cocks, but no fucking idea why.

Mike L Brown
e-mail

Lame to FAME

I WORK with someone whose dog had a fight with Billy Bragg's dog when on a walking holiday last year.

Roger Cantwell, e-mail

Your Stars at Night

With Gypsy Patrick Moore

Seventh astrolomer of a seventh astrolomer

IT'S been a fascinating week in the heavens. Astronomers at Arizona's Flagstaff Observatory have identified what they believe to be a supernova in the Horsehead Nebula. The 94-inch reflecting telescope recorded the star as it rose from magnitude 11 to magnitude 8 in three days. At its maximum it was clearly visible to the naked eye, but it has started to fall by 0.1 magnitudes per day, so now is the perfect time for any Capricorns or Geminis thinking about changing jobs to act.

SAGGITARIANS, Librans and the other water signs may have been experiencing problems with close relationships and money recently, but they should not despair. NASA's Cassini probe landed on Triton, Saturn's largest moon last week and discovered evidence of dried up river beds and methane rain, so things should begin to look up towards the middle of the week.

VIRGOS and Taureans will be thinking about travelling fairly soon, a round the world cruise or perhaps just a summer break. So it's a very good time for them to point their telescopes towards the constellation of Leo, where the planet Jupiter with its red spot, a giant thunderstorm of sulphuric acid 2000 miles across, is visible.

THE HUBBLE Space Telescope made a remarkable discovery last week when it spotted a cepheid variable star over 23 billion billion light years away. The star, referred to as HT301d is the most distant object ever observed, so it is an ideal moment for any Cancerians who have been putting off making an important decision to finally grasp the nettle.

❑ Once again the BBC are guilty of 'dumbing down'. A magnificent programme like *The Natural History of the British Isles* was marred by the choice of a distinctly lightweight presenter in Alan Titchmarsh. The programme would have been far more interesting had it been presented by an academic in the field of biology or geology. They may not have been a natural in front of camera, but they would has brought enthusiasm and intelect to the narrative. Failing that, Charlie Dimmock would have done. Just imagine her bra-less in her vest at the top of Ben Nevis. Them nips of hers would have put the camera lens through.

G. Dyke
London

UP THE ARSE CORNER

More from Up the Arse Corner on page 65

POL POT and IDI AMIN
GENOCIDAL JAPES WITH THE DICTATORIAL DUO
SAY, IDI. IS EVERYTHING SET FOR TONIGHT?
MR+MRS AMIN
YES. OUR WIVES WILL BE GOING OUT TO THE BINGO IN A MINUTE.
I HOPE YOU TWO BOYS WILL BE ALRIGHT ON YOUR OWN. WE'LL BE BACK ABOUT ELEVEN.
DON'T WORRY DEAREST. POL AND I WILL BE JUST FINE.
AND YOU BETTER NOT BE THINKING OF COMMITTING ANY ACTS OF GENOCIDE WHILE WE'RE OUT.
IF WE FIND OUT THAT YOU'VE MASS-MURDERED ANY BISHOPS AND INTELLECTUALS, WE'LL HAVE YOUR GUTS FOR GARTERS!
WHY, NOTHING COULD BE FURTHER FROM OUR MINDS. WE'RE JUST GOING TO HAVE A NICE QUIET EVENING PLAYING CARDS.
AREN'T WE, POL?
WE SURE ARE.
AND-
OK IDI — THEY'VE GONE
TEE HEE! I'LL FETCH IN THE BISHOPS AND INTELLECTUALS FOR US TO MASS MURDER
THERE. A TOP-NOTCH SELECTION OF BOFFINS AND GOD-BOTHERERS.
THEY LOOK JUST SWELL.
WE'LL START BEATING THEM TO A PULP WITH THIS AGRICULTURAL IMPLEMENT
THAT'S A GOOD IDEA.
CLONK!
YEOW! WATCH WHAT YOU'RE DOING!
YOU CLUMSY IDIOT
GIVE ME THAT RAKE!
POIT!
STRE-E-ETCH
PING!
WHOOSH
SLAP!
AND MAY THAT BE A LESSON TO YOU.
NOW IF YOU DON'T MIND, I'D LIKE TO GET ON WITH THIS GENOCIDE.
PASS ME THOSE GARDEN SHEARS.
SNIP!
FLUMPH!
WUMF! WUMF! WUMF!
PLOIP!
GLOOP GLOOP GLOOP
STRAWBERRY JAM
GLOOP GLOOP GLOOP
WUMFATA WUMFATA WUMFATA WUMFATA
STRAWBERRY JAM
BZZ BZZ
WASPS NEST
BZZ
BZZ BZZ BZZ BZZ
BZZ BZZ BZZ
WASPS NEST
PLOMP
BZZ BZZ BZZ
BLAM! BLAM!
BLAM! BLAM!
BZZ BZZ BZZ BZZ
EE-YARGH!
BZZ BZZ
THEY'RE SWARMING RIGHT UP MY BOTTOM!

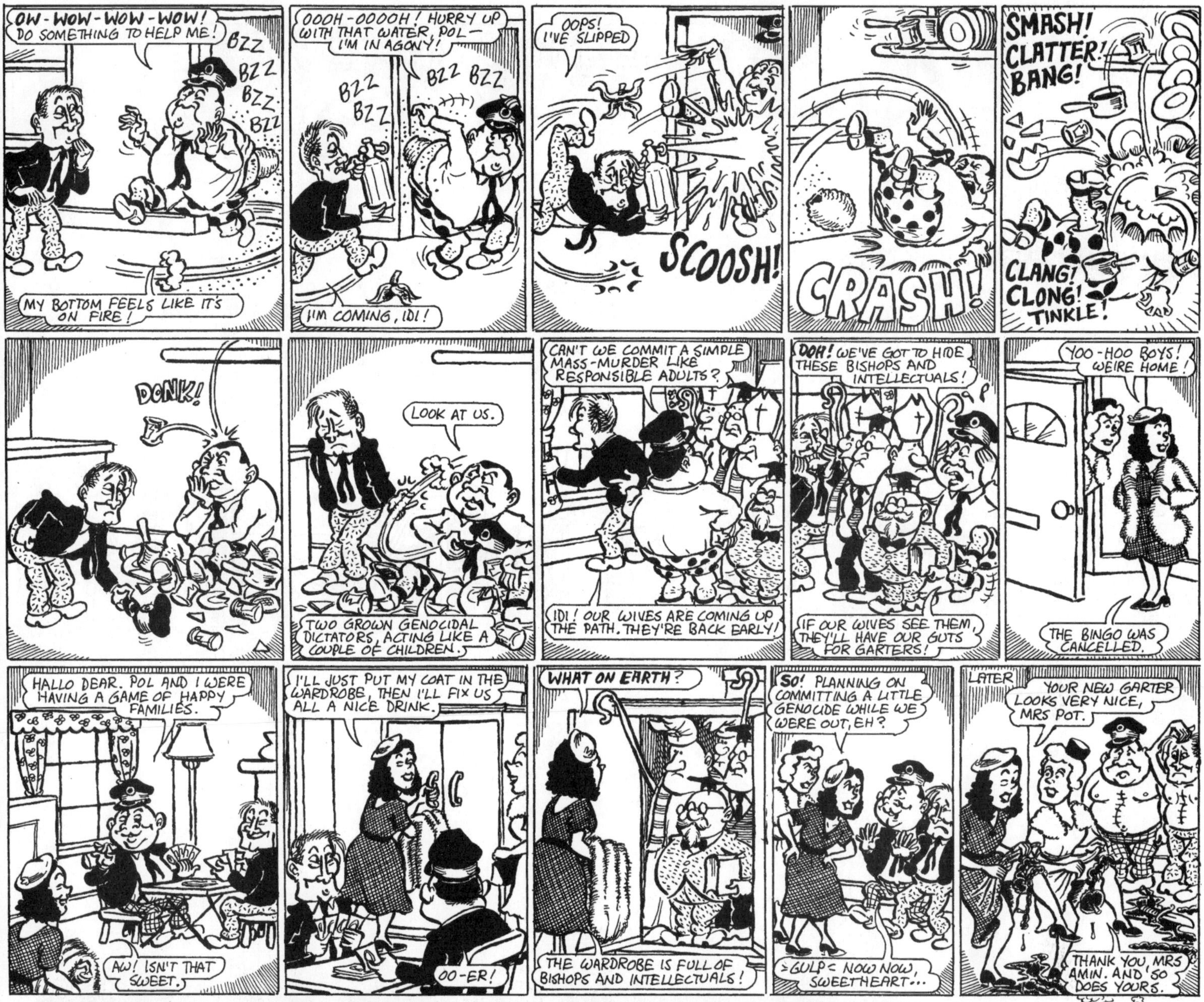
OW-WOW-WOW-WOW! DO SOMETHING TO HELP ME!
BZZ BZZ BZZ BZZ
MY BOTTOM FEELS LIKE IT'S ON FIRE!
OOOH-OOOOH! HURRY UP WITH THAT WATER, POL— I'M IN AGONY!
BZZ BZZ BZZ BZZ
I'M COMING, IDI!
OOPS! I'VE SLIPPED
SCOOSH!
CRASH!
SMASH! CLATTER! BANG!
CLANG! CLONG! TINKLE!
DONK!
LOOK AT US.
TWO GROWN GENOCIDAL DICTATORS, ACTING LIKE A COUPLE OF CHILDREN.
CAN'T WE COMMIT A SIMPLE MASS-MURDER LIKE RESPONSIBLE ADULTS?
IDI! OUR WIVES ARE COMING UP THE PATH. THEY'RE BACK EARLY!
OOH! WE'VE GOT TO HIDE THESE BISHOPS AND INTELLECTUALS!
IF OUR WIVES SEE THEM, THEY'LL HAVE OUR GUTS FOR GARTERS!
YOO-HOO BOYS! WE'RE HOME!
THE BINGO WAS CANCELLED.
HALLO DEAR. POL AND I WERE HAVING A GAME OF HAPPY FAMILIES.
AW! ISN'T THAT SWEET.
I'LL JUST PUT MY COAT IN THE WARDROBE, THEN I'LL FIX US ALL A NICE DRINK.
OO-ER!
WHAT ON EARTH?
THE WARDROBE IS FULL OF BISHOPS AND INTELLECTUALS!
SO! PLANNING ON COMMITTING A LITTLE GENOCIDE WHILE WE WERE OUT, EH?
>GULP< NOW NOW, SWEETHEART...
LATER
YOUR NEW GARTER LOOKS VERY NICE, MRS POT.
THANK YOU, MRS AMIN. AND SO DOES YOURS.

FARMER PALMER
MUCH INCEST-IN-THE-MARSH ANNUAL FELL RACE START
FINIS
FINIS

OH, LORDY! IT'S THE FAT SLAGS
ONE MORNING...
MUNCH! MUNCH!
ARIES
ARE Y' GOIN' TO 'AVE SOME BREAKFAST BEFORE Y' GO?
NAH! I'VE GOT T' GET T' WORK, SAN
WORK!?... I DIDN'T KNOW Y'D GORRA JOB, BAZ
EH!?... I'M NOT BAZ...
...I'M DENNIS...Y'KNOW, DENNIS FROM THE FISH VAN
FUCKIN' 'ELL, IT IS AN'ALL
I THOUGHT YER COCK WERE THICKER THAN USUAL
WELL, I'VE NEVER 'AD ANY COMPLAINTS SANDRA, LOVE.
EEH, TRAY... MY EYES ARE FUCKIN' TERRIBLE
WHY? WOT'S UP?
I'VE JUST SPENT THE NIGHT 'AVIN' IT OFF WI' DENNIS
WOT?.. SCAMPI DENNIS OFF THE FISH VAN?
AYE!
WELL SO WOT?
BAARP!
WELL, I THOUGHT HE W' BAZ!
'OW DID Y' THINK IT WERE BAZ? HE STINKS TO FUCK!
ARIES
AYE, BUT BAZ CAN HUM A BIT AT TIMES THOUGH, CAN'T HE?
AYE! S'POSE HE CAN
WELL, SAN. YOU'LL 'AVE T' GET YER EYES TESTED AN' GET YERSELF A PAIR OF SPECS
NO! NO! I CAN'T, TRAY. BAZ WON'T FANCY ME IN GEPS...
...Y'KNOW WOT THEY SAY... BOYS DON'T MAKE PASSES AT GIRLS WOT WEAR GLASSES
DON'T BE DAFT, SAN. BAZ RESPECTS YOU AS A PERSON... HIS LOVE GOES DEEPER THAN JUST OUTWARD APPEARENCES
D' YOU THINK SO?
I DO! ANYWAY, HE BANGED THAT WOMAN WHO WORKS IN THE LIBRARY, AND SHE'S GOT BINS LIKE FUCKIN' BOTTLE BOTTOMS
MORNIN', GIRLS.
SPEAK O' THE DEVIL
WHO IS IT?
IT'S BAZ
HEY, I'VE JUST SEEN SCAMPI DENNIS AT THE END OF YOUR STREET
AYE! HE BANGED ME LAST NIGHT, BUT I THOUGHT HE WAS YOU, BAZ.
Y' THOUGHT HE WAS ME!?
AYE! I'VE GOT BAD EYES Y'SEE, BAZ
Y' MUST 'AVE A BAD NOSE AN' ALL, SAN. I COULD SMELL HIM FROM THE BUS STOP
I TOLD 'ER SHE NEEDS SOME GLASSES, BUT SHE WON'T GET ANY BECAUSE SHE SEZ YOU WON'T FANCY 'ER ANY MORE
TELL 'ER, BAZ... TELL 'ER YOU'D STILL FANCY 'ER IF SHE 'AD GEPS ON
WELL... I DON'T KNOW AS I WOULD, TRAY... NOT WI' GLASSES.
BAZ!?!
...THEY DON'T DO MUCH FOR ME
YOU FUCKIN' HYPOCRITE!... YOU BANGED HER FROM THE LIBRARY
AYE, I DID...
BUT SHE DIDN'T 'AVE GLASSES ON ...SHE WERE WEARIN' 'SEXY SPECS'
SEXY SPECS?.. WOT'S THEM?
WELL, THEY'RE GLASSES... WOT... WHEN A BIRD'S GOT 'EM ON, THE BLOKE CAN STILL GET ON THE BONK!
WOT DO THEY LOOK LIKE?
WELL, IT'S HARD T' SAY... TELL YOU WOT, I'LL COME TO THE OPTICIANS WITH YOU... YOU TRY SOME OUT AN' I'LL TELL YOU IF I GET A BIT OF A TWITCH-ON
IF I DON'T GET A SEMI-ON, YOU'LL JUST 'AVE T' GET SOME CONTACT LENSES OR SUMMAT.
SO...
SPECS MANIAC
OPTICIAN
OPTICIA

SHORTLY...
WELL, THAT CONCLUDES YOUR EYE EXAMINATION, MISS BURKE...HERE'S YOUR PRESCRIPTION.
HOW DID IT GO, SAN? D'Y' NEED BINS?
AYE!
NOW, IT'S QUITE A STRONG PRESCRIPTION THAT YOU NEED, SO I RECOMMEND YOU PERHAPS GET A PAIR OF BIFOCALS
WOT'S THEM?
WELL... LIKE MINE. THEY HAVE TWO LENSES IN ONE. THE HALF MOON AT THE BOTTOM IS FOR CLOSE UP VISION, THE TOP PART IS FOR SEEING INTO THE DISTANCE
I STILL DON'T GET IT
WELL, IMAGINE YER GIVIN' ME A NOSH, SAN... WI' BIFOCALS ON, Y' COULD LOOK DOWN AN' SEE THE END OF ME COCK IN PINPOINT DETAIL... THEN Y' COULD LOOK UP AN' SEE ME STOOD AT THE OTHER END OF IT IN THE DISTANCE
AYE...
...IN YER DREAMS
WOT DO Y' THINK ANYWAY, BAZ? DO THESE DO OWT FOR YER?
NOT REALLY SAN...
...THEY'RE A BIT 'DAME EDNA'... AN' I'LL NOT GET WOOD COS SHE'S A BLOKE.
WOT ABOUT THESE, THEN? I LIKE THESE
CHRIST, NO! THEM'S LEZZERS GLASSES THEM
WELL THAT'S GOOD, IN'T IT? JUDGIN' BY ALL THEM FILMS Y' WATCH ON 'TELEVISION X'
NO, NOT THAT KIND... PROPER LEZZERS, SAN... PRISON WARDER RATHER THAN PORN CHANNEL
'ERE- TRY THESE... THEY'RE A BIT LIKE SCARY SPICE'S.
THERE! WHAT D' Y' RECKON?
OCH, AYE... ACTUALLY.
DO A BIT OF A SEXY POSE, SAN
OOH, YEAH! THAT'S IT, SAN. I'M DEFINITELY GETTIN' A BIT O' BLOOD IN IT... OOH, AYE... THEM'S THE ONES. THEM'S **SEXY SPECS** ALRIGHT.
YOU GET THEM, SAN, AN' WE'LL TRY 'EM OUT TONIGHT... I'LL GIVE YOU WHAT FOR IN YER BINS, EH?
AYE! SOUNDS GREAT, BAZ
SEE Y' ABOUT NINE IN THE PUB, EH?
AYE! SEE Y' THERE
NEXT MORNING...
DID Y'AVE A GOOD NIGHT WI' BAZ, SAN? DID HE MANAGE T' GEDDIT UP WI' YER GEPS ON?
DID HE GEDDIT UP? HE WAS LIKE A FUCKIN' **ROLLIN' PIN**, TRAY, I TELL YER.
HE WERE GOIN' AT IT ALL NIGHT LIKE A BULL AT A GATE... I WISH I'D GOT THESE GEPS YEARS AGO... THEY'RE TEN TIMES BETTER THAN THAT VIAGRA OFF THE NET.
EEH... I'LL HAVE T' GET MESELF A PAIR OF...
...**'ANG ON!**... THIS IS JUST **PLAIN GLASS!**
WELL, THEY W' THE ONES I TRIED ON IN THE SHOP!
AYE, BUT DIDN'T Y' GET YER PRESCRIPTION LENSES PUT IN?
NAH!
THEY WANTED ANOTHER 'UNDRED QUID FOR LENSES... I TOLD 'EM I'D NOT BOTHER.
SEE YOU, LOVE.
AYE, SEE Y' BAZ

SID the SEXIST
TITS OOT!
TYNESIDE'S SILVER-TONGUED CAVALIER
LOOK OOT, LADS. WOMAN DRIVER, STAY ON THE PAVEMENT.
LORNER AN' AALL. BEST GAN BACK IN THE PUB, EH? HEH-HEH.
VROOM! CRUNCH!
BAR
LEATHERHEAD DRIVING SCHOOL
CANNY PAIR O' HEADLAMPS ON 'ER, MIND.
GOOD JOB THAT THOUGH, DRIVIN' INSTRUCTOR... F'PULLIN' THE BORDS LIKE...
I SEEN THIS DOCUMENTARY ONCE...
THIS BLURK, REET, HE RAN A DRIVIN' SCHOOL ... COULDN'T FIGHT THE FANNY OFF, MAN. EVERY TIME HE TOOK A LASS OOT FOR A LESSON, HE ENDED UP PARKED UP SOMEWHERES BANGIN' 'ER.
FUCKIN' 'ELL.
AYE. THIS ONE LASS, HE DROVE OOT TO SOME WOODS, LIKE, AN' SCUTTED 'ER THAT HARD, THAT AALL THE DOORS OF HIS CAR FELL OFF.
ERM... ARE YEE SURE THIS WAS A DOCUMENTARY, JOE?
OH AYE...
FUCKIN' 'ELL.
...THE SAME BLURK DONE ONE WHERE HE WAS A WINDUR-CLEANER AN' AALL.
SHORTLY...
THERE YOU GAN, SON, ONE DUAL CONTRURL CAR.
Mc DOUGLE & SON plc PANEL BEATING, SPOT WELDING, CUT & SHUTS, SMUGGLED BACCY, STOLEN VIDEOS.
FUCKIN' MAGIC.
Smutt's School of motoring
AN' I'VE STRENGTHENED THE HINGES TO STOP THE DOORS FALLIN' OFF LIKE YUZ ASKED AN' AALL.
OH YEAH, I HAD TO CROSS 'EM AWA TO FIT THEM IN, SO THE BRAKE'S ON THE RIGHT AND THE CLUTCH IS ON THE LEFT.
AYE. CANNY.
NEXT MORNING...
POST OFF
RING! RING!
LOST CAT! TEL 123 4567
HELLO? SMUTT'S SCHOOL OF MOTORING?
SMUTT'S SCHOOL OF MOTORING
SCROGG ROAD, BYKER.
PROP. SIDNEY SMUTT
NERVOUS YOUNG BIRDS A SPECIALITY
SATISFACTION GUARANTEED
"IF YOU'RE A LASS, I'LL HELP YOU PASS"
(20% OFF FOR 38DD + ABOVE)
STUFFED CAT FOR SALE
I'D LIKE TO BOOK A COURSE OF LESSONS PLEASE.
SHORTLY...
Pa-Parp!
COMING, MR SMUTT.
I'M A BIT NERVOUS. THIS IS MY FIRST TIME.
DIVVEN'T WORRY, PET. I'LL BE GENTLE WI' YUZ. ANYWAY, DRIVIN' CARS IS EASY. EVEN LASSES CAN DEE IT...
...AS LONG AS THEY GET A BLURK TO PARK IT FOR 'EM, LIKE.
I'LL JUST RUN THROUGH THE CONTROLS, PET.
REET. VOLUME... BASS... TREBLE... LOODNESS... AND THIS 'UN EJECTS THE CASSETTE.
Smutt's School of motoring
I THOUGHT YOU WERE GOING TO TEACH ME TO DRIVE.
ALL REET, PET, I'M GETTIN' THERE. NEE NEED TO GET YER KNICKAS IN A TWIST...
...MEDIUM WAVE... LONG WAVE... FM...
ALL THESE PEDALS LOOK VERY COMPLICATED. I WOULDN'T KNOW WHERE TO PUT MY FEET.
RUB! RUB!
ONE OOT OF EACH WINDUR'LL SUIT ME FINE, LOVE.
HEH! HEH!
REET THEN, PET. LET'S GET SET OFF SHALL WE?
SO...
VROOM! VROOM!
CRUNCH! GRIND!
LURCH!
BANG! V-V-V-VROOM! K-K-K-K-CRUNCH!
HOP! HOP! HOP!
WOULD YOU LIKE ME TO HAVE A GO, MR SMUTT?
STOMP!

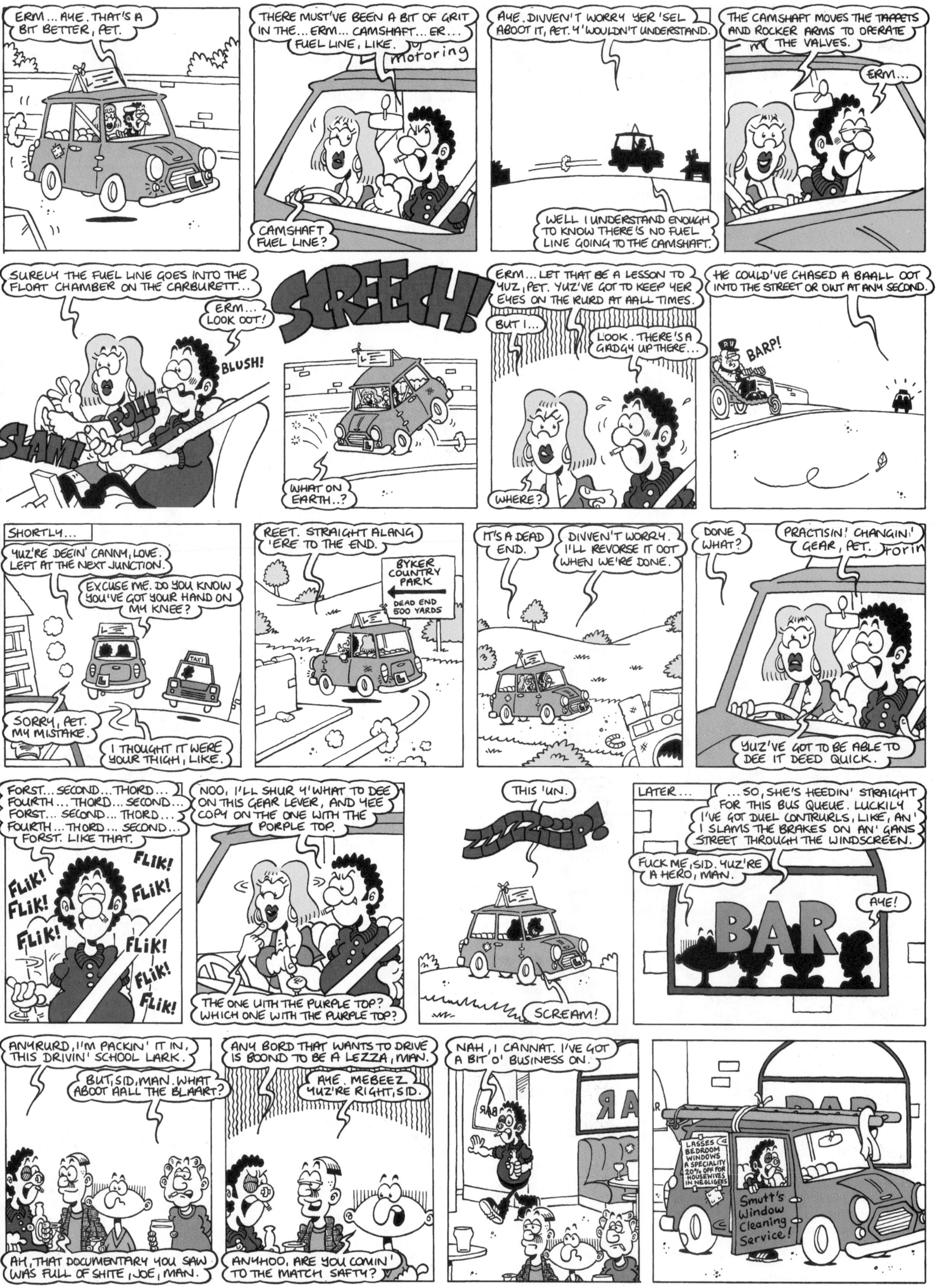
ERM... AYE. THAT'S A BIT BETTER, PET.
THERE MUST'VE BEEN A BIT OF GRIT IN THE... ERM... CAMSHAFT... ER... FUEL LINE, LIKE.
CAMSHAFT FUEL LINE?
AYE. DIVVEN'T WORRY YER 'SEL ABOOT IT, PET. Y'WOULDN'T UNDERSTAND.
WELL I UNDERSTAND ENOUGH TO KNOW THERE'S NO FUEL LINE GOING TO THE CAMSHAFT.
THE CAMSHAFT MOVES THE TAPPETS AND ROCKER ARMS TO OPERATE THE VALVES.
ERM...
SURELY THE FUEL LINE GOES INTO THE FLOAT CHAMBER ON THE CARBURETT...
ERM... LOOK OOT!
BLUSH!
PULL!
SLAM!
SCREECH!
WHAT ON EARTH..?
ERM... LET THAT BE A LESSON TO YUZ, PET. YUZ'VE GOT TO KEEP YER EYES ON THE RURD AT AALL TIMES.
BUT I...
LOOK. THERE'S A GADGY UP THERE...
WHERE?
HE COULD'VE CHASED A BAALL OOT INTO THE STREET OR OWT AT ANY SECOND.
BARP!
SHORTLY...
YUZ'RE DEEIN' CANNY, LOVE. LEFT AT THE NEXT JUNCTION.
EXCUSE ME. DO YOU KNOW YOU'VE GOT YOUR HAND ON MY KNEE?
TAXI
SORRY, PET. MY MISTAKE.
I THOUGHT IT WERE YOUR THIGH, LIKE.
REET. STRAIGHT ALANG 'ERE TO THE END.
BYKER COUNTRY PARK
DEAD END 500 YARDS
IT'S A DEAD END.
DIVVEN'T WORRY. I'LL REVORSE IT OOT WHEN WE'RE DONE.
DONE WHAT?
PRACTISIN' CHANGIN' GEAR, PET.
YUZ'VE GOT TO BE ABLE TO DEE IT DEED QUICK.
FORST... SECOND... THORD... FOURTH... THORD... SECOND... FORST... SECOND... THORD... FOURTH... THORD... SECOND... FORST. LIKE THAT.
FLIK! FLIK! FLIK! FLIK! FLIK! FLIK! FLIK! FLIK!
NOO, I'LL SHUR Y'WHAT TO DEE ON THIS GEAR LEVER, AND YEE COPY ON THE ONE WITH THE PORPLE TOP.
THE ONE WITH THE PURPLE TOP? WHICH ONE WITH THE PURPLE TOP?
THIS 'UN.
ZZZZIIIP!
SCREAM!
LATER...
...SO, SHE'S HEEDIN' STRAIGHT FOR THIS BUS QUEUE. LUCKILY I'VE GOT DUEL CONTRURLS, LIKE, AN' I SLAMS THE BRAKES ON AN' GANS STREET THROUGH THE WINDSCREEN.
FUCK ME, SID. YUZ'RE A HERO, MAN.
BAR
AYE!
ANYRURD, I'M PACKIN' IT IN, THIS DRIVIN' SCHOOL LARK.
BUT, SID, MAN. WHAT ABOOT AALL THE BLAART?
AH, THAT DOCUMENTARY YOU SAW WAS FULL OF SHITE, JOE, MAN.
ANY BORD THAT WANTS TO DRIVE IS BOOND TO BE A LEZZA, MAN.
AYE. MEBEEZ YUZ'RE RIGHT, SID.
ANYHOO, ARE YOU COMIN' TO THE MATCH SAFTY?
NAH, I CANNAT. I'VE GOT A BIT O' BUSINESS ON.
LASSES BEDROOM WINDOWS A SPECIALITY 20% OFF FOR HOUSEWIVES IN NEGLIGEES
Smutt's Window Cleaning Service!

Ursine 'o' the Times

King of Pop survives another bear attack

PINT-sized popstar Prince has been forced to put the release of his latest album back by twelve months following a bizarre break-in at his Paisley Park studios. However, the intruder wasn't an internet bootlegger after his master-tapes... it was a 30-stone black bear bent on pinching his packed lunch, the *fourth* such attack in his career.

Prince was about to tuck into a mackerel paste sandwich during a break in recording when the ravenous animal tore its way through a studio wall. "Prince stopped singing and yelled 'Bear!'" bass player Hamilton Winter told reporters.

grizzly

"All us members of his backing band *The Revolution* fled for our lives as the giant grizzly cornered the 4'11" funk svengali, whose hits include Purple Rain, When Doves Cry and Cream, against a piano."

By our Pop Correspondent
Labia Seepage
in Mineapolis, USA

The 11' 4" brown bear (above) which burst into the recording studio where 4" 11' Prince (left) was recording.

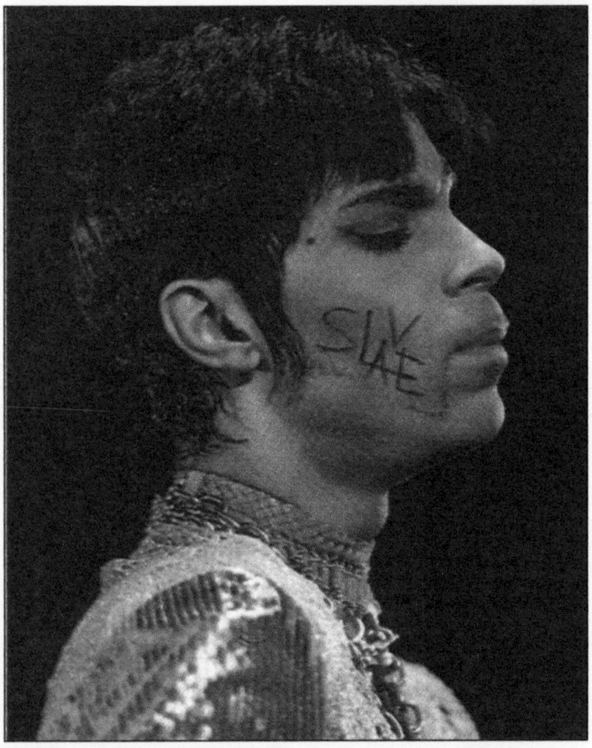

"It was terrifying," agreed producer Todd Rundgren, who watched the drama unfold.

matchwood

"The artist formerly known as the artist formerly known as Prince tried to fend it off with his guitar, but one blow from the bear's paw smashed it to so much matchwood. In the end he had to throw his sandwiches to the other side of the studio to distract it long enough to make his escape."

The 10 foot bear then spent half an hour lumbering round the $12 million studio complex, ripping up master tapes, destroying mixing desks and shitting on the drums. By the time Mineapolis State Wildlife Rangers arrived to shoot it with a tranquiliser dart, a year's work on Prince's latest album had been destroyed.

The tiny singer, who has penned hits for stars such as *Cyndi Lauper, Sinead O'Connor, the Bangles* and *Clive Dunn*, had been hoping for a January release, but the bear attack now makes that deadline look increasingly unlikely.

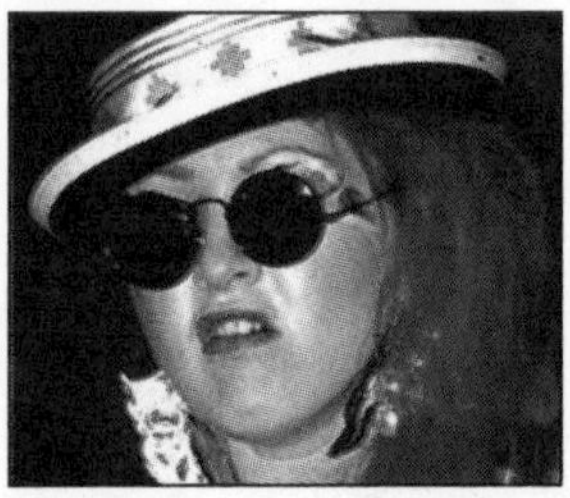

Lauper - True Colours

Prince, who recently changed his name to a squiggle and then back again when nobody noticed, is believed to be particularly angered by the attack since he recently shelled out over $3 million having his recording studio bear-proofed

It's the Scare B

THIS bear attack is just the latest in a terrifying series which have plagued the purple pocket rocker throughout his career:

- **Attack 1:** *Sessions to record Prince's 1984 chart-topper '1999' were interrupted when a confused kodiak bear which had woken early from hibernation wandered into the recording studio after apparently smelling a Toblerone which Prince was eating. The singer managed to hold it at bay by sticking a microphone stand up its arse until help arrived.*
- **Attack 2:** *During a 1987 UK tour to promote Prince's album 'Sign 'o' the Times', a female polar bear and her cubs which had escaped from the North Wales Mountain Zoo sneaked onto his tour bus while it was parked in a layby near Colwyn Bay. Prince and his band the New Power Generation were having a wee in a field when heard the horn tooting. Retur to the coach Prince was horr to discover the 11 foot arctic nivore sitting in the driver's whilst her cubs played in the a "Everything would have been if Prince hadn't made the mis of somehow getting between bear and her cubs," reca drummer Sheila E. "That's the rule when you're dealing*

THEY'RE cuddly, they're grizzly, they're brown, they're polar and they're the bane of Prince's life. That's right, they're bears and they're the world's biggest animal beginning with 'B'. Apart from blue whales. We see them everywhere we go, from the North Pole to toy shops, But we "bearly" know anything about them. Here's the "bear" essentials, a dozen furry facts about our favourite cave-dwelling carnivores.

12 THINGS YOU NEVER KNEW about BEARS

1 Evolution has played a cruel trick on bears, giving them short front legs. This means that their arses stick up higher than their heads, making bears a tempting target for angry bees.

2 Like Fred Astaire and Ginger Rogers, bears just love to dance. In Turkey and Greece proud bear owners teach their pets to trip the light fantastic, a process which involves snapping their teeth out with pliers and beating their shins with sticks.

3 Contrary to what you might think, not all bears are bears. For example, koala bears aren't bears at all. They're actually koalas, a type of small Australian bear which eats eucalyptus leaves.

4 What's more, some things that aren't called bears are bears. For example, the giant panda of China isn't really a panda. Scientists now believe that these bear-like black and white bamboo-chomping mammals are actually a special kind of bear called a panda.

5 Not all bears shit in the woods. Polar bears live in the Arctic, at least 3000 miles from the nearest tree, so they probably just have to do it behind some snow and then wipe their arse on a penguin. Other bears that don't shit in the woods include the Coventry Bears, a rugby team from the West Midlands. They probably shit in pint glasses in pubs.

6 Ask TV naturist David Attenborough what the biggest bear in the world is and chances are he'll tell you it's the Kodiak bear, which can top the scales at ten foot tall. However he'd be wrong, because the biggest bear in the world is actually the Great Bear, a constellation made of stars in the night sky which is hundreds of miles across.

7 Like British old age pensioners, bears curl up and go to sleep in the winter. However, unlike many British old age pensioners, bears tend to wake up again in the spring.

8 In the old days it was often said that if you stepped on the cracks in the pavement, the bears would get you. However, nowadays if you step on the cracks in the pavement you may be entitled to compensation worth thousands of pounds from the local authority on a no-win, no-fee basis. If you'd like to find out more about making a claim, call the Accident Advice Helpline on 0800 180 4060.

9 If you go down to the woods today and interrupt a bears' picnic, you could be in for a big surprise. That's because not only is a bear an animal, it's also a big, hairy homosexual. Small, bald homosexuals are called Jimmy Somerville.

10 Bears have featured in many films such as *The Jungle Book*, *BJ and the Bear* and *The Adventures of Grizzly Adams*. In 1978, Clyde the orange bear became the first bear to win an Oscar when he co-starred alongside Clint Eastwood and Geoffrey Palmer in the action comedy *Every Which Way But Loose*.

11 Insufferable TV favourite Gyles Brandreth has an amazing secret. For the ganzy-clad ex-MP owns 8,000 teddy bears, which he keeps at a museum in Stratford-upon-Avon. Every evening before Brandreth goes to bed he kisses each one of them goodnight - a process which bear-kissing boffins estimate takes 16,000 seconds!

12 The world's largest bear is the kodiak bear of Alaska, which stands over ten feet tall - that's equivalent to the height of Kylie Minogue standing on Ronnie Corbett's head. And it weighs nearly three quarters of a ton - the same as the Krankies... *carrying twenty-six car batteries!*

Bunch

ears, but Prince clean forgot. All ell broke loose and he ended up iding in the parcel shelf until Clwyd Police arrived and lured it ff the bus with a dead seal."

• Attack 3: *Whilst shooting a cene in a marmalade factory for is film debut 'Purple Rain', Prince arrowly escaped death when a arauding Peruvian spectacled ear smashed its way through a kylight and dropped onto the set. ten minute static chase on a onveyor belt ensued which only nded when Prince vanished into n automatic bottling machine, merging moments later in a bigger than usual jar of marmalade. All we could see was his eyes linking above the label," said irector Trevor Brooking. "It would ave made a great scene for the lm, but Prince insisted it ended p on the cutting room floor."*

Could YOU survive a bear attack? ...Yes! With your FREE Gerry 'Grizzly' Adams' Bear-ometer!

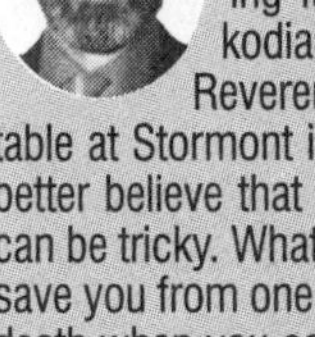

"As leader of Sinn Fein, I'm used to pressure. But let me tell you, compared to coming face to face with a hungry kodiak bear, negotiating with the Reverend Ian Paisley across the table at Stormont is a *walk in the park!* You'd better believe that coping with an angry bear can be tricky. What's more, a tactic that might save you from one species could spell certain death when you come up against another.

Over the years, I've amassed a huge amount of data about how to cope with angry bears of all types. Now I'm making the fruits of my research available to Viz readers in the form of this handsome pocket Bear-ometer fact file. Keep it with you at all times to ensure complete safety in the event of an attack."

Gerry 'Grizzly' Adams' Bear-ometer! ~ Pocket Bear Survival Guide

Breed of Bear	Danger Rating	Risk Factor	Peril Ratio	Escape Strategy
Koala Bear	10%	1/10	0.1	*Throw Lockets or mentholyptus flavoured Tunes to distract the bear before walking calmly away.*
Sun Bear	30%	3/10	0.3	*Keep it at bay with a stick or snooker cue until help arrives.*
Sloth Bear	30%	3/10	0.3	*Sloth bears are scared of fire and loud noises, so brandish a burning faggot and shout "Hyah! Hyah! Gertcha!"*
Spectacled Bear	40%	4/10	0.4	*Dig a shallow pit filled with bamboo spikes between you and the bear, then goad it into falling in.*
Giant Panda	40%	4/10	0.4	*Pandas have very poor eyesight, so run upstairs and hide in the wardrobe.*
Black Bear	60%	6/10	0.6	*Clap loudly to confuse the bear whilst retreating slowly to a place of safety.*
Brown Bear	70%	7/10	0.7	*Smear yourself with your own excreta and lie perfectly still - the bear will soon move on.*
Kodiak Bear	70%	7/10	0.7	*Avoid eye contact, don't bare your teeth and run away backwards in a haphazard zig-zag.*
Polar Bear	90%	9/10	0.9	*Polar bears can run at speeds in excess of 60mph so you have no chance of outrunning one. Head towards thinnish ice which will support your weight but crack under that of a polar bear. But make sure it's not too thin, if you fall in as well you're a goner. A polar bear can swim at speeds in excess of 50 nautical miles an hour.*
Grizzly Bear	100%	10/10	1.0	*The grizzly is perhaps the world's most gullible bear so tell it that 30-stone darts star Andy Fordham is coming across the bridge next, and he will will make much finer eating than you.*

COPPER KETTLE
The 'PC' who LOVES his 'PG'
I'VE GOT THE MOST IMPORTANT JOB IN THE LAND, READERS. I'M GUARDING THE PRIME MINISTER!
10
I'M LIKE A COILED SPRING, CONSTANTLY ON THE ALERT FOR AL QU'AEDA SUICIDE BOMBERS OR OTIS FERRY.
I CAN'T ALLOW MY ATTENTION TO WANDER FOR EVEN A SPLIT SECOND.
AH. HALF TEN, TIME FOR ME TEA-BREAK. AND NOT A MOMENT TOO SOON. I'M GASPING FOR A BREW.
AY-UP. HERE COMES THE P.M. TO ADDRESS THE PRESS WHILE I DRINK THIS NICE MUG OF CHAR.
BUT...
I'LL HAVE THAT. A CUP OF TEA IS JUST WHAT MY SPIN-DOCTORS SAID I NEEDED TO LOOK LIKE A MAN OF THE PEOPLE IN FRONT OF THE CAMERAS.
SNATCH!
HUNH!?
...TRULY SHE IS THE PRETEND SCHOOLBOY OF HEARTS AND MY THOUGHTS ARE, OBVIOUSLY WITH HER AT THIS DIFFICULT TIME...
WHAT A MAN OF THE PEOPLE.
YES. LOOK AT HIS CUP OF TEA.
RIGHT, BUGGER IT. I'M SPITTING FEATHERS.
I THINK I'LL CALL IN AT THE HOLLYBUSH TEA ROOMS FOR A CHAT ABOUT COUNTER TERRORISM MEASURES...
...AND WHILE I'M TELLING THEM THE BEST WAY TO COPE WITH 9-11s, ANTHRAX ATTACKS AND DIRTY BOMBS, I MIGHT JUST HAVE A NICE CUP OF ROSY LEE!
HEH-HEH!
TING!
OPEN
CUP OF TEA, PLEASE. MILK AND TWO SUGARS.
SORRY, DEAR. WE DON'T DO TEA ANY MORE. WE'VE BEEN TAKEN OVER.
WELCOME TO COSTBUCKS FRAPPACHINO REPUBLIC
NO TEA
PAPER CUPS FIZZY COFFEE FROM £6
SUGAR £3 EACH BIT OF WOOD TO STIR IT WITH £5
HAVE YOU TRIED OUR OVERPRICED FUCKING BISCUITS FROM £4?
WE DON'T SELL TEA
BLOODY NORA, WHAT DOES A BOBBY HAVE TO DO TO GET A PLAIN, OLD-FASHIONED CUP OF TEA THESE DAYS?
BUCKS
UNLESS...
TO THE ZOO
DON'T MISS THE CHIMPS' TEA PARTY EVERY DAY AT NOON!
SO...
...AND YOU'RE SURE YOU WANT TO GO IN WITH THE MONKEYS?
STAFF ONLY
OOH, YES. IT'S IMPORTANT POLICE BUSINESS. I HAVE TO TASTE THEIR TEA TO MAKE SURE... ERM... THEY'RE NOT BEING PLIED WITH DATE RAPE DRUGS BY... ER... INTERNET PAEDOPHILES.
CHIMPS
HA! I'M IN! NOW TO POUR MESELF A LOVELY HOT CUP OF THE DRINK WHICH REFRESHETH BUT DOTH NOT INEBRIATE.
SLOOP!
GAK!! JESUS! THAT'S THE WORST THING I'VE EVER TASTED!
FUCK ME!
SPIT! SPIT! I CAN ONLY CONCLUDE THAT THE DIRTY DEVILS HAVE BEEN URINATING AND DEFECATING IN THE TEAPOT.
OOH, NO. IT'S REAL TEA ALRIGHT, OFFICER. ONLY WE MAKE IT WITH SAFEWAYS VALUE TEABAGS, WHICH WOULD EXPLAIN WHY IT TASTES LIKE CHIMPANZEE SHIT.
BAH!
SHORTLY...
AT LAST! MY LUCK'S IN!
TODAY! FREE CUPS OF TEA FOR POLICEMEN
THERE'S QUITE A QUEUE...
FREE CUPS OF TEA FOR POLICEMEN!
FREE CUPS OF TEA!
QUEUE HERE
...BUT IT'LL BE WORTH IT TO GET A GRATIS CUPPA!
2 HOURS LATER...
RIGHT! WHO'S NEXT FOR A FREE CUP OF TEA?
ACE!
I'M PARCHED!
OH NO. IT'S THAT KIND OF "FREE CUP OF TEA".
METROPOLITAN POLICE HERNIA AWARENESS WEEK FRONTED BY A-TEAM ACTOR MR TEA
LOOK TO THE RIGHT AND COUGH, FOOL.
CUP!
K-HEUGH

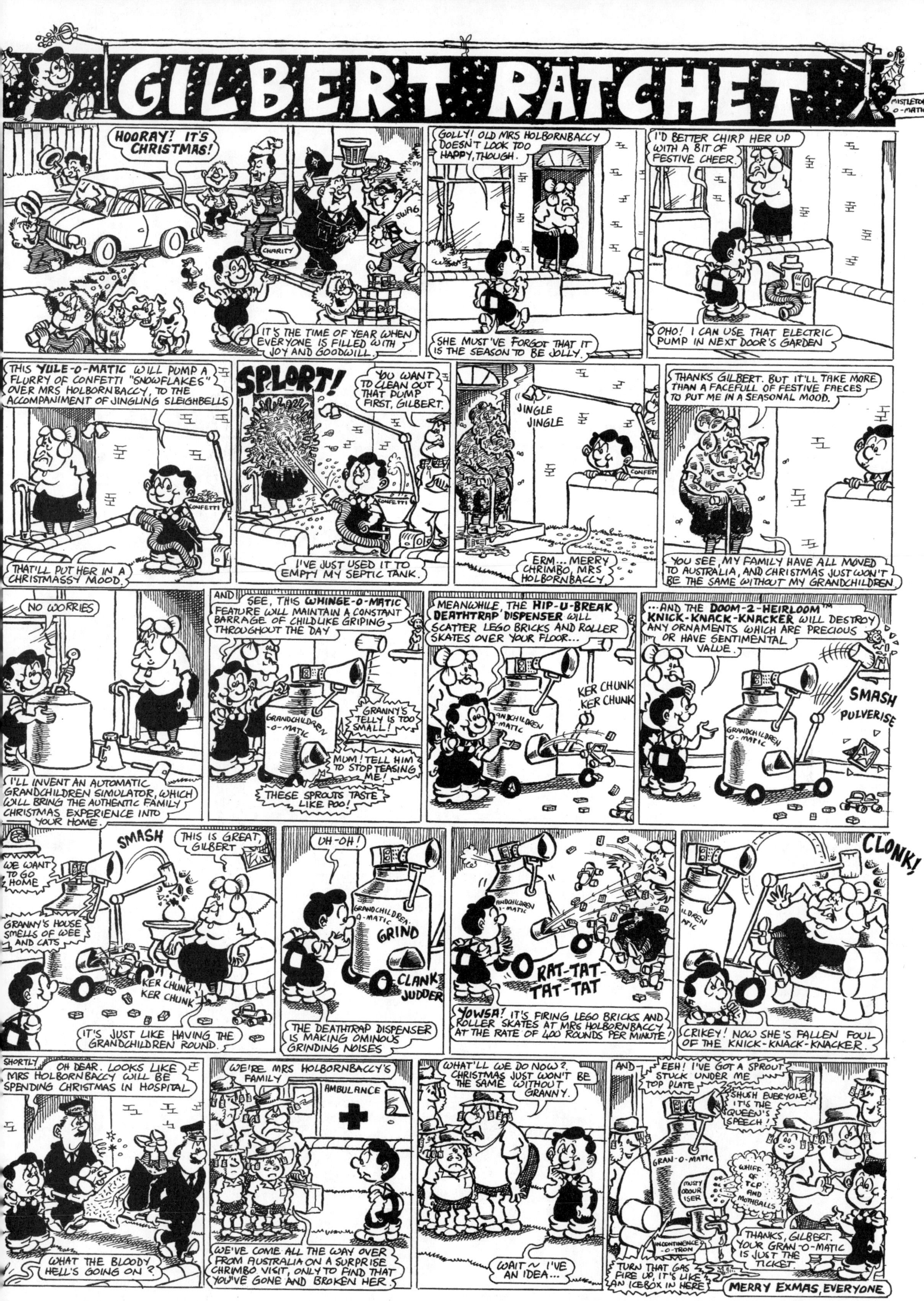
GILBERT RATCHET
MISTLETOE -O-MATIC
HOORAY! IT'S CHRISTMAS!
CHARITY
SWAG
IT'S THE TIME OF YEAR WHEN EVERYONE IS FILLED WITH JOY AND GOODWILL.
GOLLY! OLD MRS HOLBORNBACCY DOESN'T LOOK TOO HAPPY, THOUGH.
SHE MUST'VE FORGOT THAT IT IS THE SEASON TO BE JOLLY.
I'D BETTER CHIRP HER UP WITH A BIT OF FESTIVE CHEER.
OHO! I CAN USE THAT ELECTRIC PUMP IN NEXT DOOR'S GARDEN
THIS YULE-O-MATIC WILL PUMP A FLURRY OF CONFETTI "SNOWFLAKES" OVER MRS HOLBORNBACCY, TO THE ACCOMPANIMENT OF JINGLING SLEIGHBELLS
CONFETTI
THAT'LL PUT HER IN A CHRISTMASSY MOOD.
SPLORT!
YOU WANT TO CLEAN OUT THAT PUMP FIRST, GILBERT.
CONFETTI
I'VE JUST USED IT TO EMPTY MY SEPTIC TANK.
JINGLE JINGLE
CONFETTI
ERM... MERRY CHRIMBO, MRS HOLBORNBACCY.
THANKS GILBERT. BUT IT'LL TAKE MORE THAN A FACEFULL OF FESTIVE FAECES TO PUT ME IN A SEASONAL MOOD.
YOU SEE, MY FAMILY HAVE ALL MOVED TO AUSTRALIA, AND CHRISTMAS JUST WON'T BE THE SAME WITHOUT MY GRANDCHILDREN.
NO WORRIES
I'LL INVENT AN AUTOMATIC GRANDCHILDREN SIMULATOR, WHICH WILL BRING THE AUTHENTIC FAMILY CHRISTMAS EXPERIENCE INTO YOUR HOME.
AND SEE, THIS WHINGE-O-MATIC FEATURE WILL MAINTAIN A CONSTANT BARRAGE OF CHILDLIKE GRIPING THROUGHOUT THE DAY
GRANDCHILDREN -O-MATIC
GRANNY'S TELLY IS TOO SMALL!
MUM! TELL HIM TO STOP TEASING ME!
THESE SPROUTS TASTE LIKE POO!
MEANWHILE, THE HIP-U-BREAK DEATHTRAP DISPENSER WILL SCATTER LEGO BRICKS AND ROLLER SKATES OVER YOUR FLOOR...
KER CHUNK KER CHUNK
...AND THE DOOM-2-HEIRLOOM™ KNICK-KNACK-KNACKER WILL DESTROY ANY ORNAMENTS WHICH ARE PRECIOUS OR HAVE SENTIMENTAL VALUE.
SMASH
PULVERISE
GRANDCHILDREN -O-MATIC
SMASH
THIS IS GREAT, GILBERT
WE WANT TO GO HOME
GRANNY'S HOUSE SMELLS OF WEE AND CATS
KER CHUNK KER CHUNK
IT'S JUST LIKE HAVING THE GRANDCHILDREN ROUND.
UH-OH!
GRANDCHILDREN -O-MATIC
GRIND
CLANK
JUDDER
THE DEATHTRAP DISPENSER IS MAKING OMINOUS GRINDING NOISES
RAT-TAT-TAT-TAT
YOWSA! IT'S FIRING LEGO BRICKS AND ROLLER SKATES AT MRS HOLBORNBACCY AT THE RATE OF 400 ROUNDS PER MINUTE!
CLONK!
CRIKEY! NOW SHE'S FALLEN FOUL OF THE KNICK-KNACK-KNACKER.
SHORTLY
OH DEAR. LOOKS LIKE MRS HOLBORNBACCY WILL BE SPENDING CHRISTMAS IN HOSPITAL
WHAT THE BLOODY HELL'S GOING ON?
WE'RE MRS HOLBORNBACCY'S FAMILY
AMBULANCE
WE'VE COME ALL THE WAY OVER FROM AUSTRALIA ON A SURPRISE CHRIMBO VISIT, ONLY TO FIND THAT YOU'VE GONE AND BROKEN HER.
WHAT'LL WE DO NOW? CHRISTMAS JUST WON'T BE THE SAME WITHOUT GRANNY.
WAIT ~ I'VE AN IDEA...
AND
EEH! I'VE GOT A SPROUT STUCK UNDER ME TOP PLATE
SHUSH EVERYONE. IT'S THE QUEEN'S SPEECH!
GRAN-O-MATIC
MUSTY ODOUR ISER
WHIFF OF TCP AND MOTHBALLS
INCONTINENCE -O-TRON
TURN THAT GAS FIRE UP, IT'S LIKE AN ICEBOX IN HERE
THANKS, GILBERT. YOUR GRAN-O-MATIC IS JUST THE TICKET
MERRY EXMAS, EVERYONE

No Sex, Please... we're Dinosaurs!

Suffolk Postie Solves Age-Old Riddle of Dinosaurs' Death

We all know that dinosaurs, the one time rulers of the earth died out over ten million years ago following some huge, catastrophic event. But new evidence shows that it wasn't a meteorite that brought about their demise. Neither was it global climate change brought on by a huge volcanic eruption. It was because the giant, scaly lizards were *rubbish at sex!*

Diplodocuses, Stegasauruses and Pteridactyls were so bad between the prehistoric sheets, that the females of the species seldom fancied 'a bit of the other'. And it was this poor performance in the Jurassic bedroom that eventualy led to the extinction of these beasts.

That's the conclusion of a Suffolk postman who has spent a lunchtime researching the 'how's your father' habits of the largest animals that ever stalked the earth.

Malcolm Knott, 52, came to his astonishing conclusion between the ninth and tenth pints of his regular mid-day drinking session at the Lowestoft Post Office Club. And according to him, the new theory has got dinosaur boffins in a tiswas.

Malcolm Knott - new theory has literally turned the dinosaur world upside down

Shift

"I always have a few drinks with the lads at the end of an early shift," said the East Anglian postie. "It'll usually turn into a serious discussion about matters of scientific interest after seven or eight pints, especially if someone else is at the dartboard.

"On this particular day we'd just been laughing at Judy Finnegan's tits in the paper when I caught sight of an artist's impression of a Brachiosaurus on the following page. It just made me think, what with its incredibly long and flexible neck, it probably have been able to suck itself off - and which dinosaur in its right mind would ever bother having sex again if it could do that?"

control

Encouraged by the positive reaction of his workmates, Malcolm soon postulated that the Diplodocus was an ugly bastard with a bit of a temper on it, meaning that it would have been very unlikely to ever pull a lady Diplodocus.

He then went on to theorise that the Tyrannosaurus would never have been able reach its cock to have a wank because its arms were far too short.

"When it did have sex, it would be so frustrated it would probably go off after two pushes," he hypothesised. "And as for the Stegasaurus, well, do you know any bloke who would bang his missus if she had four massive spikes sticking out of her arse? It's no wonder they're all extinct."

Knott was so convinced by his findings that he immediately wrote it all down on a beer mat and posted it to the Natural History Museum on the way home.

"I completely forgot I'd even done it," he says, "I just went back to my usual routine for the next few weeks. I didn't think about dinosaurs once." But when the museum did finally speak to Malcolm, he received the shock of his life.

Caps lock

"They left me a message on my answerphone, which I accidentally deleted, congratulating me on my groundbreaking theories. They told me that the scientific community had already adopted them, and said I'd get my name in a book. All the scientists in the world were now absolutely convinced that dinosaurs weren't any good at rumpy pumpy, and it's all down to me. It's ironic, really, because I'm not interested in dinosaurs at all. I even fell asleep at the pictures in the middle bit of *Jurassic Park*.

According to himself, Knott was then whisked off to meet Sir David Attenborough at his house in central London.

"It was wonderful. There were all lions and pandas running around everywhere," Knott told reporters. "Sir David told me that the answer to the dinosaurs' extinction was so glaringly obvious that he couldn't understand why they'd never realised it before. We drank his best brandy and laughed for hours and hours and hours at all those stupid stories about enormous meteorites and drastic climate change."

f4

We contacted Sir David who spoke to us from a safari suit he was wearing at the time. The veteran broadcaster said that he had never met a Mr. Knott and was very surprised to learn of his claims, which he described as 'interesting'.

Malcolm later got in touch with us to say that he had meant David Bellamy, not David Attenborough, before saying that the reception on his mobile phone was really bad and that we were breaking up.

How the dinosaurs shaped up for sex:

WE asked paeleontologists from the Natural History Museum to speculate on what sexual problems the dinosaurs may have suffered from, and then give each an 'in-bed sexual performance' rating. Here's what they may have said, had they rung us back:

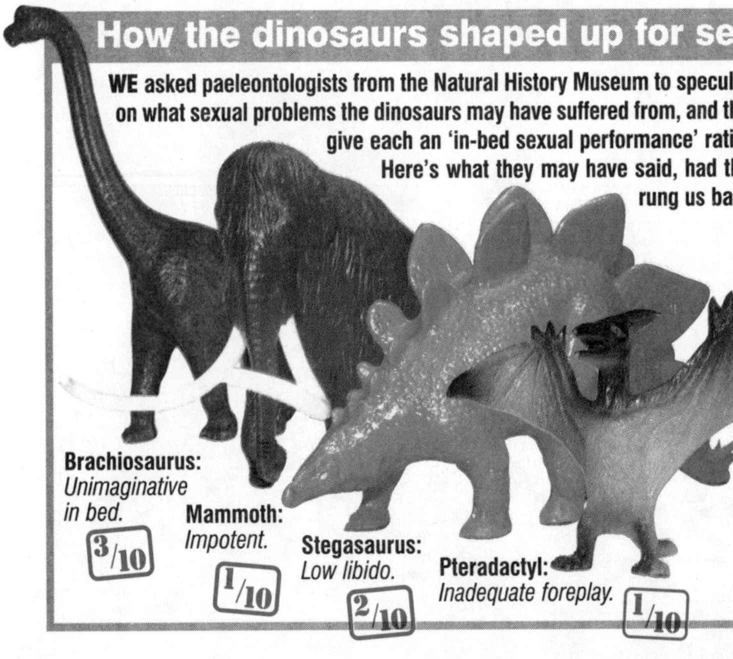

Brachiosaurus: *Unimaginative in bed.* 3/10

Mammoth: *Impotent.* 1/10

Stegasaurus: *Low libido.* 2/10

Pteradactyl: *Inadequate foreplay.* 1/10

AH, F-FF-FFUCKIN' F-FFUCKIT... THAT WOH ME LAST F-FFUCKIN' TIN.
GALLERIE de POSH Exclusive Luxuries
OPEN
TRIP!
WELCOME TO OUR 1,000,000th CUSTOMER!
!?
HUNH...?
CONGRATULATIONS, SIR! YOU'RE THE MILLIONTH CUSTOMER OF THE GALLERIE de POSH EMPORIUM OF EXCLUSIVE LUXURY ITEMS. YOU'VE WON A 3-MINUTE TROLLEY DASH!
F-FF-CHAMPION...
RIGHT... ON YOUR MARKS... GET SET...
ROLEX WATCHES
LEICA CAMERAS
BOLLY CHAMPAGNE
PLASMA TVs
CUBAN CIGARS
MONTBLANC PENS
FABERGÉ EGGS
FERRERO ROCHERS
BANG!
...GO...!?
PATEL'S 24-HOUR NANO-MART
WHACK-WHARK!
ONE FORTY-NINE.

JOHNNY FART-PANTS
FULCHESTER CATHEDRAL
MIDNIGHT MASS TONITE
IT'S CHRISTMAS EVE, READERS, SO I'M OFF TO MIDNIGHT MASS AT FULCHESTER CATHEDRAL.
OH DEAR, JOHNNY. I'VE LEFT THE COMMUNION WAFERS IN THE OVEN TOO LONG, AND THEY'RE RUINED
NOW I'VE GOT NO HOLY BISCUITS TO GIVE MY PARISHONERS FOR THEIR COMMUNION
HANG ON, VICAR ~ I'LL JUST SCOFF THIS JAR OF OLD EL PASO'S TANGY BARBECUE FAJITA SAUCE
OLD EL PASO
THEN MY BOTTOM WILL PROVIDE YOU WITH PLENTY OF HOLY COMMUNION AIR-BISCUITS.
THAT'S IT, VICAR ~ CATCH THE GUFF IN YOUR CUPPED HANDS
QUACK
GOT IT, JOHNNY!
"...AND THE LORD TOOK THE BREAD, AND HE BROKE IT"
"AND HE SAIETH UNTO THE DISCIPLES, DO THIS IN REMEMBRANCE OF ME..."
XXXX
CUPCAKE!
SNACK ON THAT!
CHOKE
ARCHBISHOP FATTY FORBISHER WANTS HIS COMMUNION NEXT, AND HE'S GOT A BIG APPETITE FOR THE BODY OF CHRIST.
I'LL NEED AN EXTRA-LARGE AIR-WAFER THIS TIME, JOHNNY
ONE SUPERSIZE EUCHARIST CHUFF COMING UP, VICAR
RUMBLE
GNNNNN...
BRAP!
YOIKS! THAT PUMP WAS SUCH A SCORCHER, IT'S BURNT RIGHT THROUGH THE VICAR'S HANDS!
SIZZLE
MELT
I'M IN FOR A RIGHT WHACKING, NOW
NICE ONE, JOHNNY! THESE MIRACULOUS EGGY STIGMATA WILL MAKE ME THE ENVY OF ALL THE CLERGY IN THE CHURCH OF ENGLAND
HELP YOURSELF TO A TENNER FROM THE COLLECTION PLATE.

LETTER

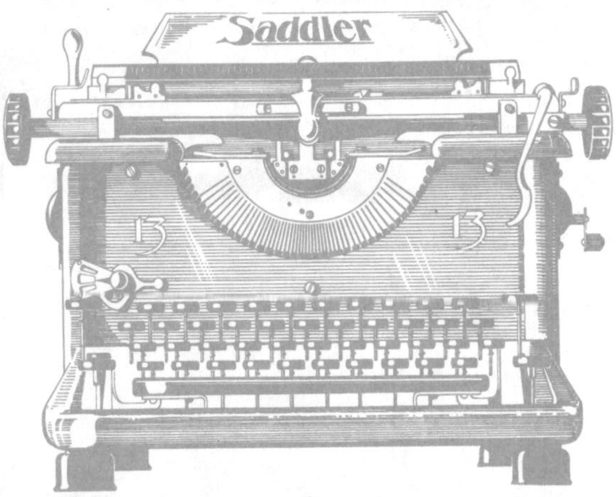

Saddler

BOCKS

Viz Comic, PO Box 656, North Shields ★ NE29 1BT. Email: letters@viz.co.uk ★

★ **'HOT TRAMP,** I love you so!' sang David Bowie on his 1974 hit single *Rebel Rebel*. Well I once had the misfortune to catch the stale odour of a hot tramp warming himself up under the hand dryer in a London subway toilet. The stench was overpowering and I couldn't get away quick enough. I certainly wasn't going to sing his praises to the whole world.

Lee Bates e-mail

★ **SURELY** it's time *Viz* gave an award for the best tabloid newspaper Soap Opera Punch-Up Let-Down. This from *Emmerdale Farm (News of the World)* is a real knockout!

P Thornton Aylesbury

★ **I HEARTILY** applaud the religious lobby group Christian Voice whose campaign stopped a cancer charity accepting £3000 raised by the cast of *Jerry Springer the Opera*. This show was blasphemous in every regard, and so it is quite right that charities should steer clear of money donated by blasphemers. I am a millionaire, and I was so impressed by Christian Voice's moral stance, that I decided to donate £500,000 to their cause. Unfortunately, on the way to post their cheque, I trod in a dog dirt and in a moment of weakness, took the Lord's name in vain. I realised that Christian Voice could not accept money from me as a blasphemer, and so I tore up their cheque.

Arthur Getty III London

★ **IN THE PUB** the other night, a man tried to pick a fight with me. "I know where you live," he shouted. I would have been scared, but he works for DHL and so his threat was almost certainly untrue.

A Langley Broadstairs

★ **DAME** Ellen MacArthur's remarkable voyage around the world would make a great film, and who better to play her than her looky-likey Little Jimmy Krankie. She's even had some recent experience of falling from a great height, so could heighten the drama by plummeting from the crow's nest.

Derek Coster e-mail

★ **WHILST I** agree with the stance that Christian Voice took over the charitable donation of money raised by *Jerry Springer the Opera*, I feel that their leader, Stephen Green should put his own house in order. On the *Newsnight* programme, he was sporting a beard which appeared to be trimmed round the edges, in direct contravention of Levitcus ch.xix v.27. He also seemed to be wearing a woollen suit with a cotton lining, in direct contravention of Leviticus ch.xix v.19. Might I suggest to Mr Green that he brush up on his scripture. Then he might remember the words of Luke ch.vi v.41, and before criticising the motes in other people's eyes, he first considereth the beam in his own.

Henry Cretis Wales

★ **I AM GAY**, but I am only attracted to homosexual policemen. As you can imagine, finding boyfriends to have anal sex with is proving quite a challenge. Does anyone know of a website which tells me which areas of the country are most likely to have gay policemen?

Bartram Tayleforth e-mail

• *Yes, Bartram. You can find the list you are looking for on the Christian Voice website at www.repentuk.com/police.htm*

★ **TYPICAL** isn't it? Jack the Ripper slaughters six prostitutes in the most gruesome way imaginable, and he gets away scot free. I slap one barmaid on the arse and I get banned from my local. Where's the justice?

Nick Pettigrew London

★ **I'VE JUST** met Peter Gabriel in my local supermarket. Whilst finding him to be a thoroughly nice bloke, I was bitterly disappointed that when he spoke, a small steam train didn't appear from his mouth. Have any of your other readers been disappointed by a celebrity in this way?

Aaron Delays e-mail

★ **I WOULD** like to congratulate my wife on the completion of her breast reduction operation. It was only a bit of back ache, you selfish bitch.

E Bright e-mail

★ **WHO SAYS** time travel isn't possible? Just tune in to one of your local radio stations and you will be transported back to a time when Phil Collins and T'Pau were always on the radio, with the added bonus of adverts about half-price suites, car finance and pile cream.

J Simmons e-mail

ST★R LETT★R

***THE POLICE** say they doubt there will be many prosecutions for illegal fox hunting as it is almost impossible to catch fox hunters in the act of killing a fox. As a burglar, this is quite heartening. If the coppers can't catch thirty odd blokes with bright red coats on horses with a pack of dogs barking their presence, they're never going to catch a sneaky little scamp like me.*

Ryan, e-mail

★ **CONGRATULATIONS** to Ellen MacArthur. It must be nice playing Captain Pugwash year in, year out. Most of us have to go to fucking work.

Jones the Steam Chesterfield

★ **WHY SHOULD** I abide by British road traffic laws? I live in Germany. And I don't even have a car.

Karl Schmidt Heidelburg

★ **WITH REFERENCE** to P Thornton's letter *(this page)*, I reckon this punch from *Coronation Street (The Sun)* should win the *Viz* Wet Paper Bag Award for the most feeble soap punch.

T Cadbury Peking

★ **THE** Ocean Finance advert say 'When you're in the worst situation you can imagine, call Ocean Finance.' So when I was kidnapped by Islamic Fundamentalist terrorists in Iraq recently, I gave them a call. To their credit, they swiftly arranged my release, had me and my family repatriated to Britain and combined all my debts into one easy to manage monthly payment. Well done Ocean Finance.

Robbie Knox Ealing

★ **AS THE** debate about Britain's involvement in the Iraq war rages on, I'm going to reserve judgement until the Hollywood movie version of the war is released. After all, it may turn out that Uncle Sam, played by Mel Gibson, had the whole thing under control from the off, and our boys might not have even been there in the first place. So let's just wait and see, eh?

H Cleft e-mail

★ **I IMAGINE** Hell to be full of recruitment consultants talking about house prices in Brummie accents whilst eating loudly. Do any other readers have similar visions of Hades?

Jake Brown e-mail

★ **I THINK** the Renault Clio adverts have really gone downhill. In the good old days of 'Nicole and Papa,' I could finish my game of five against one before the end of the advert. Now it's Thierry Henry in Las Vegas, I'm hardly past the lard-on stage before it ends. No offence, Thierry.

F Nietzsche e-mail

★ **FEMINISTS** would have us believe that all women are chained to the kitchen sink. Not me. I'm married to a lorry driver and I have been rolled up in a carpet under the stairs for the past 17 years.

Cecilia Smart London

★ **ANYONE** wishing for a thorough pasting at the hands of three lesbians for what I considered to be humourous asides, could do far worse than go out for the night in Burnley, Lancashire. I certainly didn't read about that in the tourist guide.

S Scholfield Scarborough

★ **WHEN** Tony Blair says he is worried about the threat of terrorists, I reckon he's only worried about the threat to himself. I saw him last week and he had 800 police looking after him, and that was while he was in Gateshead. If he's so worried about the rest of us, why doesn't he give us all 800 coppers to look after us while we go about our business?

T Smith Newcastle

★ **A GOOD** friend of mine once old me he that after a heavy ight on the sauce, he woke up n a field next to a 'homosexual cquaintance', with a lump on his ead and jam round his mouth.)oes anyone have any idea as to vhat could have happened?

Captain Neilos
e-mail

★ **THE OTHER** night in a pub, I vas greeted in the lavatories by n inebriated man attempting to orrectly use the urinal. On finshing, he shook his jolly roger a ew times and said to me 'I don't vant it to taste salty for my lady's ps'. I was astounded that even s this man was fighting to stay onscious, he was still thinking f his girlfriend's comfort. And ney say chivalry is dead.

D York
e-mail

★ **THIS** government prides itself n leading by example. Well John 'rescott wasn't prosectued when e thumped that bloke twice who bbed an egg at him. That's two thumps for one egg, which costs about 15p. So that means that when I catch someone pinching my £90 video, I can give them 1200 pops in the kisser without fear of being prosecuted. Just so as we know.

H Hennesy
London

★ **DURING** a recent journey on a packed commuter train, I felt the urge to do a big, rip-snorting stinky fart, but I was too embarrassed to let rip, so I fell asleep. When I awoke ten minutes later, the urge to fart had gone! I have since tried this 'falling asleep' method of flatulence cure in the library and the theatre, and it works every time. Don't ask me how, but it does. Amazing or what?

D Shitlips
e-mail

Great Moments in Rock! *by Smedley*

MY FIRST BLOW JOB

Where Ad They NOW?

WHATEVER happed to Mr hifter, the PG Tips Chimp?

Mrs Olive
Familygonetonewzealand

Vith his famous catch phrase 'You um it, son, I'll play it', Blimbo the himp shot to fame as the removal nan Mr Shifter in the popular V ad campaign that ran from 1975-78. After the axing of the ampaign, Blimbo was sold to Chipperfield's Circus where he vorked for two years with kiddies' favourite Charlie Cairoli. As howbiz fashions changed, work started to dry up and a small valk-on part in the James Bond film *Moonraker* was his last creen role. In 1994, he was bought at auction by an anonynous bidder who sold him on to a vivisection laboratory in the vest of England. For the past three years he has been taking art in a series of experiments examining primate brain funcions, clamped in a cage with a Perspex skull.

NEXT DAY...
'ERE. HAVEN'T I SEEN YOU ON THE TELLY?

TOP TIPS

MURDERERS. Need to dispose of a body? Simply parcel it up and post it to yourself via DHL. You will never see it again.

A Langley
Broadstairs

CONSTIPATED driving instructors. Alleviate your discomfort by disconnecting the dual controls on the car when instructing a new pupil. If a stronger laxative effect is required, do the same thing but with a female learner.

Stanley Etherington
e-mail

LANDLORDS. Save thousands of pounds paying hugely inflated monthly rates for Sky Sports by simply painting a small white pint glass with Tippex in the bottom right-hand corner of your TV screen.

Ross Bill
e-mail

GILLETTE. Now that you have been out-manouvred by Wilkinson's Sword with their 4 blade razor as opposed to your pathetic 3, why not catch them off their guard and make a 5 blade model?

Anonymous
e-mail

SOLDIERS. Invest in a digital camera to avoid all that court martial tomfoolery after a trip to Trueprint.

Phil
e-mail

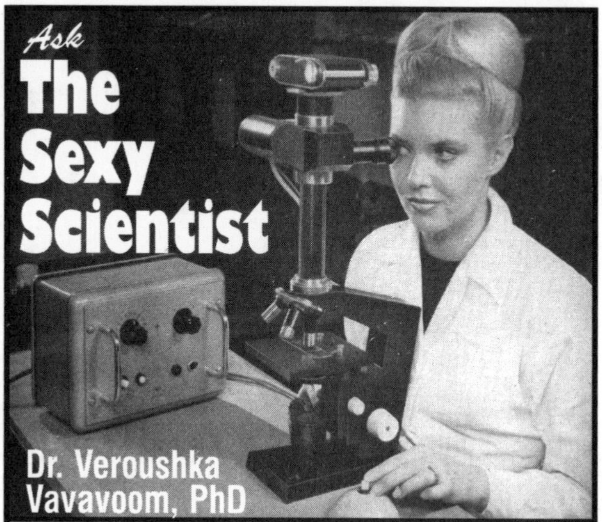
Ask
The Sexy Scientist
Dr. Veroushka Vavavoom, PhD

Dear Dr Vavavoom,

I understand that the only practical way to shrink a close-tolerance metal or ceramic component is to chill it to extreme sub zero temperatures. To do this, I know that one could use an electric refrigerator, pack it in solid CO_2, or use a cryogenically cooled liquid gas. But are there any more efficient means, and if not, which is the best liquifying gas to use?

Professor Dirk Ramrod, University of Colorado

★ Dr Vavavoom says ~ Liquid nitrogen is the most efficient gas, as the component can be completely submerged in the liquid for maximum surface contact. But another approach you might consider when fitting close tolerance components is to heat the outer member, but this can create an oxide coating and introduce metalurgical problems. Furthermore, it is very hot work. When I do it, I start to get very hot and sticky. Just imagine the way my crisp white lab coat clings to every supple curve of my body. Oooh! Sometimes I get so hot, I have to strip down to my skimpy bra and panties in the laboratory. Imagine that.

Dear Dr Vavavoom,

I am a PhD student and I am about to start work on a project to examine the nature and structure of lysozyme. How would you recommend I approach the mapping of this particular enzyme's molecular structure?

Glint Thrust BSc, University College London

★ Dr Vavavoom says ~ The amino acid sequence of protein molecules can be worked out by relatively straightforward chemical analysis, and with respect to lysozyme, this was demonstrated by P Joles and RE Canfield in the early 1960s. However, the use of physical methods, such as x-ray diffraction is required to enable the spacial arrangements of all the atoms in the molecule to be... oh, bother! I've spilt phenolpthalene all down my dress. I guess I'll just have to take it off. Oh, and it's soaked my underwear, too. I wish you were here to help me out of these wet things, Glint. But you'd have to promise not to look.

Dear Dr Vavavoom,

I'm conducting reserach into the methods of gene transfer in tobacco plants *(Nicotiana tabacum)* as a model for general gene transfer, but I have been having limited sucess using the chloramphenicol acetyl transferase assay as a method of looking at the sucess of transformation. I've heard of a similar, non radioactive assay using ß-glucuronidase as a marker, and wonder if it can be applied to the same experiments.

Professor Rock Haard, University of Amsterdam

★ Dr Vavavoom says ~ Well, there are... Oh no! I've laddered my stockings on a retort stand. Bother! They were so expensive, too. They're not the modern stay up type. I like the old fashioned style with suspenders. Look, they're real silk. Here, feel them. Aren't they smooth, hmm? Oooh, yes! That feels nice! Mmmm! Oooh, yes! Higher. That's right...

To hear the rest of Dr Vavavoom's answer to this question, call

0898 000 001

Calls to Dr Vavavoom terminate at the Faculty of Science, University College London. All calls cost £1.50/min at peak times, 90p/minute at all other times.

MICK O'THE MIDGES
BORNE ALOFT BY A DENSE CLOUD OF MIDGES, MICK JOHNSON HOVERED OVER THE WILD COUNTRYSIDE OF DARKEST SCOTLAND
SEVERAL YEARS AGO MICK'S PARENTS HAD BEEN KILLED BY AN OUT-OF-DATE PIE WHILST ON HOLIDAY IN THE SCOTTISH HIGHLANDS ~ AND THE YOUNG ENGLISH LAD HAD BEEN ADOPTED AND RAISED BY THE SWARM OF TINY ANNOYING INSECTS
MICK WAS PATROLLING THE DANK, UNCHARTED SCOTTISH JUNGLE THAT HAD BECOME HIS HOME
LOOKS LIKE ANOTHER QUIET DAY, MIDGES
SUDDENLY HE SPOTTED TWO FIGURES DOWN BELOW
ENGLISH EXPLORERS! WHAT CAN THEY BE DOING SO FAR FROM CIVILISATION?
HELP! HELP!
HELP! SAVE US! THAT HIGHLAND COW IS GAZING AT US CONTEMPTUOUSLY
IT'S LOOKING AT US LIKE WE'RE THE SHIT ON ITS HOOVES
DROPPING DOWN INTO THE CLEARING, MICK UTTERED A HIGH-PITCHED WHINING COMMAND TO HIS MIDGE PALS
GNEEEE! GNEEE!
INSTANTLY, THE SWARM OF FLYING BLOODSUCKERS SET TO WORK PESTERING THE HIGHLAND COW
IT'S WORKING! THE BRUTE HAS GOT FED UP WITH BEING HASSLED BY MIDGES AND IS WANDERING OFF!
THANK YOU, YOUNG MAN. YOU AND YOUR MIDGES SAVED OUR LIVES.
MY NAME IS KEITH HOLLAND-BARRET, AND THIS IS MY WIFE DAPHNE
WE HAVE COME HERE TO THE SCOTTISH HIGHLANDS IN SEARCH OF THE LEGENDARY LOST TEMPLE OF MEMU
I KNOW OF THE TEMPLE WHICH YOU SEEK. IT IS REGARDED AS A SACRED PLACE BY THE PRIMITIVE SCOTTISH NATIVES.
COME I WILL TAKE YOU THERE
FOR THE NEXT TWO HOURS THE MIDGE BOY LED KEITH AND DAPHNE THROUGH THE THICK SCOTTISH UNDERGROWTH
UNTIL EVENTUALLY
GOOD HEAVENS! THERE IT IS ~ THE FABLED LOST TEMPLE OF MEMU
BACK IN THE MISTS OF TIME, SCOTCH TRIBESMEN BUILT THIS TEMPLE IN HONOUR OF THEIR PAGAN GODS OF SHORTBREAD AND THISTLES
IT'S INCREDIBLE TO THINK WE ARE THE FIRST ENGLISH PEOPLE TO SET FOOT HERE.
YES. FOR THOUSANDS OF YEARS IT HAS SURVIVED UNTOUCHED BY THE RAVAGES OF OUR ENGLISH CIVILISATION.
WE WILL BEGIN RENOVATING IT IMMEDIATELY.
KEITH AND I HAVE MOVED UP HERE FROM LONDON IN ORDER TO CONVERT THIS OLD TEMPLE INTO A LITTLE SHOP SELLING OUTLANDISHLY-PRICED ORGANIC WHOLEFOODS, HERBAL TEA AND SCENTED CANDLES
CUBAN RICE
YES. WE SIMPLY HAD TO GET AWAY FROM ALL THE HURLY-BURLY OF LIVING IN NOTTING HILL.
MICK GLADLY LENT A HAND IN RENOVATING THE ANCIENT SCOTTISH TEMPLE
KEITH AND DAPHNE'S NUT HOUSE
FAIR TRADE BEAN BAGS
ORGANIC VEG
OPEN FOR HOMEOPATHIC RY COODER CDS
PAINT

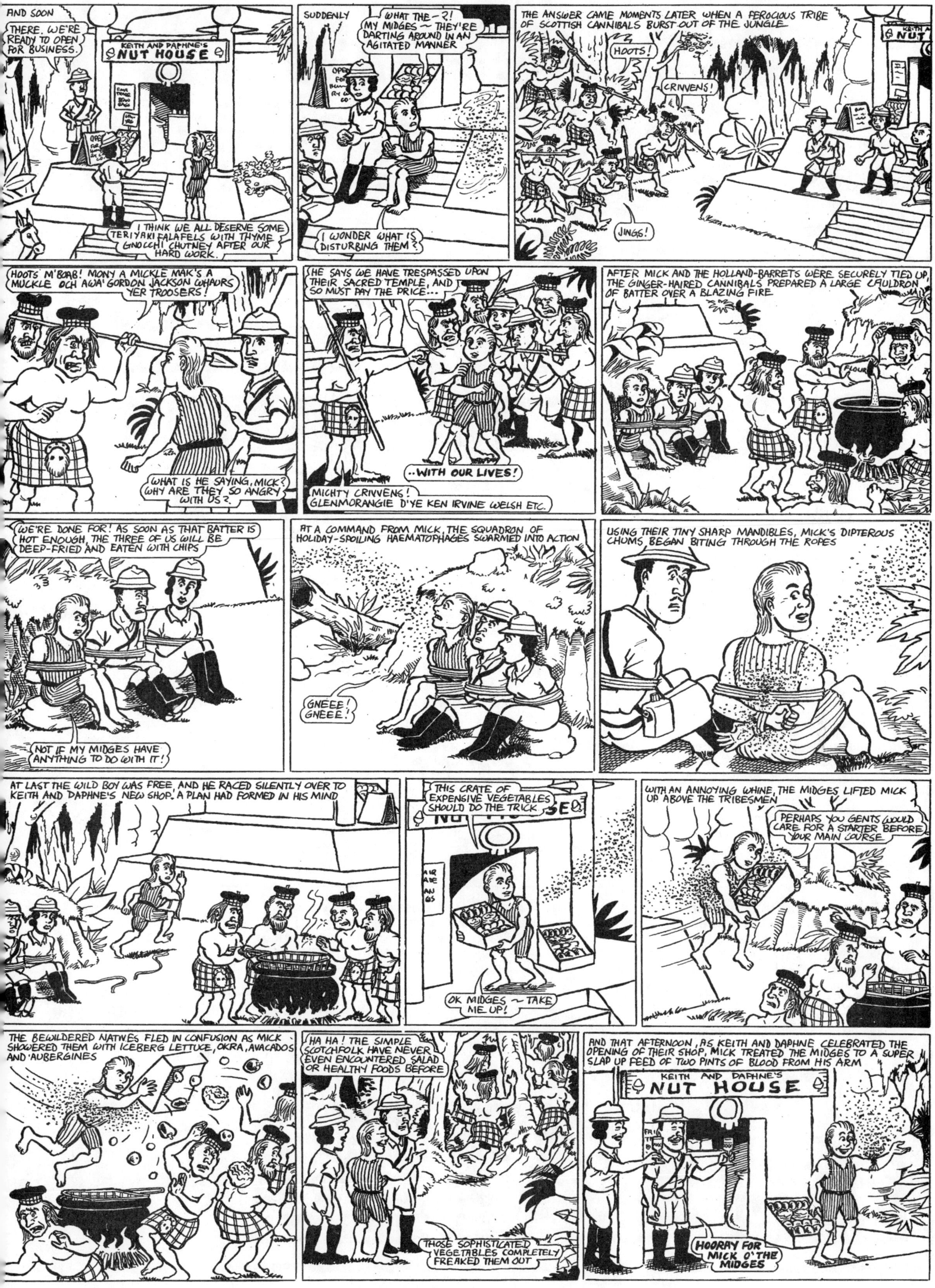
AND SOON
THERE. WE'RE READY TO OPEN FOR BUSINESS.
KEITH AND DAPHNE'S NUT HOUSE
I THINK WE ALL DESERVE SOME TERIYAKI FALAFELS WITH THYME GNOCCHI CHUTNEY AFTER OUR HARD WORK.
SUDDENLY
WHAT THE -?! MY MIDGES ~ THEY'RE DARTING AROUND IN AN AGITATED MANNER
I WONDER WHAT IS DISTURBING THEM?
THE ANSWER CAME MOMENTS LATER WHEN A FEROCIOUS TRIBE OF SCOTTISH CANNIBALS BURST OUT OF THE JUNGLE
HOOTS!
CRIVVENS!
JINGS!
HOOTS M'BOAB! MONY A MICKLE MAK'S A MUCKLE OCH AWA' GORDON JACKSON WHAUR'S YER TROOSERS!
WHAT IS HE SAYING, MICK? WHY ARE THEY SO ANGRY WITH US?
HE SAYS WE HAVE TRESPASSED UPON THEIR SACRED TEMPLE, AND SO MUST PAY THE PRICE...
..WITH OUR LIVES!
MICHTY CRIVVENS! GLENMORANGIE D'YE KEN IRVINE WELSH ETC.
AFTER MICK AND THE HOLLAND-BARRETS WERE SECURELY TIED UP, THE GINGER-HAIRED CANNIBALS PREPARED A LARGE CAULDRON OF BATTER OVER A BLAZING FIRE
FLOUR
WE'RE DONE FOR! AS SOON AS THAT BATTER IS HOT ENOUGH, THE THREE OF US WILL BE DEEP-FRIED AND EATEN WITH CHIPS
NOT IF MY MIDGES HAVE ANYTHING TO DO WITH IT!
AT A COMMAND FROM MICK, THE SQUADRON OF HOLIDAY-SPOILING HAEMATOPHAGES SWARMED INTO ACTION
GNEEE! GNEEE!
USING THEIR TINY SHARP MANDIBLES, MICK'S DIPTEROUS CHUMS BEGAN BITING THROUGH THE ROPES
AT LAST THE WILD BOY WAS FREE, AND HE RACED SILENTLY OVER TO KEITH AND DAPHNE'S NEW SHOP. A PLAN HAD FORMED IN HIS MIND
THIS CRATE OF EXPENSIVE VEGETABLES SHOULD DO THE TRICK
OK MIDGES ~ TAKE ME UP!
WITH AN ANNOYING WHINE, THE MIDGES LIFTED MICK UP ABOVE THE TRIBESMEN
PERHAPS YOU GENTS WOULD CARE FOR A STARTER BEFORE YOUR MAIN COURSE
THE BEWILDERED NATIVES FLED IN CONFUSION AS MICK SHOWERED THEM WITH ICEBERG LETTUCE, OKRA, AVACADOS AND AUBERGINES
HA HA! THE SIMPLE SCOTCHFOLK HAVE NEVER EVEN ENCOUNTERED SALAD OR HEALTHY FOODS BEFORE
THOSE SOPHISTICATED VEGETABLES COMPLETELY FREAKED THEM OUT
AND THAT AFTERNOON, AS KEITH AND DAPHNE CELEBRATED THE OPENING OF THEIR SHOP, MICK TREATED THE MIDGES TO A SUPER SLAP UP FEED OF TWO PINTS OF BLOOD FROM HIS ARM
KEITH AND DAPHNE'S NUT HOUSE
HOORAY FOR MICK O' THE MIDGES

Who is th
Deadliest

Ask anyone in the street to list their top 20 comedy actors, a chances are that hangdog-faced funnyman Geoffrey Palm will be somewhere in the middle teens, below Buster Merryfi but definitely above Windsor Davies. With his tradem gloomy jowls and deadpan delivery, he keeps viewers rolling the aisles with his wisecracking performances in shows s as Butterflies, Fairly Secret Army and The Last Song.

DAHMER

Any serial killer worth his salt has to be a good actor, and on many occasions Dahmer gave Oscar-worthy performances which convinced police and neighbours that nothing was amiss at his house of horrors. On one occasion he even convinced cops that a semi-murdered naked teenager he was chasing down the street with a power drill was his lover, with whom he'd had a tiff. He earns a standing ovation and a surprisingly high score in this round.

8

ROU
Act

According to psychologists, murderers are always quiet loners who keep themselves to themselves and Dahmer fits this blueprint exactly. Spending long hours cooped up in his house talking to his gruesome collection of severed human heads and genitals, it wasn't long before he found himself drifting towards mental illness and sexual perversion. Consequently he scores impressively in this section.

7

ROU
Keepin

During his fourteen year killing spree, Dahmer turned murdering into an art form. Using a variety of techniques, including strangulation, drowning, trepanning and poisoning, he quickly became a skilled executioner. One thing's for certain, of the seventeen victims he killed, not one of them lived to tell the tale of the grisly fate he met.

9

ROUN
Killin

Dahmer always had his victims for dinner, quite literally. Not content with simply killing them, the Milwaukee mentalist put the 'men' into 'menu' by boiling their brains, stir-frying their spleens, and doing some cooking proceedure beginning with a silent k to their knackers.

8

ROU
Ca

When Milwaukee police finally raided the cannibal madman's house on 22nd July 1991, they were unprepared for what they saw when they opened his refrigerator. Horrified cops found four human heads, a selection of severed hands and a penis which Dahmer had stashed in a jar of pickled onions, as well as a large quantity of unidentified human flesh. Dahmer's stomach-turning stash of snacks was a dreadful sight, but guarantees him a cracking score in this round.

8

ROU
Fridg

Officers who questioned Dahmer after his arrest were horrified when the full extent of their prisoner's sick behaviour became clear. For it emerged that at the same time he was carrying out his series of bizarre murders and decapitations, necrophile Dahmer had also regularly been touching himself in the nether regions. Cops were sickened to learn that as his descent into madness began, the serial cannibal would regularly take a severed head out of his fridge before performing a sick sex act onto it.

7

ROU
Mastu
Seve

At his trial in 1992, Dahmer pleaded guilty to seventeen slayings and was sentenced to fifteen consecutive life terms. However, two years into his sentence he ironically became the innocent victim of a murder himself, when another prisoner killed him in the laundry room of Milwaukee State Penetentiary. For the last eleven years he has been securely buried under six feet of earth in the prison exercise yard, where he poses no further threat to the public at large, and his score in this round reflects this fact.

0

ROUN
Ability

He may have taken seventeen innocent lives, but Geoffrey Dahmer doesn't manage to take the deadliness title from Geoffrey Palmer. He may have been dangerous in his day, but more than a decade after his death he's certainly lost his edge when it comes to preparing himself a three corpse dinner. At the end of the day, the Milwaukee Cannibal has become the Milwaukee Can't-ibal!

47

FINA

e World's Geoffrey?

while family favourite Palmer was carving out his career on British television, ıg a string of BAFTAs for his sidesplitting performances, another Geoffrey was ıg an impact 5000 miles away on the other side of the Atlantic. Milwaukee bal Geoffrey Dahmer was hard at work torturing, killing and disembowelling his ıteen victims.

the face of it, Dahmer appears to win the deadliness contest hands down. But e leaping to any conclusions, let's examine the evidence in a head to severed contest. Not until we've totted up the scores will we know for certain who is inner of our Palmer-Dahmer Ding-Dong.

PALMER

ONE
'ity

6

Despite a long career on stage and screen, Palmer has seldom been called upon to do any proper acting. In his numerous TV appearances he has relied upon his unmatched ability to recite his lines in a bored, slightly sarcastic voice whilst sitting at a breakfast table in a shirt and tie and raising an eyebrow. He was once called upon to lower a copy of the Daily Telegraph and look faintly surprised instead. Palmer took over 500 takes before he got it right, a British Film Institute record which stands to this day!

WO
o Self

6

On the face of it, it would seem impossible for a TV star to keep his private life private, but that's exactly what Palmer has achieved. Sinisterly, in the 1991 book 'Who's Who on Television', he refuses to list any cherished possessions or favourite memories. Furthermore, a cursory internet search of his name on Google revealed no information whatsoever about this secretive actor's private life or sexual predilections.

IREE
ique

7

Palmer shows no respect whatsoever for life, albeit only that of insects. In the gentle 80s comedy Butterflies, the walls of his study were lined with the framed corpses of his innocent, winged victims whom he had gassed in their hundreds before impaling them on pins. The sadistic lepidopterist nets himself a good score in this round.

OUR
sm

6

As far as is known, Palmer has no particular penchant for nibbling on human flesh. But in an episode of Fauwlty Towers, he finds no difficulty working up an appetite for sausages whilst a guest lies dead in the kitchen. Although somewhat disturbing, this trait does not prove conclusively that Palmer is capable of consuming his fellow man.

IVE
ents

7

Although police have never found any human remains in Geoffrey Palmer's fridge, its contents are likely to be just as grisly as that of his US counterpart. Stored on its shelves, there may well be sliced up pig remains, chicken corpses and various butchered lamb bodyparts. It is believed that after dark, the flesh-hungry Palmer may well often retire to his kitchen in order to feast hungrily on his gruesome trophies.

SIX
onto
ads

6

It would be nice to be able to report that popular actor Palmer has never pleasured himself to orgasm over a corpse's noggin. Certainly a Google search of "Geoffrey Palmer" and "masturbating onto severed heads" failed to find any matches. However, in the 1991 book 'Who's Who on Television', the notoriously secretive star fails to list any hobbies. Consequently it is impossible to say whether Palmer has or hasn't commited such a vile act. As a result of this uncertainty, he is awarded a middling score in this round.

EVEN
Again

10

At the age of 78, the bloodhound-chopped actor is still much in demand in the world of TV comedy. It is not known how many people have so far died laughing at his hilarious shows such as Executive Stress and Season's Greetings. But if just a tiny percentage of his millions of viewers were to succumb whilst rolling around in hysterics over his sidesplitting performances, the death toll could run into thousands.

ORE

48

It's official - Palmer's the deadliest Geoffrey by a country mile! When it comes to killing, the glum-faced sitcom star certainly puts canned s-laughter on the menu every time he appears on the screen. So next time you switch on your television to watch an episode of As Time Goes By, be afraid...be very afraid. Your time may well be up.

FINBARR SAUNDERS
& HIS DOUBLE ENTENDRES
MRS. SAUNDERS AND HER FRIEND MR. GIMLET HAVE TAKEN FINBARR TO THE LOCAL CAR BOOT SALE...
OOH, MR. GIMLET. HERE COMES SERGEI, OUR RUSSIAN EXCHANGE VISITOR.
YES. AND THERE'S SOMETHING UNDER HIS COAT, LOOK.
WHAT HAVE YOU GOT THERE, SERGEI?
IS SERGEI'S ROCK-HARD DICK, MRS. SAUNDERS.
ARP! ARP!
HOO! HOO!
WIB! WIB!
WOULD YOU LIKE TO SEE IT, MRS. SAUNDERS? IS SPUNKING NOW!
WELL... ER... I... ER...
FNARR! FNARR!
SNEED! SNEED!
YAK! YAK!
AH! I SEE. IT'S A RECORD DECK, SERGEI.
DA. IS BRUND SPUNKING NOW. I BUY FROM MAN ON STALL FOR 10p.
HMM. A TURNTABLE, EH?
THAT BRINGS BACK THE MEMORIES. AS A YOUNG MAN I SPENT MANY A HAPPY EVENING JUST SITTING IN MY ROOM, OCCASIONALLY LOWERING MY ARM ONTO A SHINY SEVEN INCHER.
K-YIK! K-YIK!
WOO! WOO!
HAR! HAR!
IN FACT, WHEN WE WERE FIRST MARRIED, MY WIFE ALSO OWNED QUITE AN IMPRESSIVE HI-FI SYSTEM.
DID SHE HAVE BIG LOUDSPEAKERS, MR. GIMLET..?
OH YES. IN THOSE DAYS MRS GIMLET HAD A SMASHING PAIR OF WOOFERS.
YUB! YUB!
CHOT! CHOT!
THE STEREO EFFECT WAS AMAZING. WHEN I STUCK MY HEAD RIGHT BETWEEN THEM IT USED TO MAKE MY TROUSERS FLAP.
FERBIT! FERBIT!
YOP! YOP!
ARB! ARB!
GLEP! GLEP!
I MYSELF WAS THE PROUD POSSESSOR OF A MASSIVE FOLDED HORN.
YURBLE! YURBLE!
NOMP! NOMP!
HOO! HOO!
WOK! WOK!
SADLY IT EXPIRED DURING A RATHER WILD PARTY IN THE 60'S. MY WIFE - AN ERIC CLAPTON FAN - TRIED TO GET SOME CREAM OUT OF IT AND RATHER FOOLISHLY BLEW IT IN FRONT OF ALL OUR NEIGHBOURS.
STREE! STREE!
BOOP! BOOP!
KWUK! KWUK!
MOST EMBARRASSING.
OF COURSE, IT WAS ALL VALVE AMPLIFICATION IN THOSE DAYS. THERE WERE NO TRANSISTORS. MY WIFE'S OLD BUSH USED TO GET TOO HOT TO TOUCH SOMETIMES.
FNURP! FNURP!
... AND I COULD ALWAYS TELL IF SHE'D BEEN LISTENING TO PETE MURRAY ON THE RADIO BECAUSE THE WHOLE ROOM WOULD SMELL OF WARM TUNER.
BLIP! BLIP!
NOOT! NOOT!
ARK! ARK!
LATER ON, OF COURSE, WE GOT HEAVILY INTO PUNK. MANY OF THOSE OLD EPs AND SINGLES ARE NOW VALUABLE COLLECTORS' ITEMS.
GOSH. I NEVER REALISED, MR. GIMLET.
OH YES. IT BRINGS TEARS TO MY EYES TO REMEMBER THE NIGHT MRS GIMLET SAT ON MY TEN INCHES OF THROBBING GRISTLE AND SNAPPED IT CLEAN IN TWO.
CHUFT! CHUFT!
SPLP! SPLP!
K-YAK! K-YAK!
HOO! HOO!
GWAFF! GWAFF!
WHAT SORT OF STEREO DO YOU HAVE NOW?
WELL EVERYTHING'S MINIATURISED THESE DAYS, ISN'T IT. MINE USED TO BE HUGE BUT NOW IT'S QUITE SMALL.
SPANG! SPANG!
CHEBB! CHEBB!
GURK! GURK!
FNIP! FNIP!
EVERYTHING'S IN MP3 FORMAT, DOWNLOADED FROM THE INTERNET AND STORED ON A PORTABLE DISK DRIVE. I'VE GOT A HARD ONE IN MY POCKET RIGHT NOW.
GAM! GAM!
FNNB! FNNB!
P-FFMMP! P-FFMMP!
WIBB! WIBB!
FANCY A FUCK?
ER.. YEAH. GO ON THEN.

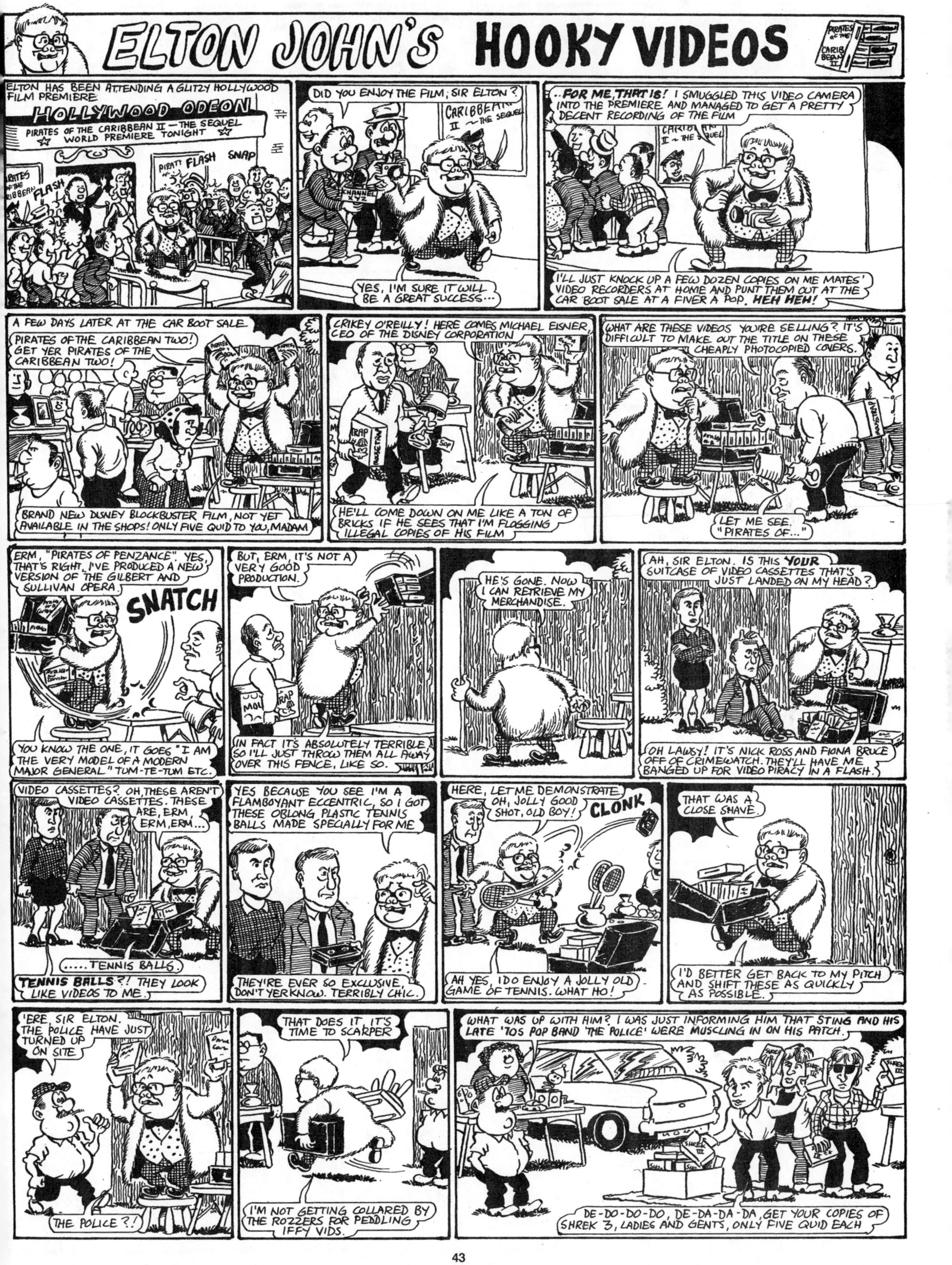
ELTON JOHN'S HOOKY VIDEOS
PIRATES OF THE CARIBBEAN II
ELTON HAS BEEN ATTENDING A GLITZY HOLLYWOOD FILM PREMIERE
HOLLYWOOD ODEON
PIRATES OF THE CARIBBEAN II — THE SEQUEL
WORLD PREMIERE TONIGHT
FLASH
SNAP
FLASH
DID YOU ENJOY THE FILM, SIR ELTON?
CARIBBEAN II ~ THE SEQUEL
CHANNEL XYZ
YES, I'M SURE IT WILL BE A GREAT SUCCESS...
..FOR ME, THAT IS! I SMUGGLED THIS VIDEO CAMERA INTO THE PREMIERE AND MANAGED TO GET A PRETTY DECENT RECORDING OF THE FILM
I'LL JUST KNOCK UP A FEW DOZEN COPIES ON ME MATES' VIDEO RECORDERS AT HOME AND PUNT THEM OUT AT THE CAR BOOT SALE AT A FIVER A POP. HEH HEH!
A FEW DAYS LATER AT THE CAR BOOT SALE
PIRATES OF THE CARIBBEAN TWO! GET YER PIRATES OF THE CARIBBEAN TWO!
BRAND NEW DISNEY BLOCKBUSTER FILM, NOT YET AVAILABLE IN THE SHOPS! ONLY FIVE QUID TO YOU, MADAM
CRIKEY O'REILLY! HERE COMES MICHAEL EISNER, CEO OF THE DISNEY CORPORATION
HE'LL COME DOWN ON ME LIKE A TON OF BRICKS IF HE SEES THAT I'M FLOGGING ILLEGAL COPIES OF HIS FILM
WHAT ARE THESE VIDEOS YOU'RE SELLING? IT'S DIFFICULT TO MAKE OUT THE TITLE ON THESE CHEAPLY PHOTOCOPIED COVERS.
LET ME SEE. "PIRATES OF..."
ERM, "PIRATES OF PENZANCE". YES, THAT'S RIGHT, I'VE PRODUCED A NEW VERSION OF THE GILBERT AND SULLIVAN OPERA.
SNATCH
YOU KNOW THE ONE, IT GOES "I AM THE VERY MODEL OF A MODERN MAJOR GENERAL" TUM-TE-TUM ETC.
BUT, ERM, IT'S NOT A VERY GOOD PRODUCTION.
IN FACT IT'S ABSOLUTELY TERRIBLE SO I'LL JUST THROW THEM ALL AWAY OVER THIS FENCE, LIKE SO.
HE'S GONE. NOW I CAN RETRIEVE MY MERCHANDISE.
AH, SIR ELTON. IS THIS YOUR SUITCASE OF VIDEO CASSETTES THAT'S JUST LANDED ON MY HEAD?
OH LAWSY! IT'S NICK ROSS AND FIONA BRUCE OFF OF CRIMEWATCH. THEY'LL HAVE ME BANGED UP FOR VIDEO PIRACY IN A FLASH.
VIDEO CASSETTES? OH, THESE AREN'T VIDEO CASSETTES. THESE ARE, ERM, ERM, ERM...
.....TENNIS BALLS.
TENNIS BALLS?! THEY LOOK LIKE VIDEOS TO ME.
YES BECAUSE YOU SEE I'M A FLAMBOYANT ECCENTRIC, SO I GOT THESE OBLONG PLASTIC TENNIS BALLS MADE SPECIALLY FOR ME
THEY'RE EVER SO EXCLUSIVE, DON'T YER KNOW. TERRIBLY CHIC.
HERE, LET ME DEMONSTRATE.
OH, JOLLY GOOD SHOT, OLD BOY!
CLONK
AH YES, I DO ENJOY A JOLLY OLD GAME OF TENNIS. WHAT HO!
THAT WAS A CLOSE SHAVE.
I'D BETTER GET BACK TO MY PITCH AND SHIFT THESE AS QUICKLY AS POSSIBLE.
'ERE, SIR ELTON. THE POLICE HAVE JUST TURNED UP ON SITE
THE POLICE?!
THAT DOES IT, IT'S TIME TO SCARPER
I'M NOT GETTING COLLARED BY THE ROZZERS FOR PEDDLING IFFY VIDS.
WHAT WAS UP WITH HIM? I WAS JUST INFORMING HIM THAT STING AND HIS LATE '70S POP BAND 'THE POLICE' WERE MUSCLING IN ON HIS PATCH.
DE-DO-DO-DO, DE-DA-DA-DA, GET YOUR COPIES OF SHREK 3, LADIES AND GENTS, ONLY FIVE QUID EACH

TOM FOOLERY!

HOLLYWOOD heart throb Tom Cruise's recent emotional outburst after he was squirted with water by a stunt Channel 4 microphone hit headlines throughout the world. Many people took the actor's side, arguing that a sensitive artiste should not be expected to put up with childish practical tricks. But one man who thinks differently is Les Kellet, proprietor of *Les' Joke Shop*, a novelty store on Hollywood Boulevard, just a plastic dog turd's throw from Cruise's Sunset Strip mansion.

LES' JOKE SHOP

Laughing Stock: Les's shop in Hollywood.

Joke Shop Les Spills the Beans on Tinsel Town Short Arse

EXCLUSIVE

Ex-pat Kellet has been in the joke business longer than he cares to remember. He previously spent thirty years behind the counter of the Laff Kabin, a popular shop selling tricks and novelties in the Shadwell district of Leeds. Eventually, an escalating series of break-ins and attacks which culminated in the firebombing of his premises prompted Les to try his luck across the pond, and in 1992 he upped sticks to set up shop in Tinseltown.

Last night Les had this to say about the pint-size *War of the Worlds* celebrity: "Tom Cruise is one of my best customers, and he's a bloody hypocrite. He's quite happy to dish it out but he just can't take it when the tables are turned."

"Over the last twelve years, Tom Cruise must have spent a hundred dollars or more in my shop. Every Friday when he gets his wages from the studio, he's in here without fail buying jokes. Looking back, he must have bought just about every novelty going; stink bombs, handshake buzzers, whoopee cushions. You name it, Tom Cruise has bought it. Apparently he liked to try them out on his then wife Moulin Rouge beauty Nicole Kidman, who at first took it all in her leggy stride.

Kidman: Nicole saw red over black-face soap.

"But the strain soon began to show. During filming for *Eyes Wide Shut,* Cruise put a bar of Black Face Soap on the sink in her dressing room. When she came onto the set to film an intense sex scene, she looked like she'd just done a shift down a coal mine! The whole crew burst out laughing and Kidman ran away in floods of tears.

"Director Stanley Kubrick was furious, and ordered Tom to apologise. Cruise admitted he'd probably gone too far this time, and went to his wife's trailer with a bunch of flowers. However, what Nicole didn't realise was that he'd bought the bouquet from my shop. A quick squeeze of a hidden bulb, and her face was covered in blue ink. Tom then blew a handful of sneezing powder at her for good measure.

"Tom thought it was the funniest thing he'd ever seen, but Kubrick didn't agree. He had to stop filming for three days while Kidman recovered from her ordeal.

Les could sense that Cruise's obsession with practical jokes was beginning to drive a wedge between the star and his wife. Kidman was reaching the end of her tether, but Tom just couldn't see it.

"The final straw was later that same week. Cruise told me he was planning a romantic meal with Nicole, where he was going to promise to give up playing tricks on her.

"The plan went smoothly. Tom vowed to put a stop to his joking ways, and Nicole was delighted. But it was all an act. At the end of the candlelit meal, Tom leaned over and offered Kidman a salted peanut from a can he had just taken out of his

...A PLACE FOR EVERYTHING AND EVERYTHING IN ITS PLACE, THAT'S WHAT I ALWAYS SAY...
CAREFUL DEAR. THAT'S NEAT VODKA.

Zeta-Jones Saw Through Specs Maniac Douglas

HOLLYWOOD marriages are notoriously rocky, but one of the strongest and most enduring of recent years is that between Welsh beauty Catherine Zeta-Jones and her elderly husband Michael Douglas. But Les was there when a pair of magic glasses showed up the cracks in their fairytale relationship.

"I was unpacking a box of rubber vomit pools when in walked *Romancing the Stone* star Michael Douglas. He explained he was just killing time whilst his wife, Catherine Zeta-Jones out of *The Darling Buds of May,* was in Argos next door buying some pans. But he didn't look like he was browsing to me. He went straight over to the X-Ray Spectacles display and tried on a pair."

Douglas seemed impressed and bought the 75 cent novelties on the spot. It was just another sale for Les, but he wasn't prepared for what happened next.

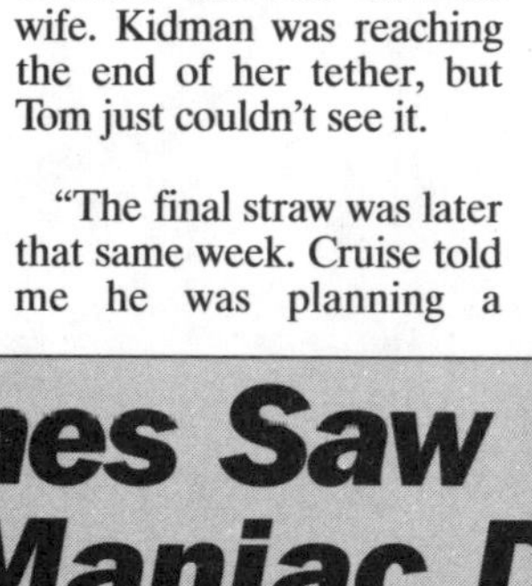
Focal objection: Zeta-Jones and Douglas in happier times.

"Zeta-Jones came in carrying a large frying pan. She was really pleased with herself because she had got it for half price, but her smile soon evaporated when she saw Douglas wearing his glasses. She started shouting and screaming, calling him a dirty old man. She accused him of buying the X-Ray Specs so he could look at women's bras and pants through their dresses. Douglas tried to calm her down, insisting he just wanted them so he could look at the bones in his hand, but his wife wasn't having any of it.

"She was really upset and kept hitting him with the pan, threatening to go back to her mum's in Wales. In the end she stormed out of the shop, leaving me and a very sheepish-looking Michael Douglas. He explained that he'd had second thoughts about buying the glasses, and asked for his money back. I explained that I couldn't give him a refund, as he'd already torn them off the card.

"Of course, nobody but Michael Douglas himself knows what *Basic Instinct* led him to buy those X-Ray spectacles. But I do know that they held a *Fatal Attraction* for him that very nearly cost him his marriage."

pocket. Cruise watched, grinning as his unsuspecting wife prised the lid off the can and...Boing! A gaily coloured spring-loaded cloth snake shot out and hurtled past her ear.

"Of course, as an Australian Kidman is absolutely terrified of snakes, and so she became hysterical. Tom was hysterical too... with laughter. He took the opportunity to empty a tin of itching powder down her back.

"The marriage didn't survive long after that, and I wasn't surprised to read in the next day's paper that Hollywood's golden couple had got divorced. Now Tom is engaged to his *War of the Worlds* co-star Katy Holmes. I only hope for both their sakes that she doesn't mind getting a ring of soot round her eye every time Tom hands her a suspiciously small telescope to look through."

And the miniature *Top Gun* actor isn't the only star of the silver screen to be found browsing through the racks of novelties in Les's shop. He told us: "If I told you who' I've had in here, you'd think I was making it up. My list of customers reads like a Who's Who of Hollywood!"

Now, in these exclusive extracts from his brand new 6-page autobiography 'Make 'Em Laff' (Kellet Publishing), Les lifts the lid on the secret world of practical jokes the stars don't want us to see.

Sweet Joke Turned Sour for Phoenix

Most of the tricks and novelties that Les sells are nothing more than a harmless bit of fun. But in the wrong hands they can have serious consequences. One such occasion occurred on Halloween 1993, when a couple of familiar faces turned up in Kellet's shop.

"I recognised them immediately as Johnny Depp out of *Edward Scissorhands* and *Matrix* star Keanu Reeves. They were giggling and nudging each other, wasting my time. Eventually I gave it to them straight; either buy something or get out of the shop.

"Reeves explained they were going to a brat pack party that night at Los Angeles's notorious Viper Club, and they wanted some fart powder to slip into their pal River Phoenix's drink. I told them I'd sold my last packet to Katherine Hepburn that very morning, but that

Turd time unlucky: A photo of Johnny Depp.

I still had several doses of Crap-A-Lot sugar in stock. They bought three sachets, joking that the *Stand by Me* actor would be spending his night sitting on a lavatory. I warned them that emptying more than one sachet into their friend's tea could be dangerous, but I don't think they were listening.

"I thought nothing more about it until I turned on the *News at Ten* the next night, and discovered that Phoenix had collapsed on the pavement outside the nightclub and had later been pronounced dead. An inquest concluded that Phoenix had succumbed to a lethal cocktail of heroin and cocaine, but I'm not so sure.

"Did River Phoenix die after taking a massive overdose of Crap-A-Lot sugar? Perhaps we'll never know. All I do know is that my conscience is clear. I'm not so sure that Keanu Reeves and Johnny Depp can say the same."

Crowe's Feat Ruffled Studio Feathers

SOMETIMES the most unlikely person turns out to have the best sense of fun. Australian hard man actor Russell Crowe has a humourless reputation, but according to Les nothing could be further from the truth.

"During the filming of *Gladiator,* Russell came into the shop and bought a few things. The next day at the studios they were filming the scene where Maximus takes off his helmet in the arena and reveals his true identity to the emperor.

"Imagine director Ridley Scott's surprise when the visor went up to reveal Crowe wearing a pair of comedy Willy Nose Glasses and a set of Austin Powers buck teeth.

There were fifty thousand extras on the Colosseum set and they all just cracked up. It was such a funny shot that Scott wanted to leave it in the final film, but the humourless bosses at MGM said no. I guess we'll just have to wait a few years for the 'Director's Cut' DVD to come out before we can see Russell with a pink winkle for a nose!"

Chuddy Rap Left Biggie Smalls Hip-Hopping Mad

IT'S quite usual for the victim of a practical joke to want to get their own back. Les remembers the time Clint Eastwood put some rubber fried eggs into Tim Roth's sandwich, only to find a plastic spider in the bottom of his own tea the next day - courtesy of the *Reservoir Dogs* actor. But sometimes, the scale of the revenge can be out of all proportion to the trick originally played.

"One of my best customers was gangsta rapper Tupac Shakur. He was always in the shop. I remember one time he came in with his posse and they all bought those things that make it look like you've stuck a nail through your finger. Tupac also bought a trick pack of

Murder Rap: Biggie and Tupac yesterday.

mousetrap chewing gum

"The next day he came in and explained that he'd tried it out on his rap rival Biggie Smalls, aka The Notorious B.I.G. backstage at a concert. Tupac had offered the unsuspecting Smalls a stick of gum and the spring-loaded wire had snapped down on his finger. Apparently everybody laughed except Biggie, who called Shakur every name under the Sun, threatening to get even.

"I thought nothing more about it until about a week later, when I read that Tupac had been killed in a drive-by shooting. Now that The Notorious B.I.G. is also dead, we'll never know whether Shakur's murder was part of a drug-related gangland turf war, or simply revenge for a mousetrap chewing gum prank."

NEXT WEEK - The time all the girls from Desperate Housewives and Sex & The City came in to buy French maid outfits and PVC nurse costumes... and insisted on trying them on in the shop!

To order a copy of Les's book, send stamps to the value of 50p to L. Kellet, 48a Bramley Apple Lane, Shadwell, Leeds. Please allow up to two weeks for delivery, as each copy is photocopied to order at the library.

Innocent Osmonds Set to Die

The Osmonds: Goin' Home in a box this Christmas.

SEVENTIES singing sensations the Osmonds were last night languishing on Utah State Prison's Death Row, after being mistakenly sentenced to death for a murder they didn't commit. The cleancut pop brothers Donny, Jay, Merril, Wayne and Alan are set to face the electric chair on Christmas morning after a computer mix-up at the District Attorney's office.

A 58-year-old shopkeeper was shot dead in March during a bungled raid on his Alabama liquor store. Three days later, police arrested 32-year-old unemployed local man Ricky-Bob Mullet, who confessed to the killing. However, instead of the murderer, the name of the popular mormon supergroup was mistakenly filled in on Mullet's execution warrant.

District Attorney's office secretary Terrylene Koswalski told reporters: "I was typing up the warrant on my computer, and I stopped to see if I could find a copy of 'Love Me for a Reason' going cheap on the internet. I guess I must have accidentally typed 'The Osmonds' into the death warrant instead of the eBay search engine."

late

Koswalski spotted her mistake after a couple of hours, but it was already too late. The warrant had been countersigned by the state governor and the Osmonds had been taken into custody. "It's a terrible thing, what's going to happen, but there's simply no way out," prison boss Nylon Hogg told Fox News reporter Hymen Prepuce. "It's going to break my heart to fry those good old Osmond boys, but the law's the law."

espreso

District Attorney Spiro Theocropolis said: "All legal avenues have been exhausted. Under state law, once the warrant has been authorised there is no appeal process. Sadly, in this case that means the Osmonds are going to have to be executed even though we know for a fact that they are innocent."

Theocropolis continued: "We have already set up an enquiry to find out what went went wrong in this case."

capucino

"Unfortunately, miscarriages of justice happen all the time. I'm sure that one day we'll look back at what we're about to do to the Osmonds and see how it could have been avoided, but that will be with the benefit of hindsight. At the moment, we just have to learn from our mistakes, and try to make sure that this sort of thing doesn't happen again too often," he added.

Meanwhile, the real killer has been released and is making the most of his new-found freedom. Ricky-Bob Mullet told NBC's Smegma Glans III: "I just couldn't believe my luck when I heard those innocent brothers were going to die in my place. I know I've done some bad things in my life, but I've done good things too. I feel the Osmonds getting electrocuted on Christmas Day may be God's way of saying thank-you. I guess I feel a bit sorry for them, but that's life I suppose." And Mullet revealed what he plans to be doing on the morning of December 25th when governor Hogg pulls the lever that will send 20,000 volts crackling through Donny, Jay, Merril, Wayne and Alan, wiping their trademark grins from their faces forever.

maxwel house

"I'll be having me a nice quiet day," he said. "Just me, my girlfriend and my little baby daughter. I'll try not to think about what's happening in the jailhouse too much, because Christmas is supposed to be a happy time."

"But I just might drink me a toast to the Osmonds," he added. "Because if it wasn't for them I wouldn't be here."

This is not the first time that members of the Osmond family have found themselves at the wrong end of a miscarriage of justice. In 1996, Marie and Little Jimmy were sentenced to 35 consecutive life sentences after a jury foreman inadvertantly doodled their names on his notepad during a Minnesota kidnapping trial.

OSAMA
BIN LADEN
ANNUAL 2006
FACTS ★ FEATURES ★ PICS ★ STORIES
OUT NOW! Only £6.99

TINRIBS
11-YEAR OLD TOMMY TAYLOR'S BEST FRIEND WAS A REMARKABLE ROBOT CALLED TINRIBS
WHAT DO YOU THINK THIS IS ALL ABOUT, TINRIBS?
SCHOOL NOTICEBOARD
A SPECIAL ASSEMBLY WILL BE HELD TODAY IN THE SCHOOL FIRST-AID ROOM.
BY ORDER The Headmaster
HI. I'M BARBIE. I LOVE YOU VERY MUCH.
AND –
GATHER ROUND, EVERYONE.
FIRST AID ROOM
SCHOOL NURSE
THE SCHOOL INSPECTORS WILL BE COMING TODAY AND I'M VERY ANXIOUS TO IMPRESS THEM.
CONSEQUENTLY I HAVE INSTRUCTED THE SCHOOL NURSE TO SURGICALLY ENLARGE MY PENIS SO THAT IT IS ABSOLUTELY MASSIVE
FWIP
ROOM
IF THIS WHOPPER DOESN'T IMPRESS THE SCHOOL INSPECTORS THEN I DON'T KNOW WHAT WILL
MR SNODWORTHY, YOU WILL KINDLY UNWRAP THE BANDAGES AND UNVEIL MY ENORMOUS GENITAL
SNAP
UGH! VERY WELL, HEADMASTER
UNWIND UNWIND UNWIND UNWIND
SCHOOL NURSE
UNWIND UNWIND UNWIND UNWIND
UNWIND UNWIND UNWIND UNWIND
WHAT TH–? NURSE! YOU HAVEN'T MADE MY PENIS BIGGER AT ALL – YOU JUST STUCK A JUNIOR DISPRIN IN THE END AND THEN BANDAGED IT UP!
WELL I'M SORRY HEADMASTER, BUT I DON'T KNOW HOW TO DO PENILE SURGERY. I AM JUST A SCHOOL NURSE, AFTER ALL.
OH LORDY, WHAT WILL I DO NOW?
HEAD MASTER
THE SCHOOL INSPECTORS ARE DUE ANY MINUTE, AND I'VE NOTHING TO IMPRESS THEM WITH.
WHAT YOU NEED IS BIG MUSCULAR ARMS, HEADMASTER. EVERYONE IS IMPRESSED BY BIG MUSCLES.
HMM..
AND MY ROBOT PAL CAN HELP YOU GET SOME
I'VE TIED ONE OF TINRIBS'S TIN CANS TO THE END OF HIS ARMPIECE
SCRAPE SCRAPE
NOW I CAN SCRAPE AWAY THE PUTTY WHICH HOLDS THE GLASS PANE IN THAT HIGH WINDOW – LIKE SO.
TOPPLE
NOW, WATCH THIS
HEAD MASTER
ERM...
EEYARGH
SHLONK
THAT SHEET OF GLASS HAS SLICED MY BOTTOM CLEAN OFF!
THERE. MR SNODWORTHY'S BUMCHEEKS WILL MAKE SUPER ARTIFICIAL ARM MUSCLES
HMI
JUST POP ONE BUTTOCK INTO EACH OF YOUR JACKET SLEEVES.
JUST IN TIME – HERE'S THE SCHOOL INSPECTORS
THOSE BULGING BICEPS ARE VERY IMPRESSIVE. JOLLY GOOD SHOW!
HMI
HEAD MASTER
YES, TOP MARKS HEADMASTER!
WELL REALLY! ONE OF YOUR MUSCLES HAS JUST BROKEN WIND!
BROMP
H.M.I
OOPS!
DISGUSTING! FOR THAT, WE SHALL RECOMMEND THAT THE SCHOOL IS CLOSED DOWN IMMEDIATELY
HOORAY! THE SCHOOL IS GOING TO BE CLOSED DOWN!
CAPER
HEAD MASTER
JIG
I'LL NEVER HAVE TO TEACH THOSE HORRIBLE BRATS EVER AGAIN!
WAH! I'VE SKIDDED ON THAT DRATTED ROBOT!
SLIP!
YEEARGH!
HMI
HEAD MASTER
BY JOVE! THAT'S THE MOST IMPRESSIVE TRIPLE-BACK SOMERSAULT I'VE EVER SEEN.
CONGRATULATIONS! THAT MAGNIFICENT DISPLAY MEANS YOU'VE PASSED THE SCHOOL INSPECTION.
HMI
AND IT'S ALL THANKS TO TINRIBS.
GROAN...
HI. I'M BARBIE. I LOVE YOU VERY MUCH.

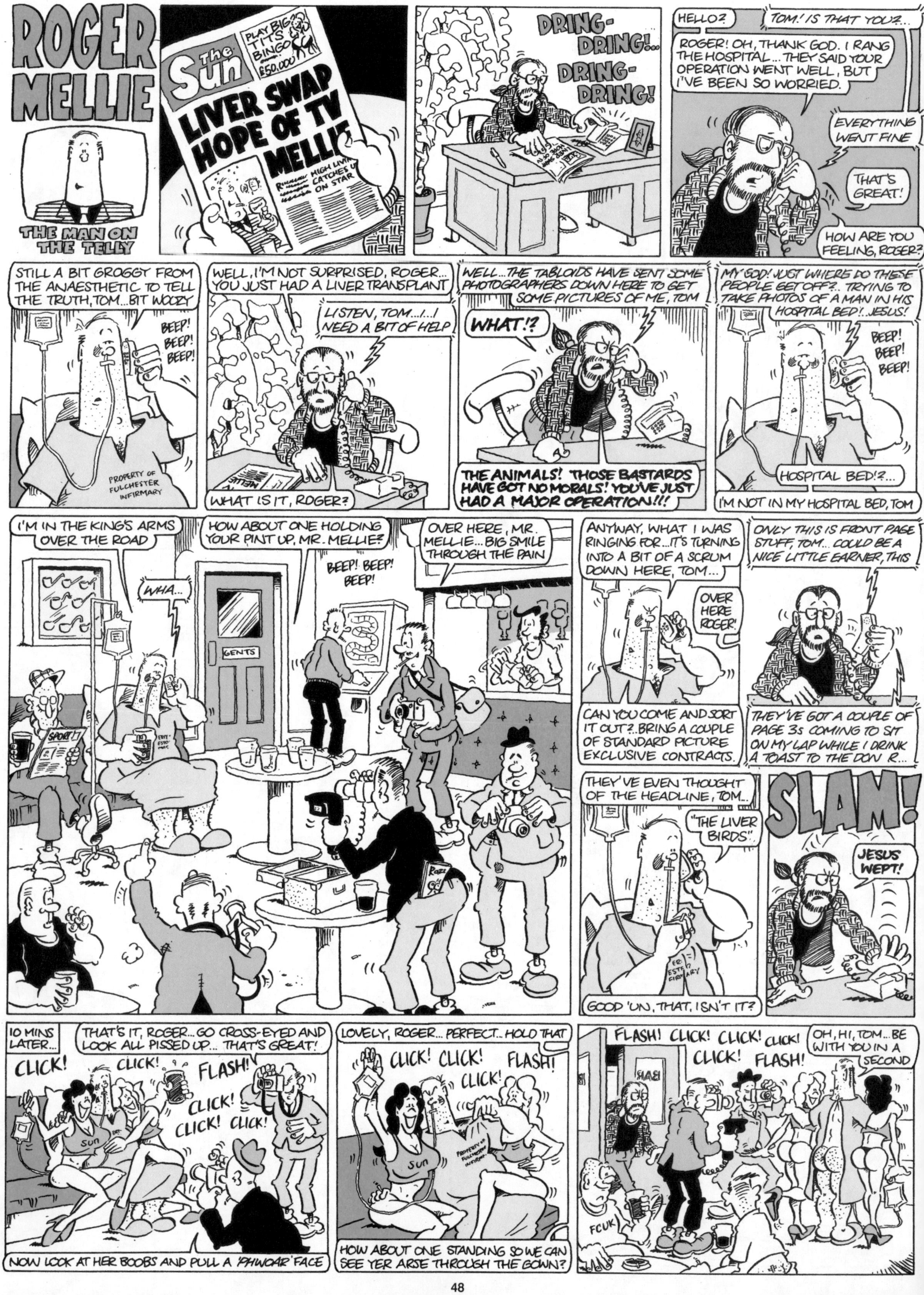

ROGER MELLIE
THE MAN ON THE TELLY
The Sun
PLAY BIG TITS BINGO £50,000
LIVER SWAP HOPE OF TV MELLIE
HIGH LIVING CATCHES UP ON STAR
DRING-DRING!... DRING-DRING!
HELLO?
TOM! IS THAT YOU?...
ROGER! OH, THANK GOD. I RANG THE HOSPITAL... THEY SAID YOUR OPERATION WENT WELL, BUT I'VE BEEN SO WORRIED.
EVERYTHING WENT FINE
THAT'S GREAT!
HOW ARE YOU FEELING, ROGER?
STILL A BIT GROGGY FROM THE ANAESTHETIC TO TELL THE TRUTH, TOM... BIT WOOZY
BEEP! BEEP! BEEP!
PROPERTY OF FULCHESTER INFIRMARY
WELL, I'M NOT SURPRISED, ROGER... YOU JUST HAD A LIVER TRANSPLANT
LISTEN, TOM... I... I NEED A BIT OF HELP
WHAT IS IT, ROGER?
WELL... THE TABLOIDS HAVE SENT SOME PHOTOGRAPHERS DOWN HERE TO GET SOME PICTURES OF ME, TOM
WHAT!?
THE ANIMALS! THOSE BASTARDS HAVE GOT NO MORALS! YOU'VE JUST HAD A MAJOR OPERATION!!!
MY GOD! JUST WHERE DO THESE PEOPLE GET OFF?.. TRYING TO TAKE PHOTOS OF A MAN IN HIS HOSPITAL BED!.. JESUS!
BEEP! BEEP! BEEP!
HOSPITAL BED!?...
I'M NOT IN MY HOSPITAL BED, TOM
I'M IN THE KING'S ARMS OVER THE ROAD
WHA...
HOW ABOUT ONE HOLDING YOUR PINT UP, MR. MELLIE?
BEEP! BEEP! BEEP!
OVER HERE, MR. MELLIE... BIG SMILE THROUGH THE PAIN
GENTS
SPORT
ANYWAY, WHAT I WAS RINGING FOR... IT'S TURNING INTO A BIT OF A SCRUM DOWN HERE, TOM...
OVER HERE ROGER!
CAN YOU COME AND SORT IT OUT?.. BRING A COUPLE OF STANDARD PICTURE EXCLUSIVE CONTRACTS.
ONLY THIS IS FRONT PAGE STUFF, TOM... COULD BE A NICE LITTLE EARNER, THIS
THEY'VE GOT A COUPLE OF PAGE 3s COMING TO SIT ON MY LAP WHILE I DRINK A TOAST TO THE DON R...
THEY'VE EVEN THOUGHT OF THE HEADLINE, TOM...
"THE LIVER BIRDS".
GOOD 'UN, THAT, ISN'T IT?
SLAM!
JESUS WEPT!
10 MINS LATER...
THAT'S IT, ROGER... GO CROSS-EYED AND LOOK ALL PISSED UP... THAT'S GREAT!
CLICK! CLICK! FLASH! CLICK! CLICK! CLICK!
SUN
NOW LOOK AT HER BOOBS AND PULL A 'PHWOAR' FACE
LOVELY, ROGER... PERFECT... HOLD THAT
CLICK! CLICK! FLASH! CLICK!
SUN
HOW ABOUT ONE STANDING SO WE CAN SEE YER ARSE THROUGH THE GOWN?
FLASH! CLICK! CLICK! CLICK! CLICK! FLASH!
OH, HI, TOM... BE WITH YOU IN A SECOND
BAR
FCUK

JUST A QUICK ONE OVER HERE, MR. MELLIE... CAN WE HAVE A QUICK LOOK AT THE SCAR?
COME ON, ROGER... LET'S GO!
JUST ONE MORE, TOM... THEY WANT ONE OF ME PULLING A PINT WITH MY DRIP HOOKED UP TO ONE OF THE OPTICS
CLICK!
CLICK!
CLICK!
LET'S GET YOU BACK TO THE HOSPITAL
KINGS ARMS
BAR
JESUS WEPT... I JUST DON'T BELIEVE YOU SOMETIMES ROGER, I REALLY DON'T! YOU'RE YOUR OWN WORST ENEMY
SHOP
SHORTLY...
BLOODY RIDICULOUS BEHAVIOUR!
DON'T GO ON, TOM. YOU CAN'T BUY PUBLICITY LIKE THAT... FRONT PAGE OF TOMORROWS PAPERS... EVERY ONE.
YOU WON'T LIVE LONG ENOUGH TO SEE TOMORROW'S PAPERS IF YOU CARRY ON AT THAT RATE. YOU ONLY GOT YOUR NEW LIVER THIS MORNING
OH, DON'T OVER-REACT, TOM... I WAS HARDLY SPANKING IT. I WAS ONLY WETTING ITS HEAD
WETTING ITS HEAD!?.. ROGER, YOU ABSOLUTELY STINK OF BOOZE!
YES, BUT THAT'S NOT FROM DRINKING, TOM... THE STAR WANTED A SHOT OF ME DRINKING A YARD OF ALE AND SOME CAME OUT MY NOSE
ANYWAY, THIS LIVER'S GOT NOTHING ON THE CLOCK, TOM... GOT TO RUN IT IN A BIT.
FOR GOD'S SAKE, ROGER... SOME POOR SOUL DIED SO AS YOU COULD HAVE THAT TRANSPLANT
HOW DO YOU THINK THEIR FAMILY WILL FEEL WHEN THEY SEE YOU ON THE FRONT OF EVERY PAPER SWIGGING A YARD OF ALE WITH YOUR GRINNING FACE SQUEEZED BETWEEN TWO PAIR OF TITS?
WHERE'S YOUR DIGNITY, ROGER?
HMM! YOU'RE RIGHT, TOM...
...YOU'RE RIGHT!... I SHOULD THINK OF THE DONOR'S FAMILY
IT MUST BE AN AWFUL TIME FOR THEM...
I'LL SEND THEM A SIGNED PHOTO, THAT SHOULD CHEER THEM UP A BIT
AND COULD YOU SORT OUT A COUPLE OF FTV 'GOODIE BAGS' FOR THEM, TOM?
WHO WAS HE, ANYWAY?
I DON'T KNOW, ROGER. HE WAS A YOUNG LAD ON A MOTORBIKE
cheers for the liver
SOME IDIOT IN A BLUE JAG KNOCKED HIM OFF IN THE HIGHSTREET LAST NIGHT... NEVER EVEN STOPPED.
HMM?.. THE BASTARD
Racing POST
PROBABLY DRUNK
HMM!
I HOPE THEY CATCH HIM AND THROW THE BOOK AT HIM
SOMEONE TO SEE YOU, MR. MELLIE
HMM!
NIP TO THE BOOKIES FOR ME, WOULD YOU, TOM?
MR. MELLIE?
THAT'S ME
ARE YOU THE OWNER OF A BLUE JAGUAR SOVEREIGN?
YEAH!
LISTEN, IF IT'S ABOUT THE TAX DISC, IT'S APPLIED FOR. I'M JUST WAITING ON DVLC.

LETTER BOCKS

Viz Comic, PO Box 656, North Shields, NE29 1BT. Email: letters@viz.co.uk

■ I am pleased to hear that the new Home Secretary Charles Clarke will be given 'special powers' to combat terrorism. I hope he chooses super strength, or the ability to fly. Or even X-ray vision. In any case, he will be better than the last one. he couldn't even see.

M Johnson
e-mail

■ Whilst enjoying the fantastic TV coverage of the royal wedding, I was especially stirred, as always, by the rousing rendition of the national anthem. However, I was shocked to see that the Queen did not seem to know the words and remained stone-faced throughout. Personally, I think that if the head of state is going to let the side down in public like this, then we should replace her with someone who is prepared to try a little harder, like David Beckham, or those fat chaps that play in the England rugby team.

Bongo Benjamin
London

■ I never worry about the destination when I'm going on holiday. My dad is Iranian and my mum is Irish, so I spend most of the time in customs.

Stan
e-mail

■ So the Tories reckon that the NHS would be better if hospitals were run by matrons. Clearly they haven't seen *Carry On, Doctor.* Hattie Jacques spends all her time trying to bed keneth Williams, the patients revolt and the whole place descends into anarchy. Where's the sense in that?

Gaz Baker
e-mail

■ I am a schools inspector of several years standing, and was appalled when my son showed me his recent copy of *Viz*. In what passed for humour in the Tinribs cartoon, a headmaster was depicted trying to cosmetically enhance the length of his manhood in an attempt to get a favourable school report. Our job is difficult enough without this kind of puerile mockery. School inspection is a very complicated and exacting process. Amongst other things, we look in detail at the standards of teaching, the ethos of the school and the levels of pupil attainment. Occasionally a school is deemed to be failing in one of these three key areas, and then and only then, is the headmaster's cock size taken into consideration.

J Clapham
Sutton Coldfield

■ Just a quick note to bosses at Esure Insurance; whenever Michael Winner comes on the telly in one of your adverts, I change the channel. Can I put it any more simply than that?

Jamie Groves
e-mail

■ The other day I was having a wank whilst watching *Neighbours* when my mobile phone rang. It was my mate, but I was already in the vinegar strokes, and I just managed to say hello when I went off. I'm worried that this might mean I am gay. And do I win £5?

Rob
Morpeth

■ Can anyone imagine the mountain of socks they must have found under the Pope's bed after 27 years of tugging his bellend?

el Tel
e-mail

■ I was saddened to see that, because of sheer numbers, many thousands of pilgrims were denied the right to say goodbye to the Pope. Rather than having the crowds file past him, I think it would have made more sense to prop him up in a car and drive him round the crowd-filled city. They didn't even need to use his Popemobile, they could have used a Fiat Panda. No one was going to bother having another pot shot, were they?

Stu Holt
South Shields

■ I'm feeling a little bit down, and wonder if you could print a picture of Donald Trump's 'hair' to cheer me up.

Terry
e-mail

STAR *Letter...*

★ Considering men of the cloth are supposed to lead humble lives, I find it a little strange that the Pope had not one, but three coffins during his funeral... I suppose he wanted to be buried eighteen feet under too.

Catboy
Rowlands Gill

■ I have discovered that masturbation does indeed send you blind. After years of knocking one off over Marilyn Monroe, through Agnetha from Abba, and latterly Kylie and the bird from Yes Car Credit, I am now paying the price for my self abuse. I am now 78 and have cataracts in both eyes. Oh for self-restraint when I was younger. Readers take heed.

P Mandelson
e-mail

■ I was watching those insurance adverts on the telly where Michael Winner plays the parts of both himself and his wife. It suddenly struck me that, after years of wishing he would, he could now actually go and fuck himself.

Mike Oxlong
e-mail

■ So much for the McDonald's adverts proclaiming 'Maccas staff can deal with anything'. The wide-eyed child serving me couldn't get her head around a plain McFlurry, seeing as there isn't a button on the cash register. It took her five minutes and three other employees before someone suggested just pressing the button for another flavour.

Andrew Tremble
e-mail

ROCK LOBSTER

WOULD YOU LIKE TO SELECT YOUR LOBSTER, MONSIEUR?
HMM... LET ME SEE...
ER... YES!.. I QUITE FANCY THE LITTLE ONE AT THE BACK
LOVE
HATE
OY, PAL!... C'MERE!
FANCY MY BIRD, DO YOU, EH?
I... I... ER...
C'MON... LET'S DISCUSS THIS, EH?.. MAN TO LOBSTER...
HATE
...IN THE FUCKIN' CAR PARK!

■ I recently went paintballing and the instructor told us all about the rules and our equipment, then asked if we had any questions. I asked how the guns could use liquid carbon dioxide, as surely CO_2 is a compound that sublimates straight from solid to gas, but he had no answer. If anything he looked rather annoyed.

Chris Scaife
e-mail

■ I know who killed Tommy Harris in Coronation Street. It was Katie, his daughter. If only the police watched more television instead of trying to fine people for speeding, the world would be a safer place.

Mark Mallinson
e-mail

■ The Sun newspaper reported that 'when the Pope was put in his coffin, his bishop's hat lay on his chest'. It's a pity he was celibate. With a cock that size he could have had a lot of fun.

S Thorn
Hexham

■ How come BT can't connect new phonelines straight away? It's always "It's not as simple as that, Sir." But when they want to cut you off, it's just the flick of a bloody switch.

Chris Peacock
e-mail

■ Yesterday in my local TK MAXX, I went into the household bit and saw a non-stick frying pan with a price sticker on it. Who the fuck are they trying to kid?

Graham Wilson
e-mail

■ An advert recently asked me to pay £5 per month to help free a mad bear. A mad bear? Christ, I'd pay three times that to keep the fucker locked up.

D Attenborough
e-mail

■ Is this article from the *Oldham Evening Chronicle* the most dull news article ever?

Mark Smith
Cheshire

Hamster dies

A HAMSTER died in a bedroom fire yesterday morning — despite fire-fighters attempts at resuscitation.

The pet was given oxygen after being brought from the house on Lime Street, Chadderton.

■ First his parents left him home alone when they went on holiday to France for Christmas, then they were separated on holiday in Florida and he ended up in New York. Then they let him go to Michael Jackson's Neverland Ranch. Can Macaulay Culkin not take a hint?

Ben Ardos
e-mail

■ Whoever said 'people say the funniest things' has never watched *Ant & Dec's Saturday Night Takeaway*.

I James
e-mail

LESS than a year after her impromptu toilet stop at the Athens Olympics, Paula Radcliffe has once again been up to her old tricks. And we have been innundated with your letters about her shocking behaviour in this year's London Marathon.

Dozens of people wrote in to complain that she was hailed as a heroine for urinating in the street, yet they were fined and bound over to keep the peace when they did the same.

However, many of you mistakenly believed that she had a shit rather than a piss mid-way through the 26 mile course and tailored your letters accordingly. Here's a selection of some of the best we recieved...

...**SO** Radcliffe thinks it's acceptable to have a shite in the middle of a Marathon, does she? Lets hope other sports stars don't start copying her example. Can you imagine the mess if Wayne Rooney left a big turd in the Old Trafford goalmouth, or of Tim Henman left a small pile of rabbit tods by the umpire's chair?

Stu Mandry, e-mail

...**I'M** an avid gambler and I know that studying form is the most important thing when trying to clean up at the bookies. With this in mind, I think a flutter on Paula to complete a shitting 'hat-trick' during her next televised race would be a good bet.

Ian Cramphorn, e-mail

...**WHEN** I take my dog for a walk, I always act responsibly and clear up after it. I think Paula Radcliffe's husband shoud be as responsible as me. During every race, he should run behind her with a little plastic bag ready to clear up any businesses that she does.

J Palmer, London

...**ATHLETES** are always going on about the amount of training they have to do. It is clear to me that Radcliffe hasn't done enough toilet training. It didn't take my Springer spaniel long to learn. Next time she shits in a race, Seb Coe should hit her firmly with a rolled up newspaper, and rub her nose in the mess whilst saying 'No! Bad girl! in a firm voice.

David Williams, e-mail

...**WHAT** on earth is wrong with this woman? Why can't she go before the race like the other 32,000 runners? I think she gets some sort of thrill out of shitting in the street.

Eric Lawton, e-mail

...**THE** woman should sort her bumhole out once and for all. You never see Kelly Holmes shitting at side of the running track. Although Geoff Capes did once, and Fatima Whitbread trod in it

Norman Bowels, e-mail

...**I THINK** the BBC should be held partly responsible for this disgusting act as they broadcast it. I do not pay my licence fee to watch grown women defecating. That is what the internet is for.

Simon Oates, e-mail

SU-DOC-WHO No. 2652

You're only on earth for a short time, so why not fritter a significant amount of it away on one of these pointless puzzles? *Su-Doc-Who* is the craze that's sweeping the nation. Inside the grid are the faces of Dr. Whos 1-9. Can you complete the grid so that each Who appears once in every row, column and block of nine? To save you those precious hours that you can never get back, we've printed the answer on page 149.

TOP TIPS

NUNS at St Cuthbert's School in the early 1970s. Demonstrate a keen sense of irony by calling yourselves the 'Sisters of mercy' whilst beating the shit out of us kids on a daily basis with bamboo canes.

Paul Bradshaw
e-mail

TIGHT-arsed blokes. At this time of year, only date girls called Natalie, Carol, Holly or Eve. Chances are their birthday is around Christmas and you won't have to shell out for a present until then, by which time they will probably have packed you in.

David Bushell
e-mail

Football Crazy Results

Manic Depression Utd **3**
Paranoid Schizophrenia City **1**

Alzheimers Academicals **0**
Dynamo Tourette's Syndrome **1**

Obsessive Compulsive Disorder FC **2**
AFC Pyromania **1**

European Cup

Lokomotiv Kleptomania **1**
Bayern Munchausen's Syndrome **1**

Real Sociopathy **1**
AC Separation Anxiety Disorder **0**

HOW'S THAT RASH ON YOUR BOTTOM?
IT'S CLEARING UP NICELY.

OH, LORDY, IT'S THE FAT SLAGS
JESUS! LADY DI'S LOOKIN' ROUGH THESE DAYS, IN'T SHE, TRAY, EH?
THAT'S NOT DI...THAT'S HIS NEW BIT, CAMILLA PARKER BOWLES. LADY DI'S DEAD
IS SHE?
AYE! BIN DEAD 'BOUT EIGHT YEAR
EEH, I NEVER PUT THE NEWS ON
DING! DONG!
GET THE DOOR, SAN
GOOD AFTERNOON, MADAM. I'M YOUR LIBERAL DEMOCRAT CANDIDATE FOR THE FORTHCOMING ELECTION... I HOPE I CAN COUNT...
COME IN, LOVER
...ON...ON...ER...YOUR SUPPORT
P'RAPS
ERM...WOULD YOU LIKE TO SEE MY ER...MANEFESTO?
AYE! FOLLOW ME UPSTAIRS AN' I'LL 'AVE A BUTCHERS.
SPROING! SPROING! SPROING!
OOH!
2 MINS LATER...
SO...ER...CAN I COUNT ON YOUR SUPPORT?
DUNNO..
...WE'VE NOT 'AD UKIP OR THE SCOTTISH NATIONALISTS ROUND YET
WHAT'S GOIN' ON?.. THAT'S THE SIXTH BLOKE CANVASSING Y'VE BANGED THIS WEEK, SAN
IT'S ME VOTIN' SYSTEM, TRAY... I'M BANGIN' ALL THE CANVASSERS WHEN THEY COME ROUND...
...AN' WHOEVER'S GOT THE BIGGEST COCK, THAT'S WHO I VOTE FOR.
WHAT!?.. THAT'S REALLY SHALLOW, THAT, SAN... YOUR GRANDADS FOUGHT IN THE WAR T' GIVE YOU THE RIGHT T' VOTE...
...AN' YOU GO CHOOSIN' WHO T' VOTE FOR BY THE LENGTH OF HIS FUCKIN' CHARLIE!
THERE'S MORE IMPORTANT THINGS T' CONSIDER THAN COCK LENGTH WHEN CHOOSIN' HOW T' VOTE...
S'POSE YER RIGHT.
ELECTION DAY...
LIBRARY
EXCUSE ME, MADAM. COULD YOU TELL ME HOW YOU VOTED?
AYE!..
POLLING STATION
POLLING STATION
POLLING STATION
I WENT FOR A COMBINATION OF GIRTH AN' LENGTH, ORAL SATISFACTION, AN' ABILITY T' FIND ME CLIT.

LUVVIE DARLING
OH GOD! THESE REVIEWS ARE TERRIBLE. IF ANYBODY IN THE BUSINESS SEES THESE, MY CAREER WILL BE RUINED, DO YOU HEAR ME..? R-R-R-R-RUINED!
DISASTER
DARLING YOU WERE RUBBISH
NONSENSE, LUVVIE. NO-ONE GETS TO SEE WHAT THE CRITICS WRITE. THOSE PAPERS ARE MERELY TOMORROW'S CHIP WRAPPERS.
YES-YES. OF COURSE YOU'RE RIGHT, DEAR.
NEXT DAY...
...I HOPE I'VE GOT THIS LUNCH ORDER CORRECT. LET ME SEE...THAT'S 500 FOR COD AND CHIPS, 500 FOR HADDOCK...
N.E.C.
TODAY-SOCIETY OF THEATRE, FILM & TV PRODUCERS, DIRECTORS & CASTING AGENTS ANNUAL CONFERENCE 2005.
FISH & CHIPS

MAJOR MISUNDERSTANDING
PARK REGULATIONS
DAILY MAIL
'SCUSE, PLEASE. I AM, HOW YOU SAY, SEEKING OF TO FIND THE CITY BUS STATION.
MAP
PLEASE TO ASK YOU FOR DIRECTING ME?
I'LL SMOKE WHERE I DAMN WELL PLEASE, SIR. THIS IS STILL A FREE COUNTRY.
I'LL NOT BE TOLD WHAT I CAN AND CAN'T DO BY PETTIFOGGING BUREAUCRATS LIKE YOU.
IT'S THE NANNY STATE GONE MAD. WE'RE BEING MOLLYCODDLED AND COSSETTED BY ALL YOU DO-GOODERS AND BUSYBODIES IN OFFICIALDOM.
YOU'LL BE ORDERING US HOW TO WIPE OUR OWN BACKSIDES, NEXT.
CHURCHILL SMOKED THIS BRAND. I SUPPOSE YOU'D TELL HIM TO STOP, AS WELL.
CALL YOURSELF A TRUE ENGLISHMAN? YOU'RE NOTHING BUT A JUMPED UP LITTLE JOBSWORTH.
WELL I'M NOT INTIMIDATED BY YOUR SORT. YOU CAN WAVE THOSE RULES AND REGULATIONS AT ME ALL YOU LIKE.
I SHALL CONTINUE WITH MY WALK, ENJOYING MY CHEROOT.
STUB STUB
LITTER

TUBBY JOHNSON
"HE'S GOT A GOOD HEALTHY APPETITE"
OOOH! I HAVEN'T EATEN FOR NEARLY TWENTY MINUTES. I'M A BIT PECKISH.
BAKER
PIES £10
BUT I'VE GOT NO MONEY TO BUY ANY PIES.
COR! THAT'S THE JOB FOR ME!
PIE TESTER WANTED APPLY WITHIN
YES, WE'VE GOT THOUSANDS OF PIES THAT ALL NEED TESTING.
GAFFER
BUT I'M AFRAID WE ONLY EMPLOY GRADUATES TO TEST OUR PIES. YOU'LL NEED TO GET A UNIVERSITY DEGREE.
QUICK – I NEED TO TAKE A UNIVERSITY DEGREE
FULCHESTER UNIVERSITY
ADMISSIONS
ANY SUBJECT WILL DO
THREE YEARS LATER
IT GIVES ME GREAT PLEASURE, ON THIS DAY OF YOUR GRADUATION, TO PRESENT YOU WITH...
SNATCH!
DEAN
DEGREE
YES, YES, HURRY UP, I'M STARVING!
GASP! THREE YEARS WITHOUT A SQUARE MEAL ~ I'M FAMISHED!
PIE TESTER WANTED APPLY WITHIN
BUT IT'LL BE WORTH IT TO GET THAT PIE-TASTING JOB
BUT
RIGHT. START MEASURING THE CIRCUMFERENCE AND DIAMETER OF EACH OF THESE CIRCLES AND CHECK THAT THE RATIO BETWEEN THEM IS 3·1415926...
OH NO! IT'S THAT SORT OF "PIE (THAT IS TO SAY, 'PI') TESTING JOB"!
...5358979323846...
MATHEMATICAL CONSTANT TESTING PLANT
ETC.
LITTER
BAH!

Too much cheese as bad for you as not enough, say boffins

EATING too much cheese can be as bad for your health as not eating enough, according to a new report which looked at the right amount of cheese to eat.

Some cheese yesterday ~ But too much, or not enough?

In the study, which looked at the medical records of people who had been fed different quantities of cheese, cheese scientists found that consuming too much cheese had just as adverse an effect on a person's well-being as consuming too little.

condemn

But condemnation of the report has come from all sides. Pro-too much cheese eating pressure group, *XS Cheese*, were quick to condemn the report's conclusion. A spokesman said: "It's nonsense. Eating too much cheese is far better for you healthwise than eating the right amount or less." And Moira Johnson, representing pro-insufficient cheese lobby group, *NotEnoughCheese*, also attacked the findings. "The study is deeply flawed. We will continue to try to educate people to eat a less than adequate quantity of this foodstuff."

condomn

However, the report was welcomed by Lord Owen, chairman of the anti too-much or not enough cheese pressure group *Just The Right Amount Of Cheese, Please*. "This report vindicates what we have said all along", the busty peer told reporters at a packed press conference. "That too much cheese is as bad for your health as not enough."

by our cheese amounts correspondent
Arthur Quanticheese

Lord Owen ~ just the right amount of cheese

Have YOUR say

THE EXPERTS have had their say, and you've had a chance to look at both sides of the argument. So what do YOU think is the correct amount of cheese to eat? Call the number below to register your vote.

Q: What do YOU think is the correct amount of cheese to eat?

Too much
☎ 01 811 8055

Right amount
☎ 01 811 8056

not enough
☎ 01 811 8057

Calls cost an absolute fucking fortune. Please wait until the bill payer has left the house before calling.

...OF COURSE, I'M TALKING OFF THE TOP OF MY HEAD HERE...

BIFFA BACON
STOP BULLYING NOW
CHARITY WRIST BAND, SIR?.. £1·50?
EH?
'STOP BULLYING' WRIST BANDS £1·50
THEY'RE ANTI-BULLYING WRIST BANDS...THEY ARE WORN TO RAISE AWARENESS OF THE PROBLEM OF BULLYING IN SCHOOLS
AYE! THEY LOOK CANNY, THEM
UNFORTUNATELY, IT'S A GROWING PROBLEM, AND MANY CHILDREN SUFFER IN SILENCE. WE WANT TO LET THEM KNOW THAT THEY'RE NOT ALONE
THE MONEY RAISED PAYS FOR TRAINED COUNSELLORS TO HELP THE VICTIMS OF BULLIES, AND WEARING ONE DEMONSTRATES YOUR COMMITMENT TO STAMPING OUT BULLYING IN SCHOOLS
THAT'S CHAMPION
ALL THE CHILDREN ARE WEARING THEM
AYE...I'LL GET ME'SEL ONE O' THEM, I WILL
HOO, CEDRIC, Y' GEET BIG PUFF!..
GIZ THAT WRISTBAND NOO!.. OR I'LL KICK YER FUCKIN' HEED IN!

GILBERT RATCHET
COO! THE LOCAL MOSQUE IS HOLDING A FÊTE.
GRAND FETE FULCHESTER MOSQUE ALL WELCOME
I LOVE FETES, ME.
I'LL POP ALONG THERE.
FULCHESTER MOSQUE
GRAND FETE TO DAY
PERHAPS THERE WILL BE THE OPPORTUNITY TO LIGHT-HEARTEDLY POKE GENTLE FUN AT ASPECTS OF THE ISLAMIC RELIGION.
ACTUALLY, READERS ~ ON SECOND THOUGHTS, I THINK I'LL JUST VISIT THE CHRISTIAN CHURCH OVER THE ROAD, INSTEAD
SWERVE
ST SWITHENS CHURCH
Jesus is your saviour
GOSH ~ WHY ARE YOU DIGGING UP THE FLOOR OF YOUR CHURCH, REVEREND BIGDAFTBUMFRIGGER?
I'M ON A QUEST, GILBERT ~ A QUEST FOR A HOLY RELIC!
HAVING READ 'THE DA VINCI CODE', IT OCCURRED TO ME THAT JESUS, BEING A RED-BLOODED MALE, MUST HAVE OWNED A SECRET STASH OF PORN MAGS.
DAN BROWN THE DA VINCI CODE
AND IT OCCURRED TO ME THAT THEY MAY WELL BE HIDDEN SOMEWHERE BENEATH THIS VERY CHURCH
BUT I'VE BEEN DIGGING FOR HOURS, AND HAVEN'T FOUND A THING.
HMM. WHAT YOU NEED IS A NUDEY-BOOK DETECTOR
SHORTLY
I'VE ATTACHED A SENSORY DEVICE TO THE TROUSERS OF RENOWNED STROKE-MAG AFICIONADO JONATHAN ROSS
AS SOON AS HE PICKS UP THE SCENT OF PORNOGRAPHY, HIS TROUSERS WILL START TWITCHING AND SET OFF THIS KLAXON ALARM
G'WAN, BOY! SEEK 'EM OUT!
SNUFFLE SNUFFLE SNUFFLE
FIND THE SACRED MUCKY BOOKS, JONATHAN
AROOGA!
THERE GOES THE ALARM ~ HE'S ON THE TRAIL OF SOME GRUMBLE
DIG DIG DIG
ARRGH! MY EARDRUMS!
AND
LOOK VICAR ~ JONATHAN ROSS HAS UNCOVERED CHRIST'S BONGO LITERATURE
PAT PAT
MEEK 'N' MILD
THAT'S ALL VERY WELL GILBERT...
...BUT THAT BLASTED ALARM THING OF YOURS HAS GIVEN ME AN AWFUL SPLITTING HEADACHE.
QUMRAN QUIM
I'VE GOT ALL THESE SAUCY PICTURES TO LOOK AT, AND SIMPLY DON'T FEEL IN THE MOOD.
DON'T WORRY, VICAR ~ I'LL INVENT A MECHANICAL PORN-PERUSER WHICH WILL READ THIS SCUD FOR YOU.
THANKS GILBERT.
SEE ~ THE OGLE-O-MATIC™ ELECTRIC EYEBALL SCRUTINISES THE PICTURES OF NUDDY LADIES, LEAVING YOU FREE TO HAVE A NICE CUP OF TEA AND A DISPRIN
BLEEP
LEAF
SMASHING.
OOPS! I'VE ACCIDENTALLY SET THE OGLE-O-MATIC TO FULL POWER
CLUNK
IT'LL GO INTO A PORN FRENZY
CRIKEY! NOW THAT'S SENT IT'S GUILT AND SELF-LOATHING LEVELS DANGEROUSLY HIGH
HISSSS
CLANK WHIRR
FRANTIC RIFFLE
RUN FOR IT ~ IT'S GOING TO BLOW UP!
BOOM
ST SWITHENS CHURCH
YOU BUNGLING YOUNG IDIOT
NOT ONLY HAVE YOU REDUCED MY LOVELY CHURCH TO RUBBLE, YOU'VE ALSO DESTROYED THE PRICELESS SCRUFF BOOKS OF JESUS
WAIT A MINUTE ~ THAT EXPLOSION HAS UNCOVERED A SECRET CHAMBER UNDERNEATH THE CHURCH
AND IT LOOKS LIKE THERE'S SOMETHING GLOSSY DOWN THERE
GASP! I DON'T BELIEVE IT!
DEITY DOLLYBIRDS
IT'S THE SECRET WANK MAG STASH OF GOD ALMIGHTY HIMSELF!
HUBBA HUBBA! THE LADIES FEATURED IN HERE ARE INFINITELY NUDE, AND HAVE GOT OMNIPRESENT KNOCKERS!
THANKS GILBERT ~ PLEASE ACCEPT THIS HOLY GRAIL AS A REWARD.

Royal *'bit on the side'* set to plumb new depths *~fear*

THE WORLD of Royal watching was last night in shock after claims that the marriage of Prince Charles to Camilla Parker-Bowles will spell *disaster* for the long-term future of the monarchy.

By our Royal Correspondent
Ingledew Botteril

In a new study looking into the relationship trends of the Prince of Wales, reserchers found that when he marries a woman, he then takes a mistress one twentieth as attractive.

report

The report from Royality boffins at the University of Birmingham could well take the shine off what was planned to be *'The Wedding of the Century'*.

"The trends were fairly obvious," said the report's author Professor Max Haystacks. "Each time Charles gets married, such as in 1981, he immediately has an affair with a woman 5% as attractive as his wife. If he repeats this behaviour pattern, and I see no reason why he shouldn't, then after marrying the unattractive Camilla Parker-Bowles, he will take a mistress only 5% as attractive as her."

Haystacks ~ report

And he had this stark message. "The figures speak for themselves. By this summer, Charles will be going behind his wife's back with a woman *one four-hundredth* as good looking as Lady Diana. That equates to somebody like Nora Batty or any of the women off the *Ocean Finance* adverts."

But friends of the Prince of Wales moved quickly to denounce the report as nonsense. "This report is nonsense," spluttered humpty-dumpty bloated tit ***Nicholas Soames***. "I know his royal Highness very well, and he has no plans to takes a mistress at present, be she ugly or attractive."

Charles ~ large ears

WOW! *~the '10' wife*

OUCH! *~the '0.5' lover*

Royal bum-nuzzler Norman St John-Stevas was more circumspect. "I disagree with the findings of the report. His royal Highness will almost certainly take a mistress, but who is to say she will be 20 times uglier than Camilla?" he told journalists. "The Prince has impeccable taste, and he may buck the trend and start doing the dirty with a really class bird like Kylie, Abi Titmuss, or Nicole out of the Renault Clio adverts."

Who Will the New Mistress Be?

IF THE REPORT turns out to be true, in 20 years time the Commonwealth could be ruled by an absolute steg. We know who the rider is, but who are the runners in the 2025 Princess of Wales Stakes? We look at the candidates and weigh up which minger is odds on to be Charlie's next darling.

Anne Widdecombe, MP for Maidstone.

Pros: Like all fairytale princesses, Anne is a virgin, so there will be no James Hewitts, Will Carlings, Dodi Fayeds or that heart surgeon bloke coming out of the woodwork. Like her potential lover, she is a conservative, so there are unlikely to be any political spats. And Charles was a pilot in the navy, so her Ark Royal landing deck-style tits will remind him of happy times.

Cons: Charles is never happier than when riding to hounds, and unfortunately, Anne cannot fit on a horse. She is also a member of the Roman Church, and it's illegal for Prince Charleses to marry Catholics. If she became the queen, under a law dating back to Henry VIII, she would have to be beheaded.

Odds: 8/1

Olive out of 'On the Busses', ugly actress.

Pros: As was seen in her famous sit-com role, Olive was very subservient, and unlike Diana, she is unlikely to rock the Royal boat. Her sit-com husband Arthur, alias real life actor Arthur Robbins died in real life, so there are unlikely to be any 'kiss and tell' stories sold to the tabloids.

Cons: Ugly Olive bursts into uncontrollable tears at the drop of a hat. The Royals are famed for their stiff upper lips, and such displays of humanity at the Cenotaph or a state funeral would be embarrassing to the family. In addition, Olive had a baby in 'On the Buses' who may well be older than Prince William and would therefore have a rightful claim on the throne.

Odds: 5/2

Janet Street-Porter, TV harridan.

Pros: The upper classes like the 'horsey' type of woman, and Ms Street-Porter resembles a carthorse form a 1930s cartoon. As a landowner, Charles has a love of the countryside, a love that Janet shares as former president of the Ramblers Society. However, the fact that she likes to walk through it and he likes to kill things in it may cause friction.

Cons: Street-Porter is famously not a virgin, having been vaginaly penetrated by former Dance Energy presenter Normski. Also, whereas Prince Charles likes culture such as Shakespeare, Michelangelo and Beethoven, Street-Porter prefers modern culture such as Playstations, rap music and modern art.

Odds: 3/2 on

Maureen out of 'Driving School', comedy driver.

Pros: Loveable halfwit Maureen is a lethal menace behind the wheel of a car, but as a member of the Royal household, she would be chauffeur driven everywhere. She is also Welsh, which means that as the Princess of Wales she would be able to talk to her subjects in their made-up vowel-free language.

Cons: Unfortunately for Prince Charles, Maureen is not posh enough to carry off the role as Royal courtesan. At a banquet, it is likely that she would embarrass the Royal family by eating her soup with a pudding spoon. She also works nights cleaning the toilets of her local police station, so it is unlikely she would get

Queen of the Jungle!

A SKELETON in the Parker-Bowles's family cupboard is once again threatening to derail the Prince of Wales's ill-fated marriage plans. Because according to a leaked document, Camilla Parker Bowles, the future Queen of England is descended from a family of hairy monkeys that lived up a tree!

EXCLUSIVE!

The document, left on a photocopier at the House of Commons revealed that her ancesters:

- *Dragged their* **knuckles** *across the floor*
- *Used* **leaves** *as rudimentary toilet paper*
- *Engaged in* **casual sex** *in banana trees*
- *Had unsightly* **blue bottoms** *and ate ants*

The anonymous author of the dossier claims that around 1 1/2 million years ago, Camilla's ancestors lived in small family groups on the plains of central Africa.

berries

In contrast to their present day comfortable lifestyle of Range Rovers, country houses and polo weekends, the Parker-Bowleses of yesteryear lived a harsh nomadic life, foraging for grubs and berries and eating fleas off each other's backs.

The dossier goes on to claim that over the millennia, the Parker-Bowleses lost their tails and began walking upright, eventually evolving into human beings around 50,000 years ago.

norrises

According to Palace insiders, Camilla is embarrassed by her humble origins and never talks about her prehistoric roots. A former Sandringham valet told us: "Camilla's family past is an open secret, but she is very touchy about it. No one is allowed to talk about monkeys, and at mealtimes it is strictly forbidden to serve bananas, nuts or PG Tips."

yeagers

Royal expert Dr David Starkey last night foresaw trouble if the marriage went ahead. "There would be many constitutional issues at stake," he told reporters. "Let's face it, blood will out, and I fear that at a Buckingham Palace reception Camilla may climb on the table and start drinking from the spout of the teapot. Either that, or at a variety performance, she may climb out of the Royal Box and start swinging from the lights, throwing handfuls of faeces at the audience."

Camilla as she is today (inset) and an artist's impression of how the Parker-Bowleses would have appeared half a million years ago.

Camilla Parker-Bowles 'Descended from Apes' ~shock

time off to open the Commonwealth Games or make state visits to Tonga aboard the Royal Yacht Britannia.

Odds: *10/1*

Lily Savage, **Scouse comedienne.**

Pros: Already popular with the British people, Lily Savage would be a breath of fresh air in Royal circles. Quick witted and humorous, she would bring much needed laughter into staid Royal proceedings. Her trademark sharp tongue would also serve her well in her new role as stepmum to the young princes.

Cons: With her working class scouse background, Lily all too often falls into the trap of using four-letter words which could be very embarrassing - with Royals, their blood is blue, not their language. As an animal lover, she would find it hard to accept Charle's love of bloodsports. Another possible obstacle to an affair with Charles might be her possession of male genitals.

Odds: *7/2*

Jackie Stallone, **actor's mum.**

Pros: Part of a high-profile Royal's job is meeting famous people, a task which could be daunting to someone unused to living in the limelight. Fortunately, Jackie has rubbed shoulders with the famous, having met such A-list stars as her son Rocky Balboa, his ex-wife Brigitte Neilson, John McCrirrick, Lisa I'Anson and Bez.

Cons: Her habit of reading the future by looking at the lines on people's bottoms may not be seen by some as a fitting pursuit for a monarch. If Jackie pulled Kofi Annan's trousers down at a UN reception and started peering at his arse, saying he's going on a long journey, it could lead to a serious diplomatic incident.

Odds: *7/3*

Public 'Split' over Royal Marriage

A NEW OPINION poll has showed that the public is as deeply divided as ever over the proposed marriage of Prince Charles to his long term lover Camilla Parker-Bowles.

EXCLUSIVE!

According to the survey, when asked whether the Divorced Prince should be allowed to marry his mistress, 51% of people said they couldn't give a toss, whilst 47% couldn't give a fuck (source 2005 *Canter* poll). 2% didn't give a shit.

Here's what the nation thought

Q. Should Camilla Parker-Bowles be allowed to use the title 'Her Royal Highness?'

Couldn't give a shit 40%
Fuck knows 23%
Who gives a fuck? 35%
Don't give a fucking monkey's 2%

Q. In the light of his marriage, should Charles give up his claim to the throne in favour of Prince William?

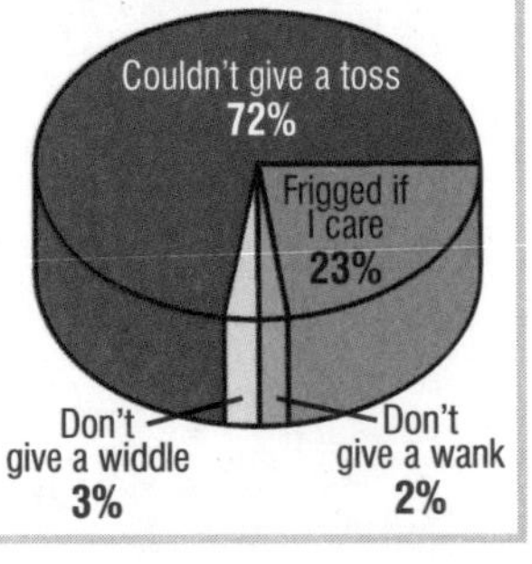
Couldn't give a toss 72%
Frigged if I care 23%
Don't give a widdle 3%
Don't give a wank 2%

Join the Debate

Here's a chance to make *YOUR* voice heard with our phone-in poll:

Q. As divorcees, many have said that Charles and Camilla should not be allowed to marry in church. What couldn't you give whether they do or not?

- **A flying fuck**
  ☎ 0800 000 001
- **Two fucking hoots**
  ☎ 0800 000 002
- **A tupenny fart**
  ☎ 0800 000 003

All calls cost £1.50/min and last a minimum of 4hours 30minutes.

TERRY FUCKWITT
He's got SHIT for brains
BOO TO THE B.B.C.
I'M SORRY, READERS. THEY'LL BE PRECIOUS FEW LAUGHS IN MY CARTOON THIS WEEK
(FILL IN YOUR OWN 'READERS VOICE' COMMENT HERE)
AS A CHRISTIAN, I'M GOING TO THE BBC TELEVISION CENTRE TO PROTEST ABOUT THEIR BLASPHEMOUS SHOWING OF 'JERRY SPINGER THE OPERA'...
...A BIG GROUP OF US ARE GOING TO BURN OUR T.V. LICENCES.
SO...
WHAT DON'T WE WANT?
JERRY SPRINGER THE OPERA!
WE ♡ JESUS
BOO TO THE B.B.C.
BBC = THE DEVIL
PENTECOSTALS 25 v 13
THE BBC IS GOING TO BURN IN A LAKE OF FIRE
?
WHEN DON'T WE WANT IT?
SEVERAL WEEKS AGO!
OKAY! OKAY! WHAT'S GOING ON, THEN
WE'RE GOING TO BURN OUR T.V. LICENCES IN PROTEST AT THE BBC
ALLELUJAH!
I SEE. WELL, HAS ANYONE BROUGHT ANY MATCHES
ER... NO
WELL, WE CAN RIP THEM UP INSTEAD
ALLELUJAH!
HAVE YOU BROUGHT THEM WITH YOU?
ER... NO.
AH! IT'S NOT MUCH OF A PROTEST, IS IT?
ER...NOT REALLY, NO!
WELL, IT DOESN'T REALLY MATTER, TERRY, BECAUSE THIS ISN'T THE BBC ANYWAY...
SECURITY BARRIER EXPO 2005
...IT'S AN OPEN-AIR SECURITY BARRIER EXHIBITION
HEY! FUCK US!
YEAH! ARE OUR BRAINS 'SHIT FOR' OR WHAT?
WE ♡ JESUS
SHORTLY...
EXCUSE ME... I'M CONDUCTING A SURVEY INTO WHICH IS THE MOST PAINFUL... HAVING YOUR TESTICLES REPEATEDLY BEATEN WITH A CRICKET BAT...
...OR HAVING THEM REPEATEDLY KICKED WITH A DIVING BOOT...
...DO YOU HAVE A FEW MOMENTS TO SPARE?
ER...YES!
SO...
THWACK! THWACK! THWACK!
HNNG! HNNG! HNNG!
GNN!
THWACK
RIGHT!.. THAT'S THE CRICKET BAT. NOW FOR THE DIVING BOOT
CLANG! CLANG! CLANG! CLANG!
HNNG! HNNG!
GNN!
WELL, WHICH, IN YOUR OPINION, WAS THE MORE PAINFUL?
ERM...OH, DEAR. I'VE FORGOTTEN.
...I DON'T S'POSE YOU COULD DO THEM AGAIN, COULD YOU?
THROB! THROB!
THWACK! CLANG! THWACK! CLANG!
HNNG!
HNNG!
SHORTLY...
TELL YOU WHAT, TERRY. I'LL PUT YOU DOWN AS A "DON'T KNOW", EH?
HYUUURGH!
HNNNNYYYEEUURGH!
JESUS, TERRY... THAT WAS THE MOST SHIT-FOR-BRAINSEST THING I'VE EVER SEEN IN MY LIFE!
BLOOOAGH!
AND AS LUCK WOULD HAVE IT, THE 'ACT OF FUCKWITTEDNESS 2005' CHAMPIONSHIPS ARE BEING HELD AT THE TOWN HALL RIGHT NOW!
BLOOOAGH!
IF THAT PERFORMANCE OF YOURS DOESN'T WIN, I'LL EAT MY HAT
AT THE TOWN HALL...
...AND FOR VOLUNTEERING HIMSELF TO BE REPEATEDLY BLUDGEONED IN THE TESTICLES AND THEN ASKING FOR THE PROCESS TO BE REPEATED, THE TITLE 'FUCKWITTED ACT OF THE YEAR 2005' GOES TO...
BLOOARGH!
WAIT!.. THERE APPEARS TO BE A LATE ENTRY...
...HIS ROYAL HIGHNESS PRINCE HARRY!
ER... HEIL HITLER, WHAT-WHAT. HAW! HAW!
FUCK ME!.. AND I THOUGHT I WAS AS THICK AS PIGSHIT.

Charles & Camilla have been banging each other for 35 years and they're still hungry for nookie. How do they do it?

20 WAYS TO SPICE UP YOUR LOVE LIFE

Our relationships, like bread, soon go stale if we don't work at them. But unlike bread, which goes hard the longer you neglect it, relationships are more like biscuits because they go soft over time. Many couples find that after several years together, their biscuits have become too soft to dunk in the tea of love. Meanwhile, the pot of desire grows cold on the draining board of your relationship, and all too often this is followed by erectile disfunction and vaginal dryness.

But the good news, according to sex experts, is that it's never too late to rewarm your teapot of love. Follow these twenty simple steps and you'll soon be guzzling down steaming mugs of hot sex with full cream milk, two sugars and biscuits which are twice as long and ten times as hard as ever before.

Role Playing
Having sex with the same person for years, perhaps decades, can soon become utterly, utterly tedious and repetitive. But, say relationship experts, we can put the spice back into our love lives by simply pretending to be someone else! Why not pretend you're a businessman going away to a conference? Then, while your wife waits at home, book into a Holiday Inn and have sex with a cheap prostitute.

Dressing Up
Whether it's policewomen, nazis or French maids, there's no denying that many of our most exciting sexual fantasies revolve around uniforms. But all too often this can become forgotten in a long term relationship. Ask your wife to dress up as a nurse, complete with a medical bag, stethoscope and black stockings. Then, plan a saucy day when she goes out to cut your nan's toenails whilst you stay home and have a wank.

Rude Food
In the film 91/2 weeks, Mickey Rourke and Kim Basinger got audiences hot under the collar when they drove each other wild with food out of the fridge. Why not try the same thing at home? You never know, it might be just what you need to tickle your jaded sexual palate back into life! Get your wife to strip and pour different foods onto her naked body. Try sticky honey, creamy yoghurt, cold ice cream or greasy sausages. Massage the food sensually into her skin and hair. Then run her a hot, foaming bath. While she's in it, tell her you're going out for a paper, then nip round to her sister's for a steamy love session.

Bondage
Bondage isn't for everyone, but it can be a wonderful way to put a bit of ooh-la-la back into a jaded marriage. The key to a successful bondage session is trust; as long as you and your partner are

comfortable with the idea of exploring the darker side of your relationship, the sex that results can be mindblowing! Select some soft rope or silken scarves and gently but firmly tie your wife's wrists and ankles to the bed. To add an extra frisson of excitement, blindfold her and then tiptoe out of the house and make your way to your local red light district. Once there, pick up a good time girl for an erotic £10 hand job behind a skip in the Matalan carpark.

Al Fresco Sex
A whiff of danger often provides all the charge that is needed to jumpstart the flattest sex batteries. And many people find that a saucy session out of doors gives them exactly that 10,000 volt thrill. Why not surprise your wife with a sexy trip to a place where there's a chance you'll be caught, somewhere like the grounds of your local convent or nurses' home? Then get her to keep a lookout by the gate whilst you treat yourself to a wristily exciting hand shandy in the shadows near the shower block.

Shared Fantasies
Dirty thirties authoress Aniis Nin kept her trans-Atlantic relationship with Henry Miller at erotic boiling point by writing down her sexual fantasies in a series of XXX-rated letters. Even though you and your wife may not be literary geniuses, there's no reason why you shouldn't follow suit. And if you do, you might just find your sword getting mightier than the pen! Ask your wife to write down all her innermost fantasies in full explicit detail. Then, while she's busy doing that, take yourself off to your local lapdancing club and fantasise about the strippers whilst pleasuring yourself through your pockets.

Talking Dirty
They say actions speak louder than words, but when it comes to spicing up a lacklustre love life, dirty words can often speak louder than actions. Even the most outwardly prudish couples find that using low down explicit language during sex helps them to achieve previously undreamed of heights of pleasure. Next time you find yourself making love to your wife in the same old way, try telling her that you "really want a fucking big shit". Then take your mobile phone with you into the toilet, dial a random number, and turn the air blue as you masturbate yourself to a shattering climax.

Wine and Roses
Although we tend to forget it, sex and romance are simply two sides of the same coin. And amazingly, many women find romance is the bigger turn on. Try to think back to the first few weeks of your relationship when you took your partner out for romantic meals and showered her with expensive wines, red roses and chocolates. Chances are, the sex you were having then was the best ever. So why not try to rekindle the passionate flame of those days? Surprise yhour wife when she comes home from work; have a candlelit meal waiting for her on the table. Ply her with glass after glass of her favourite wine while she eats it. Sooner or later she'll pass out, giving you the chance to nip into the garage for a steamy clinch with your inflatable love doll.

Sex Toys
Toys aren't just for children - they're for grown ups too! And despite their reputation, adult toys aren't meant to replace your partner, they're there to enhance the pleasures of a loving relationship. Meanwhile, programmes such as Sex and the City have brought them into the mainstream and many modern couples now say they couldn't do without their bedroom playthings. If you haven't got any you're probably in the minority...and you're certainly missing out on an awful lot of sexy fun. Go to your local Ann Summers shop and invest in a selection of his'n'hers sex aids. Take them into the bedroom and surprise your wife by waking her up and suggesting that you try some of them out. Then, while she's off down the 24-hour petrol station looking for batteries, take advantage of the Adult Channel's midnight freeview and enjoy a 10-minute sexy romp into a sailor's favourite!

FRU T. BUNN the MASTER BAKER & HIS GINGERBREAD SEX DOLLS
FRU! FRU, LOVE! HURRY UP IN THE KITCHEN, WILL YOU..? WE'RE GOING TO MISS OUR PLANE!
YES, YES! I'M JUST...
...I'M JUST... DOING... A THING. I'LL BE WITH YOU IN A MOMENT.
TING!
AH! SHE'S READY!
PHWOOAR! SHE'S ONE HOT BITCH! I COULD BANG HER DOUGHNUT RED RAW HERE AND NOW ON THE KITCHEN FLOOR...!
...BUT OLD FRU'T'S GOING TO HAVE TO CONTROL HIMSELF, MY DEAR... BECAUSE YOU AND HIM ARE GOING TO JOIN THE MILE HIGH CLUB! HEH-HEH!
SLURP!
COME ON, FRU. THE TAXI'S W... GOOD HEAVENS! WHAT HAVE YOU GOT THERE?
THIS..? ERM... IT'S MY... ER.... IT'S MY GOLF CLUBS.
I DIDN'T KNOW YOU'D TAKEN UP GOLF, FRUBERT.
YES. IT... ERM... HELPS ME RELAX AFTER ALL THE STRESS OF THE BAKERY, YOU KNOW.
SHORTLY...
FULCHESTER AIRPORT
...COULD YOU PUT YOUR CASE ON THE BELT, PLEASE SIR?
ER...NO. THIS IS MY HAND LUGGAGE. I'M KEEPING IT WITH ME.
I'M SORRY. BUT IT'S TOO BIG TO FIT IN THE OVERHEAD LOCKER.
IT'LL HAVE TO GO IN THE HOLD.
BAGGAGE CHECK-IN
NO! I'VE HEARD ALL ABOUT THESE PEOPLE WHO FLY TO SPAIN, BUT THEIR CASES END UP IN TOKYO OR SOMEWHERE. SHE'S NOT GOING IN THE HOLD. I... I'LL BUY HER A SEAT!
HER?
THEM! THEM! MY GOLF CLUBS! I'LL BUY THEM A SEAT!
I'M SORRY. THE FLIGHT'S FULL, SIR. NOW PUT THEM ON THE BELT, PLEASE.
B-BUT...
GO ON, FRUBERT. PEOPLE ARE WAITING.
DON'T WORRY, SIR. YOUR GOLF CLUBS WILL BE PERFECTLY SAFE.
RATS' COCKS.
CHEER UP, DEAR. IT'S NOT LIKE YOU WANTED TO PLAY A ROUND ON THE PLANE, IS IT?
TRUNDLE
COME ON, FRU. THEY'RE CALLING OUR FLIGHT - GATE THIRTY-SEVEN.
YES. YOU GO AHEAD. I'VE JUST GOT TO BUY A FEW THINGS.
WHAT!?
THINGS, ALRIGHT?! A BOOK... WHATEVER.
Departure Gates 1-38
WELL DON'T BE LONG WILL YOU, FRU? THE PLANE'S TAKING OFF IN 10 MINUTES.
CAMPING SUPPLIES
YES, YES! JUST GO. I'LL CATCH YOU UP, DON'T WORRY.
½ AN HOUR LATER....
...I'M AFRAID WE CAN'T HOLD THE PLANE ANY LONGER, WAITING FOR YOUR HUSBAND.
OH DEAR. I'M VERY SORRY. HE WENT FOR A BOOK, YOU SEE....
AH! HERE HE IS NOW, THANK GOODNESS!
PUFF! PANT! PUFF! PANT!
CLANK!
DID YOU GET YOUR BOOK, THEN FRUBERT?
BOOK!?.. WHAT!? OH.... ER... NO.
I FORGOT.
AT THIRTY THOUSAND FT...
BING! LADIES AND GENTLEMEN, THE CAPTAIN HAS EXTINGUISHED THE LIGHT, SO YOU MAY NOW REMOVE YOUR SEAT-BELT.
GREAT!
WHERE ARE YOU GOING TO NOW?
TOILET.
WELL DON'T TAKE THOSE BAGS. LEAVE THEM HERE...
CLANK
NO! STOP TELLING ME WHAT TO DO.

HEH-HEH! NOW FOR PLAN 'B'...!
TOILET
VACANT
RIGHT, LET'S SEE... FLOUR, EGGS, SUGAR, ROLLING PIN, STOVE... YES - THAT'S EVERYTHING I NEED TO BAKE MYSELF AN IN-FLIGHT DELIGHT.
FLOUR
RATTLE RATTLE
TOILET
ENGAGED
?
SIEVE! SIEVE!
TOILET
ENGAGED
?
WHISK! WHISK!
TOILET
ENGAGED
KNEAD! KNEAD!
ROLL! ROLL!
BAKE! BAKE!
TOILET
ENGAGED
1 HOUR LATER...
...THERE- SHE'S DONE. SHE'S NO OIL PAINTING, BUT YOU DON'T LOOK AT THE MANTLEPIECE WHEN YOU'RE POKING THE DOUGHNUT FANNY, DO YOU? - SLOOP!
RIGHT- GET READY FOR THE HIGH ALTITUDE RIDE OF YOUR LIFE, YOU DIRTY GINGERBREAD SLAG. I'M AS HARD AS LAST YEAR'S CHRISTMAS CAKE ICING.
BANG! BANG!
...UH-UH! UH-UH-UH!... OH GOD! UH! UH!...
WHAT'S GOING ON IN THERE?
ARE YOU ALRIGHT?
UH! UH! UH! UH! UH! UH! OH GOD! UH! UH!
BANG! BANG! BANG! BANG!
THIS IS THE CAPTAIN! PLEASE OPEN THE DOOR! ARE YOU IN SOME SORT OF TROUBLE IN THERE?
OOH, YES! YES! YES! YES! UH! UH! UH! UH-UH-UH-UH! UH! UHH... UH! YES! YES! OH-UH-UH-UH...!
STAND BACK EVERYONE. I'M GOING TO KICK THE DOOR DOWN.
BOOT!
OH! UH!. UH! UH! UH-UH-UH! UUUH! UH! OOOH, YEAH! UH! UH...!
NOW SIT DOWN AND BEHAVE YOURSELF, MR. BUNN. WE'RE ABOUT TO BEGIN OUR DESCENT INTO MALAGA AIRPORT.
BAH!
SO NEAR AND YET SO FAR.
SHORTLY, AT THE BAGGAGE RECLAIM...
...REALLY, FRUBERT. TRYING TO BAKE BISCUITS ON THE PLANE! STSK!
IT'S JUST AS WELL YOU'VE BROUGHT YOUR GOLF CLUBS. YOU NEED SOMETHING TO STOP YOU THINKING ABOUT WORK ALL THE TIME.
AH, YES! OF COURSE! MY... AHEM... GOLF CLUBS. I'D COMPLETELY FORGOTTEN ABOUT HER... THEM.
IN FACT, DEAR, WHEN WE GET TO THE HOTEL, WHY DON'T YOU GO AND HAVE A SIT BY THE POOL? I'LL STAY UP IN THE ROOM AND... ERM... PRACTISE PUTTING IT IN.
GOOD IDEA, LOVE.
FROTH! FROTH! FOAM!
FOAM! FROTH-FROTH! SALIVATE!
MEANWHILE, AT TOKYO INTERNATIONAL AIRPORT...

Black Ice!

Lancashire Resort Ready for Ice Age

~"Bring it on!" says Lord Mayor

Councilor Ivan Taylor who said "Bring it on" (right) and Blackpool tower (far right) yesterday

THE DINOSAURS perished when the world was plunged into a 'Day After Tomorrow'-style Ice Age a million years ago. And now it's time to turn up the central heating once more, because scientists predict there's another one just around the corner.

EXCLUSIVE!

As sea levels rise, global warming is set to go into catastrophic reverse, leading to a worldwide Doomsday scenario which will leave the entire planet looking like a giant snowball.

resort

It's a frightening thought, but one person who certainly isn't losing any sleep worrying about the coming big chill is the Lord Mayor of Britain's favourite seaside resort. That's because Blackpool is the ideal holiday destination whatever the weather... and that includes temperatures as low as minus 85 degrees F, says Councillor Ivan Taylor. And he has this message for anyone thinking of cancelling their break in the Lancashire resort: "Come to Blackpool and have a good time. It takes more than a cold snap to spoil the fun along the Golden Mile!"

Scientists estimate that a new ice age could leave Blackpool buried under a 2-mile thick sheet of rock-hard permafrost, but Councillor Taylor isn't worrying.

chance saloon

"We've been hard at work on a 10-point action plan, called 'Blackpool - Open for Business'," he told reporters. "One thing's for sure, this town isn't going to be caught napping when the Ice Age hits."

The leaflet, which is available from the rack just inside the library door, outlines the council's plans which include:

- *Borrowing extra gritting lorries from nearby Fleetwood Borough Council to tackle the encroaching Arctic ice sheet and keep main traffic routes open.*
- *In addition to a full range of cones, choc-ices and lollies, all council-licensed ice cream vans will be selling cups of hot soup and Bovril for the duration of the ice age.*
- *The weekly knobbly knees competition on the South Pier will be relocated to a marquee adjacent to the Pleasure Beach or, if temperatures drop below -88°F, to the Town Hall Assembly Rooms on Corporation Street.*
- *Boarding Houses will be required to shut guests out at 9am instead of 8am, and to allow them back indoors an hour earlier than usual, at 4pm instead of 5pm.*
- *The council dog warden will be equipped with a specially-strengthened hoop on a stick and a pair of tough gardening gauntlets to enable him to tackle any mauruading polar bears that may stray into the town's streets.*

In addition, the ladies of Blackpool, Fleetwood and Lytham Women's Institutes are hard at work knitting scarves which will be handed out free of charge to people hiring deckchairs.

Councillor Taylor said: "No matter how cold the weather gets, you're always guaranteed a warm welcome in Blackpool."

STEW-DO-KU No. 4823

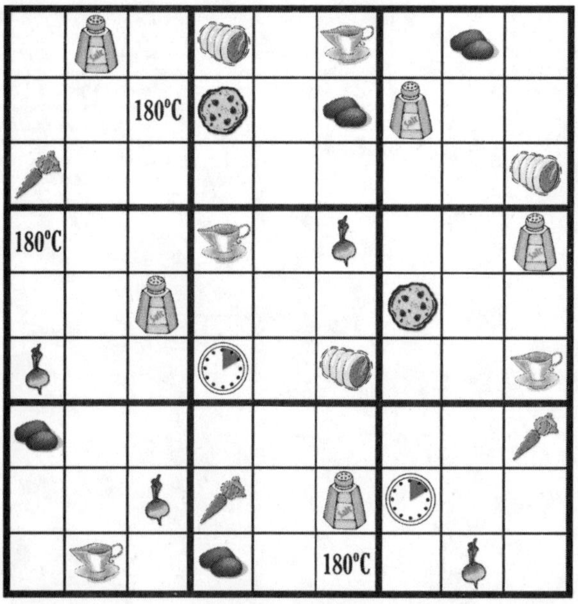

180°C
180°C
180°C

If you find it difficult relating to people in social situations, then why not do this sensational *Stew-do-ku* puzzle, the 'mental wanking' craze that's infecting the nation's brains and spreading like Creutzfeldt Jakob Syndrome.

Inside the grid are the nine elements that go in to making the ideal beef stew. All you have to do is fill in the grid so that each ingredient appears once in each column, row and nine square box. The answer is on page 49.

The Snow Must Go On!

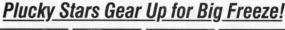

Plucky Stars Gear Up for Big Freeze!

We contacted several traditional variety stars to see if they'd get cold feet about doing a Blackpool Summer Season during the Ice Age. The answer was a resounding no. 'The show must go on!' they all told us.

"The Arctic conditions could play havoc with my career," said Strictly Come Dancing presenter **Bruce Forsyth**. *"It would be impossible for me to perform one of my trademark tap-dance routines wearing clumsy snowshoes on my feet. But it wouldn't stop me performing. I love getting up in front of an audience. It's always ice to see them, to see them ice. Even if it's just some walruses."*

"We'd still be up there on stage singing our hit every night," said **the Nolan sisters**. *"But we'd have to dress up in reindeer skin parkas and snow goggles to combat the sub-zero temperatures. If we wore the same skimpy sequinned frocks we did when we were famous, we'd get frostbite in our knockers."*

"I'd have to alter my act without a doubt,"Crackerjack stalwart **Bernie Clifton** *told us. "My comedy ostrich is a bird adapted to a temperate climate so it certainly couldn't survive an Ice Age. I'd have to adapt my routine accordingly, riding round on the back of a comical penguin. But that's showbusiness. If you want to stay at the top of the comedy tree for as long as I have, you have to keep changing your act constantly."*

"I'd like the planet to be devastated by thousands of years of plummeting temperatures, but not a lot!" quipped former celebrity **Paul Daniels**. *"I'd still be up there on stage doing tricks with my wife, the wonderful Debbie McGee, but a 2-mile thick ice shelf on top of the theatre may well keep audiences away. So it wouldn't actually make much difference to me."*

Laddism is a thing of the past, and we now live in the age of the more sensitive man. But have ***YOU*** *moved with the times? Ask yourself...*

Are *YOU* a New Man or an Old Woman?

In the hit comedy 'Three Men and a Baby', Tom Selleck, him out of 'Cheers' and the other one showed a more caring side to their nature. But how will **YOU** fare when you take our questionnaire?

IT'S OFFICIAL. Laddism has gone. The larger swilling, lecherous lout of the 80s and 90s has been swept aside, joining other out-moded stereotypes such as mods, Teddy Boys and Cro-magnons in the dust-bin of history. In their place, a new, more caring, thoughtful man has emerged; one who is just as happy to wield a feather duster as a monkey wrench. We all like to think we are new men, but are we really? How in touch are YOU with the more sensitive side of your psyche..?

Take our test to find out. Simply answer the question honestly, and then tot up your score to reveal if you are a *New Man* or an *Old Woman*.

Q1. It is Saturday morning, and you have arranged to meet your mates to play five-a-side football. However, your wife is very tired after breastfeeding your six-month-old baby all night. **What do you do?**

a) *Insist she goes back to bed to get some proper rest, phone your friends to cancel football, and then spend some quality time with your son. Take him to the park, or perhaps the local playgroup?*

b) *Feed your 12 cats, phone the doctor and describe your bowel movements then totter your way to the post office with a tartan shopping trolley, muttering about immigrants and telling passers by how old you are, before falling over and breaking your hip?*

HOW DID YOU DO?

Award yourself 1 point for each time you answered a), and 5 points for each time you answered b) and then tot up your score to see how you did:

Between 1 and 4~
Congratulations. You are a New Man. You are just as at home changing a nappy as you are a spark plug. You love to stop in and watch football on the telly, but you'll happilly go with your wife to see shit films like *Bridget Jones's Diary* instead. You have that wonderful combination of tenderness and strength that women find adorable.

Between 5 and 10~
Oh, dear. You are an old woman. You only like tea made with leaves, claiming tea bags taste of paper, and you can't tell the difference between a Gas Man and and six 12-year-old gluesniffers with a Blockbusters card. You never put the heating on because it's too expensive, yet you have £50,000 in a teapot on the mantlepiece.

Don't miss our questionaire in the next issue: ***Are you Ant & Dec or Dick & Dom?***

MAJOR MISUNDERSTANDING

TEA ROOMS
CRAFTS
GIFTS
DONATE BLOOD HERE
GIVE BLOOD
SAVE A LIFE
YOUNG LADY, I'VE LIVED IN THIS TOWN FOR THIRTY YEARS. WE ARE A CLOSE-KNIT COMMUNITY.
AND WE'VE MANAGED TO SURVIVE PERFECTLY WELL WITHOUT YOUR FISH AND CHIPS AND HAMBURGERS THANK YOU VERY MUCH.
THIS TOWN ATTRACTS HUNDREDS OF VISITORS EVERY YEAR. THEY COME FOR THE PEACE AND QUIET, THE HISTORIC BUILDINGS AND THE LOVELY TEASHOPS.
THEY DON'T COME TO SEE A SMELLY CHIP VAN PARKED SLAP IN THE MIDDLE OF OUR BEAUTIFUL TOWN SQUARE.
NO, YOUR BUSINESS IS GOING TO ATTRACT A VERY DIFFERENT TYPE OF PERSON, ISN'T IT?
I'M TALKING ABOUT THE TYPE OF PEOPLE WHO LIVE IN LOCAL AUTHORITY HOUSING.
DOES THIS TOWN REALLY WANT HOARDES OF THESE PEOPLE QUEUING UP TO BUY THEIR TURKEY TWIZZLERS AND MUSHY PEAS, WITH THEIR PUSHCHAIRS AND THEIR CHEWING GUM?
ALL YELLING AT EACH OTHER AND DROPPING THEIR CHIP WRAPPERS IN THE FLORAL TUBS? I THINK NOT.
THIS VAN IS THE THIN END OF THE WEDGE. WHAT ARE WE GOING TO GET NEXT?
A GYPSY CAMP? CAR BOOT SALES? A BINGO HALL, PERHAPS?
I THINK YOU'D BE HAPPIER IF YOU TOOK YOUR BUSINESS ELSEWHERE.
WE'RE A CLOSE-KNIT COMMUNITY HERE.

Letterbocks

Viz Comic, PO Box 656, North Shields, NE29 1BT

Electromail: letters@viz.co.uk

STAR Letter...

If Catholics want to improve their image, why don't they give all the kiddie-fiddling jobs to nuns instead of priests? There would be far fewer complaints from teenage schoolboys if they were being pulled off by a nun instead of being poked up the arse by some middle aged bloke.

C Growler, e-mail

HAS anyone noticed that if you cover Paul Simon's face from the eyebrows down on the cover of Bridge over Troubled Water, Art Garfunkel has a large Cossack moustache?

Ian Barret e-mail

IT WAS heartening to see Private Johnson Beharry awarded the first Victoria Cross in 20 years for his actions in saving 30 members of his unit in Iraq. But there are many people whose acts of bravery go unrewarded all the time. Jarvis Cocker, for instance. Any man who waves his arse at Michael Jackson deserves a hatful of medals.

J Geils Band

I DON'T know why cigarette manufacturers put those big warning stickers on the side of their packets. If anything, it is likely to put people off buying the product.

Mark Mayhem e-mail

MAYBE it's me getting old, or perhaps the tide is turning, but amongst the usual Circus of Horrors in the latest Ocean Finance advert is a bird who is half worth a bang. Don't get me wrong, she's no great shakes and would still be at the back of a very long queue, but at least it's a step in the right direction.

D Strake London

I SEE that our new Pope used to be in the Hitler Youth. It just goes to show that you can take the Pope out of Germany, but you can't take Germany out of the Pope.

B James Holloway

I WAS being chased by a police dog last week, and made the mistake of trying to escape through a little tunnel, over a see-saw and through a hoop of fire. It finally caught me as I was weaving in and out of some sticks.

Stan Herschel e-mail

PEPPERAMI claims to be 'a bit of an animal'. I'm sure it is, but which bit, exactly? My money is on a baboon's cock. And after tasting their hot, spicy one, I can see why they've all got bright red arses.

Tripod e-mail

WHEN I nipped into a McDonald's to use their toilets the other day, I was confronted by a spotty teenager mopping up vomit just by the lavatory. On the back of his T-shirt it said 'I'm Lovin' it!' Funny, but the poor sod's face told a different story.

Tommo Hull

WHO says a swan can break your arm with its wing? What bollocks! It would just be like being hit with a feather duster. Even if Mike Tyson hit you with a feather duster, it's not going to hurt.

T Pewter Leigh

TWO years after I moved out of a house, I received a council tax demand from Manchester City Council for a house I never lived in in the same road, covering a time when I was exempt from paying council tax. I was wondering if any of your readers have ever elected officials who could find their arses with both hands.

Adam Bowman e-mail

IN THE recent general election, my mate and I were going to vote, but as he was going to vote Labour, and me the Tories, we decided to just stay at home and have a spliff instead.

Dave e-mail

LAST Saturday, my mate Harry Larkin paid £15 for a blow job. Yet on my last date I spent near on £40 taking a bird out and all I got was a lousy peck on the cheek. I feel I have been ripped off considering the value my mate got for his money.

Ash e-mail

WHY don't rugby players play the game carrying a cup of tea on a saucer all the time, seeing if they can keep it in the cup throughout the game? The chances of scalding oneself or an opponent when going in for tackles and tries would add plenty of thrills and 'spills' to the game. This 'cup of tea rugby' may also challenge the dominance of League and Union, which could only be good for the game.

J Wilson St Helens

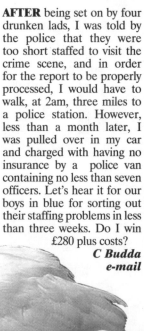

IF I was Dr Who, I'd have that Billie Piper bent over the Tardis console and given what for before you could say Jack Robinson. Then I'd use my time-twiddling powers to constantly repeat the time I was in the vinegar strokes, keeping me in a delicious state of eternally-looped space-time ecstasy. Do any other readers waste their valuable time dreaming up frankly unlikely sexual scenarios involving timelords and their beaver-faced sidekicks?

Lee Henman e-mail

AFTER being set on by four drunken lads, I was told by the police that they were too short staffed to visit the crime scene, and in order for the report to be properly processed, I would have to walk, at 2am, three miles to a police station. However, less than a month later, I was pulled over in my car and charged with having no insurance by a police van containing no less than seven officers. Let's hear it for our boys in blue for sorting out their staffing problems in less than three weeks. Do I win £280 plus costs?

C Budda e-mail

SURRIGATE ANXIETY OPPORTUNITIES

EARN EXTRA CASH! WORK FROM HOME!

Become a FREELANCE WORRIER today!!!

HOSPITAL RESULTS

You don't have to have been a major worrier in the past. In fact it's best if you haven't!

Pay a small subscription and you'll soon be rocking back and forth and fretting over a stranger's woes on their behalf... for cash! ***Just read these testimonials from delighted worriers...***

"I've got five different types of strangers' cancers and I don't even need to leave the house!" *E, Surrey*	"I'm teetering on the edge of eleven other people's bankrupcies and I'm living the high life. I'll never look back!" *M, Preston*	"My son is gripped in a crack addiction and is stealing to feed his habit. I've never met him, I hope I never do - I'm quids in!" *T, Bristol*

SEND NO CASH NOW!!!

Send £200 cash in about half an hour to Blue Sky Opportunities, The Well, Garibaldi Lane, Knutsford.

Your home is at risk if you suffer someone else's mental collapse.

HOW lucky I am to live in Newcastle. Not only were we honoured to have Carol Vorderman open the 'Centre for Life' back in 2000, but the local *Evening Chronicle* reminded us this week that she did so by pressing her ample breasts against a large plasma dome.

Michael Watson
The Toon

ON visiting the theatre last week to see a play, I was struck by how inefficient the whole process was. If the first performance was recorded on film and shown at the local cinema, many more people would be able to enjoy it. And the actors could go home and put their feet up, rather than turning out every night to say the same things over and over again.

Peter Drobinski
e-mail

THESE women who would have us believe that gay men are 'cute' and 'sweet' because they are well groomed and can discuss fabrics by name could perhaps do well to occasionally visualise some of the foul and unnatural acts I imagine these wretches get up to behind closed doors.

Col. R Conway (Rtd)
Beckenham

MY neighbour is an odd fellow. He's got a wall around his garden that is completely covered in leaves! And every week in summer, he goes out and trims it with an enormous pair of scissors! I often wonder what he'll get up to next.

J Barratt
Nottingham

THE sitcom *In Loving Memory* shows that Dame Thora Hird was all too happy to make fun of death while she was alive. But since her real life death, this show has been remarkably absent from our screens. It seems that she could dish it out, but she couldn't take it.

S Thorn
Northumberland

IF Otis Ferry likes killing stuff so much, why doesn't he get a job with Rentokil? I'm sure they would jump at the chance of employing the sadistic little shit. He'd get immense job satisfaction and he'd also find out what it's like to work for a living.

Richard Macey
e-mail

UP THE ARSE
CORNER

More chuckles from
Up the Arse Corner on page 107

TOP TIPS

FOOL everyone into thinking you have just eaten an apple by rubbing your tummy and saying loudly "Mmm! That was a lovely apple."

Brian Clark, e-mail

ENJOY indoor snorkelling by filling a bath with water, then removing the plug quickly putting your mouth over it and breathing through the overflow.

A Mawdsley, e-mail

SMALL dog owners. Too lazy to take the little fellow out for a walk? Simply place him on a record player turntable and tie his lead to the arm. Set it away at 33rpm for a gentle stroll, 45 rpm for a good walk and 78 rpm for a jog.

John Stormont, e-mail

RAPPERS. Avoid having to say 'know what I'm sayin' all the time by actually speaking clearly in the first place.

J Calabas, e-mail

BEE keepers. Avoid getting stung by bees by buying honey in a healthfood shop and getting stung there instead.

Gary D, e-mail

LADIES. Avoid parking discrepancies by aiming to park all wonky. There is a good chance you will end up perfectly straight and within the lines.

A Man, Houseville

WIG wearers. Don't waste money on new wigs. Simply turn your old ones round for the 'boy band' look.

Danny the Dog, e-mail

SINGLE men. Get a glimpse of married life by taping *Woman's Hour* on Radio 4, then playing it back at a higher volume than the TV whilst trying to watch something on Discovery Wings.

Graham Marsh, e-mail

SAVE money on toilet paper by wiping your arse on a flannel. This can be re-used once your wife or girlfriend has washed it.

Barry D, e-mail

DUTCH masters. Try a little more light in your paintings. It's often difficult to see what's happening in the corners.

Peter Drobinski, e-mail

LADIES, save money on sexy lace underwear by stapling paper doilies to your usual underwear.

Pete Turner, e-mail

EASY TIGER
THE SEXUALLY INDISCRIMINATE MEMBER OF THE CAT FAMILY
I'M NOT A SLUT...
Flick!
...I'M JUST LOOKING FOR A LITTLE AFFECTION, OK?
YOU'RE HOME EARLY, DARLING!
Flick!
YES, I'M NOT STUPID, YOU UNFAITHFUL SLAG!
SO ALRIGHT, THEN! WHERE'S HE HIDING?
Paul VIZ 05

BOT
GOSSIP

with *Krystle Klitris*

★★★★★★★★★★★★

★My spies tell me that Ginger Spice ***Geri Halliwell*** is all set to reveal her new look buttocks in the summer, and they're sure to spark a right royal rumpus because get this... They're square! Yeah! You read it right. The 48-year-old spinster has shelled out a cool £200,000 having rigid shoebox-sized plywood implants inserted into that famous derriere. And she's tickled pink with her new angular ass. But word on the street is that the rectangular rectum has hit a bum note with Geri's current beau, ***Dick*** out of ***Dick and Dom***. "It's like scuttling a stack of pallets," the disgruntled kiddies' favourite is said to have moaned.

★★★★★★★★★★★★

★Bottom collectors around the world have been in a bidding frenzy this week as World War II despot ***Adolf Hitler***'s anus came up on a popular internet auction site. The Hoola-Hoop sized farter, which was found by Russian soldiers in the Fuhrer's burnt-out Berlin bunker in 1945 has been put up for sale on eBay by its previous owner ***Lemmy*** out of Motorhead.

★★★★★★★★★★★★

★U2 frontman ***Boneo*** certainly could give a monkeys when it comes to primate welfare. And to prove it, he's going to put his monkey where his mouth is, quite literally. The big-hearted pop star is set to have a baboon's blue arse grafted onto his face in a bid to raise the profile of ape charities. "We're destroying their world with our modern ways," he told reporters from his trolley outside a makeshift operating theatre at Chessington World of Adventures. "If I can save just one monkey by having this blue arse sewn over my face, then the whole thing will have been worth while." But U2 fans will have to wait to see Boneo's new-look mush, because he is not going to reveal it until the first date of the band's 2005 world tour on 6th October at the Magnesia Bank Pub, North Shields.

More Bot Gossip next week, ass fans... Krystle

Elvis has Left the Coffin

Tomb With a View Suede Shoes: Elvis remains six foot under yesterday.

Since the day he died in 1977, rumours that Elvis is still alive have abounded. Barely a week has gone by without the King of Rock'n'Roll being spotted stacking shelves in a supermarket, working at a gas station or flipping burgers in a fast food drive-thru.

EXCLUSIVE!

But yesterday, over 28 years after his funeral, those rumours finally came to an end when the chart-topping dead star held a sensational live press conference from his Graceland coffin, confirming that he has indeed been alive since his death.

"I've just been taking things kinda easy for a while, that's all," Elvis told reporters in his trademark Tennesee drawl. "After more than twenty years living the rock'n'roll lifestyle, 1977 seemed like the right time to kick back and hang loose a little," he added.

Presley explained how he has spent nearly three decades under the ground, doing Sudoku puzzles and eating worms. He confessed that burgers were one of the things he missed most about being alive. "Them wriggly critters sure don't taste as good as one of Colonel Tom's chitterling sandwiches with a side order of hominy grits, but you get used to them eventually," he quipped.

But Elvis disappointed fans by announcing that he currently has no plans to resume his record-breaking pop career. "I've had plenty of hits down the years, but I'm seventy now and I guess rock'n'roll is a young man's game," he announced.

However, he didn't rule out the possibility of a comeback at some time in the future, perhaps to celebrate the thirtieth anniversary of his death.

He told reporters: "I never say never. If Ronnie Barker can come out of retirement to do the 'Best of the Two Ronnies' sketch compilation specials, then anything is possible. Who knows how I'll feel in two years' time?"

But he confirmed he wasn't intending to brush the moss off his blue suede shoes just yet. "Sometimes I miss my old lifestyle, with its fast cars, private jets and Las Vegas glitz," he said. "But I've never for one minute regretted dropping dead on the toilet whilst doing a big shit. Looking back, it was the best career move I ever made."

INSTANT WEIGHT LOSS

I lost 18 stone in a day with new SLIMCIUM.

says top journalist
Julie Burchill

I thought I'd never lose weight. I'd tried everything from low fat salad cream to standing with the light behind me, but the weight just stayed on...

SLIMCIUM
SOLUBLE HELIUM POWDER
1 quart

Then I discovered SLIMCIUM soluble helium powder. Just one quart of SLIMCIUM and my body had soon filled with lighter-than-air gas. I checked the scales and couldn't believe my eyes. I weighed less than an ounce! I could barely keep my feet on the ground.

BEFORE AFTER

The scales never lie. I'm the slimmest I've ever been. And I can still eat my favourite foods. Pizza, birthday cake, bags of sugar, glasses of lukewarm cooking oil... I simply take a spoonful of SLIMCIUM helium preparation with every mouthful and I never put on a pound.

With SLIMCIUM the weight takes care of itself... leaving me free to enjoy my fat life, a couple of inches higher up!

SLIMCIUM

HARNESSING BALLOON TECHNOLOGY SINCE 1997

* CAUTION: Slimcium can cause your voice to go all high and squeaky.

Heartless Thieves Steal Shopping Scooter

So-sad Edna: *In happier times sitting on her great big fat arse.*

A South Tyneside woman was recovering at her home last night after heartless thieves stole her electric mobility scooter.

EXCLUSIVE

Edna Cretin from Jarrow had gone to play her nightly game of bingo at the local Mecca Hall on Wednesday. When she came out at around 10.30pm, the 48-year-old grandmother found that her ShopRider Scooter had been taken. Bingo-goers told reporters that 20-stone Edna was distraught. Without her scooter, the lazy cow was forced to walk the 150 yards to her home.

Mrs Cretin bought the scooter two years ago after doctors told her that she was overweight. Since buying the scooter, her condition has deteriorated and the idle bitch has recently been diagnosed as being clinically obese.

"I hope these thieving monsters are proud of themselves," the tearful walkshy lardarse told us. "But I know the big-hearted folk of the north east will club together to buy me a new scooter, perhaps with a bigger seat this time.

"And a tray on the armrest for my sweets and crisps," added the idle fat pig.

STUDENT GRANT
BRITAIN... BRITAIN... BRITAIN...
OH GWEAT! IT'S WITTLE BWITAIN! I ABSOWUTEWY WOVE THIS PWOGWAMME!
YETH. IT'TH A FACKING THCREAM!
I CAN'T BELIEVE YOU WATCH THIS. IT'S SO UN-PC. IT'S WORSE THAN THE NAZIS.
WHAT DO YOU MEAN?
WELL FOR A START IT'S COMPLETELY ANTI-HOMOPHOBIC.
WHICH BIT-TH?
THAT FAT WELSH PUFF CHARACTER.
OH YEAH! I'M THE ONLY GAY IN THIS VILLAGE!
HAAR! HAAR! DO IT AGAIN, TARQUIN!
I'M THE ONLY GAY IN THIS VILLAGE! I'M THE ONLY GAY IN THIS VILLAGE!
HOOO! HOOO!
WELL THAT'S EVEN WORSE. IT'S MAKING FUN OF THE GAYS AND THE WELSH.
AND THE WELSH ARE A RACE, SO IT'S RACIST TOO. AND HITLER WAS A RACIST, ACTUALLY.
...WRITE THE FEEM CHOON, SING THE FEEM CHOON...
WELL, NUMBER ONE, WIGHT, THE WELSH AREN'T A WACE, ACTUAWWY.
REALLY?
...AND IT CAN'T BE HOMOPHOBO-ITHT.
WHY NOT?
NO. BECAUSE THEY'RE WHITE. TO BE A WACE YOU HAVE TO BE BWACK. OR AT WEAST A WITTLE BIT BWOWN...
YEAH. OR YELLOW.
...OR WEAR A TURBAN OR ONE OF THEM JEWISH CAPPY-HAT FINGS.
BECAUTHE THE ONE WHO PLAYTH THE ONLY GAY IN THE VILLAGE ITH A GAY HIMTHELF!
BLIMEY.
WHAT ABOUT THE OTHER ONE?
NO. HE'S NOT ONE OF THEM. APPARENTLY HE WENT OUT WITH PATSY KENSIT AND ABI TITMUSS.
WHAT!? YOU REALLY DON'T KNOW WHO PATSY KENSIT AND ABI TITMUSS ARE?
WELL I HARDLY WATCH TV AT ALL, SO I DON'T KNOW WHO YOU'RE TALKING ABOUT.
ABSOLUTELY NOT. I'VE NEVER SEEN EMMERDALE FARM AND I'VE NEVER DOWNLOADED ABI TITMUSS'S LESBIAN VIDEO EITHER.
...THAT... ONE...
OH, I WOVE VIS CHAWACTER! VAT... ONE... VAT... ONE... HAAAR! HAAAR!
HAAAR! HAAAR!
WELL THAT'S DEFINITELY POLITICALLY INCORRECT, MAKING FUN OF MONGRELS.
HA! NOW WHO'TH BEING POLITICALLY INCORRECT? THE CORRECT PHRATHE ITH "DOWN'TH THYNDROME" ACTUALLY. AND ANYWAY – HE'TH NOT EVEN THUPPOTHED TO BE A MONGREL, HE'TH THUPPOTHED TO BE A THPATH-TIC.
WHO'S THIS ONE, THEN? I'M A LADY! I'M A LADY!
DID YOU LISTEN TO IT WHEN IT WAS ON THE RADIO, THEN?
WELL I DON'T THINK IT'S VERY FUNNY. IT WAS MUCH BETTER ON THE RADIO.
NO. I JUST THINK IT WAS BETTER, THAT'S ALL. IF I WAS GOING TO LIKE IT, I WOULD HAVE LIKED IT THEN, BEFORE EVERYONE ELSE DID.
YEAH BUT NO BUT...
GWARNT'S GOT A POINT, ACTUAWWY. EVEWYONE WIKES WITTLE BWITAIN NOW.
WELL I THERTAINLY DON'T. I'VE GONE RIGHT OFF IT.
...ER...
...NOT THAT I EVER LIKED IT IN THE FIRTH-T PLATHE.
YETH. IT'TH JUTH-T CATCHPHRATHE COMEDY, ITHN'T IT.
YES, WELL. IT'S THE LOWEST FORM OF WIT. I LIKE A LAUGH AS MUCH AS THE NEXT FEMINIST, BUT REALLY.
YAWN-OLA! LITTLE BRITAIN IS SO OLD HAT.
I MEAN... I'M A LADY!? BO-OOO-OORING OR WHAT?
WE SHOULD FIND A BRAND NEW PROGRAMME THAT NOBODY ELSE LIKES – AND LIKE THAT INSTEAD.
AH – WHAT ABOUT THIS ONE? "10:30. DARK COMEDY DOCU-SOAP SET IN A SLOUGH PAPER MERCHANTS' OFFICE". NOW THAT SOUNDS SUITABLY OBSCURE AND INTELLECTUAL. LET'S PUT THAT ON INSTEAD, SHALL WE?
HALF AN HOUR LATER...
HEY, WOOK EVEWYONE! GWARNT'S DOING THE DAVID BWENT DARNCE!
♪ VVVV! VV-VV-VV VVV-VVV! ♪
♪ VVVV! VV-VV-VV VVV-VVV!
HAAAR! HAAAR!
HAAAR! HAAAR!
HAAA! HAAAA! HAAAAAR!
HAAAAAR! HAAAAAR!

Mrs Brady Old Lady
ELECTORAL ROLL
KNOCK-KNOCK!
LATCH! SLIDE! CLUNK!
YES?
GOOD MORNING MRS... ER... BRADY, AND WHAT A LOVELY MORNING IT IS.
ARE YOU A GYPPO?
NO. I REPRESENT MONTGOMERY OF EL-ALAMEIN EE-ZEE RISER CHAIRS LTD.
OH. ONLY I'VE HAD ME RUDDY DRIVE TARMACCED SIX TIMES THIS MONTH.
AND I WOULDN'T MIND, ONLY I DON'T EVEN HAVE A DRIVE.
YES, WELL... WE'RE IN YOUR AREA LOOKING FOR SHOW-HOMES TO DEMONSTRATE OUR EE-ZEE-RISER 3000 ELECTRIC LIFT-ASSISTANCE RECLINE-O-MATIC CHAIR...
THRIFTY VAN HIRE
OOH, CHAIR. YES.
... AND, MRS. GRADY, IF YOU'D LIKE US TO CONSIDER YOUR HOME IN OUR PROMOTION, I COULD OFFER YOU A TREMENDOUS DISCOUNT.
EEH...
... DISCOUNT, YES.
WOULD YOU BE INTERESTED IN A FREE, NO OBLIGATION DEMONSTRATION OF THE PRODUCT?
... FREE, YES.
THAT'S WONDERFUL. I'VE GOT ONE IN THE VAN.
IS IT THE FUCKING GYPPOS AGAIN, ADA?
NO DOLLY. IT'S A MAN WITH AN ELECTRIC CHAIR.
EEH. THEY SHOULD BRING THEM BACK.
THERE WAS NO MURDERS IN THE OLD DAYS WHEN WE HAD ELECTRIC CHAIRS, WAS THERE ADA?
THAT'S RIGHT, DOLLY. WE HUNG ALL THE MURDERERS. BLOODY GOOD THING AN'ALL, AND THAT'S SWEARING.
MIND YOU, SOME OF 'EM WASN'T REALLY GUILTY THOUGH, WAS THEY? LIKE HANRATTY, GEORGE KELLY, THAT TIMOTHY EVANS, MAHMOOD MATTAN OR HIM ON THAT SWEET SHOP ROOF...
YES, BUT THEY WAS TERRIBLE CRIMES, DOLLY. NO GETTING AWAY FROM THAT.
NOW, WE ALL HAVE PROBLEMS GETTING OUT OF OUR FAVOURITE ARMCHAIR, DON'T WE? BUT NOW YOU CAN SAY GOODBYE TO THOSE... BECAUSE THE MONTGOMERY OF EL-ALAMEIN EE-ZEE-RISER 3000 DOES THE HARD WORK SO YOU DON'T HAVE TO.
EEH, SMASHING. HOW MUCH IS IT?
HOW MUCH? I'LL TELL YOU WHAT, MRS. O'GRADY. IT'S PROBABLY A LOT MORE AFFORDABLE THAN YOU THINK.
OOH, THAT'S GOOD.
CONTROLLED BY THIS SIMPLE KEYPAD, IT RISES TO ALLOW YOU OUT EASILY, AND WHEN YOU SIT BACK DOWN IT EASES YOU GENTLY INTO WHICHEVER RESTFUL POSITION SUITS YOU BEST.
IT'S VERY COMFY, ADA. IT'S LIKE I'VE DIED AND WENT TO HEAVEN.
IT LOOKS LOVELY. HOW MUCH IS IT?
WELL, YOU CAN'T PUT A PRICE ON QUALITY LIKE THIS, CAN YOU MRS. O'HARA?
EEH, NO. YOU CAN'T CAN YOU.
IT'S SO CONVENIENT, AND OPERATING IT COULDN'T BE SIMPLER...
... I'LL SHOW YOU.
LET'S SAY YOUR FRIEND WANTS TO STAND UP – SIMPLY PRESS 'SELECT' TWICE UNTIL 'STAND' FLASHES ON THE SCREEN. THEN PRESS 'MODE'... 'YES'... TO ACCESS THE RISE MENU... THEN SCROLL DOWN UNTIL YOU GET TO 'RECLINE', HIGHLIGHT IT WITH THE 'OK' BUTTON... THEN PRESS 'NO'... 'ENTER'... 'PROGRAM'... 'SET'... AND 'STORE/MENU'...
PRESS PRESS PRESS
BEE BEEP!
BZZZZ
... AND UP SHE COMES! IT REALLY IS AS SIMPLE AS THAT, MRS. O'SHAUGHNESSY.
OOH! ADA! LOOK AT ME!
EEH! IT'S MARVELLOUS. HOW MUCH IS IT?
WELL, IT'S A CANCELLED ORDER, YOU SEE, SO I CAN DO YOU THIS ACTUAL CHAIR FOR AN EXTRA SPECIAL PRICE .... 20% OFF!
OOH. THAT'S A BARGAIN, THAT.
... BUT ONLY IF YOU PAY A 90% DEPOSIT.
A 90% DEPOSIT? OOH... I DON'T REALLY KNOW...
LOOK. I'LL PHONE MY BOSS... SEE IF I CAN GET YOU AN EVEN BETTER DEAL...
... BECAUSE... WELL... YOU REMIND ME OF MY MUM.
TAP TAP
HELLO. CLIVE... YES, LISTEN... I'VE GOT A LOVELY LADY HERE, INTERESTED IN THE EE-ZEE-RISER 3000. SHE'S A LOVELY LADY... LOVELY... CAN I GIVE HER 30%?
YES... HMM. I SEE.

YES... I SEE... YES.
I SEE... OKAY.
YES... YES.
YES CLIVE... OKAY...
I SEE....
谁是这喜欢？烦死！
BYE.
WHAT DID HE SAY? WHAT DID HE SAY?
WELL, I'M AFRAID HE WON'T LET ME GIVE YOU 30% OFF, MRS. McSHANE.
OH.
HE SAYS, YOU'RE SO LOVELY, IF I DON'T GIVE YOU FIFTY PERCENT OFF, I'M FIRED!
EEH! SMASHING! DID YOU HEAR THAT, DOLLY? HE'S GIVE ME 50% OFF.
...BUT ONLY IF YOU PAY IN FULL TODAY...
...CASH.
QUICK, ADA. GET YER LIFE SAVINGS OUT THE TEAPOT.
I WILL DOLLY.
'OW MUCH IS IT, THEN?
WELL - IT'S HARD TO SAY, REALLY, BECAUSE THERE'LL BE AN EXTRA DISCOUNT FOR CASH, YOU SEE...
...TELL YOU WHAT - JUST GIVE ME WHAT YOU'VE GOT AND I'LL SORT IT OUT BACK AT THE OFFICE... WE DON'T WANT TO BOTHER YOU WITH THE PAPERWORK, DO WE?
RIGHT, SO I'LL POP BACK NEXT WEEK SOME TIME WITH YOUR RECEIPT AND GUARANTEE.
...GUARANTEE, YES.
...YES, YES.
OOH, IT'S COMFORT'S OWN SELF IS THIS CHAIR, ADA...
EEH.
MIND, I NEED TO DO A NUMBER ONE. CAN YOU LIFT ME UP SO I CAN GET OUT?
RIGHT... HANG ON.
PRESS PRESS PRESS
BEEP BEEP!
SNAP! CLANG!
OO-ER...!
PRESS PRESS PRESS
BEE-BEE-BEEP!
OOH, ADA. OOH, GET ME OUT WILL YOU... I CAN'T BREATHE!
ALRIGHT... NOW... WHAT DID HE SAY TO DO..? PRESS THE MENU AND RECLINE THE SCROLL OR SUMMAT..?
EEH... AREN'T THESE BUTTONS FIDDLY?
3 HOURS LATER...
HAVE YOU FOUND OUT HOW TO WORK IT YET, ADA?
HOLD YER HORSES, DOLLY. I'VE ONLY JUST FOUND ME READERS.... NOW THEN, LET'S HAVE A LOOK...
"...DRUK OP 'UITGEZOICHT' TWEEMAAL TOT DE 'TRIBUNE' FUTSEN OP HET SCHERM. DAN DRUK OP 'WIJZE' EN UITGEZOICHT 'JA' OM TOT HET STIJGINGSMENU TOEGANG TE HEBBEN..." HANG ON - ALL THESE INSTRUCTIONS ARE IN BLOODY FOREIGN.
EZ-3000
CAN YOU HURRY UP, ADA? ONLY I'VE GOT A NUMBER TWO COMING ON NOW - AND IT FEELS LIKE A BIG 'UN.

MAJOR MISUNDERSTANDING
AH, EXCUSE ME ~ COULD YOU DIRECT ME TO PONDICHERRY CRESCENT?
CEDAR AVE
I'M VISITING MY NIECE, AND I SEEM TO HAVE GOT A BIT LOST
MADAM, THIS ISN'T BANGKOK, YOU KNOW. IF YOU WISH TO PLY YOUR TRADE UPON THE STREETS, MAY I SUGGEST YOU FIND A MORE SUITABLE DISTRICT IN WHICH TO DO SO.
THIS IS A RESPECTABLE NEIGHBOURHOOD. YOU'LL FIND NO "CUSTOMERS" ROUND HERE.
DON'T GET ME WRONG. I'M A MAN OF THE WORLD. I VISITED A WHORE WHEN I WAS STATIONED IN BURMA DURING THE WAR. WE ALL DID.
CEDAR AVE
WE WERE YOUNG MEN IN A STRANGE COUNTRY, FAR FROM HOME. IT WAS ONLY NATURAL THAT WE SHOULD SEEK COMFORT IN THE SERVICES OF A DOLLYMOP.
BUT A DISCREET TRANSACTION IN A BURMESE BORDELLO IS ONE THING. THIS BRAZEN SOLICITING ON OUR OWN STREETS IS SOMETHING ELSE ENTIRELY
WE DON'T WANT OUR FRONT GARDENS LITTERED WITH SPENT CONDOMS AND HEROIN SYRINGES, THANK YOU VERY MUCH.
NO, MADAM.
I'M AFRAID YOU'LL FIND NO "CUSTOMERS" ROUND HERE.
VERY WELL THEN. BUT I SHALL PAY YOU TEN GUINEAS AND NOT A HA'PENNY MORE.

JACK BLACK
AND HIS DOG
SILVER
THE JANUARY HOLIDAYS WERE HERE AGAIN AND BOY DETECTIVE JACK BLACK, AND HIS DOG SILVER, WERE STAYING WITH AUNT MEG AT HER CONVERTED SMUGGLERS COTTAGE IN THE CORNISH FISHING VILLAGE OF PENPASTIE.
ONE MORNING, JACK AND SILVER WERE OUT FOR A WALK...
FETCH, BOY. GO ON! FETCH!
WOOF!
SILVER! BRING THE BALL! BRING IT NOW, BEFORE I THRASH YOU!
I AM YOUR MASTER AND I WILL BE OBEYED!
HOW DARE YOU DISOBEY ME. I'M GOING TO RUDDY WELL...
HELLO?! WHAT HAVE YOU FOUND?
WHAT COULD IT BE, SILVER OLD BOY?
WOOF!
WHAT ON EARTH IS IT, SILVER? I'VE NEVER SEEN THE LIKE OF IT BEFORE.
JACK WASTED NO TIME IN BORROWING A WHEELBARROW, AND TAKING HIS EXTRA-ORDINARY FIND TO SHOW HIS AUNT MEG.
AUNT MEG! AUNT MEG! LOOK WHAT SILVER AND ME HAVE FOUND!
HAVE YOU ANY IDEA WHAT IT IS, MEG?
WELL, IT LOOKS LIKE SOME KIND OF SKULL, JACK. PERHAPS OUT OF A HORSE.
I DON'T THINK IT'S A HORSE. LOOK AT IT'S TEETH. THEY'RE A FULL FOOT LONG AND RAZOR SHARP.

Continued over...

MAYBE IT'S OUT OF A VERY BIG CAT. OR PERHAPS A CRAB.
I DON'T THINK SO, AUNT MEG.
WELL, WHY DON'T YOU TAKE IT ALONG TO MR VARDY AT THE PENPASTIE MUSEUM. HE MIGHT KNOW WHAT IT IS.
GOOD IDEA!
SHORTLY...
...AND AUNT MEG THOUGHT IT MIGHT FROM A HORSE, OR POSSIBLY A BIG CAT. OR A CRAB.
DEAR ME NO, JACK. IT'S MUCH MORE EXCITING THAN THAT.
WHAT YOU'VE GOT HERE IS THE SKULL OF A TYRANNOSAURUS.
A TY-WHAT-OSAURUS?
A TYRANNOSAURUS. A TYRANNOSAURUS REX, THE LARGEST CARNIVORE EVER TO WALK THE EARTH.
WOW!
WHERE DO THEY LIVE, MR VARDY?
THEY LIVED AROUND HERE. IN CORNWALL.
WELL I'VE NEVER SEEN ONE.
YOU WON'T HAVE DONE. THEY LIVED MILLIONS OF YEARS BEFORE MAN WAS ON THE EARTH. BY THE TIME HUMANS EVOLVED FROM APES, THESE FELLOWS HAD BEEN EXTINCT FOR 65 MILLION YEARS.
OH!
YES. YOU SEE, MAN HAS BEEN ON THIS PLANET FOR LESS THAN A MILLION YEARS, THE MEREST BLINK OF AN EYE IN GEOLOGICAL TERMS.
TIMELINE OF EVOLUTION
BUT...BUT SURELY THE EARTH IS ONLY 4000 YEARS OLD. GOD MADE IT IN SEVEN DAYS.
I DON'T KNOW ABOUT THAT, JACK, BUT LOOK AT THESE FOSSILS. THEY SHOW US THAT LIFE FIRST DEVELOPED AROUND 2000 MILLION YEARS AGO. IMAGINE THAT?
THANK YOU FOR YOUR TIME, MR VARDY, BUT I'VE GOT TO GO NOW. COME ALONG SILVER.
OH. OKAY, JACK.
JACK WASTED NO TIME AND RACED TO SEE PC BROWN, OF THE DEVON AND CORNWALL POLICE.
A TYRANNOSAURUS REX, EH JACK?
THAT'S WHAT HE TOLD ME, PC BROWN.
WELL YOU TAKE IT FROM ME, IT'S A HORSE. OR A CRAB OR A BADGER.
OR SOMETHING.
YOU'RE NOT THE FIRST PERSON TO COME IN HERE AND TELL ME ABOUT VARDY AND HIS SO-CALLED PROGRESSIVE THINKING. THE MAN'S A TROUBLEMAKER WITH HIS BLASPHEMOUS, HERETICAL NOTIONS. HE'S BEEN TO LONDON, YOU KNOW. HE ONCE TOLD MRS PENHALIGAN THE HAIRDRESSER THAT WE ALL USED TO LIVE UP TREES YEARS SINCE,
WHAT!?! LIKE MONKEYS?
YES. AND MR TRELANEY OVERHEARD HIM TELLING SOMEONE THAT MAN USED TO HAVE A TAIL. STILL GOT THE BONES OF IT AT THE BOTTOM OF YOUR SPINE, IF YOU PLEASE.
WHY DON'T YOU ARREST HIM. THAT WOULD SHUT HIM UP!
I CAN'T, JACK. HE HASN'T COMMITTED ANY CRIME.
WHAT!?! BUT HE'S DOUBTING THE LITERAL TRUTH OF THE BIBLE.
YES, BUT THAT'S NOT AN OFFENCE IN THIS WORLD. HE'LL BE BE PUNISHED IN THE NEXT WORLD, THAT'S FOR SURE. WE JUST HAVE TO CONSOLE OURSELVES WITH THAT.
AND MEANWHILE WE JUST HAVE TO SIT BACK WHILE HE PREACHES HIS HERESIES ABOUT DINOSAURS?
AS I SAY, HE'S NOT BREAKING THE LAW.
SO...IF I COULD PROVE TO YOU HE WAS COMMITTING A CRIME, YOU'D ARREST HIM?
IN A FLASH, JACK.
WELL, I'VE GOT A PLAN. MEET ME OUTSIDE THE MUSEUM AT FIVE O'CLOCK TONIGHT. AND DON'T FORGET YOUR HANDCUFFS.

JACK WASTED NO TIME IN PUTTING HIS PLAN INTO ACTION...
ALL TOO SOON, IT WAS 5 O'CLOCK.
GOOD EVENING, PC BROWN. I'M AFRAID WE'VE CLOSED FOR THE NIGHT.
OH, I HAVEN'T COME TO SEE THE MUSEUM, MR VARDY. I HAD COME TO SEE YOU...BUT IT LOOKS LIKE I'VE HAD A WASTED TRIP.
OH, WELL, I'LL GET OFF HOME THEN.
NO EVIL-UTION IN PENPASTIE!
THE WORD OF GOD, NOT THE WORD OF VARDY
GET BACK TO LONDON!
WE'RE NO MONKEYS
FUCK OFF, CUNT!
NOT SO FAST, VARDY.
PC BROWN. ARREST THAT MAN!
BUT JACK, I TOLD YOU, HE ISN'T BREAKING THE LAW.
OH YES HE IS.
THE CITIZENS OF PENPASTIE ARE SO ENRAGED BY HIS DARWINIST OPINIONS, THAT WE'RE GOING TO BURN DOWN THE MUSEUM IN PROTEST. AND IN MY BOOK, THAT MAKES VARDY GUILTY OF INCITING A CROWD TO COMMIT ARSON.
GREAT SCOTT, JACK, YOU'RE RIGHT. VARDY, YOU'RE UNDER ARREST.
BUT...BUT...
PC BROWN. CAN WE BORROW YOUR PRISONER FOR HALF AN HOUR BEFORE YOU TAKE HIM AWAY?
OF COURSE, JACK. BUT WHY?
WE'VE GOT A SPECIAL TREAT LINED UP FOR HIM.
HERE YOU GO, JACK. A WEEK'S WORTH OF HAIR CLIPPINGS.
AND HERE'S THE TAR.
GOOD!
RIGHT EVERYONE. LET'S STRIP HIM NAKED!
YES! GET HIM!
BLASPHEMER!
STOP THIS, JACK. PLEASE!
THE VARDY CHIMPANZEE (APUS BLASPHEMUS)
HA! HA!
HA! HA! HA!
YOU TRIED TO MAKE A MONKEY OUT OF US, VARDY. NOW WE'VE MADE A MONKEY OUT OF YOU.
WOOF!

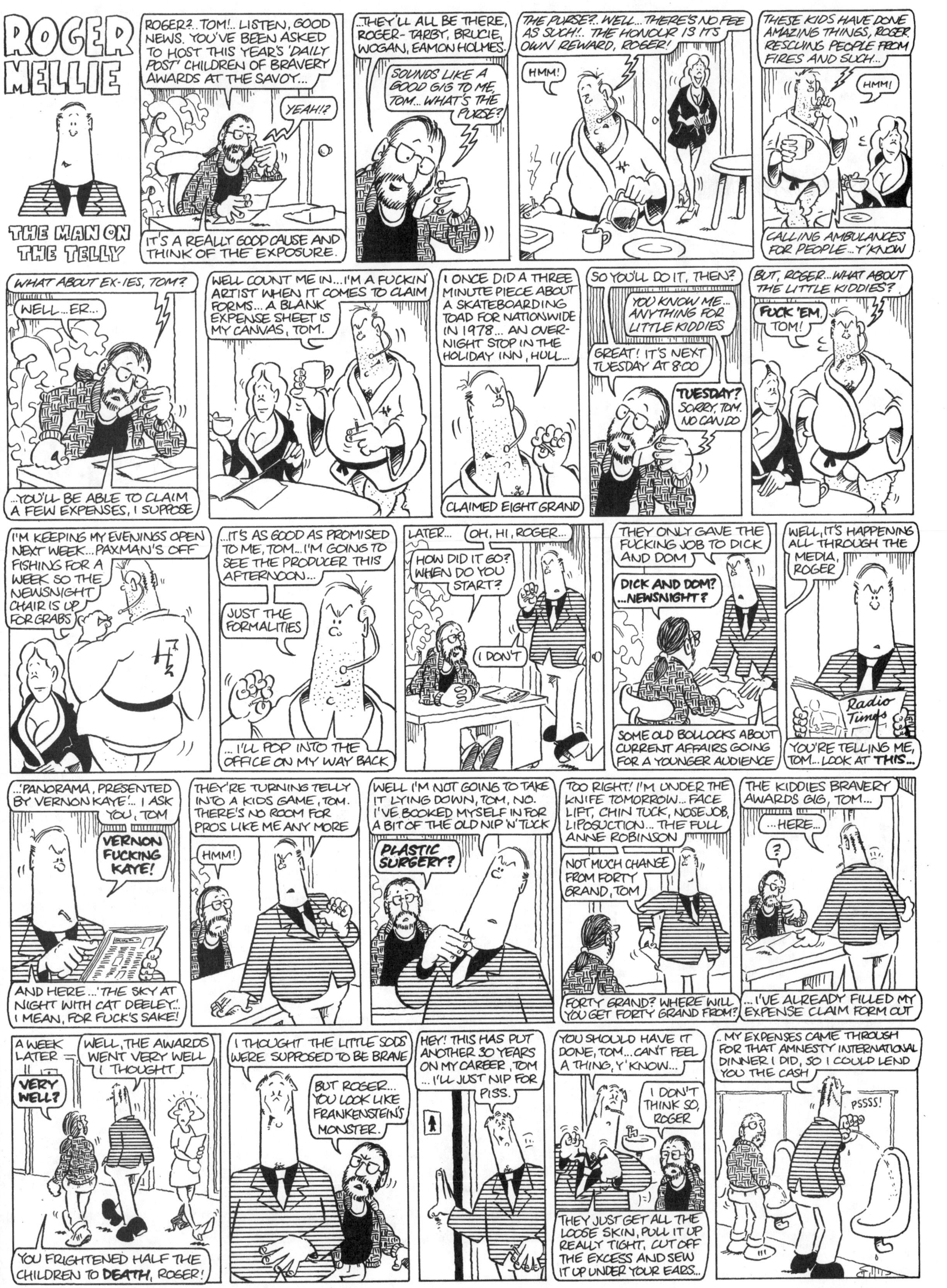
ROGER MELLIE
THE MAN ON THE TELLY
ROGER?.. TOM!.. LISTEN, GOOD NEWS. YOU'VE BEEN ASKED TO HOST THIS YEAR'S 'DAILY POST' CHILDREN OF BRAVERY AWARDS AT THE SAVOY...
YEAH!?
IT'S A REALLY GOOD CAUSE AND THINK OF THE EXPOSURE.
...THEY'LL ALL BE THERE, ROGER - TARBY, BRUCIE, WOGAN, EAMON HOLMES.
SOUNDS LIKE A GOOD GIG TO ME, TOM... WHAT'S THE PURSE?
THE PURSE?.. WELL... THERE'S NO FEE AS SUCH!.. THE HONOUR IS ITS OWN REWARD, ROGER!
HMM!
THESE KIDS HAVE DONE AMAZING THINGS, ROGER. RESCUING PEOPLE FROM FIRES AND SUCH...
HMM!
CALLING AMBULANCES FOR PEOPLE... Y'KNOW
WHAT ABOUT EX-IES, TOM?
WELL... ER...
...YOU'LL BE ABLE TO CLAIM A FEW EXPENSES, I SUPPOSE
WELL COUNT ME IN... I'M A FUCKIN' ARTIST WHEN IT COMES TO CLAIM FORMS... A BLANK EXPENSE SHEET IS MY CANVAS, TOM.
I ONCE DID A THREE MINUTE PIECE ABOUT A SKATEBOARDING TOAD FOR NATIONWIDE IN 1978... AN OVERNIGHT STOP IN THE HOLIDAY INN, HULL...
CLAIMED EIGHT GRAND
SO YOU'LL DO IT, THEN?
YOU KNOW ME... ANYTHING FOR LITTLE KIDDIES
GREAT! IT'S NEXT TUESDAY AT 8:00
TUESDAY? SORRY, TOM. NO CAN DO
BUT, ROGER... WHAT ABOUT THE LITTLE KIDDIES?
FUCK 'EM, TOM!
I'M KEEPING MY EVENINGS OPEN NEXT WEEK... PAXMAN'S OFF FISHING FOR A WEEK SO THE NEWSNIGHT CHAIR IS UP FOR GRABS
...IT'S AS GOOD AS PROMISED TO ME, TOM... I'M GOING TO SEE THE PRODUCER THIS AFTERNOON...
JUST THE FORMALITIES
... I'LL POP INTO THE OFFICE ON MY WAY BACK
LATER...
OH, HI, ROGER...
HOW DID IT GO? WHEN DO YOU START?
I DON'T
THEY ONLY GAVE THE FUCKING JOB TO DICK AND DOM
DICK AND DOM? ...NEWSNIGHT?
SOME OLD BOLLOCKS ABOUT CURRENT AFFAIRS GOING FOR A YOUNGER AUDIENCE
WELL, IT'S HAPPENING ALL THROUGH THE MEDIA, ROGER
Radio Times
YOU'RE TELLING ME, TOM... LOOK AT THIS...
...'PANORAMA, PRESENTED BY VERNON KAYE'... I ASK YOU, TOM
VERNON FUCKING KAYE!
AND HERE...'THE SKY AT NIGHT WITH CAT DEELEY'.. I MEAN, FOR FUCK'S SAKE!
THEY'RE TURNING TELLY INTO A KIDS GAME, TOM. THERE'S NO ROOM FOR PROS LIKE ME ANY MORE
HMM!
WELL I'M NOT GOING TO TAKE IT LYING DOWN, TOM, NO. I'VE BOOKED MYSELF IN FOR A BIT OF THE OLD NIP 'N' TUCK
PLASTIC SURGERY?
TOO RIGHT! I'M UNDER THE KNIFE TOMORROW... FACE LIFT, CHIN TUCK, NOSE JOB, LIPOSUCTION... THE FULL ANNE ROBINSON
NOT MUCH CHANGE FROM FORTY GRAND, TOM
FORTY GRAND? WHERE WILL YOU GET FORTY GRAND FROM?
THE KIDDIES BRAVERY AWARDS GIG, TOM...
...HERE...
?
...I'VE ALREADY FILLED MY EXPENSE CLAIM FORM OUT
A WEEK LATER
WELL, THE AWARDS WENT VERY WELL I THOUGHT
VERY WELL?
YOU FRIGHTENED HALF THE CHILDREN TO DEATH, ROGER!
I THOUGHT THE LITTLE SODS WERE SUPPOSED TO BE BRAVE
BUT ROGER... YOU LOOK LIKE FRANKENSTEIN'S MONSTER.
HEY! THIS HAS PUT ANOTHER 30 YEARS ON MY CAREER, TOM ...I'LL JUST NIP FOR PISS.
YOU SHOULD HAVE IT DONE, TOM... CAN'T FEEL A THING, Y'KNOW...
I DON'T THINK SO, ROGER
THEY JUST GET ALL THE LOOSE SKIN, PULL IT UP REALLY TIGHT, CUT OFF THE EXCESS AND SEW IT UP UNDER YOUR EARS...
.. MY EXPENSES CAME THROUGH FOR THAT AMNESTY INTERNATIONAL DINNER I DID, SO I COULD LEND YOU THE CASH
PSSSS!

Now Wash BANDS!

Government Launches Nationwide Campaign to Counter Pop Squirts

A recent survey found that a disturbing 25% of Britons don't wash their hands after wiping their bottoms. That means that one in every four people is walking about with their finger ends coated in excreta.

It's a shocking statistic for ordinary members of the public, but its implications for the pop industry are truly horrifying. For the figures prove that, thanks to their lack of hygiene in the toilet, one member out of every four-piece pop band is spreading unpleasant germs around the country's stages and recording studios.

A bout of nausea and sickness caused by turd-borne bacterias amongst the members of a group could delay the release of an album or even mean that a concert tour has to be postponed or cancelled. Lost sales of tickets and records on the high street would inevitably lead to a reduction in tax revenues, and it's a scenario that is worrying the government.

"Diaorrhea and vomiting amongst pop stars could cost the Exchequer millions of pounds a year," says entertainment minister Ord Wingate MP. "Unless something is done to address the issue of toilet

All Along the Washtowel
Soapy Hendrix sez...
CLEAN UP YOUR ACT!
Issued by the
Department of Health

Right: Part of the government's £1m campaign. One of the leaflets that will be distributed around recording studios, international stadiums and swanky hotel suites.

IT'S A FACT that one member out of every rock quartet leaves the bathroom after a pony without washing their hands. But which one is it? Here pop guru and ex-diddler *Jonathan King* sniffs out the evidence before pointing the brown finger as he names and shames...

...the Mucky Pups of Pop!

U2

FOUR-PIECE rock supergroup U2 have been cleaning up by topping the charts since 1983, but it's a fact that one member of the band can't be bothered to wash his hands after wiping his bottom. But which one is it? Let's look at the evidence.

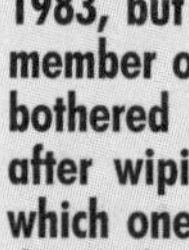

Very little is known or cared about Larry Mullins. But like most obsessive loners, chances are that the reclusive drummer keeps himself fastidiously clean. Indeed, it's quite likely that a bizarre psychological condition compells Mullins to wash his hands obsessively, often hundreds or thousands of times per day.

Hell raising bassist Adam Clayton (real name Harry Webb) is best known for false rumours accusing him of having it off with loads of prostitutes in a London Hotel. You might suppose that anyone who stoops so low wouldn't think twice about leaving a lavatory without washing their hands. But you should remember that the sort of high-class good time girls that millionaire Clayton certainly didn't go with always insist that their punters are clean before letting them do sex.

The third member of U2, hat-wearing The Edge (real name Shirley Crabtree), is known for only one thing besides his stupid hat and his stupid name - his distinctive clear-cut guitar riffs. These would become increasingly difficult to play if the strings were covered with shitcrumbs and pellets of winnity bogroll. Therefore it's highly likely that The Edge spends upwards of a minute working away with soap and water after each sit-down khazi visit.

As well as being a band member, lead singer Bono (real name George O'Dowd) is also an environmentalist, a world statesman and a chess Grandmaster. With such a hectic schedule, it's unlikely he has enough time to wash his hands. Indeed, it would be a miracle if he managed to give his soiled anus more than the briefest of rudimentary wipes after each stool.

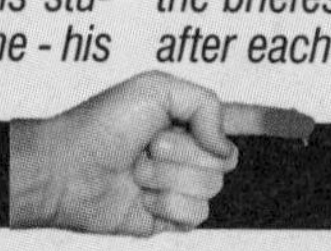

Jonathan Points the Brown Finger at: ***BONO***

T

AFTER the departure of G Halliwell, the five-piece Spi Girls were reduced to four mem bers. In their three-year reign Queens of Girlpower, they had th fingers on the nation's pop puls But statistically, only three of the had their fingers under the t after wiping up the mess from copper bolt. Baby, Posh, Scary a Sporty they may have been, b which one was Dirty Spice?

Sporty Spice Mel C (re name Declan McManu was well known for h trademark on-stage car wheels, forward rolls and pres ups. Like all sporty people s probably spent a large amount time in the shower, getting hers clean after her gruelling daily f ness routine. It is highly likely th

Jonathan Points t

Your

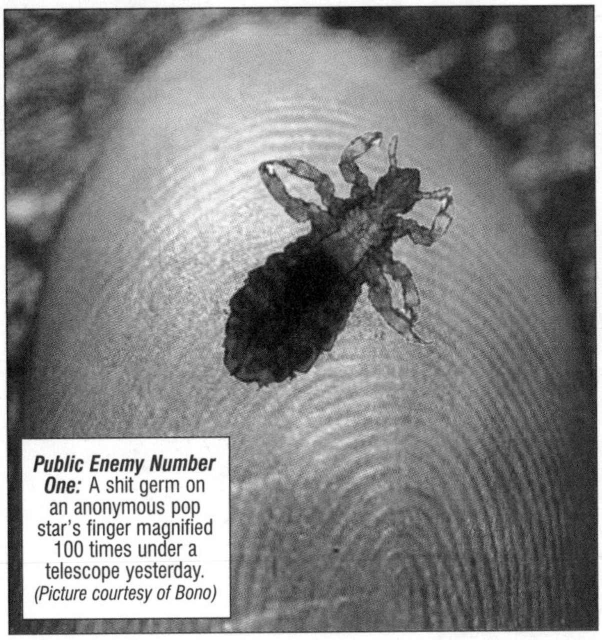

Public Enemy Number One: A shit germ on an anonymous pop star's finger magnified 100 times under a telescope yesterday. *(Picture courtesy of Bono)*

hygiene amongst British pop musicians, this country's economy could be plunged into the worst recession this century."

And the government has decided to put its money where its mouth is, by launching a £1 million poster and leaflet campaign - *'Clean Up Your Act'*, featuring Soapi Hendrix, a cartoon bar of soap that plays an electric guitar. The minister added: "We've even set up a 24-hour freephone hotline that pop stars can ring to find out more information about when they need to wash their hands."

ROCK stars are often our role models. We copy their haircuts, their clothes and their CDs on our computers, but do we copy their toilet habits? We went out on the street to get the public at large to come clean about their bog standards.

Hands Up!

Do YOU Wash After a Shite?

John Brown, Contract Publisher...
"For many years I washed my hands after going to the smallest room like everyone else. But then I found out how cheap water was, so I started to use vintage champagne instead. And a bar of gold instead of soap."

Charlene Lubbock, McDonald's Chef...
"I've had amoebic dysentery since eating a dodgy paella in Benidorm 4 years ago, and I have to go for a tom tit at least fifty times a day. If I stopped to wash my hands each time, I'd never get any burgers cooked, so I just clean them every four times or so."

Archie Turtle, Lavatory Attendant...
"Certainly not. As someone who spends most of his working day with his hands down the toilet, pulling turds out of a blocked U-bend, I see little point in it."

Mad Lennie, Gentleman of the Road...
"Yes, I wash my hands thoroughly every time I have a shit. In fact I'm going to wash them right now, because I've just done a great big one in my trousers."

Mrs. Edna Tortoise, Housewife...
"Unfortunately, I suffer from Obsessive Compulsive Disorder, which causes me to wash my hands about a hundred times a day. Fortunately I also suffer from Crohn's disease, which means I defecate about a hundred times a day, so it balances out quite nicely."

Sir Rupert Tickler, Consultant Proctologist...
"Certainly not. As someone who spends most of his working day with his hands up someone's bottom, pulling turds out of a blocked alimentary canal, I see little point in it."

Marvo, Stage Magician...
"No I do not. I simply use sleight of hand to fool the audience into thinking I have."

Rev. Trafford Lovething, Parish Priest...
"In my line of business, it's certainly true that cleanliness is next to godliness. A vicar's hands get very close to his parishioners' noses when he's handing out the communion wafers. A friend of mine who wasn't quite so fastidious in the bathroom soon got the nickname 'Father Shitty-Fingers'."

SPICE GIRLS

vashing her hands after wiping er bottom was therefore second ature.

Scary Spice Mel B was best known in the band for her frightening voice and terrifying talon-like ingernails. As a person with such harply-manicured digits, she will ave been no stranger to pushhrough. After doing a sticky number two, it's more than likely that Mel had no choice but to give her ands a thorough cleaning with oap, nailbrushes and a cocktail tick.

Giggly Emma Bunton was the youngest and prettiest member of the band. But like all babies, her personal hygiene would have left omething to be desired. As any mum will tell you, infants have no idea about protecting herself from germs. After doing a 'poo poo' in her potty, the 22-year-old blonde megastar was probably so keen to go out and play skipping and ponies to bother about washing her hands.

Posh Spice Victoria Adams was the upper class member of the group. Aristocratic people are by nature some of the most hygienic in the world, as they are able to afford refined soaps such as Imperial Leather and Lux. However, Victoria would not have needed to wash her hands after having a dump, since she would probably have delegated such menial tasks as removing her clag to one of her many servants.

inger at: *BABY SPICE*

THE ROLLING STONES

THE wrinkly rockers may have sung *'It's All Over Now'* back in 1964, but when it's all over their hands after they've wiped their arses, which member of the Greatest Rock'n'Roll Band in the World fails to wash it off?

Rubber-lipped lead singer Mick Jagger may be getting a bit long in the tooth these days, but when he gets up on stage he's still got the energy of a 40-year-old man half his age. A dope-smoking rebel in his youth, Mick would once have probably thought nothing of leaving the bathroom with stinky fingers. However, now as a respectable pillar of society, Sir Mick regularly takes tea with the Queen at Buckingham Palace and so is likely to be a stickler for post-excretory etiquette.

Very little is known or cared about Charlie Watts. But like most obsessive loners, chances are that the reclusive drummer cares little about personal hygiene. Indeed, it's quite likely that a bizarre psychological condition gives Watts an obsessive aversion to soap and water, compelling him to not wash his hands hundreds or even thousands of times per day.

Unlike his clean-living elder brother Cliff, Keith Richards has rightly earned his position as the wild man of rock. For over four decades he has lived on a diet of nothing but drugs and Jack Daniels. As a result of eating no food, Keith's anus healed over in the late 1970s. Consequently, since he only goes to the toilet to urinate, the Stones guitarist has no need to wash his hands.

The Stones guitarist Ronnie Wood is an accomplished artist, whose energetic portraits of rock stars often resemble the people they're supposed to be. Like all great painters, such as Brian Sewell and Tony Hart, Ronnie is a sensitive soul at heart. Now that he's more likely to be found washing his brushes with turps rather than nudging it, it's quite possible that genteel Wood would be deeply distressed if he failed to clean the turd off his fingerends after a doing a faece.

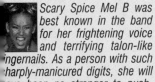

Jonathan Points the Brown Finger at:

CHARLIE WATTS

THE ALL NEW
JONATHAN ROSS
& his QUEST for a TOSS
KLEENEX
I'M OFF TO COLLECT MY OBE FWOM HER MAJESTY THE QUEEN TODAY
BUCKINGHAM PALACE
IT'S A TWEMENDOUS HONOUR FOR ME
HUNH?
RING A DING A LING
AWARDS, GONGS ETC.
WHASSAT?
CWUMBS! IT'S TIME FOR MY MID-MORNING WANK
RING A DING A LING
FULL NUTS ALARM
IN ALL THE EXCITEMENT, I FORGOT TO HAVE ONE BEFORE I LEFT MY HOUSE
WELL I'LL JUST HAVE TO NIP INTO THE PALACE LAVVY FOR A QUICK TUG BEFORE THE AWARD CEREMONY
WC
SORRY. THE TOILET IS CLOSED FOR FUMIGATION DUE TO THE DUCHESS OF YORK USING IT EARLIER TODAY
WC
LAVENDER
DANGER DO NOT CROSS
DWAT!
NO MATTER. I'LL POP BEHIND THAT CURTAIN AND CWACK ONE OUT OVER THIS NUDIE PICTURE FWOM THE WOYAL GALLEWY
HEH HEH! NO ONE WILL SEE ME BEHIND HERE
I'VE GOT MY HANKY OUT ALL WEADY.
READY FOR WHAT, MR ROSS?
GASP! THE QUEEN!
ERM..ERM.. WEADY TO CLEAN THIS LOVELY PAINTING, YOUR MAJESTY
RUB RUB
I JUST NOTICED A SPOT OF DIRT ON IT ~ AH. THAT'S GOT IT.
CWIKEY! I'VE GOT TO FIND A HIDING PLACE TO HAVE A DISCREET SHERMAN SOON!
OHO! THIS SUIT OF ARMOUR LOOKS QUITE SPACIOUS...
...BIG ENOUGH FOR ME TO FIT INSIDE AND PARTAKE IN A SWIFT BARCLAYS
AND
AY SAY, PHILIP — THET SUIT OF ARMOUR APPEARS TO BE SHAKING RHYTHMICALLY
CLANKITTY CLANKITTY WANKITTY CLANK
AY THINK IT MUST BE HAUNTED
WHAT? A GHOST?
DAMNED SPECTRAL VERMIN. I'LL BAG THE BLIGHTER WITH ME SHOTGUN
BOOM
YEOW!
IT'S ONLY ME, YOUR MAJESTIES I WAS JUST, ERM, CLEANING INSIDE THIS OLD ARMOUR
VERY DUSTY IN THERE. AHEM
SHORTLY
THE CEWEMONY IS ABOUT TO START BUT I'VE A CWAFTY IDEA.
I'VE SEWN A PAIR OF GLOVES ONTO THE CUFFS OF MY JACKET SLEEVES.
NOW I CAN HAVE A GOOD WUMMAGE IN MY TWOUSERS WHILE I'M WAITING IN LINE FOR THE QUEEN
NO ONE WILL BE ANY THE WISER. ARF ARF!
AND
UH! UH! UH!
THERE'S ONE FOR YOU... ..AND ONE FOR YOU...
OBE
JERK JERK JERK
POP
HARRODS
OOH YEH! THERE SHE BLOWS!
AH, MR ROSS. ONE DOES ENJOY YOUR TELEVISION PROGRAMMES
EH?
YOU ARE PERMITTED TO SHAKE MY HAND.
HARRODS
ERM... THANK YOU VEWY MUCH, YOUR WOYAL HIGHNESS
SQUELCH
WHAT THE-?!
GASP! ONE'S HAND IS ALL COVERED IN COCKNEY JITLER!
OO-ER!
GUARDS! SEIZE HIM!
DO YOU WANT US TO CHOP HIS HEAD OFF, YOUR MAJESTY?
WIPE WIPE
NO. MR ROSS SHALL RECEIVE A FAR HARSHER PUNISHMENT...
GWOAN! THEY'VE CHAINED ME UP IN THE TOWER OF LONDON SO THAT I CAN'T HAVE A WANK...
WRIGGLE
..FOR THE WEST OF MY LIFE!
THROB

MIRIAM'S PHOTOGRAPHIC CASEBOOK

Lady Marchmaine's Perfidious Liason - Day 3

Lord Marchmaine has taken the Stephenson's Rocket to London on business, and once again his wife has seized the opportunity to pursue her clandestine relationship with Mr Fezzywigg the chimney sweep.

He's a grubby tradesman and I'm a member of the aristocracy. I know it's wrong....but it feels so right.
Cor! Strike a light, your ladyship. I'm werry obliged, strite up I am.
That was the front door! His Lordship must have returned from the city preveniently.
Lumme! I'll scarper up the chimney, m'lady.
Egad!
What the deuce are you doing in your bedchamber at this hour, Euphemia dearest?
I'm afraid I had a fit of the melancholic vapours, Edward.
Oh? If that is so, then how, pray, do you explicate this?

CONTINUES TOMORROW...

Victorian Miriam

VICTORIAN MIRIAM ANSWERS YOUR 19TH CENTURY PROBLEMS

MP is Father of my Child

Dear Victorian Miriam...

I AM in big trouble and I don't know what to do. I am an 18-year-old chambermaid, working in a large house in Westminster. My employer, an important member of parliament, has been making improper demands of me for several months and now I find that I am going to have his baby.

He has told me to get rid of it and threatened me with dismissal if I don't. But I want to keep the child. Please help me, Victorian Miriam, I am confused. What should I do for the best?

Betty, London

You must do as your employer says and terminate your confinement. If you do not do this, and you are dismissed, you will undoubtedly end up in bad circumstances. Your baby will be put in the workhouse, get rickets and eventually freeze to death in the snow whilst you will be locked up in a lunatic asylum and spend the next forty years picking oakum. More importantly, the child's father will suffer irreparable damage to his reputation.

I am sending you my free leaflet for unmarried pregnant women, which explains how to drink a bottle of gin, take a hot bath and throw yourself down the cellar steps.

Tempted to Sin by Pianoforte

Dear Victorian Miriam...

I AM a professional, God-fearing, married gentleman, but I was recently moved to perform a sordid act of personal pollution upon my virile member, wherefore a most dreadful guilt is preying upon my mind.

I am 42 and I have been married for nearly twenty years. Until recently my wife performed her marital obligations without complaint. However, in the past year she has become most conjugally unaccommodating and thus I have found myself increasingly physically frustrated.

Last week I retired to the drawing room after dinner with the intention of imbibing a balloon of brandy, and found myself unaccountably fixated by the elegant leg of the pianoforte. Unbidden, I became roused to a state of tumescent passion by the firmness of its round curves, and the delicate pertness of its finely carved ankle.

Before I could help myself, I had dropped my breeches and wrought a foul act of onanism upon my turgid person, divesting myself of my base spendings all over the mantlepiece and everywhere.

Miriam, I am beracked by remorse at my weakness, yet at the same time I feel tempted to sin again in spite of my penitence. Please help me, as I fear for my soul.

Albert, Peterborough

Your fears regarding the welfare of your immortal soul are well-founded, for the road you have embarked upon will surely lead you to the very fires of Hell itself. Next time you feel the urge to despoil your parts of shame, try taking an icy bath or sharply rap the bellend of your unmentionable with a cold silver kedgeree spoon to dampen your ardour.

Worried that Husband is Stabbing Whores

Dear Victorian Miriam...

I AM severely vexed that my dear husband may have be pursuing a secret life that is threatening our marriage. We have been wed these five and twenty years, and until recently have been blessed by the good Lord with a state of matrimonial harmony.

However these few weeks past he has been behaving in a way strange to his previous manner, travelling to Whitechapel each night and returning in the early hours covered in blood.

Whilst going through his portmanteau, I discovered a leather apron, a butcher's knife of exceeding sharpness, miscellaneous human organs and an ink bottle filled with a congealed red fluid of some sort.

Miriam, I am afeared that my husband is Jack the Ripper, but I don't know what to do about it. Please come to my assistance, as I know not the correct direction in which to turn.

Nancy, London

Your husband certainly appears upon first glance to be Jack the Ripper, yet notwithstanding this may I caution you not to jump hastily to any unwarranted conclusions. Indeed, there may be a perfectly simple explanation for his eccentric behaviours.

Sit down and talk to him earnestly. Enquire of him in a frank manner whether he has started murdering prostitutes in the east end of the capital. If you are still worried, send a penny-blacked addressed envelope for my leaflet *'I Think my Husband is Jack the Ripper'*.

Miriam's TELEGRAPH LINES

Horrified by wife's pubic effusions
WHItehall 623

Cursed with vaginal agues
KENsington 314

Husband wants to go up fundament
HOLborn 37

Going blind due to masturbation
MAYfair 143

Is my son a sodomite?
PICcadilly 427

All telegraphs cost 3 farthings a minute, and terminate in the farthest reaches of Her Majesty's glorious Empire.

SQUASHED FLAT?

Don't just lie there... claim compensation!

"I got £3750" ~ M. Fernbear

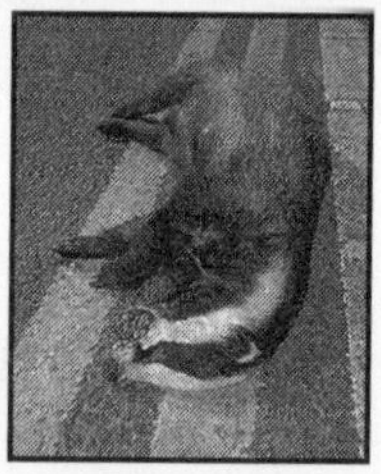

"Whilst out spreading bovine tuberculosis near the Hundred Acre Woods, I was run over by a tractor and all my guts came out. I called Woodland Claims and within minutes discovered I could claim substantial damages. A couple of weeks later I had the cheque in my paw. I'd advise any woodland creature who has suffered a personal injury to give Woodland Claims a ring now."

"I claimed £4625" ~ M. Tiggywinkle

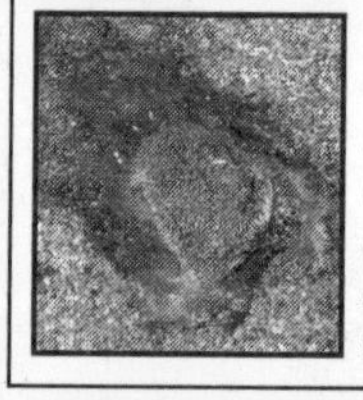

"I was scuttling along a country lane one night when I heard a car coming and instinctively rolled into a ball. I suffered multiple injuries and spent the next six weeks stuck to the tarmac, gradually drying out and being pecked by crows. Woodland Claims took on my case on a no-win no-fee basis and got me justice."

"I won £8995" ~ B. Rabbit

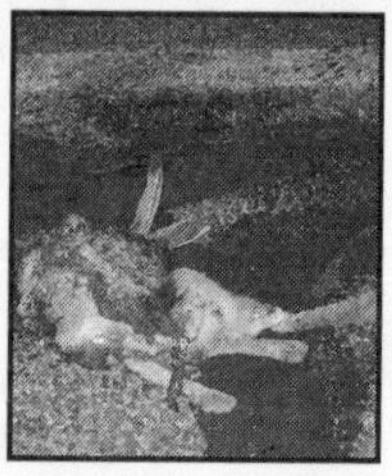

"I was crossing the road by the briar patch one evening when a car came round the corner. I was dazzled by the headlights, froze and was run over. My back was shattered and one of my eyes came out, but I was still conscious. The driver took pity on me and finished me off with a tyre iron. Woodland Claims were soon on my case and I won nearly nine thousand pounds."

Have YOU been flattened into the tarmac and it wasn't your fault?

YOU could be entitled to claim compensation.

☎ 01 811 8055

Call Woodland Claims in complete confidence, quoting VZ146. Our trained advisors are waiting to take your call.

Sex Times Table

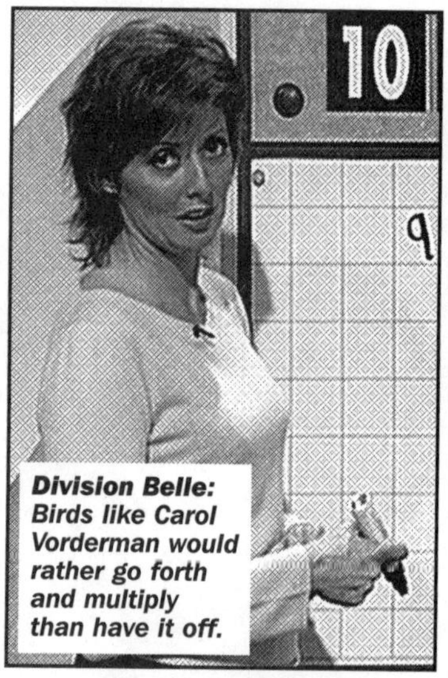

Division Belle: Birds like Carol Vorderman would rather go forth and multiply than have it off.

Calculus Beats Coitus every time, say Ladies

WOMEN prefer multiplication on their own to multiple orgasms with their fella. They would rather spend their evenings working out sums on sheets of paper than having a sexy workout between the sheets.

A new study asked women whether they preferred maths or nookie, and an astonishing 95% chose sums over rumpy pumpy.

love eggs

And it's good news for ladies' calculator manufacturers as sales of the miniature electronic adding machines look set to outstrip dildos, clitoral stimulators and Japanese love eggs by ten to one. A spokesman for Casio told us: "Today's woman just can't get enough of long division, algebra and co-ordinate geometry. Our calculator factory is working overtime, but we just can't keep up with demand."

Even celebrities are getting in on the act. Madonna was spotted buying a book of logarithm tables, a propelling pencil and some graph paper in Ryman's on Sunset Boulevard, whilst Sharron Stone last week announced that she has worked out pi to 300 decimal places.

adore bacon

Meanwhile, it was recently reported that the marriage of Hollywood golden couple Brad Pitt and Jennifer Anniston hit the rocks after the former *Friends* star began spending all her evenings working on a solution to Fermat's last theorem.

BOMBER
TINNED BREAKFASTS
It's 'Auf Wiedersehen hunger!' with these refreshing Pat-Roach-style breakfasts in a tin...
IN THREE ADVENTUROUS FLAVOURS
Each flavour commemorates one of Pat's unforgettable screen roles!
FULL ENGLISH!
BOMBER'S HUNGRY!
CONTINENTAL!
HIER, JUNGE! ACH! MEIN CROISSANTS!
SHREDDIES 'N' HOT MILK!
NO, MR BOND... I EXPECT YOU TO EAT IT ALL UP!
PAT SAID: 'Tastes great, straight from the tin!'
BOMBER TINNED BREAKFAST
ONLY 37p
Pat Roach
Farm Foods Ltd

AAARGH! AAARGH! EEEK! OH MY GOD! WE'RE ALL GOING TO DIE! AAARGH!
NEXT DAY...
DID YOU SEE THAT THING ON THE TELLY LAST NIGHT? IT WAS ABSOLUTELY HYSTERICAL.

Prices Tutu High

EXCLUSIVE!

THE ROYAL BALLET was at the centre of a storm last night after watchdogs accused it of ripping off fans. The Covent Garden-based dance company was criticised by trading chiefs for charging excessive prices for replica tutus, tights and flouncy shirts.

Cash-strapped parents led a merry dance by Royal Ballet ~ *report*

Cash-strapped parents complained that dancing strips costing as much as £55 each represented poor value for money, and that they often felt pressured to buy the latest ballet outfits for their children.

tights

Mum Kelly-Anne Fungus told us: "I've got nine kids, and they all want tutus with 'Fonteyn' on the back or tights like Rudolf Nureyev's because all their friends have them. What am I supposed to do?" She was also unhappy about the poor quality of the kits.

Hopping Mad: Fuming mum Kelly-Anne Fungus yesterday.

slacks

"For the sort of prices they charge they should last forever, but they're actually quite shoddy," she told reporters. "I bought my youngest a pair of Baryshnikov tights, and he went to the park with his mates to do some pas-de-deuxs. When he came back, they were completely ripped around his packet. I can't afford to keep shelling out £35 every time the kids want ballet tights, I'm on income support."

brambels

But Royal Ballet spokesman Quentin Bumboy was adamant that the outfits represented good value for money. "We realise that some families may have difficulty finding the money to purchase official merchandise, but at the end of the day, nobody is forcing them to do it. It's simply up to parents to resist the pressure that we put the children under through our relentless advertising." And he also hit back angrily at claims that the Royal Ballet was marking up prices excessively. "It is true that our unit cost for a Darcey Bussell tutu is £3.50, and we sell them in our shop for £45, but there is a perfectly simple reason for this. Unfortunately, it is too complicated to go into now."

thornes

But Mrs Fungus was unimpressed by Bumboy's explanation. She fumed: "It wouldn't be so bad if the costumes remained the same. I bought a Swan Lake shirt for my son a month ago. A week after he got it, they brought out a new one with different ruffles on the cuff. Not surprisingly, he won't wear it any more in case his mates laugh at him, so that's another 45 quid down the drain. Plus another £10 to have 'Wayne Sleep' printed on the back. It's a disgrace."

***Big pay-packet:** A ballet dancer with impressively prominent genitals looks up a ballerina's skirt yesterday.*

• In a similar case last week, The English National Opera was fined £4000 after Trading Standards officials prosecuted them for selling sub-standard replica viking helmets and size 48DD tin bras.

Make your dreams come sort of true!

LEARN TO PRETEND TO FLY!

with qualified pretending to fly instructors

An integrated programme of lessons in running round with your arms outstretched going 'Nnnnneoooooorrrrr!'

ALL TYPES OF PRETENDING TO FLY CATERED FOR, FROM CONCORDE TO ROBIN

ONLY **£3999.99**

Newton-le-Willows Pretend Airfield, Nr the duckpond, Sherdley Park, St Helens, Merseyside

* helmet, goggles and scarf not provided

LEGAL NOTICES

Family Planning Permission

The following applications have been received by Fulchester District Council.

Ref. 135/676/B. *13 Larch Crescent.* Application is hereby made by Mr Brian Wetherby to erect a five inch French-tickler-style sheathed penis in the bedroom of the same address.

Ref. 336/76/Y. *34a Grampian Street.* Application is hereby made by Mrs Doreen Loris to remove an existing 5-year-old inter-uterine coil and replace with similar of same dimensions.

Ref. 56/887/BH. *4 Renton Close.* Application is hereby made by Mrs Ursula Hossenpfeffer for the insertion of a pre-formed latex diaphragm across the entrance to a standing uterus.

Ref. 66/873/UH. *Fulchester Parochial House.* Application is hereby made by Father Finbarr O'Plywood for permission to remove an erection from the vulva of his housekeeper and put down a screed of viscuous ejaculate on the bottom sheet of a bed at the same address.

Any objections to the above applications should be made in writing to the Chief Family Planning Officer, Fulchester District Council, Corporation Street, Fulchester within 28 days.

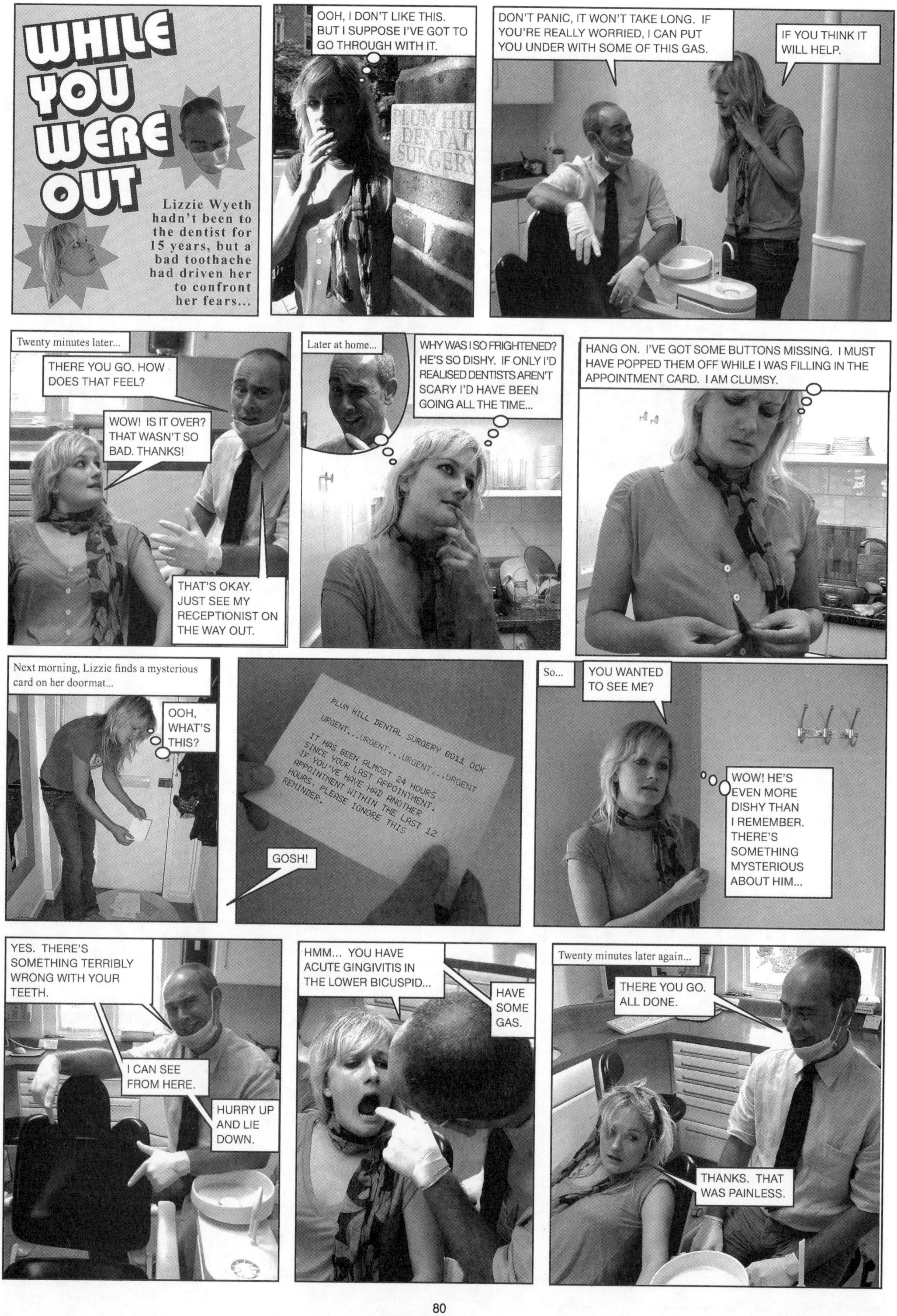
WHILE YOU WERE OUT
Lizzie Wyeth hadn't been to the dentist for 15 years, but a bad toothache had driven her to confront her fears...
OOH, I DON'T LIKE THIS. BUT I SUPPOSE I'VE GOT TO GO THROUGH WITH IT.
PLUM HILL DENTAL SURGERY
DON'T PANIC, IT WON'T TAKE LONG. IF YOU'RE REALLY WORRIED, I CAN PUT YOU UNDER WITH SOME OF THIS GAS.
IF YOU THINK IT WILL HELP.
Twenty minutes later...
THERE YOU GO. HOW DOES THAT FEEL?
WOW! IS IT OVER? THAT WASN'T SO BAD. THANKS!
THAT'S OKAY. JUST SEE MY RECEPTIONIST ON THE WAY OUT.
Later at home...
WHY WAS I SO FRIGHTENED? HE'S SO DISHY. IF ONLY I'D REALISED DENTISTS AREN'T SCARY I'D HAVE BEEN GOING ALL THE TIME...
HANG ON. I'VE GOT SOME BUTTONS MISSING. I MUST HAVE POPPED THEM OFF WHILE I WAS FILLING IN THE APPOINTMENT CARD. I AM CLUMSY.
Next morning, Lizzie finds a mysterious card on her doormat...
OOH, WHAT'S THIS?
PLUM HILL DENTAL SURGERY B011 OCK
URGENT...URGENT...URGENT...URGENT
IT HAS BEEN ALMOST 24 HOURS SINCE YOUR LAST APPOINTMENT. IF YOU'VE HAVE HAD ANOTHER APPOINTMENT WITHIN THE LAST 12 HOURS, PLEASE IGNORE THIS REMINDER.
GOSH!
So...
YOU WANTED TO SEE ME?
WOW! HE'S EVEN MORE DISHY THAN I REMEMBER. THERE'S SOMETHING MYSTERIOUS ABOUT HIM...
YES. THERE'S SOMETHING TERRIBLY WRONG WITH YOUR TEETH.
I CAN SEE FROM HERE.
HURRY UP AND LIE DOWN.
HMM... YOU HAVE ACUTE GINGIVITIS IN THE LOWER BICUSPID...
HAVE SOME GAS.
Twenty minutes later again...
THERE YOU GO. ALL DONE.
THANKS. THAT WAS PAINLESS.

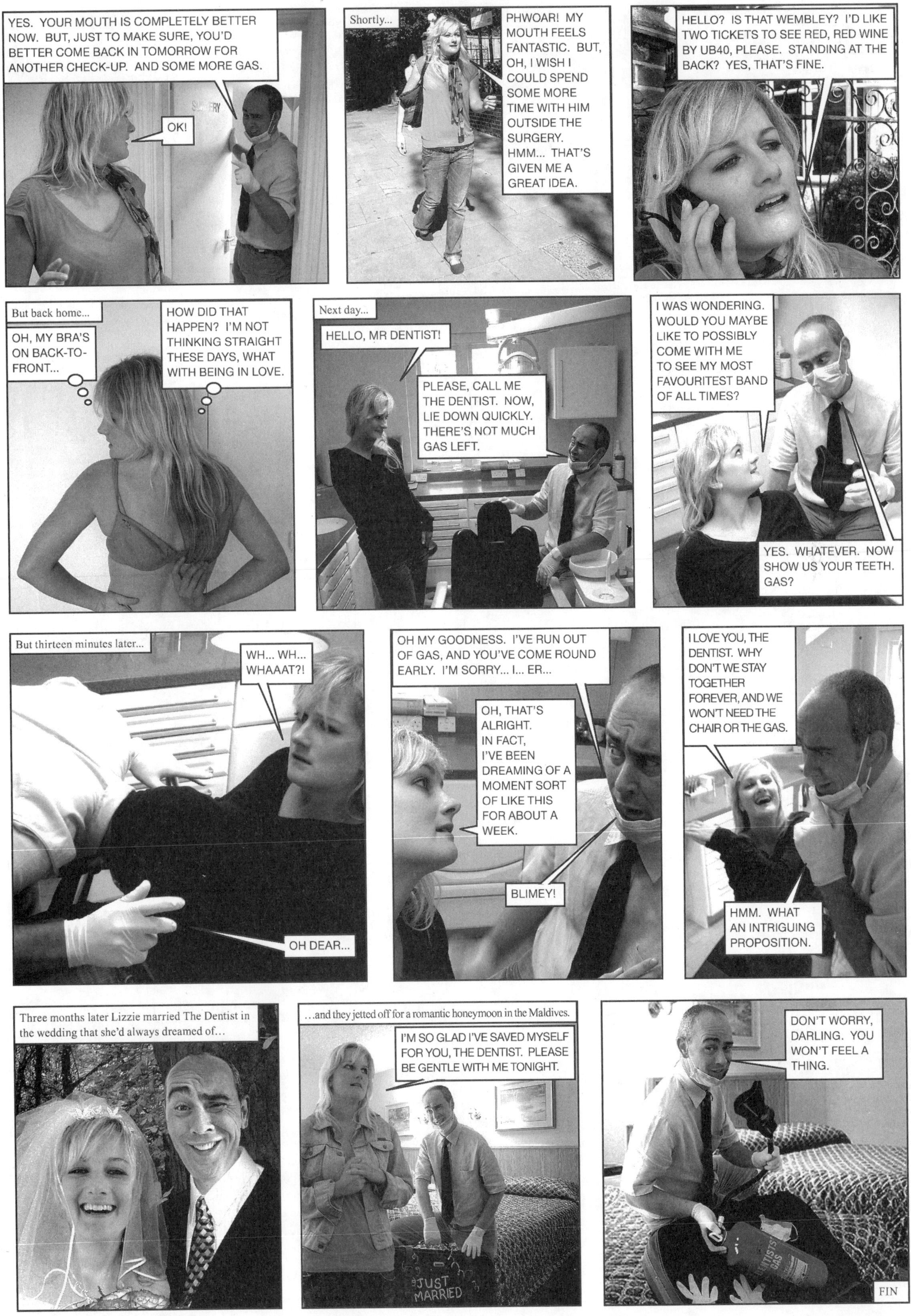
YES. YOUR MOUTH IS COMPLETELY BETTER NOW. BUT, JUST TO MAKE SURE, YOU'D BETTER COME BACK IN TOMORROW FOR ANOTHER CHECK-UP. AND SOME MORE GAS.
OK!
Shortly...
PHWOAR! MY MOUTH FEELS FANTASTIC. BUT, OH, I WISH I COULD SPEND SOME MORE TIME WITH HIM OUTSIDE THE SURGERY. HMM... THAT'S GIVEN ME A GREAT IDEA.
HELLO? IS THAT WEMBLEY? I'D LIKE TWO TICKETS TO SEE RED, RED WINE BY UB40, PLEASE. STANDING AT THE BACK? YES, THAT'S FINE.
But back home...
OH, MY BRA'S ON BACK-TO-FRONT...
HOW DID THAT HAPPEN? I'M NOT THINKING STRAIGHT THESE DAYS, WHAT WITH BEING IN LOVE.
Next day...
HELLO, MR DENTIST!
PLEASE, CALL ME THE DENTIST. NOW, LIE DOWN QUICKLY. THERE'S NOT MUCH GAS LEFT.
I WAS WONDERING. WOULD YOU MAYBE LIKE TO POSSIBLY COME WITH ME TO SEE MY MOST FAVOURITEST BAND OF ALL TIMES?
YES. WHATEVER. NOW SHOW US YOUR TEETH. GAS?
But thirteen minutes later...
WH... WH... WHAAAT?!
OH DEAR...
OH MY GOODNESS. I'VE RUN OUT OF GAS, AND YOU'VE COME ROUND EARLY. I'M SORRY... I... ER...
OH, THAT'S ALRIGHT. IN FACT, I'VE BEEN DREAMING OF A MOMENT SORT OF LIKE THIS FOR ABOUT A WEEK.
BLIMEY!
I LOVE YOU, THE DENTIST. WHY DON'T WE STAY TOGETHER FOREVER, AND WE WON'T NEED THE CHAIR OR THE GAS.
HMM. WHAT AN INTRIGUING PROPOSITION.
Three months later Lizzie married The Dentist in the wedding that she'd always dreamed of...
...and they jetted off for a romantic honeymoon in the Maldives.
I'M SO GLAD I'VE SAVED MYSELF FOR YOU, THE DENTIST. PLEASE BE GENTLE WITH ME TONIGHT.
JUST MARRIED
DON'T WORRY, DARLING. YOU WON'T FEEL A THING.
FIN

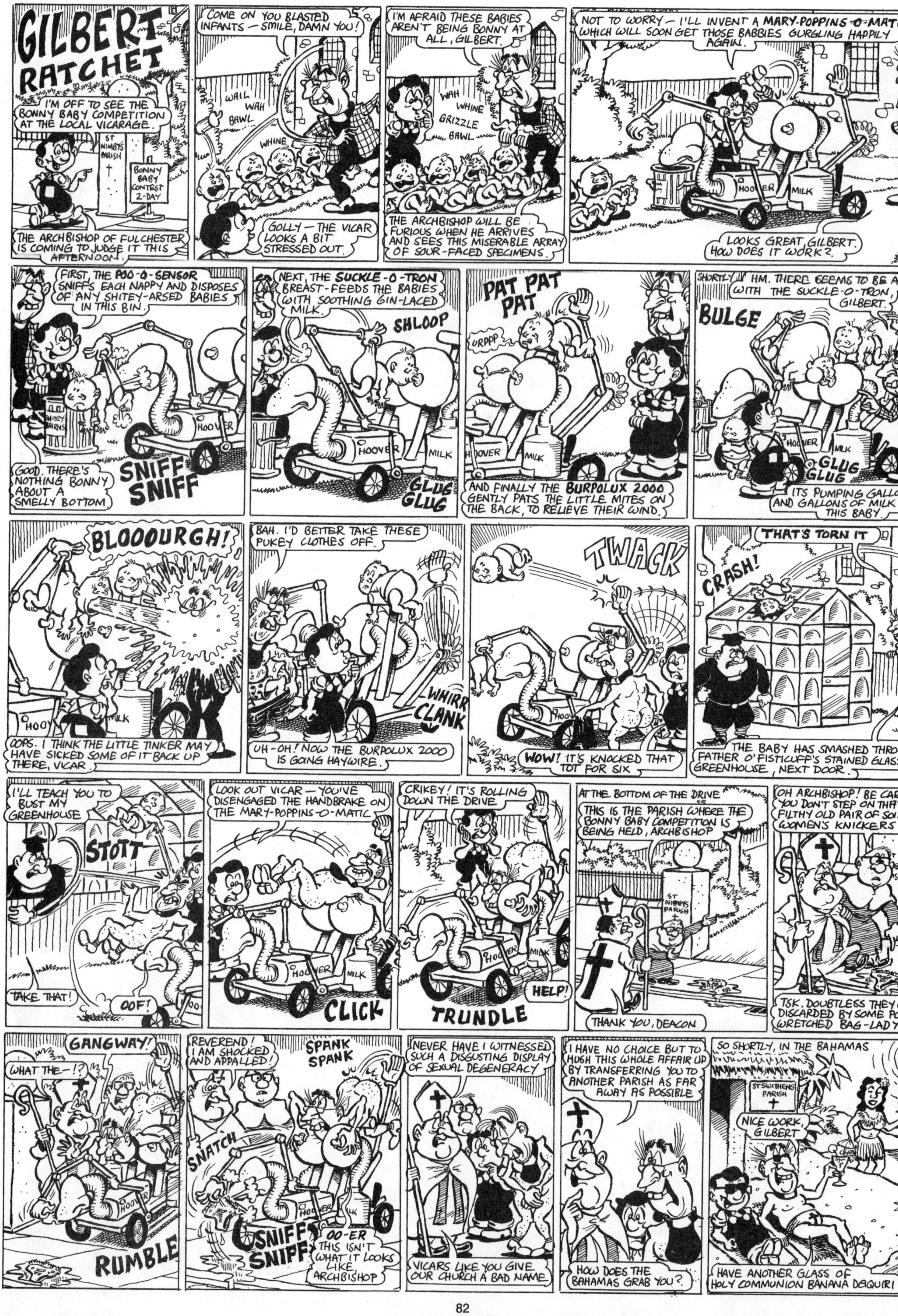
GILBERT RATCHET
I'M OFF TO SEE THE BONNY BABY COMPETITION AT THE LOCAL VICARAGE.
ST NIMBY'S PARISH
BONNY BABY CONTEST 2-DAY
THE ARCHBISHOP OF FULCHESTER IS COMING TO JUDGE IT THIS AFTERNOON.
COME ON YOU BLASTED INFANTS — SMILE, DAMN YOU!
WAIL
WAH
BAWL
WHINE
GOLLY — THE VICAR LOOKS A BIT STRESSED OUT.
I'M AFRAID THESE BABIES AREN'T BEING BONNY AT ALL, GILBERT.
WAH
WHINE
GRIZZLE
BAWL
THE ARCHBISHOP WILL BE FURIOUS WHEN HE ARRIVES AND SEES THIS MISERABLE ARRAY OF SOUR-FACED SPECIMENS.
NOT TO WORRY — I'LL INVENT A MARY-POPPINS-O-MATIC WHICH WILL SOON GET THOSE BABBIES GURGLING HAPPILY AGAIN.
HOOVER
MILK
LOOKS GREAT, GILBERT. HOW DOES IT WORK?
FIRST, THE POO-O-SENSOR SNIFFS EACH NAPPY AND DISPOSES OF ANY SHITEY-ARSED BABIES IN THIS BIN.
SHITEY BAIRNS
HOOVER
GOOD. THERE'S NOTHING BONNY ABOUT A SMELLY BOTTOM.
SNIFF SNIFF
NEXT, THE SUCKLE-O-TRON BREAST-FEEDS THE BABIES WITH SOOTHING GIN-LACED MILK.
SHLOOP
HOOVER
MILK
GLUG GLUG
PAT PAT PAT
URPPP
HOOVER
MILK
AND FINALLY THE BURPOLUX 2000 GENTLY PATS THE LITTLE MITES ON THE BACK, TO RELIEVE THEIR WIND.
SHORTLY
HM. THERE SEEMS TO BE A FAULT WITH THE SUCKLE-O-TRON, GILBERT.
BULGE
HOOVER
MILK
GLUG GLUG
ITS PUMPING GALLONS AND GALLONS OF MILK INTO THIS BABY.
BLOOOURGH!
HOOV
MILK
OOPS. I THINK THE LITTLE TINKER MAY HAVE SICKED SOME OF IT BACK UP THERE, VICAR.
BAH. I'D BETTER TAKE THESE PUKEY CLOTHES OFF.
WHIRR CLANK
UH-OH! NOW THE BURPOLUX 2000 IS GOING HAYWIRE.
TWACK
HOOV
WOW! IT'S KNOCKED THAT TOT FOR SIX
SHORTLY
THAT'S TORN IT
CRASH!
THE BABY HAS SMASHED THROUGH FATHER O'FISTICUFF'S STAINED GLASS GREENHOUSE, NEXT DOOR.
I'LL TEACH YOU TO BUST MY GREENHOUSE
STOTT
TAKE THAT!
OOF!
LOOK OUT VICAR — YOU'VE DISENGAGED THE HANDBRAKE ON THE MARY-POPPINS-O-MATIC
HOOVER
MILK
CLICK
CRIKEY! IT'S ROLLING DOWN THE DRIVE.
HOOVER
MILK
HELP!
TRUNDLE
AT THE BOTTOM OF THE DRIVE
THIS IS THE PARISH WHERE THE BONNY BABY COMPETITION IS BEING HELD, ARCHBISHOP
ST NIMBY'S PARISH
THANK YOU, DEACON.
OH ARCHBISHOP! BE CAREFUL YOU DON'T STEP ON THAT FILTHY OLD PAIR OF SOILED WOMEN'S KNICKERS
TSK. DOUBTLESS THEY WERE DISCARDED BY SOME POOR WRETCHED BAG-LADY.
GANGWAY!
WHAT THE-!?
HOOVER
RUMBLE
REVEREND! I AM SHOCKED AND APPALLED!
SPANK SPANK
SNATCH
HOOVER
SNIFF SNIFF
OO-ER THIS ISN'T WHAT IT LOOKS LIKE, ARCHBISHOP
NEVER HAVE I WITNESSED SUCH A DISGUSTING DISPLAY OF SEXUAL DEGENERACY
VICARS LIKE YOU GIVE OUR CHURCH A BAD NAME.
I HAVE NO CHOICE BUT TO HUSH THIS WHOLE AFFAIR UP BY TRANSFERRING YOU TO ANOTHER PARISH AS FAR AWAY AS POSSIBLE
HOW DOES THE BAHAMAS GRAB YOU?
SO SHORTLY, IN THE BAHAMAS
ST SWITHENS PARISH
NICE WORK, GILBERT.
HAVE ANOTHER GLASS OF HOLY COMMUNION BANANA DAQUIRI

BAXTER BASICS MP
VOTE FOR ME
...YES SIR. YOU... NO, NOT YOU... THE MAN WITH A TIE... THE BLUE TIE... NO, NOT YOU SIR... YOU. THE MAN WITH THE CURLY HAIR... NOT YOU SIR, SORRY... NEXT TO YOU...
QUESTION TI
NO... NOT YOU... YOU...
...SIGH... ALRIGHT, ALRIGHT... THE FAT CYCLOPS... YES, YOU SIR...
IN LIGHT OF THE GOVERNMENT'S RECENT CLAMPDOWN ON THE USE OF HARD DRUGS, I WOULD LIKE TO KNOW IF ANY MEMBERS OF THE PANEL HAVE EVER TAKEN HARD DRUGS, AND IF SO, DO THEY NOW REGRET THEIR ACTIONS?
DEREK TWATT?
WELL, I DON'T THINK THAT WHAT I HAVE OR HAVEN'T DONE IN THE PAST IS OF ANY RELEVANCE...
WHAT IS IMPORTANT IS THAT THE MESSAGE GOES OUT THAT DRUGS ARE...
NO! NOW COME ON, DEREK. DON'T AVOID THE ISSUE. ANSWER THE QUESTION.
NO. I'M SORRY, BUT WHAT I HAVE OR HAVE NOT DONE IN THE PAST IS NOT OF ANY...
ANSWER THE QUESTION!
FOR MY PART, I AM HAPPY TO SAY THAT I HAVE NEVER TAKEN HARD DRUGS. CAN DEREK TWATT SAY THE SAME?
HAPH!
QUESTION
I THOUGHT NOT.
WELL I THINK THE MINISTER'S SILENCE ON THIS IMPORTANT SUBJECT SPEAKS VOLUMES. IT IS NOTHING LESS THAN A TACIT ADMITTANCE OF GUILT.
RIGHT, I DON'T THINK WE'RE GOING TO GET ANY FURTHER WITH THAT TOPIC, SO LET'S MOVE ON TO THE NEXT QUESTION... WHICH IS FROM MR. LIONEL BATHYSPHERE...
QUESTION
MR. BATHYSPHERE?
THANK-YOU. A RECENT AMNESTY INTERNATIONAL REPORT ESTIMATED THAT 5000 UNDER-AGE GIRLS ARE KIDNAPPED AND SMUGGLED INTO THE UK EACH YEAR...
IT IS BELIEVED THEY ARE THEN FORCED TO WORK IN THE SEX INDUSTRY.
WOULD THE PANEL AGREE THAT THE MEN WHO USE THESE CHILD PROSTITUTES ARE AS GUILTY AS THE KIDNAPPERS?
BAXTER BASICS?
WELL, I DON'T THINK THAT WHAT I HAVE OR HAVEN'T DONE IN THE PAST IS OF ANY RELEVANCE. WHAT IS IMPORTANT IS THAT THE MESSAGE GOES OUT THAT CHILD PROSTITUTES ARE...

OH, LORDY... IT'S THE FAT SLAGS
EEH! I'M SENDIN FAR TOO MANY XMAS CARDS. IT'LL COST A FORTUNE IN STAMPS.
AYE!
20 CARDS
I CAN'T REMEMBER WHO HALF OF THESE ARE
I'M MAKIN' A NEW RULE: I'M NOT SENDIN' A CARD TO ANYONE I DIDN'T GET ONE OFF LAST YEAR.
THAT'S NOT THE XMAS SPIRIT, SAN
...NOT SENDIN' A CARD TO SOMEBODY IF YOU DIDN'T GET A CARD OFF THEM
NO, TRAY... IT'S ANYBODY I DIDN'T GET A POKE OFF LAST YEAR... NOT A CARD.
OOH! THAT'S A GOOD IDEA
RIGHT... STAN- NO, HAVEN'T HAD HIM. HE'S OFF THE LIST. FISHY NORMAN- NO
BIG TONY... I'VE NOT DONE HIM FOR YEARS. HE'S OFF.
SKRIT!... SKRIT!...
...SKRIT!
THINGY PERKINS- WELL HE'S BEEN MARRIED NEARLY A YEAR, SO HE'S OFF
'OLD ON... I THOUGHT YOU FUCKED HIM IN THE LAVS AT HIS STAG DO... REMEMBER?
SKRIT!...
AYE...
...SKRIT!
BUT HE COULDN'T GET IT UP... HE'S OFF...
YOUR GRANDAD... ...OFF...
MY GRANDAD? WHICH ONE?
BOTH OF 'EM.
CHINESE LES... OFF!
IT'S A GOOD SYSTEM OF YOURS, THIS IS, SAN... PRUNING OUT THE DEAD WOOD, SO T'SPEAK. NO FUCK THIS YEAR, NO XMAS CARD
AYE!
SHOULD SAVE US A BOB OR TWO
NEXT DAY...
743 SECOND CLASS STAMPS, PLEASE

“With This Bling,

LAST MONTH, readers of *OK* magazine drooled over page after page of photographs of the marriage between singer Peter Andre and breast model Jordan. Dubbed the Wedding of the Century, the ceremony at an expensive Berkshire Castle was the climax to a fairytale romanace that had started 18 months earlier in the jungles of Australia.

In the heavily copyright protected photographs, the D-list-celebrity-filled event appeared to go without a hitch. The pumpkin coach pulled by six white horses arrived on time, Jordan’s 10 foot-wide dress sparkled with the the lights of 1000 Swarovski crystals, and the £50,000, 18-tier cake was cut without it toppling off its specially-made £100,000 gold-plated trestle table.

EXCLUSIVE!

By our Tacky Showbiz Correspondent
Duncan Smothley

But according to one insider, away from the *OK* cameras the day went anything but smoothly.

Former SAS paratrooper **Frankie Liar** was employed by the couple to make sure than no gatecrashers or unwanted friends and family made it through the security cordon and into the star-studded bash.

According to Frankie, the day was a catalogue of cock-ups from start to finish. And in a hastily published book, he spills the beans on the Fairytale wedding that very nearly turned into a horror story. Here for the first time are exclusive extracts from his book that Peter and Jordan have not tried to ban.

“The day started badly. I was on a routine security sweep, and I was in Mr Andre’s bedroom checking there were no *Hello* photographers in his wardrobe. When he got out of bed, I heard an almighty commotion. “They’ve gone! They’ve gone!” he kept shouting.

At first I thought that someone must have broken in and stolen the wedding rings, but then I realised he was talking about his abdominal muscles.

ABS

Where they had been there was just a small, flabby pot bellly. In all the excitement, Andre had forgotten to do his abs excercises the night before, and his trademark six-pack had turned to flab. But lucky for him, I was there to save the day. I taught him a secret SAS training technique to get his muscles back, involving doing half a million sit-ups in an hour. By breakfast, his stomach looked like a bag of six burger buns once more.”

Everything went smoothly for a while. But about halfway through the morning, Frankie was doing a routine sweep of the castle when all Hell broke loose once more.

“We’d received a tip-off that a Sun photographer was hiding in the tea urn. That turned out to be a false alarm, but as I was leaving the kitchens I heard a commotion in the next room. It was Peter Andre yelling at the top of his voice. “Take them off! Take them off!” he kept shouting.

> “...Peter was furious, and because Bubble was refusing to take his shoes off, it looked like the wedding would be cancelled.”

TCS

It turned out that former Big Brother contestant Bubble had turned up wearing a pair of shoes which had cost several thousand pounds more than Peter’s. As the groom, he was adamant that his footwear should be the most expensive in the room. He was furious, and because Bubble was refusing to take his shoes off, it looked like the wedding would have to be cancelled.

4WD

Luckily, one of the guests came up with the bright idea of increasing the value of Andre’s shoes by stuffing them with fifty pound notes. It was a bit of a squeeze with nearly eight grand in each shoe, but he managed to get his feet in somehow. In fact, in the wedding photographs you can see Peter wincing as he hobbles down the aisle.”

Once the bride and groom had made it to the wedding ceremony, you could be forgiven for thinking that nothing else could go wrong. But Jordan and Peter’s troubles were only just beginning. Frankie takes up the story.

“During the service I was carrying out a routine check for hidden cameras under the vicar’s cassock while the couple were standing at the altar. When they had exchanged their vows, Peter reached in his pocket and brought out a ring the size of a man’s fist, covered in hundreds of diamonds. Talk about bling! It was the most showy thing I’ve ever seen.

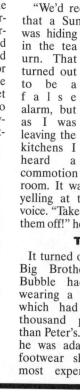

Don’t they make a lovely pair: Tit model Jordan’s wedding as it may have looked (above), and (below) a six pack similar to the one Andre lost. (Below right) Bling: Tit model Jordan’s wedding ring as it may have looked.

SRS

But it didn’t impress Jordan; she went absolutely ballistic, shouting and screaming about the ring, saying that it wasn’t gaudy enough. She told Peter in no uncertain terms that the marriage was off unless he could find a more ostentatious wedding ring ... and quick!

The call went out, and within an hour a helicopter landed on the lawn with a very important cargo - a bucket of diamonds and a tube of superglue. Peter’s best man, the winner of last

Thee Wed"

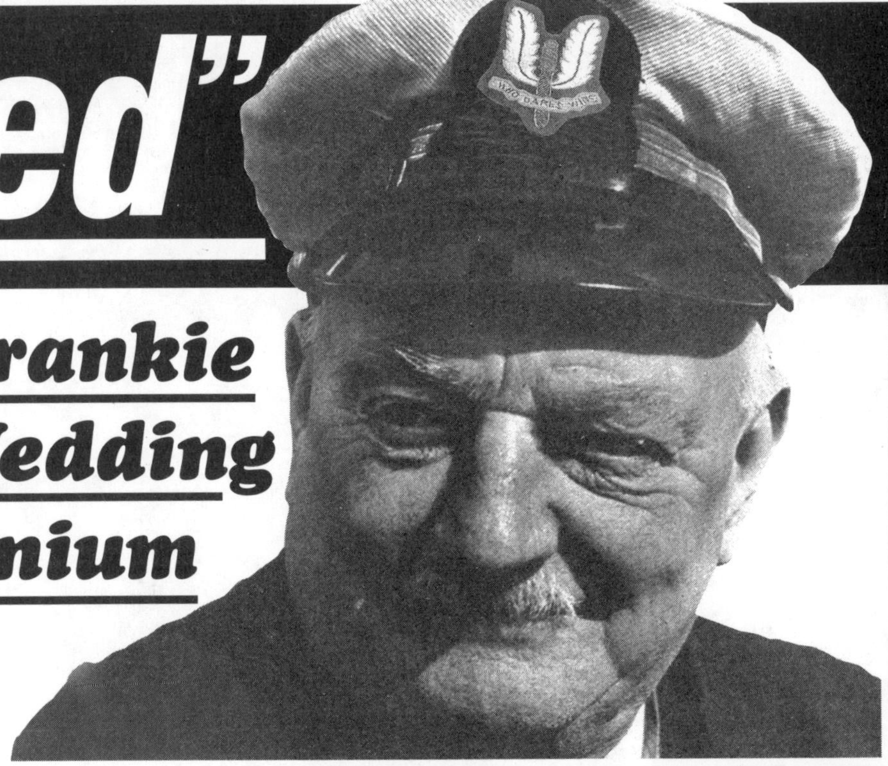

Ex SAS-man Frankie Blows Lid on Wedding of the Millennium

year's *'Fame Academy'*, then had to sit down and start sticking the jewels onto the ring. A couple of hours and about ten thousand diamonds later, Jordan decided it was tawdry enough, and the wedding ceremony went ahead."

But even as Mr and Mrs Andre left the church to get into their tacky pumpkin-shaped horse-drawn coach, things nearly went pear-shaped again.

"I was just checking up the horses' arses for concealed video equipment when Jordan and Peter came out of the church. Everyone was cheering and clapping and each guest had been given a box of very special confetti to throw over the newly-weds.

Normal confetti is fine for a normal marriage, but the wedding of the century demanded something a little more tasteless. Earlier in the day, Peter had handed a servant at the castle a paper shredder and a million pounds in notes and told him to get to work. But, amazingly, as the guests showered the shredded cash over the happy couple, the emotional bride threw another wobbly.

"...Peter handed a servant at the castle a paper shredder and £1million in notes and told him to get to work."

AQUAFRESHES

Jordan had noticed that the confetti was made of twenties, and she started crying. She threatened to divorce Andre then and there, sobbing that if he really loved her it would have been a million pounds in fifties.

Peter kept apologising, but there was no time to shred a million pounds in fifties; the couple's farcical golden Cinderella coach couldn't be kept waiting any longer. It seemed like the marriage was going to be over before it had even begun.

EUTHYMOLS

Then Peter had a brainwave. He took out his wallet and wrote a cheque for a million pounds cash in fifties, tore it into little bits and sprinkled it over his wife's head. Everyone breathed a sigh of relief. The wedding was back on! "

FRANKIE LIAR
Love at Any Price

Copies of Frankie Liar's book ***'Love at Any Price - Behind the Scenes with the SAS at the Wedding of the Century'*** (Ex-SAS Man Publishing) are available from the author in the snug of the Winning Post, Clifton, every night from 6pm, price 1 pint.

Here's YOUR chance to
Win Your Own Wedding List!

JORDAN AND PETER'S wedding was a magical day in every one of our lives. All *Viz* readers join together in wishing the couple a long and happy marriage. ***But how long exactly do YOU give it?***

Send us ***YOUR*** guess on the entry form below, and when the happy couple announce they've split up, the reader who has come closest to predicting the length of their marriage will receive a fantastic ***Wedding Day Gift Selection,*** comprising of a set of coffee cups, a set of wine glasses, a kitchen wall clock and 18 toasters.

I think Jordan and Peter Andre's marriage will last ☐ months and ☐ days.

Name..

Address..

....

...............................Post Code......................

Send to: *Viz Jordan and Peter Andre Separation Lottery, PO Box 1PT, Newcastle upon Tyne NE99 1PT.*

KRISSMÜSTAGEN MIT
Das Bacons
BIFFLA
MUTTA
VATTA
HEH HEH! ES IST KRISSMÜSTAGEN
HEY! ICH LIEBE KRISSMÜSTAGEN, MICHT!
GUTEN TAG, BIFFLA. DAS IST SEINE KRISSMÜSTAGEN GIFTENWRAPPEN
BIFFLA
EH?
NEIN, VATTA. SIE MÜSSE ZINKEN ICH BIN EINE RICHT KUNTENDAFTEN
BIFFLA
MEINE MUTTA IST IN DAS, UND SIE SPRINGT AUS UND HOOFEN MEINE TESTICULISCHE.
NEIN, NEIN, BIFFLA SOHN.
MUTTA IST STUFFENZWEIGEN DAS GOBBLEVOGEL IN DIE KOOKENSTRASSE.
AALRICHT, VATTA.
HEH HEH. VAS IST IN MEINE KRISSMÜSTAGEN GIFTENWRAPPEN?
EINE RUSSISCHE DOLLSCHAFT! DANKE, VATTA.
OPPEN SIE AUS, BIFFLA.
EIN DOLLSCHAFT... UND ZWEI DOLLSCHAFT... UND DREI DOLLSCHAFT...
HEH HEH!
HÜNH?
DAS ULTIMATE DOLLSCHAFT RESEMBLICHT MUTTA!
SMACK
HEH HEH! WIR AANLICHT KIDDENZWEIGEN, BIFFLA
EIR SINT EINE KOUPLEN PAIREN KUNTENFRIGGEN

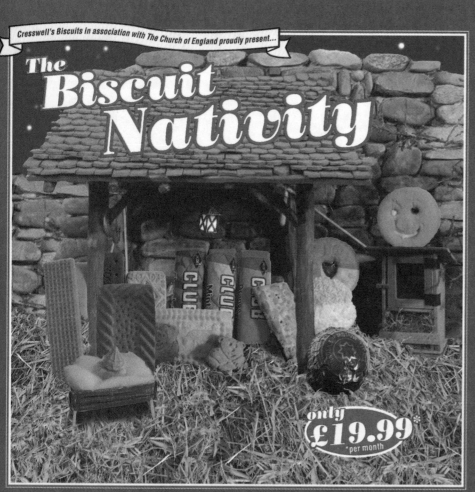

Cresswell's Biscuits in association with The Church of England proudly present...

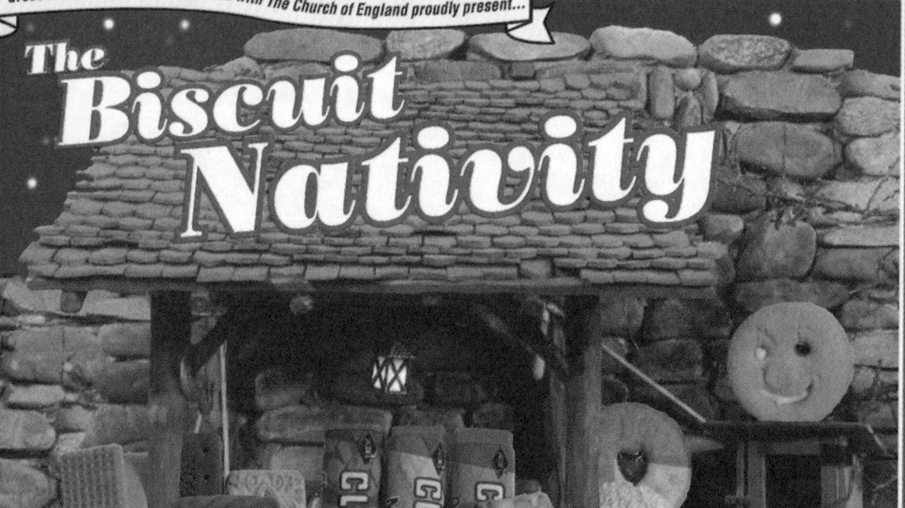
The Biscuit Nativity
only £19.99*
*per month

The Pink Wafer as the Virgin Mary

With its slim figure and meek and mild nature this teatime treat simply glows with that just-given-birth look. And it's pink like a lady should be.

The Shortcake as Joseph

Loyal and dependable, no biscuit asks fewer questions than the shortcake, just as Joseph probably didn't ask enough questions 2,000 years ago.

The Iced Gem as the Little Baby Jesus

Tiny and sweet with a delightful blackcurrant-flavoured icing sugar halo, this birthday party staple is the perfect biscuit to save us all from our sins.

The 3 Club biscuits as the 3 Wise Kings

Everyone loves a Club and everyone loves wise people. With their silver crowns and shiny shoes, the Magi bring Jesus their gifts of mints, oranges and plain.

The Garibaldi as the Innkeeper

The glazed finish of the Garibaldi accurately captures the glazed expression of a man so tanked up from his own optics that he made a woman give birth in dung.

The Jammy Dodger as the Angel Gabriel

When Gabriel appeared to the shepherds, lo! they were sore afraid but they soon relaxed when they saw the glory of his raspberry jam shining all around.

The Custard Cream, the Bourbon and the Fig Roll as the Shepherds

The perfect witnesses to the glory of the coming Lord... and the perfect accompaniment to a nice hot pot of tea! Amen.

The Malted Milk and some Cadbury's Animals as the Ox, the Ass, and the Lamb

The cow bit wasn't too hard but a chocolate monkey and a chocolate bear is as good as it gets.

The Happy Face as God, the Father

The last time you enjoyed a Happy Face was probably the last time you went to church. Repent as this beaming biscuit God winks his creamy eye at his bouncing baby blackcurrant Son.

The Tunnock's Teacake as the Devil

What better biscuit to tempt us towards the dark side than the Tunnock's, with his gaudy jacket and gooey white centre? Resist the teacake or be damned for all eternity.

The Coconut Mallow as Father Christmas

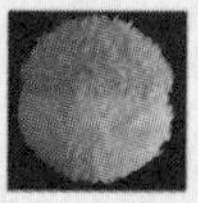

Who's that with the ruddy face and big white beard? Why it's the coconut Saint Nick, reminding us that one particular iced gem was crucified so that we might get a load of presents every year.

☐ **YES!** I want to put the cream back into Christmas with the Cresswell's Biscuit Nativity. Please rush me the first part of the scene (the straw) by second class post. I understand that the Cresswell's Biscuit Nativity is sold by instalments and it may be August before I receive any actual biscuits, and then it'll probably be the shortcake or the fig roll or one of the sturdier, duller biscuits. By the time the coconut mallow arrives, I'll more than likely have gone off the idea. Please keep debiting my card.

NAME: ____________ **ADDRESS:** ____________

____________ **CARD No.** ____________

I **do / do not** wish to be saved by the healing love of Our Lord Jesus Christ.

Send your application to Cresswell's Biscuits, 110 Farthing's Wharf, Chigley, Trumptonshire. Check with your God before applying.

Death Doc Jaunt on Public Cash

Public shells out for Shipman trip of a lifetime

THE WOMAN who lived next-door-but-two to record-breaking serial killer Harold Shipman is going on a sensational three-day luxury caravanning break in Anglesey... *and YOU'LL be footing the bill!*

By our Exclusives Correspondent
Xavier Clusive

Dr Death (above) ~ multiple mass murderer Shipman, yesterady and (left) neighbour but two Lucy Hartless

Jekyll and Hyde park ~ the luxury £85 per weekend caravan site where Hartless will live it up at YOUR expense.

Lucy Hartless, 42, who pockets a whopping £16,000 of taxpayer's money each year as a staff nurse at St Ratner's Hospital in Manchester, plans to blow almost £85 on a no-holds-barred long weekend at a top Welsh caravan park.

knees-up

The news that the woman who lived only three doors away from Britain's most notorious serial killer is planning a lavish knees-up at the expense of decent, law-abiding Britons has outraged moral indignation groups.

chin-up

"It's horrific," steamed campaigner Clive Perfect of Staying Annoyed. "This greedy woman is having a three-day beano in Anglesey, with a black-and-white television and cold running water, with money taken from our taxes – money that could be spent on schools or hospitals."

hands-up

And as Hartless prepares for the holiday, further shocking details have emerged of her extravagant lifestyle, funded by the ordinary British citizen. According to a colleague, who asked to remain nameless, the notorious late murderer's blonde ex-neighbour;

- Travels everywhere by ***BUS***, always paying in cash
- Owns a ***COLOUR TV*** set and video recorder
- Takes her mother to ***BINGO*** every Saturday
- Plans to replace her twin tub with a ***BRAND NEW*** washing machine

cock-up

"It beggars belief," fumed Perfect. "I am sickened that this woman can continue to grab government salary handouts working in the Accident & Emergency ward of a hospital, whilst the late Shipman's victims don't get a penny. I'm sure many of them would have loved the chance to go gallavanting off to Anglesey."

Tomorrow, a 25-signature petition will be handed to the Prime Minister's driver by a group of protesters from Staying Annoyed. In it, they describe heartless Lucy's luxury holiday as "an outrage," and call for her to be killed.

Not only of TOAST...but also of GOLF!

No. 318

Celebrities choose their favourite words that are not only of TOAST, but also of GOLF.

This week:~
Wife-swap Benefits Queen
Lizzie Bardsey

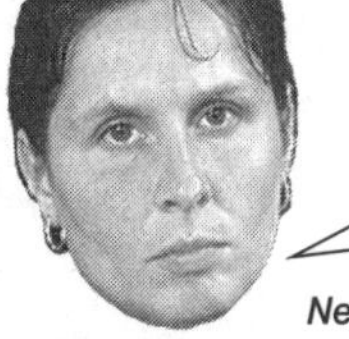

A 'ROUND'

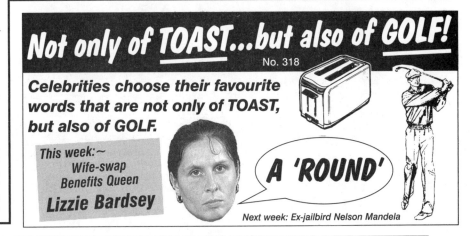

Next week: Ex-jailbird Nelson Mandela

the
SLOW-MOVING DUCK
NOBODY WANTS ME.
SNIFF!
REDUCED
W-WHY?
Paul Palmer
SIGH! NOBODY WANTS ME. I'LL NEVER FIND A HOME.
DON'T BE DAFT. YOU JUST NEED TO BE POSITIVE.
NOW PULL YOURSELF TOGETHER... HERE COME SOME PUNTERS NOW!
SALE
REDUCED
AND
OH, MUMMY! LOOK!! CAN I HAVE THAT ONE PLEASE? CAN I? CAN I!?!
PET
SALE!
SOME DUCK
SHRUG!
SOME DUCK
ORANGE SAUCE.
SNIFF!
FINAL REDUCTION
SNIFF!

BIG VERN
IN THE LIBRARY...
SILENCE
LET ME SEE... ALL'S WELL THAT ENDS WELL... ...AS YOU LIKE IT... HMMM...
SHAKESPEARE
AH! HERE IT IS...
COMEDY OF ERRORS
WOTCHA ERNIE. REMEMBER ME, DO YA?
VERN!
WHAT THE..?
...ONLY I AIN'T CLOCKED YER BOAT RAHND THE MANOR LATELY, THAT'S ALL.
RUDDY HELL, VERN! YOU REALLY MADE ME JUMP THERE.
BIT EDGY, ARE WE, ERNIE? I 'OPE YOU AIN'T GOT NAFFINK TO HIDE...
WELL, NO. OF COURSE I HAVEN'T ANYTHING TO...
NOT TRYING TO FREEZE ME AHT, ARE YOU ERNIE? I DON'T LIKE PEOPLE FREEZIN' ME AHT.
FREEZE YOU OUT..!?
IT MAKES ME ANGRY, ERNIE. AND BELIEVE YOU ME, YOU WOULDN'T LIKE ME WHEN I'M ANGRY.
NO, IT'S JUST I'VE BEEN VERY BUSY LATELY. I'M A MEMBER OF THE VILLAGE DRAMA GROUP, AND WE'RE PUTTING ON A PLAY AT THE MOMENT. ACTUALLY, WHY DON'T YOU JOIN US? THERE'S STILL A FEW PARTS UP FOR GRABS.
TELL ME MORE, ERNIE. I'M ALL SHELL-LIKES.
WELL, WE'RE DOING A PRODUCTION OF 'COMEDY OF ERRORS' IN THE VILLAGE HALL.
A PRODUCTION, EH? I LIKE IT, ERNIE, I DO. VILLAGE HALL, EH?... NICE TOUCH...
...NO PLOD, NO GUARDS WANTIN' TO MAKE A NAME FOR THEMSELVES... STRAIGHT IN... STRAIGHT AHT...
SWEET AS, ERNIE.
'OO'VE Y'GOT ON THE FIRM, THEN? THE USUAL FACES, IS IT? SMILER EDDIE, STAN THE HAT, GENTLEMAN ROB, MICKEY THE CHIN..?
NO. IT'S JUST THE LOCAL AMATEUR DRAMATICS SOCIETY, VERN.
DO WOT!? WELL YER CAN COUNT ME AHT, ERNIE. I DON'T WORK WIV AMATEURS.
OH, BUT WE'RE NOT BAD, VERN...
NOT FACKIN' BAD!?... ERNIE, I'VE BEEN DOIN' BLAGS LIKE THIS SINCE I WAS SUCKIN' ME MUM'S TITS, AN' I'VE SEEN TOO MANY AMATEURS GET STAGE FRIGHT...
TAKE IT FROM ME, ERN. WHEN THE TOYS COME AHT, THEY BOTTLE IT... I'VE SEEN 'EM SHIT THEIR-SELVES, ERNIE, AN' IT AIN'T A PRETTY SIGHT, I CAN TELL YER.
WELL I DON'T KNOW ABOUT THAT, BUT WE DID 'MOTHER GOOSE' LAST CHRISTMAS, AND THAT SEEMED TO GO DOWN QUITE WELL.
COME ON VERN. COME AND JOIN IN. IT'LL BE FUN...
LATER THAT WEEK...
FULCHESTER VILLAGE HALL
TONIGHT FULCHESTER AMATEUR DRAMATIC SOCIETY presents "COMEDY OF ERRORS" by W. Shakespeare TICKETS 50p.
BACK-STAGE...
HOW'S IT LOOKING OUT THERE, VERN. IS THERE A BIG CROWD?
IT'S FILLIN' UP, ERNIE.
I JUST 'OPE NONE OF 'EM TRIES TO PLAY THE HERO, ERNIE, 'COS I DON'T WANT TO 'AVE TO WASTE NOBODY... BUT I'M NOT GOIN' BACK INSIDE.
STILL NO SIGN OF THE WAGES VAN, ERNIE.
WAGES VAN?! THIS IS A SHAKESPEARE PLAY, VERN. ARE YOU SURE YOU KNOW WHAT YOU'VE GOT TO DO?
I FINK SO, VERN. BUT IT'S A FUNNY OLD CAPER, THIS ONE.
NOT SURE I LIKE IT, ERNIE. IT JUST DON'T FEEL RIGHT.
I'M SURE THAT'S JUST FIRST NIGHT NERVES, VERN.
DON'T WORRY, YOU'LL BE FINE. WHEN YOU GET YOUR CUE, JUST COME ON THE STAGE AND STAND NEXT TO ME.

YOU'RE THE GUV'NOR, ERNIE. WHAT'S MY COVER?
COVER? WELL, YOU'RE ANTIPHOLUS OF EPHESUS AND I'M DROMIO OF SYRACUSE, REMEMBER?
STREWF, ERNIE. THAT'S A BIT OF A NORF AN' SARF-FULL, INNIT? WHATEVER 'APPENED TO MR. PINK AN' MR. BRAHN?
STILL - YOUR TICKLE, YOUR RULES, I S'POSE.
BUT I'M WARNIN' YOU, ERNIE. THE CODE OF 'ONOUR'S AHT THE BLEEDIN' WINDER ON THIS ONE. WE GO A LONG WAY BACK, YOU AN' ME, BUT IF IT ALL GOES SHIT-SHAPED, IT'S EMFH I TELL YER.
SHORTLY...
THE PLAY'S GOING WELL, ISN'T IT, VERN. OUR SCENE'S COMING UP SOON. YOU'RE NOT GETTING NERVOUS, ARE YOU?
I'LL LEVEL WITH YOU, ERN. I DON'T LIKE THIS ONE BIT.
...NOT KNOW MY VOICE? O, TIME'S EXTREMITY...
TOO MANY FACES, ERNIE. THIS SHOULD'VE BEEN A TWO MAN JOB, BUT YOU 'AD TO GET GREEDY, DINCHA?
...HAST THOU SO CRACK'D AND SPLITTED MY POOR TONGUE IN SEVEN SHORT YEARS...
...MY WASTING LAMPS SOME FADING GLIMMER LEFT... MY DULL DEAF EARS ARE LITTLE USE TO HEAR...
'OO'S THIS JOKER, EH? I DON'T LIKE THE LOOK OF 'IM, ERNIE.
'E LOOKS LIKE A NARK TO ME.
YOU'VE COCKED UP 'ERE, ERNIE, BIG TIME. I WISH I'D NEVER LET YOU TALK ME INTO THIS JOB...
...I SEE THY AGE AND DANGERS MAKE THEE DOTE...
COME ON, VERN. THAT'S OUR CUE. WE'RE ON!
BUT WITH THESE NAILS I'LL PLUCK OUT THESE FALSE EYES THAT WOULD BEHOLD IN ME THIS SHAMEFUL SPOT..!
...OH BIND HIM, BIND HIM. LET HIM NOT COME NEAR ME..!
ERNIE! LOOK AHT!
IT'S THE FACKIN' COZZAS!
I TOLD YOU, ERNIE! WE'VE BEEN STITCHED UP LIKE A BLEEDIN' KIPPAH!
SHH! PLEASE! REMEMBER THE PLAY, VERN!
JESUS CHRIST, ERNIE! NO NAMES, YOU SLAAAAAG!!
SORRY, VERN...
TOO LATE, ERN! EVERYONE IN THE ROOM'S MADE ME MUSH, THEN YOU GO AND PIN A MONICKER ON IT!
YOU FACKIN' SCHT-YOOPID TOERAG, ERNIE! I TOLD YA BEFORE, I AIN'T NEVAH DOIN' NO MORE PORRIDGE!
...AN' I BLEEDIN' MEANT IT!
I'VE SPENT TOO MANY YEARS SHITTIN' IN A BUCKET, ERNIE. I'M TOO OLD TO DO ANAVAH TWO-WAY STRETCH!
TELL ME MUM I LAV 'ER!
K-CLICK!
BLAM!
ERM... MAY IT PLEASE YOUR GRACE, ANTIPHOLUS MY HUSBAND WHO I MADE LORD OF ME AND ALL I HAD AT YOUR IMPORTANT LETTERS THIS ILL DAY, A MOST OUTRAGEOUS FIT OF MADNESS TOOK HIM...

SPOT THE CLUE
WITH MTV'S
TIM WESTWOOD
YO! CHECK IT OUT, MA MAIN MAN!
WHEN I'M NOT HELPING MY FATHER, WHO IS A BISHOP, TO PREPARE HIS SERMONS FOR SUNDAY SERVICE, I LIKE NOTHING BETTER THAN TO RELAX WITH A GOOD WHODUNNIT. THIS ONE IS CALLED THE CASE OF THE POISONED CHIN.
SCOTLAND YARD – THE OFFICE OF INSPECTOR SHARPE
SHARPE! YOU'D BETTER GET OVER TO HOCKLEBY HALL – LORD HOCKLEBY HAS BEEN MURDERED
I'M ON MY WAY, CHIEF.
SOON, AT HOCKLEBY HALL
AFTERNOON, CONSTABLE. YOU'D BETTER SHOW ME THE BODY.
RIGHT THIS WAY, INSPECTOR.
LORD HOCKLEBY WAS FOUND DEAD HERE IN HIS STUDY. SOMEONE HAD STABBED HIM THROUGH THE CHEST WITH THE FAMOUSLY POINTY CHIN OF TV PERSONALITY BRUCE FORSYTH.
NICE TO SEE YOU, TO SEE YOU NICE.
HM. BRUCE FORSYTH'S CHIN HAS BEEN COATED WITH A FAST-ACTING DEADLY POISON. WHOEVER DID THIS INTENDED LORD HOCKLEBY TO DIE INSTANTLY.
GOOD GAME, GOOD GAME
THE OLD FOOL HAD IT COMING, INSPECTOR...
AND WHO ARE YOU?
I AM RUPERT HOCKLEBY, THE NE'ER DO WELL YOUNGER BROTHER OF LORD HOCKLEBY. HERE IS MY CARD.
HM. I SEE YOU ARE A MANUFACTURER OF FAST-ACTING DEADLY POISONS, MR HOCKLEBY.
R. HOCKLEBY FAST-ACTING DEADLY POISONS
THAT'S RIGHT. MY BUSINESS WAS ON THE VERGE OF BANKRUPTCY BECAUSE OF MY GAMBLING DEBTS...
I ASKED MY BROTHER FOR A LOAN, BUT THE SWINE REFUSED.
LUCKILY, NOW THAT HE IS DEAD, I STAND TO INHERIT HIS VAST FORTUNE
MOST INTERESTING. CONSTABLE, WHO DISCOVERED THE BODY?
IT WAS LADY HOCKLEBY, SIR. HIS LORDSHIP'S WIFE. SHE'S THROUGH HERE IN THE DRAWING ROOM.
OH, INSPECTOR! WHO COULD HAVE DONE THIS TO MY POOR HUSBAND?
CALM YOURSELF, YOUR LADYSHIP, AND TELL ME WHAT HAPPENED.
I SAW MY HUSBAND GO INTO HIS STUDY AT AROUND 2PM, FOLLOWING A VIOLENT ARGUMENT WITH HIS BROTHER RUPERT
I REMEMBER HEARING RUPERT SHOUT, "IF YOU DON'T GIVE ME THAT LOAN, I'LL KILL YOU WITH THE CHIN OF BRITAIN'S PREMIER STAR OF LIGHT ENTERTAINMENT."
NATURALLY I THOUGHT NO MORE ABOUT IT – UNTIL I LOOKED IN THE STUDY ABOUT HALF AN HOUR LATER
AND THERE WAS MY HUSBAND... SOB = DEAD!
SO YOU WERE IN THE ADJOINING ROOM TO WHERE THE MURDER TOOK PLACE
YOU GET NOTHING FOR A PAIR – NOT IN THIS GAME!
SURELY THEN YOU MUST HAVE HEARD BRUCE FORSYTH UTTER ONE OF HIS CATCHPHRASES AS THE MURDERER PLUNGED THE CHIN INTO YOUR HUSBAND'S CHEST?
I'M AFRAID I DIDN'T HEAR A THING, INSPECTOR.
THE RECORD PLAYER WAS ON RATHER LOUD. I WAS LISTENING TO SOME OF MY OLD VINYL LPS.
WELL INSPECTOR, ALL THE EVIDENCE SEEMS TO POINT TO LORD HOCKLEBY'S BROTHER RUPERT BEING THE MURDERER.
I WOULDN'T BE SO SURE!
CAN YOU SPOT THE CLUE?
THE MURDERER OF LORD HOCKLEBY WAS... LADY HOCKLEBY
IT WAS YOU WHO STABBED YOUR HUSBAND WITH THE POISONED CHIN OF BRUCE FORSYTH.
IT'S A FAIR COP. I KILLED HIM BECAUSE HE USED TO FART IN BED
WELL THERE'LL BE NO BEDS WHERE YOU'RE GOING, LADY HOCKLEBY – TO PRISON!
WELL, ACTUALLY THERE WILL BE BEDS.
CONGRATULATIONS, INSPECTOR. BUT WHAT MADE YOU SUSPECT LADY HOCKLEBY?
HER LADYSHIP WAS A CLEVER WOMAN ~ BUT SHE MADE ONE SILLY MISTAKE
DID YOU SPOT THE CLUE?
LADY HOCKLBY SAID THAT SHE HAD BEEN LISTENING TO HER OLD VINYL LPS – AND AMONGST THEM I NOTICED THE CLASSIC STRAWBS ALBUM "HEARTBREAK HILL".
STRAWBS HEARTBREAK HILL
BUT "HEARTBREAK HILL" WAS NEVER ACTUALLY RELEASED ON VINYL – RECORDED IN 1978/79, IT WAS ONLY AVAILABLE ON CASSETTE TAPE (UNDER THE TITLE "STARTING OVER") UNTIL 1995 WHEN IT WAS FINALLY RELEASED ON CD.

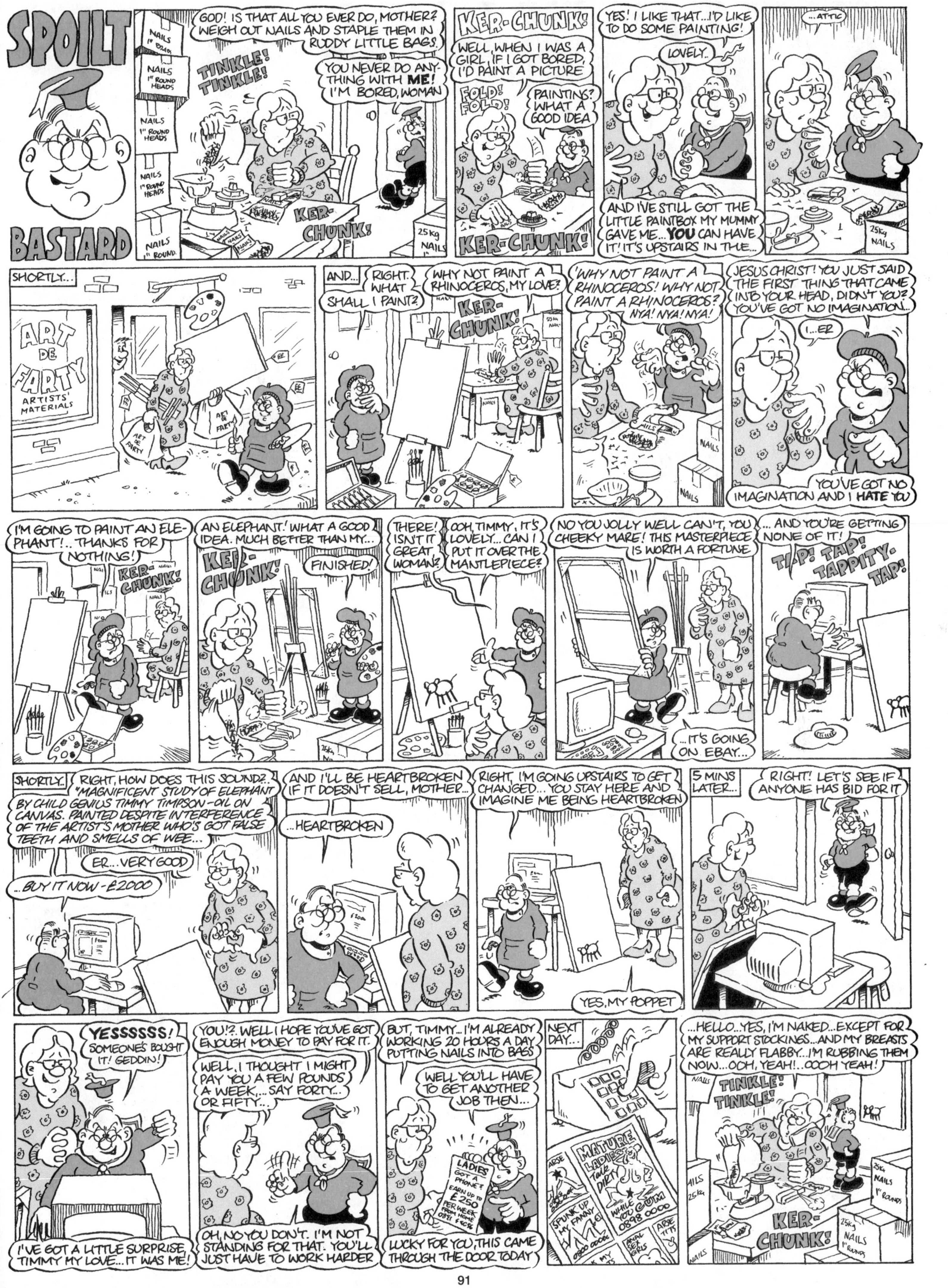
SPOILT BASTARD
NAILS 1" BRADS
NAILS 1" ROUND HEADS
NAILS 1" ROUND HEADS
NAILS 1" ROUND HEADS
NAILS 1" ROUND
GOD! IS THAT ALL YOU EVER DO, MOTHER? WEIGH OUT NAILS AND STAPLE THEM IN RUDDY LITTLE BAGS.
TINKLE! TINKLE!
YOU NEVER DO ANYTHING WITH ME! I'M BORED, WOMAN
KER-CHUNK!
25kg NAILS
KER-CHUNK!
WELL, WHEN I WAS A GIRL, IF I GOT BORED, I'D PAINT A PICTURE
FOLD! FOLD!
PAINTING? WHAT A GOOD IDEA
KER-CHUNK!
YES! I LIKE THAT...I'D LIKE TO DO SOME PAINTING!
LOVELY..
AND I'VE STILL GOT THE LITTLE PAINTBOX MY MUMMY GAVE ME... YOU CAN HAVE IT! IT'S UPSTAIRS IN THE...
...ATTIC
25kg NAILS
SHORTLY...
ART DE FARTY ARTISTS' MATERIALS
ART DE FARTY
AND...
RIGHT. WHAT SHALL I PAINT?
WHY NOT PAINT A RHINOCEROS, MY LOVE?
KER-CHUNK!
'WHY NOT PAINT A RHINOCEROS! WHY NOT PAINT A RHINOCEROS?' NYA! NYA! NYA!
NAILS
JESUS CHRIST! YOU JUST SAID THE FIRST THING THAT CAME INTO YOUR HEAD, DIDN'T YOU? YOU'VE GOT NO IMAGINATION...
I...ER
YOU'VE GOT NO IMAGINATION AND I HATE YOU
I'M GOING TO PAINT AN ELEPHANT!...THANKS FOR NOTHING!
KER-CHUNK!
AN ELEPHANT! WHAT A GOOD IDEA. MUCH BETTER THAN MY...
KER-CHUNK!
FINISHED!
THERE! ISN'T IT GREAT, WOMAN?
OOH, TIMMY, IT'S LOVELY... CAN I PUT IT OVER THE MANTLEPIECE?
NO YOU JOLLY WELL CAN'T, YOU CHEEKY MARE! THIS MASTERPIECE IS WORTH A FORTUNE
...IT'S GOING ON EBAY...
...AND YOU'RE GETTING NONE OF IT!
TAP! TAP! TAPPITY-TAP!
SHORTLY..
RIGHT, HOW DOES THIS SOUND?.. "MAGNIFICENT STUDY OF ELEPHANT BY CHILD GENIUS TIMMY TIMPSON - OIL ON CANVAS. PAINTED DESPITE INTERFERENCE OF THE ARTIST'S MOTHER WHO'S GOT FALSE TEETH AND SMELLS OF WEE...
ER...VERY GOOD
...BUY IT NOW - £2000
AND I'LL BE HEARTBROKEN IF IT DOESN'T SELL, MOTHER...
...HEARTBROKEN
RIGHT, I'M GOING UPSTAIRS TO GET CHANGED... YOU STAY HERE AND IMAGINE ME BEING HEARTBROKEN
YES, MY POPPET
5 MINS LATER...
RIGHT! LET'S SEE IF ANYONE HAS BID FOR IT
YESSSSSS! SOMEONE'S BOUGHT IT! GEDDIN!
I'VE GOT A LITTLE SURPRISE, TIMMY MY LOVE... IT WAS ME!
YOU!?. WELL I HOPE YOU'VE GOT ENOUGH MONEY TO PAY FOR IT.
WELL, I THOUGHT I MIGHT PAY YOU A FEW POUNDS A WEEK... SAY FORTY... OR FIFTY...
OH, NO YOU DON'T. I'M NOT STANDING FOR THAT. YOU'LL JUST HAVE TO WORK HARDER
BUT, TIMMY... I'M ALREADY WORKING 20 HOURS A DAY PUTTING NAILS INTO BAGS
WELL YOU'LL HAVE TO GET ANOTHER JOB THEN...
LADIES GOT A PHONE? EARN UP TO £250 PER WEEK FROM HOME
LUCKY FOR YOU, THIS CAME THROUGH THE DOOR TODAY
NEXT DAY...
MATURE LADIES Talk DIRTY
WHILE YOU CUM 0898 0000
SPUNK UP MY FANNY
ARSE TITS
...HELLO...YES, I'M NAKED...EXCEPT FOR MY SUPPORT STOCKINGS...AND MY BREASTS ARE REALLY FLABBY...I'M RUBBING THEM NOW...OOH, YEAH!...OOOH YEAH!
TINKLE! TINKLE!
NAILS 25kg
25kg NAILS 1" ROUNDS
KER-CHUNK!
25kg NAILS 1" ROUNDS

Letterbocks

Viz Comic, PO Box 656, North Shields NE29 1BT
Email: letters@viz.co.uk

STAR LETTER

★★★★★★★★★★★★★★★★★★★★★★★★★

How is it that Channel 4's Big Brother are allowed to install loads of cameras in a house and watch the residents' every move. But when I put one tiny camera in my neighbour's bathroom I get bound over for 12 months. There's no justice.

Simon Eldritch, e-mail

I get utterly fed up with disabled activists banging on about how unfortunate they are, and how they want equal treatment with non-disabled persons. Maybe, then, they shouldn't be given the best parking spaces at the supermarket, or be allowed to take their dogs into shops when nobody else can. I'm just in favour of equality.

C Mitchell
e-mail

I was delighted to hear that the new identity card introduced by the government will be brought in as a voluntary scheme in the first instance. Let's hope that the drug dealers and terrorists the government hope to catch are amongst the first to apply for their card.

T Thorne
Hexham

After discussing our favourite song of all time recently, a friend of mine said her favourite song ever was *Tainted Love* by Soft Cell. Although I agree that it is a fantastic tune, and a wonderful reworking of a classic song, I still find it hard not to picture Marc Almond lying on a hospital bed having two pints of Harry Monk pumped out of his stomach. TWO PINTS!

R Chowdhury
Sarfend on Sea

I was extremely saddened to hear of Richard Whiteley's recent death. But I was cheered to imagine his life support machine making the famous *Countdown* "da-da, da-da, da-da-da-da! Booooooo!" sound as he took his final breaths.

Tripod
e-mail

It's all very well prosecuting paedophiles for looking at images of naked children on computer screens, but isn't it about time we named and shamed these obstetricians?

My wife is six months pregnant, and whilst having a scan the other day, the pervert doctor sat there looking at an image of my naked unborn child on screen. He even asked me if I wanted a picture of it.

P Smith
London

In the *Sunday Times*, Jeremy Clarkson said he found it a real pain being a celebrity. I wholeheartedly agree, as I find him being a celebrity a complete pain.

P Lorimer
Leeds

Like Tim Henman, I have absolutely no fucking chance of winning Wimbledon. But unlike the whey-faced ponce, I don't have legions of women sat on a hillside outside my flat shouting "Come on, Nick!"

Nick Pettigrew
London

They say that truth is stranger than fiction. Well last night I read a story about a giant dragon that lived in a castle made out of clouds in the sky. I'd love to see that in real life.

Adam Lee
e-mail

I was at the U2 gig at Twickenham Stadium last week. Seeing Bono's speech it was clear he is concerned about poverty and fair trade. Perhaps, then, he can explain why I paid seventy quid to get in, and six quid for a fucking cheese pasty and a bottle of pop?

Reg Reggington
Email

In the court case of the fifteen year old schoolboy seduced by his attractive teacher, it was decided that the victim should give his evidence from behind a screen. This was a good move by the prosecution. If I had been the victim, the mile wide grin on my face could well have played into the hands of the defence.

J Hughes
Carlisle

FIST FURY ALERT

Regarding P Thornton and T Cadbury's nominations for Soap Opera Punch-Up Let Downs on page 36, surely these two, from *the Sun* and *the Sun's TV mag*, win 'hands down'.

Richard Karslake
Oxford

I walked past a mirror the other day, and it didn't look like I was doing a moonwalk. What's going on? I thought they were supposed to make everything look opposite.

Graeme Patterson
e-mail

During an early morning walk I was amazed to see an elderly gentleman collecting his dog's excrement and taking it home with him. Jesus Christ, I shudder to think what his other hobbies are.

Alan Thackray
e-mail

Isn't it about time we stopped spelling Hitler with a capital H? The man doesn't deserve the respect, and who's going to get upset apart from the Pope?

Pete James
e-mail

They say 'what doesn't kill you makes you stronger'. Try telling that to my cousin. He was a champion weight lifter untill he got hit by a BT van. Now he drinks his food through a straw.

M Hirst
e-mail

I was pleased to notice that Prince William is going bald. It's true, look at the photos. Meanwhile, his idiot brother has hair like a ginger bog brush. What's going on there?

Henry the Thirst
e-mail

I have never been a fan of U2 or Take That. Several years ago my two children bought a copy of U2's latest album and Take That's *Back for Good* single from our local HMV. What I said to them was this: "You two can take back U2 and Back for Good by Take That back for good and that." I still find this amusing. Do I win a fiver?

Bill Newton
e-mail

I have to disagree with Richard Karslake *(this page)*. This must be the shittest, most unconvincing fight ever. I know it's two girls, but for fuck's sake.

R Evans
Bridgend

TOP TIPS

SHOPPERS. When buying oranges, get more for your money by peeling them before taking them to the counter to be weighed.
Jason Orange
Manchester

US GOVERNMENT. Repay the millions of pounds, all the lives of British soldiers and the embarrassment of everyone supporting the US invasion of Iraq by increasing the cost of paperwork needed for UK citizens to visit your country for 6 months to $600, then make them wait half a day at immigration and treat them like shit. Underline the irony of the situation by repeatedly banging on about how the USA has no truer friend than Great Britain.
Diccon Cooper
e-mail

LEFT wing celebrities. When offered an OBE or similar gong, don't 'accept it begrudgingly', saying you disagree with system, but it is churlish to turn it down. Simply tell them to fuck off and keep your credibility.
T Thorne
Hexham

Jam Jarre

The Page that's Jam-Packed with Jam Facts, brought to you by synth wizard JEAN-MICHEL JARRE

JAM SPOTs

IF *someone tells you their car is being followed by a "jam sandwich", they don't mean they are being tailed by two slices of bread with a fruit preserve filling. That's because "jam sandwich" is another way of saying police car. However, in a bizarre twist, policemen refer to the jam sandwiches in their packed lunches as "police cars"!*

JAM *even gets a mention in the bible. In 1 Kings 6, verse 31, King Solomon makes some "jambs" out of olive wood. Yuk!*

WHEN *a jazz musician talks about a "jam session", he's not referring to a period of time spent eating jam. In fact, he means a sort of formless, overlong, drug-fuelled tuning up process which nobody in their right mind would want to listen to.*

DON'T *ask for jam in America, they won't know what you mean. That's because jam is called something else in America.*

UNLIKE *other sandwich fillings, such as marmalade (A dam lamer), marmite (Rat mime) and sandwich spread (Can add hers wisp), the word "jam" has no anagrams in the English language.*

QUESTIONS & JAMSWERS

WHAT *is the difference between jam and marmalade?* **asks** *Edward Gooch of Beaconsfield.*

"Well Edward, jam and marmalade are both fruit preserves. The difference is in how they are made. To make marmalade, oranges are cooked whole in water, then simmered in a lidded saucepan for several hours. When they are thoroughly softened, the oranges are removed and allowed to cool, before having their flesh and pips scooped out and placed in a small saucepan. Water is then added and the resulting mixture is simmered for about ten minutes. Meanwhile, the remaining orange peels are thinly sliced and placed in a preserving pan with the saved water from the saucepan, together with the juice and grated rind of some lemons. The simmered pith and pip mixture is then sieved and added to the preserving pan before the whole lot is brought to the boil. Sugar is added and the whole lot is boiled for ten or twenty minutes until setting point is reached. Then the mixture is allowed to stand for a further twenty minutes before being potted. Jam is made in a jam factory. I hope this answers your question."

Jean~Michel Jarre

PIPS TO THE POST: YOUR JAM LETTERS

A Sticky Moment!

I recently went out to buy a jar of raspberry jam, but the supermarket shelf was empty. The shopkeeper explained that the delivery lorry had been held up ... in a traffic JAM!!! When I finally stopped laughing I bought some lemon curd instead.

Mr F Renton
Penge

Top of the Charts!

My three favourite jams are; 1. Raspberry, 2. Blackberry, 3. Strawberry, in that order.

Mrs BTR Read
Welwyn Garden City

I must disagree with Mrs Read's letter *(above)*. In my opinion, the top three jams are apricot, blueberry and raspberry seedless. In future Mrs Read should check her facts before rushing into print.

Mike Scoltock
Sheffield

Jammy Dodge!

I recently tried to open a jam jar, but it was stuck tight. In the end I had to lodge the lid in a doorframe to get enough grip to loosen it. Imagine my amusement when my wife pointed out that I had "jammed the jam into the jamb".

Paul Weller
London

JEAN-MICHEL'S JAR-TOON TIME

SORRY I'M LATE. I GOT STUCK IN A JAM!
© Jean-Michel Jarre 2005.

Q. *What's a strawberry's favourite pop group?*
A. The Jam.
Mrs G Bishop, Knutsford

Q. *What sort of university course would some jam go on?*
A. A "sandwich" course.
T Poulson, Grantham

Q. *When is a door like something you keep jam in?*
A. When it's ajar. (A jar)
Mrs Hutton, Coalbrookdale

LAUGH JAM-BOREE

Q. *When is a door like the lid of a jam jar?*
A. When it keeps jamming. (Keeps jam in)
Mrs Hutton, Coalbrookdale

Q. *What is a guinea pig's favourite jam?*
A. Hamster jam. (Amsterdam)
Mrs Hutton, Coalbrookdale

JAMWORD

Across
1. Something you keep in a jar.
Down
1. Something you keep jam in.

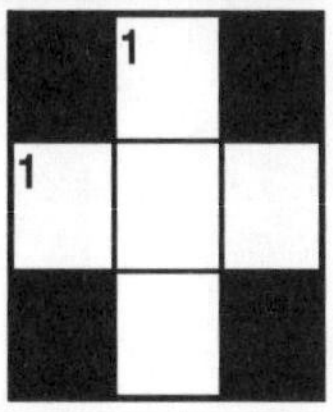
1
1

Answers: 1.Across. Jam. 1.Down. Jar.

THE VIZ ISSUE

THE world was gripped by the trial of ***Michael Jackson*** **and his dramatic let-off on child molestation charges. We were deluged with letters following the announcement of the verdict, so here we we give you a chance to voice your opinions...**

...so Michael Jackson is a free man – but for how long? I reckon it's just a matter of time before he is caught red-handed and put in prison for crimes I and many ordinary people imagine he has committed. The jury, confused by the facts, saw fit to ignore public opinion. Just because he is the most successful recording artist of all time doesn't mean he is above the law. Would the jury let Jackson look after their sons or daughters, knowing the filthy things he does in my head every day? I think not!

Polly Wannacracker, Stourbridge

...am I the only person to think that this trial was a farce? The jury should have found Jackson guilty regardless of the evidence. In serious cases where children are at risk, it's essential to find the accused guilty.

Richard Clog, Enderby

...they say that there is no smoke without fire. Well, tell that to the jury. If they saw the number of emails and humorous images I receive every day in which Michael Jackson commits paedophile acts, they'd have no hesitation in electrocuting him and throwing away the key. Surely it can't be right for a grown man to dance in a jerky way with a clipart baby, his cutout hand waggling over the child's groin? It seems that these days there's one rule for the politically correct, another for the gone mad!

Clarityn Tablet, Hornchurch

...while I now accept that Michael Jackson has done nothing wrong, is it wise to set him free to molest children should he decide to? If it had been me in the dock and not superstar Jackson, I'm sure the jury would have found me guilty, and I have never slept with an underage boy in my life. It's one law for the rich and another for the poor, as usual.

Gruber Paddington-Bear, North Shields

...initially I thought Michael Jackson was guilty and posed a risk to youngsters. But now that he has been found innocent by a jury of his peers, I would happily let him share a bed with my children.

Wainright Turdbridge, Spelter-upon-Lisk

...thank goodness the jury saw sense and acquitted Michael Jackson. The prosecution didn't bring forward one credible witness. The case hung on the evidence of a woman who was the kind of person who would let her children sleep with a suspected paedophile. How could they believe anything she said?

Renton Chimpanzee, Woking

...I was pleased Michael Jackson was acquitted, but I think he could have been a bit more grateful to the jury. A short medley of his greatest hits, and perhaps a little moonwalking across the judge's desk would have been a fitting 'thank you' for the verdict. But oh, no! He just skulked out without singing a single note.

Ingledew Botteril, Sutton-under-Buttocks

...the prosecution alleged that the only way Jackson's accusers could have described the characteristic marks on the underside of his penis was if they had seen him with an erection. Nonsense. There are many completely innocent explanations – perhaps he was performing a series of naked handstands or cartwheels for his young pals' amusement.

Genevieve Spartacus, Tunbridge Wells

...Jackson vowed after his trial that he would not sleep with any more youngsters. But if at some time in the future he finds himself again being tempted to share his bed with a schoolboy, a safe alternative that would avoid wagging tongues would be to invite septuagenarian cross-dresser Little Jimmy Krankie for a sleepover at Neverland.

Franklin Gothic, Font

OH NO... IT'S THOSE
PATHETIC SHARKS
NOV 5TH
HEY! I LOVE BONFIRE NIGHT!
ME TOO!..
...LET'S STICK A BANGER UP THIS CAT'S ARSE!
HERE, KITTY! KITTY! KITTY!
GOTCHA!
HE! HE! I'LL GET THE BANGER OUT...
WEEOW!
...THIS IS GOING TO BE MINT!
WHAT'S THAT?
SCRAPE!
PHEW! FRESH AIR AT LAST!
SHARKS!
SCREAM!
THAT'S THE LAST TIME I TAKE ONE OF YOUR SHORTCUTS... I'M ALL COVERED IN PLOPS... AND WEE
SO!?.. WEE IS STERILE ACTUALLY
YES, BUT PLOPS ISN'T! IT'S FULL OF GERMS!
WHAT ABOUT MANURE? THEY PUT THAT ON VEGETABLES AND YOU EAT THOSE
NO I DON'T...
...I HATE VEGETABLES!
YOU EAT TOMATOES
NO I DON'T. ANYWAY THEY'RE FRUITS
NONSENSE!
LOOK. ALL I'M SAYING IS I DON'T LIKE SWIMMING THROUGH PLOPS THAT'S ALL
ANYWAY, LET'S STOP ARGUING AND DO SOME SHOPPING...
...I THINK OXFORD STREET IS THIS WAY.
OOH, GOOD. I'VE GOT MY SHOPPING LIST
I THINK IT'S TOO EARLY TO DO CHRISTMAS SHOPPING. IT TAKES ALL THE FUN OUT OF IT
WELL I THINK IT'S SENSIBLE TO GET IT ALL DONE BEFORE THE MAD RUSH STARTS
HANG ON!.. IT'S ALRIGHT! THESE SHARKS ARE PANTS!... THEY'RE ABSOLUTELY PATHETIC!
Anyway, it's far too commercial these days. And it starts earlier each year
Well its my best time of the year. I've got my tree up already
I put mine up Christmas eve and not a day earlier
FIREWORKS
HEY, YOU'RE RIGHT!
I'M NOT HAVING A REAL TREE AGAIN. YOU'RE FOREVER SWEEPING UP NEEDLES
HEY, LOOK. FIREWORKS
WELL WHOEVER LEFT THE LID OFF THE BOX OUGHT TO BE ASHAMED OF THEMSELVES
THEY SHOULD BE IN A BISCUIT TIN WITH A TIGHT FITTING LID
LET'S LET THEM OFF! WE'LL HAVE A DISPLAY!
Not if you get a Norway fir. They never drop their needles.
You mean a NORDMAN fir
Show off!
HEY YOU TWO!.. FIREWORKS!
FIREWORKS! ARE THERE SPARKLERS?
I HOPE SO. I DON'T LIKE THE ONES THAT GO BANG!
WE SHOULD BE INDOORS ... THE FIREWORK CODE SAYS ANIMALS SHOULD BE KEPT INDOORS ON BONFIRE NIGHT
THAT DOESN'T MEAN WILD ANIMALS, THAT MEANS PETS. WE'RE NOT PETS
LET'S LIGHT THIS ONE...
MAKE SURE YOU READ THE INSTRUCTIONS FIRST
HERE'S A SPARKLER!
AND USE A TAPER...NOT MATCHES
YES... "MATCHES, MATCHES, NEVER TOUCH. THEY CAN HURT YOU VERY MUCH!"
ISN'T IT PRETTY?
YES, IT'S GORGEOUS!
LOOK!.. I'M WRITING MY NAME IN SPARKLER!
HEY, YOU LOT!.. DOES ONE OF YOU WANT TO DO A DEAD GOOD TRICK WITH SOME BANGERS?
YES! ME! ME! OOH, PLEASE! ME!
THAT'S NOT FAIR! YOU'RE ALWAYS FIRST
HEE! HEE! THIS IS GOING TO BE FANTACKA
SHORTLY...
WHAT DO I DO NOW?
FSSSS!
SSS!
FSSSSS!
BANG!
WELL I THINK IT NEEDS A PLASTER
NO! IT NEEDS TO BE BATHED IN T.C.P.
THAT'LL STING
YES, BUT IT ONLY STINGS BECAUSE IT'S DOING GOOD
GNNN!

ELTON JOHN'S DOLE FIDDLE

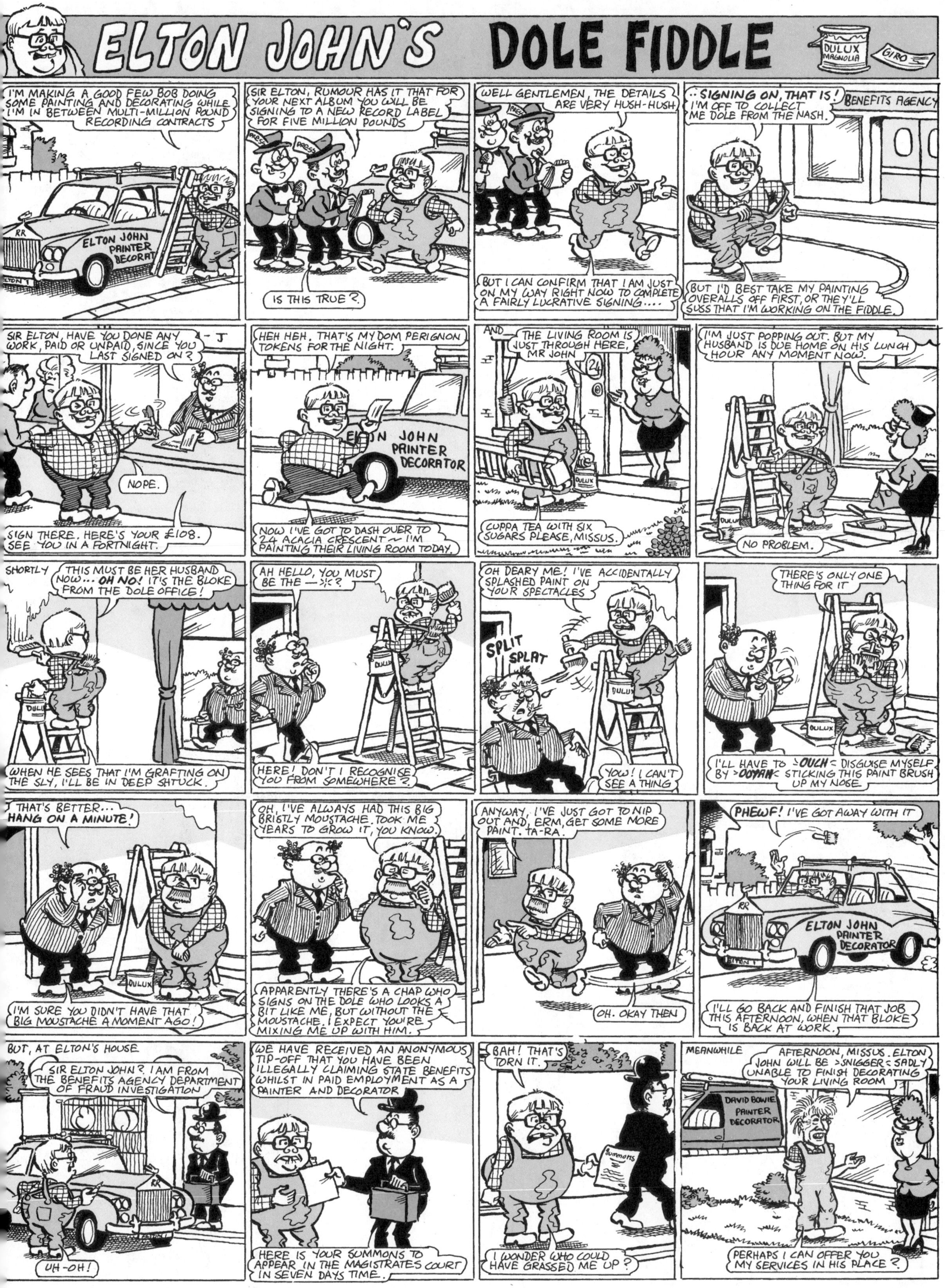
DULUX MAGNOLIA
GIRO
I'M MAKING A GOOD FEW BOB DOING SOME PAINTING AND DECORATING WHILE I'M IN BETWEEN MULTI-MILLION POUND RECORDING CONTRACTS
ELTON JOHN PAINTER DECORAT
SIR ELTON, RUMOUR HAS IT THAT FOR YOUR NEXT ALBUM YOU WILL BE SIGNING TO A NEW RECORD LABEL FOR FIVE MILLION POUNDS
PRESS
IS THIS TRUE?
WELL GENTLEMEN, THE DETAILS ARE VERY HUSH-HUSH
BUT I CAN CONFIRM THAT I AM JUST ON MY WAY RIGHT NOW TO COMPLETE A FAIRLY LUCRATIVE SIGNING....
..SIGNING ON, THAT IS! I'M OFF TO COLLECT ME DOLE FROM THE NASH.
BENEFITS AGENCY
BUT I'D BEST TAKE MY PAINTING OVERALLS OFF FIRST, OR THEY'LL SUSS THAT I'M WORKING ON THE FIDDLE.
SIR ELTON, HAVE YOU DONE ANY WORK, PAID OR UNPAID, SINCE YOU LAST SIGNED ON?
NOPE.
SIGN THERE. HERE'S YOUR £108. SEE YOU IN A FORTNIGHT.
HEH HEH. THAT'S MY DOM PERIGNON TOKENS FOR THE NIGHT.
ELTON JOHN PAINTER DECORATOR
NOW I'VE GOT TO DASH OVER TO 24 ACACIA CRESCENT ~ I'M PAINTING THEIR LIVING ROOM TODAY.
AND—
THE LIVING ROOM IS JUST THROUGH HERE, MR JOHN
24
CUPPA TEA WITH SIX SUGARS PLEASE, MISSUS.
DULUX
I'M JUST POPPING OUT. BUT MY HUSBAND IS DUE HOME ON HIS LUNCH HOUR ANY MOMENT NOW.
NO PROBLEM.
SHORTLY
THIS MUST BE HER HUSBAND NOW... OH NO! IT'S THE BLOKE FROM THE DOLE OFFICE!
WHEN HE SEES THAT I'M GRAFTING ON THE SLY, I'LL BE IN DEEP SHTUCK.
AH HELLO, YOU MUST BE THE —*?
HERE! DON'T I RECOGNISE YOU FROM SOMEWHERE?
OH DEARY ME! I'VE ACCIDENTALLY SPLASHED PAINT ON YOUR SPECTACLES
SPLIT SPLAT
YOW! I CAN'T SEE A THING
THERE'S ONLY ONE THING FOR IT
I'LL HAVE TO >OUCH< DISGUISE MYSELF BY >OOYAH< STICKING THIS PAINT BRUSH UP MY NOSE.
THAT'S BETTER... HANG ON A MINUTE!
I'M SURE YOU DIDN'T HAVE THAT BIG MOUSTACHE A MOMENT AGO!
OH, I'VE ALWAYS HAD THIS BIG BRISTLY MOUSTACHE. TOOK ME YEARS TO GROW IT, YOU KNOW.
APPARENTLY THERE'S A CHAP WHO SIGNS ON THE DOLE WHO LOOKS A BIT LIKE ME, BUT WITHOUT THE MOUSTACHE. I EXPECT YOU'RE MIXING ME UP WITH HIM.
ANYWAY, I'VE JUST GOT TO NIP OUT AND, ERM, GET SOME MORE PAINT. TA-RA.
OH. OKAY THEN
PHEWF! I'VE GOT AWAY WITH IT
ELTON JOHN PAINTER DECORATOR
I'LL GO BACK AND FINISH THAT JOB THIS AFTERNOON, WHEN THAT BLOKE IS BACK AT WORK.
BUT, AT ELTON'S HOUSE
SIR ELTON JOHN? I AM FROM THE BENEFITS AGENCY DEPARTMENT OF FRAUD INVESTIGATION
UH-OH!
WE HAVE RECEIVED AN ANONYMOUS TIP-OFF THAT YOU HAVE BEEN ILLEGALLY CLAIMING STATE BENEFITS WHILST IN PAID EMPLOYMENT AS A PAINTER AND DECORATOR
HERE IS YOUR SUMMONS TO APPEAR IN THE MAGISTRATES COURT IN SEVEN DAYS TIME.
BAH! THAT'S TORN IT.
SUMMONS
I WONDER WHO COULD HAVE GRASSED ME UP?
MEANWHILE
AFTERNOON, MISSUS. ELTON JOHN WILL BE >SNIGGER< SADLY UNABLE TO FINISH DECORATING YOUR LIVING ROOM
DAVID BOWIE PAINTER DECORATOR
PERHAPS I CAN OFFER YOU MY SERVICES IN HIS PLACE?

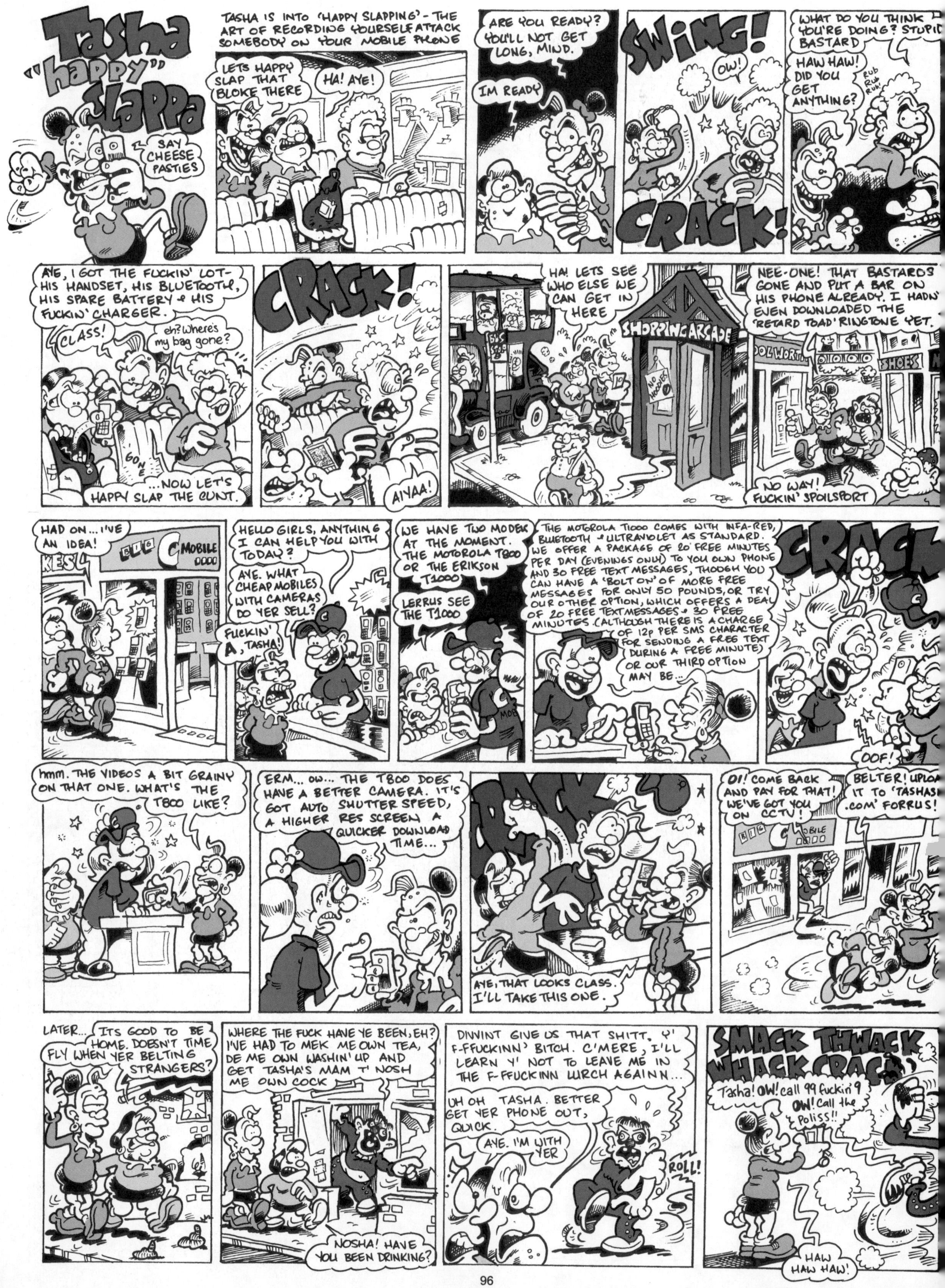

Tasha "happy" Slappa
SAY CHEESE PASTIES
TASHA IS INTO 'HAPPY SLAPPING' - THE ART OF RECORDING YOURSELF ATTACK SOMEBODY ON YOUR MOBILE PHONE
LETS HAPPY SLAP THAT BLOKE THERE
HA! AYE!
ARE YOU READY? YOU'LL NOT GET LONG, MIND.
IM READY
SWING!
OW!
CRACK!
WHAT DO YOU THINK YOU'RE DOING? STUPID BASTARD
HAW HAW! DID YOU GET ANYTHING?
Rub Rub Rub!
AYE, I GOT THE FUCKIN' LOT- HIS HANDSET, HIS BLUETOOTH, HIS SPARE BATTERY & HIS FUCKIN' CHARGER.
CLASS!
eh? Where's my bag gone?
GONE
...NOW LET'S HAPPY SLAP THE CUNT.
CRACK!
AIYAA!
HA! LETS SEE WHO ELSE WE CAN GET IN HERE
SHOPPING ARCADE
NO HOODIES
NEE-ONE! THAT BASTARDS GONE AND PUT A BAR ON HIS PHONE ALREADY. I HADN' EVEN DOWNLOADED THE 'RETARD TOAD' RINGTONE YET.
SHOES
NO WAY! FUCKIN' SPOILSPORT
HAD ON... I'VE AN IDEA!
BIG C MOBILE
HELLO GIRLS, ANYTHING I CAN HELP YOU WITH TODAY?
AYE. WHAT CHEAP MOBILES WITH CAMERAS DO YER SELL?
FUCKIN' A, TASHA!
WE HAVE TWO MODELS AT THE MOMENT. THE MOTOROLA T800 OR THE ERIKSON T1000
LERRUS SEE THE T1000
THE MOTOROLA T1000 COMES WITH INFA-RED, BLUETOOTH & ULTRAVIOLET AS STANDARD. WE OFFER A PACKAGE OF 20 FREE MINUTES PER DAY (EVENINGS ONLY) TO YOU OWN PHONE AND 30 FREE TEXT MESSAGES, THOUGH YOU CAN HAVE A 'BOLT ON' OF MORE FREE MESSAGES FOR ONLY 50 POUNDS, OR TRY OUR OTHER OPTION, WHICH OFFERS A DEAL OF 20 FREE TEXT MESSAGES & 30 FREE MINUTES. (ALTHOUGH THERE IS A CHARGE OF 12p PER SMS CHARACTER FOR SENDING A FREE TEXT DURING A FREE MINUTE) OR OUR THIRD OPTION MAY BE...
CRACK
OOF!
hmm. THE VIDEOS A BIT GRAINY ON THAT ONE. WHAT'S THE T800 LIKE?
ERM... OW... THE T800 DOES HAVE A BETTER CAMERA. IT'S GOT AUTO SHUTTER SPEED, A HIGHER RES SCREEN & QUICKER DOWNLOAD TIME...
CRACK
AYE, THAT LOOKS CLASS. I'LL TAKE THIS ONE.
OI! COME BACK AND PAY FOR THAT! WE'VE GOT YOU ON CCTV!
BELTER! UPLOAD IT TO 'TASHASH .COM' FORRUS!
LATER...
ITS GOOD TO BE HOME. DOESN'T TIME FLY WHEN YER BELTING STRANGERS?
WHERE THE FUCK HAVE YE BEEN, EH? I'VE HAD TO MEK ME OWN TEA, DE ME OWN WASHIN' UP AND GET TASHA'S MAM T' NOSH ME OWN COCK
NOSHA! HAVE YOU BEEN DRINKING?
DIVVINT GIVE US THAT SHITT, Y' F-FFUCKINN' BITCH. C'MERE, I'LL LEARN Y' NOT TO LEAVE ME IN THE F-FFUCKINN LURCH AGAINN...
UH OH TASHA. BETTER GET YER PHONE OUT, QUICK.
AYE. I'M WITH YER
ROLL!
SMACK THWACK WHACK CRACK
Tasha! OW! call 99 fuckin' 9 OW! Call the Poliss!!
HAW HAW HAW!

Bridge Over Jamiroquai

LIGHTWEIGHT pretend funkster Jay Kay was at the centre of a planning storm last night after the Highways Agency attempted to serve a compulsory purchase order on him.

By our Pop Correspondent
Trafford Lovething

Plans for the new A267 dual carriageway linking Deal and Colchester was given the go ahead by Essex Council's planning committee in April, despite the fact that it would have to pass straight through the be-tittered Jamiroquai frontman.

At a public enquiry, an application by the McAlpine group to compulsorily purchase and bulldoze Mr Kay was turned down following a successful appeal from the Sony record company. A spokesman said: "We argued that being flattened by a twelve ton demolition ball before being shovelled into a landfill site may have adversely affected Jay's musical career. Thankfully the committee saw sense and turned down the application."

flyover

However an ammended plan was approved. Essex County Council chief planning officer Mike Sausages told reporters: "McAlpine's secondary plan incorporated an eight foot high concrete flyover so the road could pass straight over the top of the 32-year-old star whose hits include *Virtual Insanity* and *When You Gonna Learn*."

Jay Kay yes-ter-day

But record chiefs are set to appeal once again in the hope of derailing the road scheme. A Sony spokesman said: "We believe we have a good chance of stopping the construction if we can convince the Minister of the Environment to declare Jay a Site of Special Scientific Interest."

Win a Luxury Weekend Break for Two in Jay Kay's Hat!

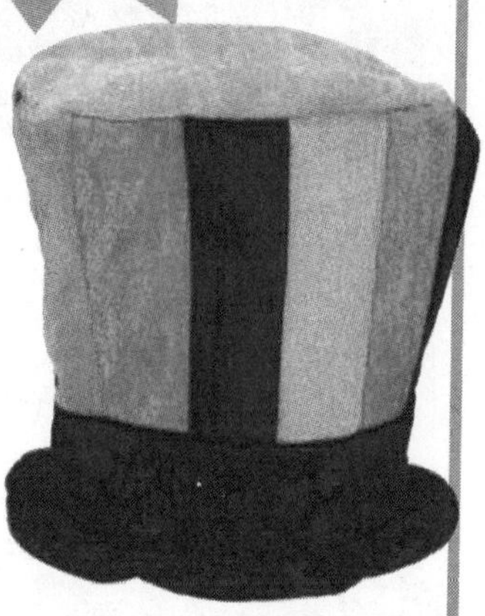

IN A MATTER of weeks Britain's most famous funk artiste could be standing directly underneath a monstrous concrete flyover. So this could be your last chance to enjoy a fantastic couple of days in the picturesque surroundings of his hat. We'll whisk the lucky winners off to Jay Kay, where they'll spend a relaxing weekend being pampered in his enormous luxury titfer.

For a chance to win, just answer this simple question:

What was the name of the now dead husband of the woman that Jay Kay's mother always used to do an impression of on Blankety Blank?

Send your entries to ***Jay Kay Holiday Competition, Viz, PO box 1PT, Newcastle upon Tyne, NE99 1PT****. Please mark your envelope "I know the name of the now dead husband of the woman that Jay Kay's mother always used to do an impression of on Blankety Blank. It's Bobby."*

The Bilderberg Group Shoe Warehouse's Unrepeatable Offer!

FREE* SHOES!

It's the footwear giveaway of the decade!

EVEN BETTER THAN A SALE!

Not *Half Price!* Not *Quarter Price!*
These shoes are *NO PRICE!*

PEOPLE say that there's no such thing as a free pair of shoes...well they are WRONG! Because we've got thousands to GIVE AWAY, and you won't pay A PENNY!

Thanks to a foreman inadvertantly pressing the 'fast' button on our shoe-making machine before going on a summer holiday, we've got millions of pairs of top quality, men's hand-stitched leather shoes in all sizes and styles. Our warehouse is so full that the roof is lifting off and as a result, all these shoes must be given away.

How do we do it? We simply don't know. All we do know is that these shoes are absolutely **FREE!** And to prove it, with every **FREE PAIR** you order, we'll send you another pair **ABSOLUTELY FREE!** What's more, there is no limit on the number of free pairs you can order.

IMPORTANT INFORMATION

REAL
LEATHER

The quality of these shoes are truely unbelievable. Stitched in the softest kid leather and with welted soles, these shoes rival the sort of shoes worn by kings and film stars and costing up to £1000 per pair.

Look at these testimonials:

"...I thought it sounded too good to be true, so I only sent off for one pair. They arrived the next day with no bill or anything. So I sent off for another 100 pairs," **Mr B, Essex**

"...I sent off for 1500 pairs of size 9 Blenheims, and they arrived by return of post. Nothing has happened yet, but I've got this awful feeling in the pit of my stomach that something will very soon." **Mr T, Hendon**

"...I don't get it. I've had 10,000 pairs of perfectly good shoes in my garage for a week, and I haven't paid a penny for them. I don't get it. I can't eat or sleep for worry." **J Francis, Luton**

"...I got 1200 free pairs of brogues, size 61/2 back in 1962, but I very quickly found the catch." **Lee Harvey Oswald, Dallas**

"...My 2000 pairs of shoes arrived two days after I ordered them, and my instructions about a week after that." **Sirhan Sirhan, Louisiana State Penetentiary**

"...These free shoes are great. Thanks!" **Barry Bulsara, Fulham**

The Irish Brogue
Brown/black
sizes 6~11
(inc 1/2 sizes)

The Blenheim
Brown/black/
oxblood
sizes 6~11

The Lake Palmer
black/beige/grey
sizes 6~11

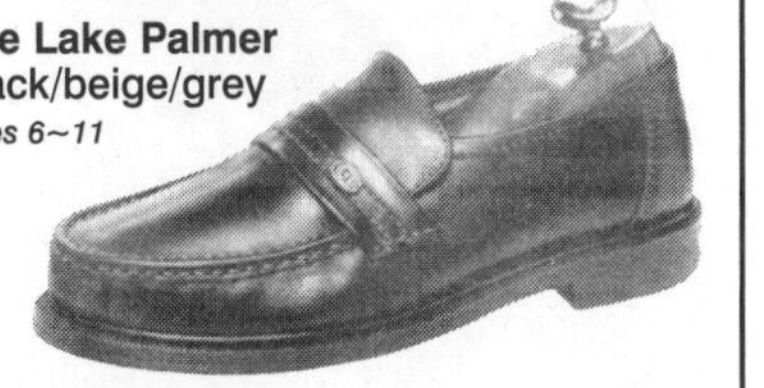

The Kensington
Black/brown/
blacky-brown/
browny-black
sizes 6~11

The Bilderberg Group Shoe Warehouse

Enter details below for your FREE shoes

Name.............................Address.......................
....
.... Post Code..........................

I have scoured this advert for some sort of catch, but I am fucked if I can find it. However, I am sure it will soon become apparent when you send me my free shoes. Signed..

**The Bilderberg Group Shoe Warehouse occasionally require their customers to carry out small favours in return for their free shoes. The more shoes you order, the bigger the favour that may be required. The Bilderberg Group does not tolerate failure or ingratitude.*

Post Coupon NOW without delay

Hot Pants!

Rocker Elton offers a cool million for space-age trunks

ROLY-POLY pop queen Elton John is offering a £1million prize for the first scientist to make him a pair of heat-proof swimming trunks. And it's all because the balding bumboy wants to be the first man in the world to go for a swim... *in liquid gold!*

KEXCLUSIVE!

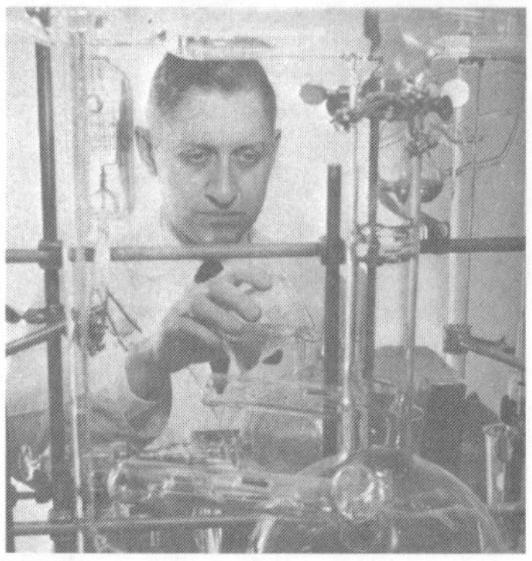

Trunk and disorderly ~ John (left) and (above) the shorts that fell short of his expectations. (far left) A scientist works round the clock on new heat proof bathing trunks.

Elton, 55, had a special £750million olympic sized pool installed in his Kent mansion filled with liquid gold intending to take a 24 carat luxury dip each morning before breakfast. But what he didn't realise was that to maintain its liquid state, the precious metal has to be kept piping hot - over **1000°centigrade** to be precise. That's enough to turn homosexual John, including his wig and big glasses, into a puff of smoke.

toe

A source told us that after having the pool installed, Elton went to try it out and lost the big toe of his right foot testing the termperature. "It's a good job he didn't just jump in off the top board. It would have been a case of Sir Elton Gone," the source added.

An advert placed in *Scientific American* and *New Scientist* offers the six figure purse to the first boffin to provide John with 'a pair of swimming trunks with a 46 inch waist, that can withstand an ambient temperature of at least 1064.18°c.'

A friend of the singer told reporters yesterday: "Elton is desperate for these trunks. He keeps standing on the side of his pool looking longingly at the molten gold, wishing he could jump in for a splash around. It's heartbreaking."

monster

But any budding boffin should take note; the famously fussy rocker is not prepared to take a dip in just any old pair of heatproof bathers. A team of material scientists from the Max Planck Institute department of thermophysics recently sent him a pair of teflon treated pyroplasticised microceramic trunks which they claim would withstand temperatures as high as 2265°c.

cattle

But John threw a four-letter tantrum on seeing them and refused to put them on. "They're f*cking swim shorts! That's so f*cking last year!" he is reported to have stormed. "They've got a f*cking drawsrtring waist! I want a f*cking swim-brief style with a f*cking elasticated waist and a f*ucking high thigh-line. Not this f*cking fashion disaster."

HALLELUJAH
IVAN JELICAL
PRAISE BE! TODAY IS THE FIRST DAY OF LENT
FOR IT IS WRITTEN - "AND JESUS WENT FORTH INTO THE WILDERNESS AND FASTED FOR FORTY DAYS AND FORTY NIGHTS, AND THOUGH THE DEVIL TEMPTED HIM, JESUS ATETH-ETH NOT". LUKE 29 VERSE 2.
A SINGLE GLASS OF WATER WILL BE ALL MY BODY NEEDS FOR THE NEXT FORTY DAYS AND NIGHTS
FOR I SHALL BE FED BY GOD'S LOVE, WHICH DROPPETH DOWN LIKE BREAD FROM HEAVEN. AND IT SHALL BE BUTTERED BY THE GRACE OF CHRIST JESUS, AND SPREAD WITH THE JAM OF THE HOLY SPIRIT
12 HOURS LATER
ANOTHER 12 HOURS LATER
RUMBLE
ANOTHER 12 HOURS LATER
HALLELUJAH! I HEAR THE VOICE OF GOD ~ AND HE SAYETH UNTO ME, "GO FORTH UNTO THE FRIDGE AND FEAST YE UPON THE THINGS WHICH ARE THERE."
"DO THIS IN REMEMBRANCE OF ME. FOR THOU ART MY BELOVED SON, AND WITH THEE I AM WELL PLEASED."
PRAISE THE LORD! I AM HIS FAITHFUL SERVANT, AND HE SHALL REWARD ME WITH HIS BOUNTEOUS GIFTS OF PLENTY.
"I WAS HUNGRY, AND YE GAVE ME FOOD; I WAS THIRSTY AND YE GAVE ME DRINK". ALOPECIA 13 VERSES 4-7
HMM.
EMPTY
MY HEART IS FILLED WITH JOY, FOR IT IS THE LORD'S WILL THAT I GO FORTH INTO THE WORLD AND SEEK OUT THE VENDERS OF FOOD
AND I SHALL SIT AT THE TABLES OF SINNERS AND BREAK BREAD WITH THEM, AND SPREAD THE GOOD NEWS OF THE WORD OF THE GOSPEL OF THE RISEN CHRIST

IT'S A MIRACLE! GOD HAS DELIVERED UNTO ME AN ALL-NIGHT CAFE
JOES CAFF
24 HOUR CAFE
I WONDER IF IT'S OPEN...
IT'S A MIRACLE! GOD LOOKED UPON THIS CAFE, AND LO HE MADE IT OPEN.
JOE'S CAFF
OPEN
I WONDER IF THE DOORHANDLE WORKS...
IT'S A MIRACLE!
JOE'S CAFF
OPEN
GLORY BE TO HOSANNA IN THE HIGHEST FOR HE HATH BLESSED ME THRICE BEFORE THE COCK HATH CREW.
I'LL HAVE THE ALL-DAY BREAKFAST PLEASE, BROTHER. YOU KNOW, JESUS IS A LITTLE BIT LIKE AN ALL-DAY BREAKFAST...
ALL DAY BREAKFAST —3.50 SAUSAGE EGG CHIPS —3
FOR HE IS NOT JUST AVAILABLE IN THE MORNING, BUT AT ANY TIME OF THE DAY, WHENEVER WE WANT HIM.
YOU WANT BLACK PUDDING WITH THAT?
BLACK PUDDING? BROTHER, DOES NOT THE SCRIPTURE TELL US...
"NEITHER SHALT THOU EAT THE BLOOD OF ANY CREATURE WHICH IS CLOVEN IN THE HOOF; NOR SHALT THOU EAT OF THE OWL OR THE PUMA; NOR SHALT THOU SHAVE THE BEARD OF THE OSSIFRAGE". GENITALS 7 VERSES 11-14
OK, OK, THAT'S ONE ALL-DAY BREAKFAST WITHOUT ANY BLACK PUDDING, OWL, PUMA OR OSSIFRAGE...
SUN TITS OF EVIL
...Y' FUCKIN' FRUITCAKE
SHORTLY
COUGH! CHOKE! GASP!
THAT MAN'S CHOKING ON SOMETHING
WHEEZE! GASP! CHOKE!
BRETHREN, DO NOT BE AFRAID! THIS MAN IS POSSESSED BY DEMONS
BUT IN GOD'S NAME I WILL CAST THEM OUT
CHOKE... GASP... ..WHEEZE..
I COMMAND THEE, O DEMONS, TO LEAVE THIS MAN! LEAVE HIM! LEAVE HIM! LEAVE HIM!
LE-E-E-E-AVE HIM
CHOKE.... GASP
HANG ON — I'LL TRY THE HEIMLICH MANOEUVRE
..TWO, THREE, PRESS TWO, THREE, PRESS
HURP! HURP!
I CAST THEE OUT, O SATAN, IN THE NAME OF ALMIGHTY GOD, KING OF KINGS
SAN-CTUS, DOM-INUS, LIN-CTUS, MINI-BUS..
URP!
WUP. THERE WE GO. A CHICKEN BONE, BY THE LOOKS OF IT.
PANT PANT PANT
DON'T THANK ME, BROTHER...
PANT PANT I AM BUT A CONDUIT THROUGH WHICH THE LORD PERFORMS HIS WONDROUS WORKS PANT PANT
SHORTLY
ONE ALL-DAY BREAKFAST. THAT'S THREE POUND FIFTY.
MY BROTHER, WHY DO YOU CONCERN YOURSELF WITH MONEY AND MATERIAL THINGS? CONSIDER THE LILIES OF THE FIELD — THEY NEITHER SOW NOR REAP.
NO, AND THEY DON'T COME IN HERE ORDERING ALL-DAY BREAKFASTS, EITHER. THREE POUND FIFTY.
"DO NOT LAY UP FOR YOURSELF TREASURES ON EARTH. FOR THE LOVE OF MONEY IS THE ROOT OF ALL EVIL". ZEBEDEE 7:16
ARE YOU GONNA PAY THIS BILL OR NOT?
TRULY, THOUGH I AM POOR IN EARTHLY THINGS, YET HAVE I RICHES IN MY HEART BEYOND COMPARE. LET ME PAY YOU IN LOVE, BROTHER.
KNEEL AND PRAY WITH ME. OPEN YOUR HEART TO JESUS, AND YOU TOO CAN SHARE IN THE WEALTH OF GOD'S LOVE WITH WHICH MY CUP OVERFLOWETH.
RIGHT. I'LL SHOW YOU HOW WE DEAL WITH BILL-DODGERS
SPANG
NON STICK
GLORY, GLORY. HALLE-OOYAH
ONE VICIOUS BEATING LATER
OH LORD, MY FAITH IS LIKE A MUSTARD SEED WHICH MOVETH MOUNTAINS. I KNOW THAT YOU HAVE NOT FORSAKEN ME
JOE'S CAFF — BACK DOOR
YET I AM SORELY TROUBLED, LORD, AND IN NEED OF THY GUIDANCE.
SHOW ME A SIGN, LORD
SHOW ME A SIGN THAT I MAY TAKE COMFORT FROM THY BOUNDLESS MERCY
SNIFF SNIFF
TSSSSSSSSS

Oliver's ARMY
LITTLE JAMIE OLIVER WAS THE LUCKIEST CHEF IN LONDON, FOR HIS UNCLE, AN ECCENTRIC INVENTOR, HAD MADE HIM A CATERING CORPS OF REMOTE CONTROL MINIATURE CHEFS...
ONE DAY...
COME ON, CHEFS... WE'VE GOT AN APPOINTMENT AT THE LOCAL PRIMARY SCHOOL
LEFT, RIGHT! LEFT, RIGHT!
BUT...
'ERE... WOT DO YOU WANT, EH, KID?
WE'VE COME TO SHOW THE DINNER LADIES HOW TO COOK DELICIOUS, NUTRITIOUS MEALS ALL FOR 37p PER HEAD
FULCHESTER PRIMARY SCHOOL
HENCH-MAN
OH, YEAH!?.. WELL, SORRY, KID... IT'S BEEN CANCELLED, OKAY
BUT WHAT ABOUT MY PUKKA GRUB?
THE 'EADMASTER CHANGED HIS MIND, ALRIGHT?. NOW SHOVE IT.
...AND TAKE YER CLOCKWORK COOKS WITH YOU!
COME ON, CHEFS
LOOKS LIKE WE'RE NOT WANTED
SUDDENLY...
MMF! MMF!
EH?. WHAT'S THAT?..
LIFT ME UP, CHEFS!
GAW, LUV A DUCK! THE OLD HEADMASTER'S BEEN TAKEN PRISONER BY NORFOLK TURKEY BARON MATTHEW BERNARDS!
OKAY, MUNGO, THAT'S THE HEADMASTER DEALT WITH... GO AND FETCH THE LORRY FULL OF TURKEY PIZZLERS AND TAKE THEM TO THE KITCHENS!
YUS, MASTER!
MMMF! PLMMF!
HEH! HEH! HEH!.. MY PLAN IS WORKING BOOTIFULLY!
SO THAT'S HIS GAME... HE WANTS TO GET THE KIDS HOOKED ON ALL THAT DISGUST-IN FATTY PROCESSED MULLARKY... GAW!
BY THE KITCHENS...
COME ON, CHEFS... WE'VE GOT TO STOP HIM...
...IN WE GO!
KITCHEN
RUBBISH CHUTE
GET THE PIZZLERS IN THE DEEP FAT FRYER, IGOR... THE CHILDREN WILL BE HERE FOR THEIR LUNCH ANY MINUTE
YUS, MASTER!
TURKEY PIZZLERS
TODAY TURKEY PIZZLERS
TODAY CHIPS
WE'VE GOT TO ACT FAST... SALAD SQUAD-RUN UP A BIT OF THE OLD VINAIGRETTE DRESSING... PASTA PATROL - I NEED A LOAD OF SPAGHETTI DONE 'AL DENTE'
MOVE! MOVE! MOVE!
THAT NEEDS A BIT MORE WHOLEGRAIN MUSTARD... AND QUICK - GET THAT LEMON SQUEEZED
COME ON!
AWAY YOU GO!
EH!?! WHAT THE..?
GLOOP!
TAKE THAT
VWOOSH!
CLUNK! DUNK!
RIGHT, PASTA CHEFS... GET GOING WITH THAT SPAGHETTI... BISH BOSH!
I SAY! GOOD SHOW, OLIVER!
SORTED!
GROAN!
THANKS TO YOU AND YOUR ROBOT ARMY, OUR KIDS HAVE BEEN SAVED FROM A LIFE OF OBESITY, HEART DISEASE AND VOMITING UP SEMI-FORMED FAECES!
THANKS, HEADMASTER... BUT IF YOU'LL EXCUSE ME, MY ARMY AND I HAVE GOT 250 NUTRITIOUS SCHOOL DINNERS TO PREPARE
SHORTLY...
THERE YOU GO, MY SON... BRAGADOCCIO CIABATTA WITH TOFU AND ROCKET PESTO! GET ON THE OUTSIDE OF THAT, WHY DON'TCHA!
THREE CHEERS FOR JAMIE!
CHRIST!.. I'M NOT EATING THIS!
IT LOOKS LIKE DO SHIT ON TOAST
I WANT TURKEY PIZZLERS LIKE AT HOME!
GIZ ONE OF YOUR DAIRY LEA LUNCHABLES!
FUCK OFF!

The Queen of Farts

Queen: Lit one of her farts

FIRE engines were called to Buckingham Palace last night after the Queen set fire to the curtains on her four-poster bed.

The blaze was swiftly brought under control and no-one was hurt, although her majesty and two friends, Queen Julianna of the Netherlands and Queen Noor of Belgium, were treated for smoke inhalation at the scene.

According to reports, the three monarchs had been having a sleepover when the incident happened. It is believed that the curtains caught fire when the Queen lit one of her farts with a match. The flames quickly spread to the canopy over the bed and the Queens were forced to take refuge on the balcony in their pyjamas.

A palace insider told reporters: "Their Royal Highnesses had been making a lot of noise all evening. Their giggling and shrieks of raucous laughter were keeping everybody awake. In fact, the footman had already had to go in two or three times to tell them to go to sleep at the time the blaze happened."

The Queen later apologised for all the trouble she'd caused, and praised firemen for their swift action. Reading from a prepared statement, she said: "I now realise that lighting my fart was a silly thing to do. It is only thanks to the quick-thinking and bravery of the emergency services that the consequences were not far worse."

This was the first time the Queen had had a sleepover since she was forbidden from holding them by her late mother. The last time the three European monarchs got together for a sleepover was at Windsor Castle in November 1992, when the resulting blaze caused damage estimated at over forty million pounds.

Windsor Castle: Blaze blamed on 'worker's blowtorch'

Who's the new Bond

MOVIE bosses have revealed the next James Bond, and fans are delighted - because it's going to be *Doctor Who!*

Old Bond, Moore and new Bond Who

Doctor Who will take over from Pierce Brosnan in the next 007 spectacular, which starts filming later this year. The timelord won the role against stiff competition from the usual suspects like Clive Owen and a footballer.

Have Your Say

TWO YEARS ago, trigger-happy farmer Tony Martin shot dead an intruder in his home and was convicted of manslaughter. Instead of a two year jail sentence, the tabloids believed he should have been given a medal. Every week, the papers are full of stories of burglars murdering innocent householders in their beds, so is it finally time to change the law? Is it time parliament gave us the green light to murder them first? We went on the street to find out what YOU think...

...I **BELIEVE** that an Englishman's home is his castle. As a consequence, I keep a cauldron of boiling oil by the bedroom window at night, and I wouldn't hesitate to tip it onto anybody trying to break into my house.

Peter Scott
dentist

...**BURGLARS** are vermin, and if I caught one burgling my house I would treat him like the vermin he was and hold his head in a cup of water.

Mike Cable
chiropodist

...**I AGREE** with Mr Cable that burglars are vermin. But they are still God's creatures, so if I caught one, I would drive him some distance from my house and let him go in some woods.

Frank Mozart
osteopath

...**I KEEP** a cricket bat by my bed in case a burglar breaks into my house during the night and throws a cricket ball at me.

Hector Strauss
trichologist

...**I AM** a barrister, and I have simply attached a set of terms and conditions to each door and window in my house. They state that 'any party or parties attempting to gain unlawful entry to these premises is likely to be attacked and/or killed as deemed necessary and in any way deemed necessary by the householder and/or his agents or appointees without redress, and that breaking into the premises constitutes full acceptance of these terms'.

Mike Mansfield
barrister

...**MY HEART** goes out to Tony Martin. Not only was he prosecuted for defending his home, but he had to spend two years in prison surrounded by burglars that he couldn't shoot. He must have felt like a kid with no money in a sweet shop.

J Wells
trichologist

...**HOME** owners often feel powerless to protect their homes, but allowing them to kill burglars is the thin end of the wedge. Perhaps the Home Secretary should look for a halfway house and take a leaf from the 'Carry On' team's book and allow the shooting of burglars with a blunderbuss. In Carry On Camping, Terry Scott gets shot in the buttocks with such a weapon and has to suffer the indignity of his wife extracting the pellets with tweezers. The removal of each pellet is accompanied by a swanee whistle noise, followed by a loud pop and a howl of pain. Surely, the thought of this happening would act as a deterent to any burglar.

T Rothwell
trichologist

...**MY WIFE** recently had the heart-stopping experience of waking up one night and coming face to face with a burglar on the stairs. She was absolutely hysterical until I calmed her down and reminded her that it was me, her husband Handy Andy off 'Changing Rooms'.

H Andy
odd job man

...**I STRONGLY** oppose the majority that thinks we should be allowed to shoot thieves. I work for a top London advertising agency, and it would look like the St Valentine's Day massacre in here every day.

Dickey Beasley
creative

...**IF IT** does ever become law that you can shoot people who steal things from you, then could the woman who wrote that short story about the cat, which ended up in one of Jeffrey Archer's books please get in touch. I would love to watch when she puts a cap in the lying bastard's thieving arse.

Steven Marbles
masseur

...**I DON'T** know what the world is coming to. A man can break into a pensioner's house, murder us with a baseball cap and get off with a slap on the wrist. Meanwhile, the innocent householder is sent to prison for burgling his own home. Eeeh! It's a disgrace.

Ada Brady,
grandmother

...**I OWN** my own home, and I recently broke into a prison to steal a television from a cell. Whilst in the process, I was attacked by an inmate who was serving two years for burglary. In order to defend myself, I had to use excessive force. The upshot of all this? The burglar was released, and I, a householder, was sentenced to six months in prison. What a topsy-turvy world we live in.

J Harper
dentist

...**I REGULARLY** shoot burglars, but I am never prosecuted. That's because I teach a human cannonball course at Risley Remand Centre.

Keith Stromboli
human cannonball

REASONABLE QUALITY JOKE

HAVE YOU GOT A MOMENT TO LOOK AT THESE WALLPAPER SAMPLES, DARLING?
NOT NOW DEAR. CAN'T YOU SEE I'M IN THE MIDDLE OF SOMETHING?

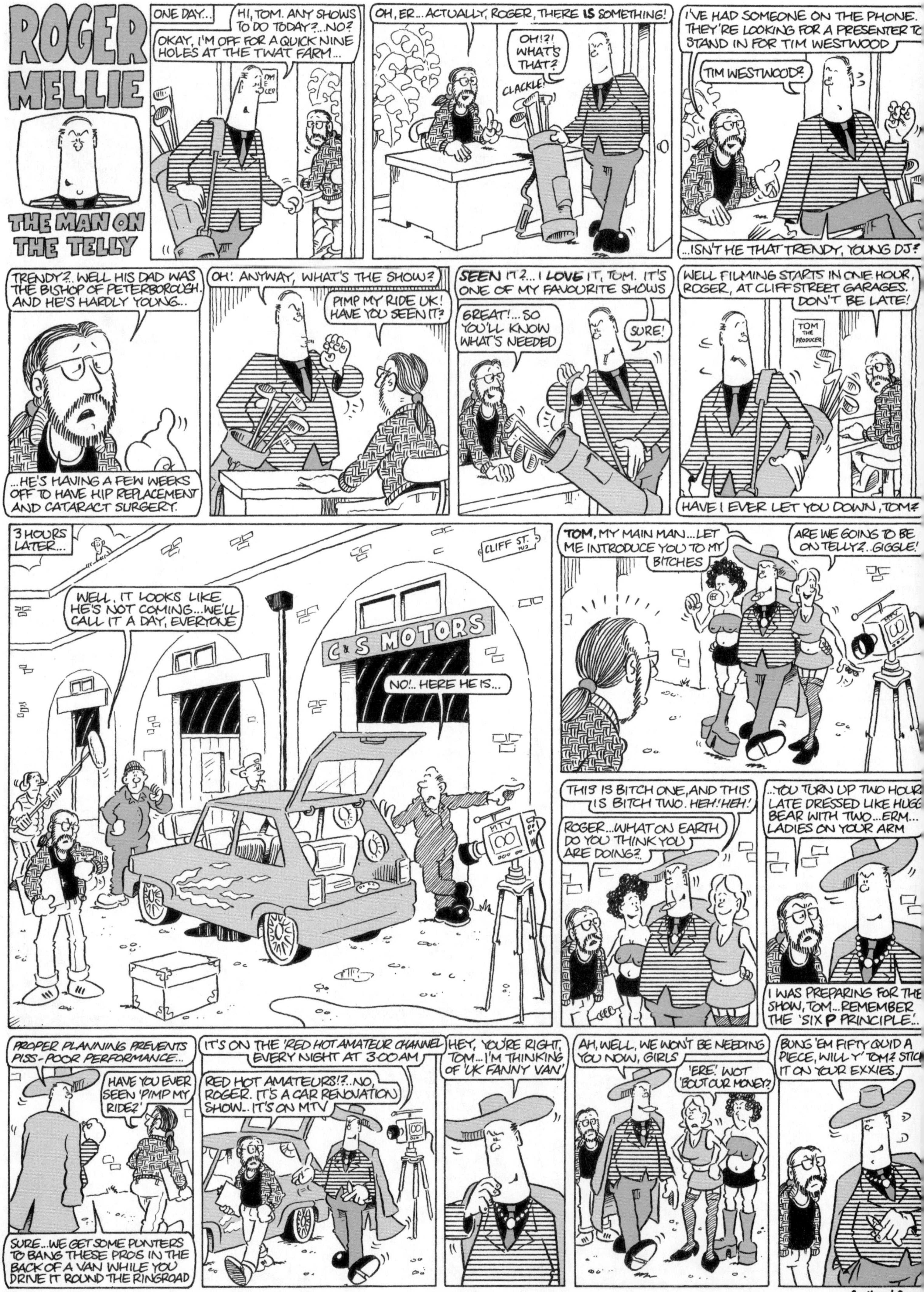
ROGER MELLIE
THE MAN ON THE TELLY
ONE DAY...
HI, TOM. ANY SHOWS TO DO TODAY?...NO?
OKAY, I'M OFF FOR A QUICK NINE HOLES AT THE TWAT FARM...
OH, ER... ACTUALLY, ROGER, THERE IS SOMETHING!
OH!?! WHAT'S THAT?
CLACKLE!
I'VE HAD SOMEONE ON THE PHONE. THEY'RE LOOKING FOR A PRESENTER TO STAND IN FOR TIM WESTWOOD
TIM WESTWOOD?
...ISN'T HE THAT TRENDY, YOUNG DJ?
TRENDY?.. WELL HIS DAD WAS THE BISHOP OF PETERBOROUGH. AND HE'S HARDLY YOUNG...
...HE'S HAVING A FEW WEEKS OFF TO HAVE HIP REPLACEMENT AND CATARACT SURGERY.
OH! ANYWAY, WHAT'S THE SHOW?
PIMP MY RIDE UK! HAVE YOU SEEN IT?
SEEN IT?... I LOVE IT, TOM. IT'S ONE OF MY FAVOURITE SHOWS
GREAT!... SO YOU'LL KNOW WHAT'S NEEDED
SURE!
WELL FILMING STARTS IN ONE HOUR, ROGER, AT CLIFF STREET GARAGES. DON'T BE LATE!
TOM THE PRODUCER
HAVE I EVER LET YOU DOWN, TOM?
3 HOURS LATER...
CLIFF ST.
WELL, IT LOOKS LIKE HE'S NOT COMING... WE'LL CALL IT A DAY, EVERYONE
C & S MOTORS
NO!.. HERE HE IS...
MTV
TOM, MY MAIN MAN... LET ME INTRODUCE YOU TO MY BITCHES
ARE WE GOING TO BE ON TELLY?.. GIGGLE!
THIS IS BITCH ONE, AND THIS IS BITCH TWO. HEH! HEH!
ROGER... WHAT ON EARTH DO YOU THINK YOU ARE DOING?
...YOU TURN UP TWO HOURS LATE DRESSED LIKE HUGGY BEAR WITH TWO... ERM... LADIES ON YOUR ARM
I WAS PREPARING FOR THE SHOW, TOM... REMEMBER THE 'SIX P PRINCIPLE'.
PROPER PLANNING PREVENTS PISS-POOR PERFORMANCE...
HAVE YOU EVER SEEN 'PIMP MY RIDE?'
SURE... WE GET SOME PUNTERS TO BANG THESE PROS IN THE BACK OF A VAN WHILE YOU DRIVE IT ROUND THE RINGROAD
IT'S ON THE 'RED HOT AMATEUR CHANNEL' EVERY NIGHT AT 3:00AM
RED HOT AMATEURS!?.. NO, ROGER. IT'S A CAR RENOVATION SHOW.. IT'S ON MTV
HEY, YOU'RE RIGHT, TOM... I'M THINKING OF 'UK FANNY VAN'
AH, WELL, WE WON'T BE NEEDING YOU NOW, GIRLS
'ERE! WOT 'BOUT OUR MONEY?
BUNG 'EM FIFTY QUID A PIECE, WILL Y' TOM? STICK IT ON YOUR EXXIES.

Continued Over..

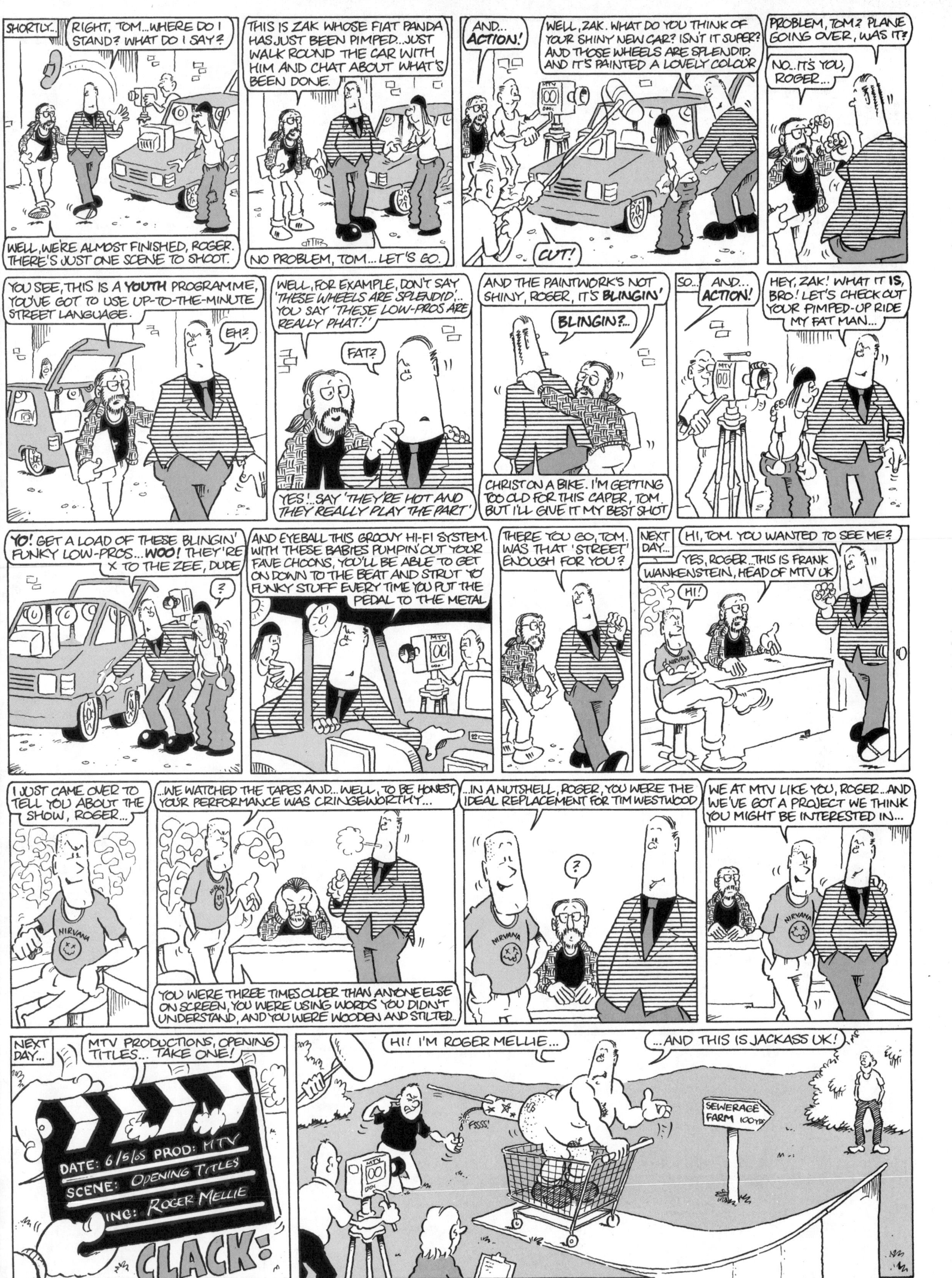
SHORTLY...
RIGHT, TOM... WHERE DO I STAND? WHAT DO I SAY?
WELL, WE'RE ALMOST FINISHED, ROGER. THERE'S JUST ONE SCENE TO SHOOT.
THIS IS ZAK WHOSE FIAT PANDA HAS JUST BEEN PIMPED... JUST WALK ROUND THE CAR WITH HIM AND CHAT ABOUT WHAT'S BEEN DONE.
NO PROBLEM, TOM... LET'S GO.
AND... ACTION!
WELL, ZAK. WHAT DO YOU THINK OF YOUR SHINY NEW CAR? ISN'T IT SUPER? AND THOSE WHEELS ARE SPLENDID. AND IT'S PAINTED A LOVELY COLOUR
CUT!
PROBLEM, TOM? PLANE GOING OVER, WAS IT?
NO... IT'S YOU, ROGER...
YOU SEE, THIS IS A YOUTH PROGRAMME, YOU'VE GOT TO USE UP-TO-THE-MINUTE STREET LANGUAGE.
EH?
WELL, FOR EXAMPLE, DON'T SAY 'THESE WHEELS ARE SPLENDID'... YOU SAY 'THESE LOW-PROS ARE REALLY PHAT!'
FAT?
YES!.. SAY 'THEY'RE HOT AND THEY REALLY PLAY THE PART'
AND THE PAINTWORK'S NOT SHINY, ROGER, IT'S BLINGIN'
BLINGIN?...
CHRIST ON A BIKE. I'M GETTING TOO OLD FOR THIS CAPER, TOM. BUT I'LL GIVE IT MY BEST SHOT
SO...
AND... ACTION!
HEY, ZAK! WHAT IT IS, BRO! LET'S CHECK OUT YOUR PIMPED-UP RIDE MY FAT MAN...
YO! GET A LOAD OF THESE BLINGIN' FUNKY LOW-PROS... WOO! THEY'RE X TO THE ZEE, DUDE
?
AND EYEBALL THIS GROOVY HI-FI SYSTEM. WITH THESE BABIES PUMPIN' OUT YOUR FAVE CHOONS, YOU'LL BE ABLE TO GET ON DOWN TO THE BEAT AND STRUT 'YO' FUNKY STUFF EVERY TIME YOU PUT THE PEDAL TO THE METAL
THERE YOU GO, TOM. WAS THAT 'STREET' ENOUGH FOR YOU?
NEXT DAY...
HI, TOM. YOU WANTED TO SEE ME?
YES, ROGER... THIS IS FRANK WANKENSTEIN, HEAD OF MTV UK
HI!
I JUST CAME OVER TO TELL YOU ABOUT THE SHOW, ROGER...
...WE WATCHED THE TAPES AND... WELL, TO BE HONEST, YOUR PERFORMANCE WAS CRINGEWORTHY...
YOU WERE THREE TIMES OLDER THAN ANYONE ELSE ON SCREEN, YOU WERE USING WORDS YOU DIDN'T UNDERSTAND, AND YOU WERE WOODEN AND STILTED...
...IN A NUTSHELL, ROGER, YOU WERE THE IDEAL REPLACEMENT FOR TIM WESTWOOD
?
WE AT MTV LIKE YOU, ROGER... AND WE'VE GOT A PROJECT WE THINK YOU MIGHT BE INTERESTED IN...
NEXT DAY...
MTV PRODUCTIONS, OPENING TITLES... TAKE ONE!
DATE: 6/5/05 PROD: MTV
SCENE: OPENING TITLES
ING: ROGER MELLIE
CLACK!
HI! I'M ROGER MELLIE...
...AND THIS IS JACKASS UK!
FSSSS!
SEWERAGE FARM 100YDS

ABRAHAM LINCOLN
THE TALL-HATTED 16TH PRESIDENT OF THE UNITED STATES
Gettysburg Address
Four Score and seven years
MARY-BETH, WHERE IN TARNATION IS MY BIG STOVE-PIPE HAT?
ABE LINCOLN
I WANT TO WEAR IT WHILE I DELIVER MY GETTYSBURG ADDRESS TODAY.
IT'S RIGHT HERE, ABE.
HOT DAMN! AIN'T THAT JUST THE TALLEST HAT YOU EVER CLAPPED EYES ON?
WHEN THE FOLKS AT GETTYSBURG GET A LOAD OF THIS, THEY'LL BE KNOCKED FLAT ON THEIR ASS.
SAY, LOOKEE THERE ABE. OUR NEW NEIGHBOURS ARE MOVING IN NEXT DOOR
FOR SALE SOLD
IT'S THE BRITISH INVENTOR ISAMBARD KINGDOM BRUNEL AND HIS WIFE
HOLY FREAKIN' SHIT! LOOK AT THE SIZE OF THAT GUY'S HAT!
IT MAKES MINE LOOK LIKE A GOD DAMNED MIDGET
LATER
NOW YOU STOP THIS MOPING AROUND, ABE LINCOLN. YOUR HAT IS PLENTY BIG ENOUGH, Y'HEAR?
THE GOOD FOLKS OF GETTYSBURG WON'T THINK ANY LESS OF YOU JUST BECAUSE MR BRUNEL'S HAT IS AN INCH OR SO TALLER.
DAGNABBIT, MARY-BETH, THAT AIN'T THE POINT! I'M THE GODDAM PRESIDENT, FER CHRISSAKES
AND I AIN'T GONNA STAND FER SOME CHICKENSHIT INVENTOR HAVING A TALLER HAT THAN MINE
AND
I'M JUST POPPING DOWN TO MY SHED, DEAR
I'M GOING TO INVENT THE GREAT EASTERN STEAMSHIP
THAT'S NICE LOVE
I'LL JUST WHUP A FEW INCHES OFF THAT LIMEY FAGGOT'S TOPPER
PROPERTY OF GEO. WASHINGTON
HEH HEH! I CANNOT TELL A LIE ~ I'M GONNA DO IT WITH GEORGE WASHINGTON'S LITTLE AXE.
SWIPE
CLANG
WHUT THE BLUE BLAZES-?!
B-B-BAH
THIS IRON FUNNEL WILL FIT MY STEAMSHIP NICELY.
LATER
RECKON I'LL CUT BRUNEL'S HAT DOWN TO SIZE WITH THIS JAR OF LI'L OLD MOTH LARVAS
INVENTING NEWS
YES SIRREE-BOB, THEY'LL EAT AWAY THE SILK FABRIC RIGHT DOWN TO THE GODDAM BRIM
HOLD ON ONE CONSARNED MINUTE! THIS AIN'T NO JAR OF MOTH LARVAS...
SILK WORMS
... THESE ARE SILKWORMS!
MOTHERFUCKER!
WEAVE WEAVE WEAVE
INVENTING NEWS
THE SILKWORMS HAVE WOVEN ANOTHER SIX INCHES ONTO HIS HAT!
SHORTLY
I'LL LEAVE MY HAT THERE WHILE I GO AND FETCH ANOTHER DRINK
NOW'S MY CHANCE! I'LL BURN IT TO DIDDLYSQUAT WITH HIS OWN CIGAR LIGHTER
YEE-HAW!
CRACKLE CRACKLE
I LOVE THE SMELL OF BURNING TIFTER IN THE MORNING
JESUS H. FUCKIN' CHRIST!
I'VE DONE SET FIRE TO MY ROOTIN' TOOTIN' BEARD!
DON'T WORRY MR LINCOLN — I'LL PUT YOUR BEARD OUT
SODA
SCOOSH
UGH!
WELP, I GOT A SOAKIN', BUT IT WAS WORTH IT
ONCE AGAIN I'VE GOT THE TALLEST HAT IN THESE HERE PARTS. YES SIRREE!
NOW I CAN GO AND DELIVER MY GETTYSBURG ADDRESS WITH MY HEAD HELD HIGH!
LAN' SAKES! THAT WATER IS MAKING ABE'S HAT SHRINK!
"FOUR SCORE AND SEVEN YEARS AGO OUR FATHERS BROUGHT FORTH ON THIS CONTINENT A NEW NATION..."
GETTYSBURG
SAY! WHAT IN THE SAM HILL ARE Y'ALL LAUGHING AT, Y'ALL?

Death of the Milkman

BRITAIN'S traditional randy milkman is set to become a thing of the past as demand for one of his doorstep services has slumped to an all time low. According to figures released this week, the number of scantily clad housewives demanding early morning sexual intercourse with their delivery of milk has declined tenfold in the last thirty years.

EXCLUSIVE!

Sid Hill, a spokesman for Carrion Dairies, one of Britain's biggest providers of early morning extra-marital romps told us: "Back in the halcyon days of the seventies, you couldn't walk down a street without seeing a negligee-clad bit of crumpet waving goodbye to a milkman as he staggered down the path covered in lipstick and with his collar rumpled and his hat askew. A typical milkman in these days would deliver a bit of slap and tickle to one housewife in three. These days he'd be lucky to get his leg over one or two suburban nymphos a week."

Under threat: Britain's traditional morning routine of slap 'n' tickle

The decline of the milkman's morning crumpet round has been linked to a reduction in the amount of sexual frustration felt by voluptuous, overbearing women. Hill continued: "A generation ago the average married man was a henpecked weakling with a little moustache and a cardigan. Sexually, he was unable to satisfy the needs and desires of his highly-sexed wife. Nowadays, thanks to gyms and viagra, he's far more likely to be able to keep her happy in the bedroom, which is bad news for our milkmen."

In fact, says Hill, the situation is so serious that Carrion Dairies has actually considered giving up providing door to door how's-your-father to its customers.

"It's a shame to see this traditional service go, but if the present trends continue, I can foresee the day when our employees are reduced to delivering just milk, cream and yoghurts."

Mrs Francis Batter, president of the Federation of Women's Institutes mourned the decline of the service but declared it was simply a sign of the times. "I remember the days when only the milkman and the window cleaner called while our hubbies were at the office," she told us. "These days, there are so many daytime callers that my members can't be expected to have hanky panky with all of them," she continued, before slipping into a fur-trimmed see-through nightie and asking if we'd mind coming upstairs to change a lightbulb in her bedroom.

COME ON HOUSEWIVES! FLOAT MY SKIN BOAT!

Dear Milkman,

Along with my milk, yoghurt and cream, please can you deliver...

- ❑ Saucy Romp
- ❑ Slap 'n' Tickle
- ❑ Ooh la-la!
- ❑ A bit of the other
- ❑ How's-your-father
- ❑ Vaginal penetration

VIZ

More Cream Please!

We're Backing Britain's Bonking Milkos

WE BELIEVE THAT PRIAPIC milkmen are just one more thing that makes Britain Great, and we don't want to see them go. That's why we are asking the nation's housewives to show a bit of bottle and back our campaign to save our bonking milkmen.

To join our campaign, simply cut out the bottle collar and order up your favourite sexual services. Then pop it round the neck of one of your empties after your hubby has gone to work.

LETTERBOCKS

Viz Comic, PO Box 656,
North Shields NE29 1BT
Email: letters@viz.co.uk

'12,000 people can't be wrong' say the makers of Pantene conditioner in their latest advert. What about the 12,000 that regularly used to turn up at Adolf Hitler's rallies?

Renton Pollard
Radcliffe

I recently witnessed a car accident involving a Vauxhall Nova and a Renault Clio. I was just about to run over and see if everyone was okay, but then I noticed that both of the drivers were wearing track suits and baseball caps.

L Granville
e-mail

I'VE just watched some kid on BBC *Newsround* doing a report about the launch of the new Harry Potter book. He sounded nervous, stumbled on one of his lines and lacked any real screen presence. Surely with so many presenters at their disposal, the BBC could send a more experienced and professional sounding journalist to cover such a big story.

Ciro Castaldo
London

'TONIGHT there's gonna be a jailbreak', sang Thin Lizzy in 1976, 'somewhere in this town'. Well, I'm guessing it's going to be at the prison.

Raymond Wankybollocks
e-mail

IS Spider-man the real hero? In *Spider-man 2,* Aunt May is being thrown around a huge skyscraper, only just being caught by Spider-man, and the very next day, she is smiling and having a jolly good giggle about things. Now *that's* heroic. My granny just saved herself from tripping over a kerb and managed to shit herself.

Danny
e-mail

YOU don't get many letters from Grantham, do you?

Mark
Grantham

CONGRATULATIONS to Seb Coe and his team for bringing the 2012 Olympics to these shores. One tip for any visiting marathon runners making their way through the East End - don't spend too much money on your footwear, or you might find yourself being held up at knifepoint for your new £80 Nikes like I was last Friday.

Andy Bryant
Bristol

I WAS part of the crowd that took part in the naked art installation in Newcas-tle recently. To be part of this conceptual art construct was truly a once-in-a-lifetime opportunity, but like most of the blokes I was there for the tits and bush. Sorry.

Duane
e-mail

THEY say that muscle is heavier than fat, but my husband weighs thirty stone and he doesn't look like a Mr Universe.

Mrs S Romagnoli
e-mail

I'M good looking, intelligent, well-off and fairly well-endowed, yet I was born in Middlesbrough. Do any other readers have similar 'impossible but true' stories?

Craig McManus
e-mail

'WE know the places you work' claim the benefit fraud squad. Funny that, because I poured a pint of Fosters for the nice lady who works at the dole office where I sign on, and she didn't give me a second glance.

John Smith
e-mail

I RECENTLY bought a fridge freezer from Currys, and after I had paid for it they asked me for my address to arrange delivery. I told them that I lived between Gateshead and Hexham, and if they rang me a week next Tuesday between 8am and 7pm, I night be able to give them a six hour slot when I would be able to take delivery. When they rang me, I told them that my house was out of stock and they should ring back on Saturday. The shoe's on the other foot now, isn't it, Currys?

DF Kant
e-mail

Star ★ Letter

★ **HAS anyone stopped to consider just how unlikely this whole lesbian sex business really is? I mean honestly - two women kissing passionately and rubbing their hands all over each other's soft, smoooth, naked bodies, tumbling around together on the eiderdown in a sensuous embrace and gently feeling their way to mutual ecstacy. That has to be a hoax up there with the Hitler diaries and crop circles.**

Brian Battenberg-Cake, Derbyshire

I HAVE been wondering whether the actors operating the Daleks in *Dr Who* have ever been tempted to 'bang one out' whilst safely encased in their own private booths, especially with Ms Piper cavorting around the set. I know I would.

Martin Osborn
e-mail

CONGRATULATIONS to the level-headed guard at Grays Station who fined my girlfriend who lost her season ticket travel pass in the confusion at Fenchurch Street Station following the London bombings. It was a relief to know that whilst others were concentrating on getting people home safely, she hadn't forgotten revenue streams.

Alex Palmer
e-mail

WERE you at the Minnack Theatre on 9th June watching *Pygmalion*? Were you that man who accidentally farted during the quiet bit of the play? If you are, this is to let you know that me and my wife are still pissing ourselves laughing.

Alan and Sandra
Westbury

I JUST bought some pills designed to make men last longer in bed, and I'm delighted to say that they really work - this morning I didn't wake up until 11.30. Mind you, the wife didn't seem too pleased, although I can't see what her problem is. If I'm asleep, she has more time to watch women's TV and shop for clothes, not to mention the housework.

Alan Heath
e-mail

AS I write this letter, I am being fellated by a major Hollywood star. Obviously, I wouldn't be so indiscreet as to name them.

Reg Spennythwaite
Cheadle

TOP TIPS

MINIMISE the chance of stepping in canine pavement deposits when it's too dark to see by taking full length strides with every pace.

Trev, e-mail

McDONALD'S. Save money on glass by not building a 'window number 1' in your drive throughs as there is invariably never anybody there.

M. B. Lloyd, Fawdon

SKATEBOARDERS. When buying trousers, choose a pair which stop around about your ankles as opposed to some point about 10 inches further on.

Ben Keen, Whitley Bay

LADIES. When treating genital thrush, always ensure you use natural bio-yoghurt and not raspberry flavoured Munch Bunch.

Lee Henman, e-mail

SKATEBOARDERS. Stop your trousers from falling halfway down your arse by wearing a strip of perforated leather with a buckle around your waist.

Lee Christopher, e-mail

IOW about this feeble soap unch I recently spotted in the *nternational Herald Tribune?* orry, come to think of it, it as in *Soaplife* magazine.

W Lothian
Gateshead

IEY, I spotted it first.

Andrew Tait
Newcastle

WONDER what curly-aired nineties crooner Michael Bolton is up to these ays. Very little I expect. Ie's probably sat on his big, hestnut-tanned backside aking in loads of money n royalties for doing cock ll. I never had much time or the man or his so-called nusic, so I'm glad he's no onger in the limelight. But he thought of him sat on a olden toilet, knocking one out into a silk hankie, then oing for another round of golf while the rest of us have to work for a living makes my fucking blood boil.

Mathias Octopuss
email

MY friend Andy Chamberlain has just got two puppies and has called them Titian and Balthus. I believe these to be the most pretentious names ever given to dogs. Can any of your readers beat that?

R. Fotherington-Smythe
e-mail

UP THE ARSE CORNER

More from Up the Arse Corner on page 134

HAVE YOUR SAY...

With the publication of her sixth book *Harry Potter and the Half Blood Prince,* JK Rowling officially became the richest woman in Britain - richer even than Her Majesty the Queen. And our postbag has been full to bursting with letters telling us exactly what YOU thought about the matter. Here's a selection of some of the vitriol we received...

...I READ with despair that so-called author JK Rowling has more money than Her Majesty the Queen. I find that disgusting. After serving her country by selflessly reigning over it for fifty years, is this how we repay her - by making her play second financial fiddle to someone who writes fairy stories?

Edna Patriot, Kent

...JK ROWLING with more money than the Queen? Is that what my husband died in the war for? It's probably a good thing he did die, because if he had lived to see this day he would be turning in his grave.

Doris Britannia, Berkshire

...A single mother the richest woman in Britain? What an example to set the young folk today. No wonder all kids these days are turning to drugs and gayness.

Ada Bigot, Tewksbury

...My heart breaks for the Queen. JK Rowling should be made to give the Queen a million pounds a week until Her Majesty is back in her rightful place as the richest woman in Britain.

Dolly Pomp, Croydon

...It is so unfair that this woman should have more money than the Queen. Any Tom, Dick or Harry can write a children's book, but it takes a certain, special something to be born a princess - something few of us could achieve even if we tried for a thousand years.

Irene Majestic, London

...I fear we will become the laughing stock of the world, having someone richer than our Queen. The Government should either take half of Ms Rowling's money off her and give it to Her Majesty, or else crown the woman Queen JK I of England.

Hector Margold, Cheam

...JK Rowling was not born into that kind of money, and she will have no idea how to spend it wisely. Like the worst kind of lottery winner, she will splash out on gaudy jewellery, flashy houses and expensive cars. The Queen, however, who has known nothing but opulence all her life would buy tasteful diamond encrusted crowns, palatial stately homes and royal yachts.

Doreen Poison, London

...When a drunken tramp broke into the Queen's bedroom and felt her tits in 1981, she reacted with great dignity, in a calm, stately manner. Now JK Rowling is the richest woman in the world, let's hope that, should the same thing happen to her, he doesn't let her country down and acts with similar aplomb.

Mavis Angina, Swindon

...Her Majesty costs each of us a mere 61p per year. The latest Harry Potter book on the other hand costs a whopping £12.99. No wonder she's richer than the Queen. Parliament should pass a law forcing her to drop the price of her books to 61p, then we'd soon see who was the richer.

Ida Gangrene, Hull

...I'm not a royalist, but I wept openly when I heard that the Queen had less money than JK Rowling. I sold everything I owned, including my wedding ring, furniture and clothes, and sent her the proceeds. I received a nice letter from her secretary thanking me for the money, but stating that unfortunately it wasn't enough. Can I urge everyone to sell everything they have and send the money to Buckingham Palace? If we all pull together, like we did during the war, we can make Her Majesty the top of the heap once more.

Edna Hypothermia, Luton

...JK Rowling may have overtaken the Queen in the rich list, but I say hats off to her. She works very hard, travelling the country doing signings in bookshops and shopping centres. Perhaps if Her Majesty embarked on a tour of Post Offices, signing stamps and banknotes, she would make a few more sales and improve her position in the wealth charts.

Una Beelzebub, Torquay

...Parliament should pass a law making it illegal to have more money that the Queen as she does the most difficult and demanding job in the country. I'm not exactly sure what's difficult or demanding about waving out of a Rolls Royce, or being given a racehorse by the Sultan of Brunei, but it can't be as easy as it looks.

Gladys Emphasema, Rhyll

...JK Rowling should be ashamed of herself. She says her books are original, but the vast majority of the words are copied out of the dictionary - she just jumbles them up in a different order. It's plagarism at its worst. The Queen on the other hand doesn't copy any other Queen.

Phyllis Thrombosis, Brighton

TV Miseryguts Victor Meldrew's
Amazing World of Foliage

I don't be-LEAVES it!

• WHEN APOLLO 12 astronaut Al Bean stepped onto the lunar surface in 1969 he was amazed to see hundreds of leaves blowing about in the solar wind. Baffled NASA scientists could offer no theory as to how the leaves had reached the moon, over a quarter of a million miles from the nearest tree. The most likely explanation is that they had been cast up into space when a meteorite hit a tree on earth back in dinosaur times. The crew of the next lunar mission, Apollo 13, carried rakes and a wheelbarrow but due to an accident just after launch they were unable to carry out their plan to have a bonfire on the moon. *I don't be-leaf it!*

• THE LEAVES of the Giant Waterlily (*Victoria regia*) are so strong that they can sometimes support the weight of a fully grown man. Crowds at the opening of Kew Gardens in 1852 were amazed when Prince Albert leapt from the dais and landed squarely on a lily pad floating in the great Palm House pond. Unfortunately, the weight of the German pervert's penis jewellery - a large iron dumbell piercing his glans and attached to his scrotum with a heavy chain - proved too much for the leaf to support, and the Prince consort sank uncermoniously into the water. Needless to say his wife Queen Victoria was not amused. *I don't be-leaf it!*

• LEAVES MAY be small, green and flat, but botanists believe that inside they are just like a human body. Like a person, a leaf breathes, grows and eats. Even more amazingly, it even goes to the toilet! But unlike people leaves don't have meals of food as we understand it. Every leaf - and there can be hundreds on a single tree - tucks in to a meal of carbon dioxide and sunlight before shitting out oxygen. So remember, next time you take a breath of air, chances are it's come out of a leaf's arse. *I don't be-leaf it!*

GOLDFISH BOY
AFTER LOSING HIS PARENTS IN A BIZARRE FAIRGROUND ACCIDENT, YOUNG JOHNNY JOHNSON WAS TAKEN IN AND RAISED BY KINDLY GOLDFISH ON THE HOOK-A-DUCK STALL. AFTER SEVERAL YEARS HE HAD BEEN WON BY FATHER BROWN THE LOCAL VICAR, WITH WHOM HE NOW LIVED.
DECEMBER 20TH...
DO NOT BE AFRAID, FOR I BRING GLAD TIDINGS OF GREAT JOY FOR YOU AND ALL MANKIND...
BARNTON-ON-THE-WATER PARISH CHURCH NATIVITY PLAY TOMORROW 5 p.m. TICKETS 10p. REHEARSALS NOW IN PROGRESS KEEP OUT!
I'M SORRY FATHER BROWN. I'VE FORGOTTEN THE NEXT BIT
OH, FOR GOD'S SAKE, BOY..! "TO YOU IN DAVID'S TOWN THIS DAY IS BORN A CHILD WHO IS CHRIST THE LORD"
NOW, FATHER, DON'T TAKE THE LORD'S NAME IN VAIN
TO YOU IN... DAVID'S... DAVID'S... TO YOU IN DAVID'S
...HOW DOES IT GO, AGAIN?
OH, DEAR, FATHER. THE BABY JESUS'S HEAD'S FALLEN OFF
OH, CHRIST ALMIGHTY!
HAVING A FEW PROBLEMS, ARE WE, FATHER?
FATHER O'SHAUGHNESSY! DO YOU MIND? THIS IS A PRIVATE REHEARSAL!
WELL, WE'VE JUST FINISHED THE FINAL DRESS REHEARSAL FOR THE NATIVITY AT SAINT PATRICK'S. I THOUGHT I'D JUST POP IN AND CHECK OUT THE PROTESTANT OPPOSITION...
...NOT GOING TOO WELL BY THE LOOK OF THINGS
IT'S GOING FINE THANK YOU. WE'LL SELL MORE TICKETS THAN YOUR LOT THIS YEAR
WITH THE WIDOW ERNSHAW AS THE VIRGIN MARY AGAIN? PULL THE OTHER ONE, BROWN, IT'S GOT CHURCH BELLS ON IT
WHAT'S WRONG WITH THE WIDOW ERNSHAW?
WELL, CASTING HER AS A YOUNG VIRGIN IS STRETCHING THE CREDULITY OF YOUR PARISHIONERS A TAD, DON'T YOU THINK?
THAT'S A BIT RICH COMING FROM YOU, O'SHAUSNESSY. FROM WHAT I HEAR, YOUR VIRGIN DOESN'T NEED A DONKEY SO MUCH AS A ZIMMER FRAME
WHAT ARE YOU TALKING ABOUT, BROWN
YOUR HOUSEKEEPER, MRS. MAGUIRE. SHE MUST BE IN HER FORTIETH YEAR IN THE ROLE. SHE'S BEEN GOING LONGER THAN THE MOUSETRAP
OH, NO. I HAD TO LET MRS. MAGUIRE GO. I CAUGHT HER WITH HER FINGERS IN THE COLLECTION PLATE
...SHE'LL BE TAKING THE PART OF THE HOLY MOTHER THIS YEAR
THIS IS MY NEW HOUSEKEEPER, SHINADE...
SHE'S VERY GOOD, YOU KNOW. SHE WAS MISS KILKENNY 2004, AND SHE'S NO STRANGER TO THE STAGE...
...SHE HAD A WALK-ON PART IN BALLYKISSANGEL DIDN'T YOU, MY DEAR?
YES, FATHER O'SHAUGHNESSY
ANYWAY, I MUST BE GETTING HOME. I MAY POP OVER TOMORROW TO BORROW SOME OF YOUR EMPTY PEWS, ONLY WE'RE EXPECTING QUITE A CROWD OVER AT SAINT PATRICK'S
LATER...
THE TROUBLE IS, GOLDFISH BOY, FATHER O'SHAUGHNESSY'S RIGHT. THE BEAD-JIGGLING BUGGER IS GOING TO PULL THE CROWDS TOMORROW WITH THAT CRACKING BIT OF CATHOLIC CRUMPET HE'S GOT IN THE LEAD ROLE...
...AND WHO HAVE WE GOT PLAYING OUR CHASTE VIRGIN? SOMEONE WITH MORE CANDLES ON HER CAKE THAN METHUSELAH
AH, WELL. NO GOOD WORRYING ABOUT IT. I'LL JUST SETTLE BACK AND WATCH EUROTRASH...
CLICK!
...THERE'S AN ITEM ABOUT PAGE THREE MODEL CANDY WONDERBRA. SHE REALLY RENOVATES MY BELLTOWER, I CAN TELL YOU, GOLDFISH BOY
'ELLO, MY EENGLEESH CHUMS. AND TONIGHT, NEWS OF CANDEE WONDAIRBRA, 'OO AS QUEET THE CEETY AND GONE TO LEEVE IN THE LEETLE EENGLEESH VILLAGE OF BARNTON ON ZE WATER...
WHAT!?! DID YOU HEAR THAT, GOLDFISH BOY? CANDY WONDERBRA IS COMING TO LIVE IN OUR VILLAGE!
MY GOD! THERE SHE IS! SHE'S MOVING INTO THE COTTAGE ACROSS THE ROAD...
PHWOAR!
DO YOU KNOW, GOLDFISH BOY, I THINK MY PRAYERS HAVE BEEN ANSWERED. AND I HAVEN'T EVEN SAID THEM YET
DING! DONG!
OH, SOMEONE AT THE DOOR. I WONDER IF IT'S MY AGENT WITH ANOTHER LUCRATIVE LINGERIE MODELLING CONTRACT
HELLO
HELLO, MISS WONDERBRA. I COULDN'T HELP NOTICING THAT YOU HAD MOVED IN, AND I THOUGHT I'D POP OUT... I MEAN POP OVER AND WELCOME YOU TO OUR PAIR OF... I MEAN PARISH
THANK YOU, VICAR. DO COME IN A HAVE A CUP OF TEA

ACTUALLY, MISS WONDERBRA, I DO ADMIT THAT I HAVE A POSTERIOR – I MEAN ULTERIOR – MOTIVE FOR MY VISIT
OH YES, VICAR? WHAT IS THAT?
WELL, WE HAVE THE ANNUAL NATIVITY PLAY TOMORROW, AND IT WOULD BE A GREAT HONOUR FOR THE PARISH IF YOU WOULD PLAY THE PART OF THE VIRGIN MAMMARY... I MEAN TITS... MARY THE VIRGIN MARY
WHY, VICAR, I'D BE DELIGHTED
WHY THAT'S SPLENDID NEWS. I'LL SET TO GETTING SOME POSTERS RUN OFF...
...HAVE YOU GOT ANY PUBLICITY PHOTOS I COULD USE?
BARNTON-ON-THE-WATER PARISH CHURCH
TODAY
STARRING PAGE 3 STUNNA
CANDY WONDERBRA
(38DD)
TICKETS - STALLS £10 each
SNIFFERS' ROW £20
BUT FATHER BROWN, I'VE PLAYED MARY FOR THE PAST THIRTY YEARS
YES, WELL I'M SORRY, WIDOW ERNSHAW, BUT THAT'S SHOW BUSINESS, I'M AFRAID. IT'S ALL ABOUT BUMS ON PEWS...
...THIS GIRL IS STACKED. HER ASSETS ARE BOX OFFICE DYNAMITE. FATHER O'SHAUGHNESSY IS GOING TO BE PLAYING TO AN EMPTY HOUSE OF GOD THIS AFTERNOON, I CAN TELL YOU
THAT AFTERNOON...
LOOK, GOLDFISH BOY. PACKED TO THE RAFTERS. WE'VE TAKEN NEARLY TWO GRAND. ALL THANKS TO CANDY
MISS WONDERBRA. HOW LOVELY TO SEE YOU BOTH
I'M SORRY, NO MEMBERS OF THE PUBLIC BACKSTAGE. CANDY WILL BE SIGNING PUBLICITY PHOTOGRAPHS LATER. COME ON - OUT YOU GO
SORRY, SQUIRE, YOU DON'T UNDERSTAND. I'M MISS WONDERBRA'S AGENT. I'VE COME TO COLLECT HER FEE
F... F... F... FEE? WHAT FEE?
HER APPEARANCE FEE, VICAR. EIGHTY GRAND. FORTY UP FRONT, THE OTHER FORTY AFTER THE SHOW...
...CASH!
BUT... NOBODY MENTIONED MONEY. I... I THOUGHT SHE WAS DOING THIS FOR FREE
FREE!?! MISS WONDERBRA DOESN'T GET OUT OF BED FOR LESS THAN TEN GRAND. PLUS SEVENTY FOR A P.A. LIKE THIS, THAT'S YOUR EIGHTY GRAND
BUT I HAVEN'T GOT EIGHTY THOUSAND POUNDS. I'VE ONLY TAKEN TWO THOUSAND ON THE DOOR
TWO THOUSAND? WELL, YOU'RE IN LUCK. THAT JUST COVERS YOUR CANCELLATION FEE
COME ON, CANDY. BACK TO BED. YOU'VE GOT TO BE UP EARLY IN THE MORNING. YOU'RE DOING A GIRL ON GIRL SPREAD FOR 'NUTS' TOMORROW...
...THEN ONE FOR 'ZOO' IN THE AFTERNOON
WE WANT CANDY! WE WANT CANDY! WE WANT CANDY!
OH, LORD. WHAT ARE WE GOING TO DO, GOLDFISH BOY? THE CROWD ARE TURNING UGLY, AND I CAN'T GIVE THEM THEIR MONEY BACK...
THERE'S NOTHING ELSE FOR IT. I'M GOING TO HAVE TO PRAY FOR INSPIRATION...
SHORTLY...
DO NOT BE AFRAID, FOR I BRING GLAD TIDINGS OF GREAT JOY FOR YOU AND ALL MANKIND...
...ERM, I'M SORRY FATHER BROWN, I'VE FORGOTTEN THE NEXT BIT
BOOO!
WHAT A LOAD OF RUBBISH!
LET'S GO TO SAINT PATRICK'S. THEIR MARY'S A CRACKER
BW
THE END

BIFFA BACON
LOVE
HATE
4.a.m...
zZZZzzzZZ!
zzZZZZZZZZz!
BLAM! BLAM!
EH!?!
...WASSAFUCK!?....
BOOT!
NEEBODY MOVE... IT'S THE BIZZIES!
MUTHA!.. FATHA. WOT THE FUCK'S GANNIN' ON?
IT'S WPC MUTHA, AN SERGEANT FATHA T' YEE, SUNSHINE...
AYE!
WUZ'VE JOINED THE FUCKIN' POLISS!
THAT'S REET... WUZ'RE THE FILTH NOO, BIFFA... AN' WUZ'VE GOT A WARRANT T' SORCH YOUR BEDROOM
EH?
SORCH WARRANT
WOT THE FUCK FAWA?
WUZ'VE BIN TIPPED OFF THAT YEES GOT SOME CLASS 'A' DRUGS 'ERE
AYE ! FUCK MAN
AYE!... WUZ'LL SEE, SON
WELL, Y' CAN SORCH AALL Y' LIKE... I'M GANNIN' BACK T' SLEEP...
...SHUT THE FRIGGIN' DOOR ON YER WAY OOT
ELLUR! ELLUR! ELLUR!.. WOT 'AVE WE 'ERE THEN, EH?
?
WOR BIFFA'S DRUGS
LOOKS LIKE A BAG OF CURCAIN T' ME, WPC MUTHA
AYE! AN' IT'S GOT YOUR FRIGGIN' NAME ON IT....
FLOUR WOR BIFFA'S DRUGS
EH!? Y' FUCKIN' BASTAADS. YUZ'VE PLANTED THAT FUCKER THERE, MAN
HEY! FUCKIN' GERROFUZ! LEAVE US ALAIRN
SAVE IT FER THE JUDGE, SON. YOUR FUCKIN' NICKED!
QUICK, WPC MUTHA... HE'S RESISTIN' ARREST... PEPPAH SPRAY THE CUNT
FSSSST!
AAARGH!
FLY SPRAY
ME FUCKIN' EYES!
NOO CALM DOON, SON. YUZ'RE AANLY MEKKIN IT WORSE FER YERSEL
?
PLOOF!
LOOK, SEE! LOOK! IT'S NOT DRUGS. IT'S A BAG O' FUCKIN' FLOO-AH!
FLOUR
HMM! HE'S REET, MUTHA. THIS IS SELF RAISIN' FLOO-AH
EH!?
SHALL WE DEE 'IM F' WASTIN' POLISS TIME?
NAA... THERE'S SUMMAT ELSE...
THIS YOUR CD PLAYAH, IS IT, SON?
AYE! WOT ABOOT IT, LIKE?
WELL...
...I'VE GOT REASON T' BELIEVE IT'S KNOCKED!
KNOCKED!? BUT I WAS GIVE IT AS A PRESSIE!
WAS Y' NOO? WHO OFF, EH?
ERM...ERM... I CANNAT SAY.
REET, SON. I SHALL 'AVE T' ASK YOU TO ACCOMPANY US T' THE KITCHEN T' ANSWER A FEW QUESTIONS

SHORTLY...
REET. I'LL ASK Y' ONE MORE TIME... WHO GIVE YE THE CD PLAYAH?
NEE COMMENT!
AAL REET!
IT'S NEE GOOD, SERGEANT FATHA. HE'S NOT GANNA CRACK!
WUZ'LL 'AVE T'USE THE URLD 'GOOD COP, NASTY COP' ROUTINE. BAGSY ME NASTY COP.
REET, BIFFA. THAT CD PLAYAH YUZ'VE GOT IS KNOCKED, AN' I'M AFRAID Y' MUST TELL US WHO GIVE IT YER, SON
TAB?
AYE
CLANG!
WOULD Y' LIKE ANOTHER CUPPA TEA, SON?
GROAN!
SMACK!
OOF!
WOULD Y' LIKE T' SMELL THESE FLOO-AS, BIFFA?
CRACK!
LOOK, SON... SAVE YERSEL AALL THIS TROUBLE. TELL US WHO GIVE IT YUZ AN' WE'LL LET YUZ OFF WI' A CAUTION
HEH!
GROAN!
AALL REET... AALL REET! I'LL FUCKIN' TELL YUZ.
CHAMPION
...BUT JUST T' YEE, LIKE ...NOT T' WPC MUTHA
WPC MUTHA... WOULD YOU LEAVE THE INTERVIEW KITCHEN FOR A MURMENT, PLEASE?
AYE...
I'M GANNIN' OFF DUTY NOO, ANYHOO
REET, SON... IN Y' AAN TIME... WHO GIVE Y' THAT KNOCKED OFF CD PLAYAH?
IT WAS... IT WAS...
MUTHA!
MUTHA!? FUCKIN' 'ELL...'ERE, SIGN THIS BIRRA PAPER SAYIN' IT WAS 'ER WOT KNOCKED IT OFF, REET
AYE... REET!
MIND, I WOULDN'T LIKE T' BE IN YOUR SHOES IF SHE FINDS OOT Y'VE SQUEALED
HOO, YEEZ TWOS... WOT'S GANNIN' ON?
NOWT, MUTHA... HONEST
THIS 'UNS JUST GRASSED YEE UP GOOD AN' PROPPAH, MUTHA.
SEZ YEE KNOCKED HIS FUCKIN' CD PLAYAH!
EH!?!
AYE! SIGNED A FUCKIN' STATEMENT, THE LOT!
BASTAAD! I'LL FUCKIN' MORDER THE CUNT
FUCKIN' LERRUZADDIM...
LEAVE IT, MUTHA. HE'S GOT POLISS PRUR-TECTION
HEH! HEH!.. AYE!..SO FUCK YEE!
I'M GANNA 'AVE YEE! YER FUCKIN' DEED, SON... Y' HEAR ME?... DEED!
AYE... I HEAR Y'
Y' CAN RUN, BUT Y' CANNAT HIDE!
SHE'S REET, THOUGH, BUT. US PIGS CANNAT GIVE Y' PROTECTION FOREVAH... I THINK Y' SHOULD GET YERSEL A NEW IDENTITY.
EH! HOW?
WELL, Y' KNOW... CHANGE YER APPEARANCE, LIKE.
TELL Y' WOT... COME INTO THE SHED WI ME, AN' I'LL GIVE YEE A COMPLETE NEW LOOK. I'VE GOT UNCLE DEKKA T' GIVE ME A HAND
GREAT!
AYE! WHEN WUZ'RE DONE WI' YER, YER AAN MUTHA WUVENT RECOGNISE Y' SON
10 MINS LATER...
FUCKIN' BASTAAD... GRASSIN' HIS AAN MUTHA UP... WHEN I SEE HIM AGAIN, I'LL FUCKIN' MORDER IM
GROAN!
WHO'S THIS FUCKER?

Heaven Can't

"It's Time for Change" says Pope Benedict VI

THE OLD-FASHIONED Heaven of angels, harps and fluffy clouds could soon become a thing of the past, if cold-eyed new Pope Benedict VI has his way. For the reforming pontiff has revealed plans for a revamped, bang-up-to-date afterlife that will see silicon chip technology take its place in the hereafter.

By our Religious Affairs Correspondent
Jack Smethurst

"Eternity's been stuck in the past for too long," the Holy Father told a Vatican press conference.

"Heaven's got to move with the times if it's going to appeal to a new generation of immortal souls. On earth, we live in an age of TV remote controls, fax machines and Space Invaders. People have a right to expect modern innovations like these when they get to the other side."

radical

The clearly excited ex-Hitler Youth then outlined his 15-year plan for a radical makeover of God's kingdom. He told reporters: "Anyone who dies after 2020 will see a big difference from the moment they arrive at the Pearly Gates. For a start, there'll be no St Peter to greet them. Entry to paradise will be controlled electronically.

"A laser will scan your iris, and compare it with a biometric database of people who have lived good lives. If it finds a match, the gate will slide open automatically, making a noise a bit like the doors on *Star Trek*. However, if the computer decides you've committed a sin, you'll be sent straight to Hell."

And it'll be all change inside Heaven too. Angels will fly around not upon wings of gossamer, but on James Bond-style vertical take-off jetpacks. According to the Pope: "Out will go clouds, ambrosia and harps, and in will come hover platforms, tiny food pills and Mini-Moog synthesizers."

lunch

In addition, the Pope intends to update the angels' traditional head-dress, replacing the old-fashioned halo made out of tinsel and a coat hanger with a space-age glow-in-the-dark holographic version.

OUT - Wings
IN - Jet Packs
OUT - Harps
IN - Synthesizers
OUT - Nudity
IN - Uniforms

All angels and clouds: *Heaven as we all know it today. But what does the future hold for the afterlife?*

Benedict is also planning a heavenly communications revolution that will be bad news for spiritualists like TV's Doris Stokes and Derek Acorah. He continued: "At the moment, the technology available for speaking to the dear departed is still in the stone age."

> **"..each spirit will have its own email address with a high-speed broadband connection. It's going to be an exciting time to be dead"**

gift

Our present day mediums with their table tapping, ouija boards and ectoplasm will become a thing of the past. In the hereafter of 2020, the souls of the dead will have no need for such unreliable methods of getting in touch.

"They will all be equipped with the latest camera mobiles, so they can exchange cryptic text messages and snapshots with their living relatives at the touch of a button. What's more, each spirit will have its own email address with a high-speed broadband connection. It's going to be an exciting time to be dead, I can tell you," he added.

As part of his package, the Pope plans to introduce other changes which reflect the modern world. "At the moment the cherubims and seraphims fly around Heaven stark naked, playing their little trumpets," he continued. "It's an unfortunate fact that in the afterlife, just as on earth, there is a paedophile problem. These nude, curly-haired, chubby, pre-pubescent fairies sadly make a tempting target for perverted immortal souls, especially the ex-Catholic priests.

"As a result, in the modern Heaven of 2020 baby seraphs and cherubs will be required to wear a smart uniform," he added. It is believed that British fashion designer Wayne Hemingway has already been approached to design the little costumes.

spirit

Although the plans have met with a largely positive response, certain traditionalist elements in the church have reacted more guardedly. Hirsute Archbishop of Canterbury Dr Rowan Williams admitted he was uncomfortable with the idea of a *Changing Rooms*-

Doing a buffet but can't be bothered to prepare a load of salad that won't get eaten anyway?

A&M
SALAD
HIRE

Everything from a spoonful to a skipful
Wedding salads – Fancy Dress salads
Rentals from two days to a month

FREE DUSTBIN OF COLESLAW WITH EVERY SINGLE ENQUIRY

IT'S NO WONDER OUR CUSTOMER THINKS WE'RE THE UKs #1 SINCE 2004

A&M PLANT HIRE LTD, COLESLAW HOUSE, THE GREEN, GETTEN-ON-THE-TITTS GB2 2OV. TEL. 01919 563372 FAX. 01919 563373

Wait

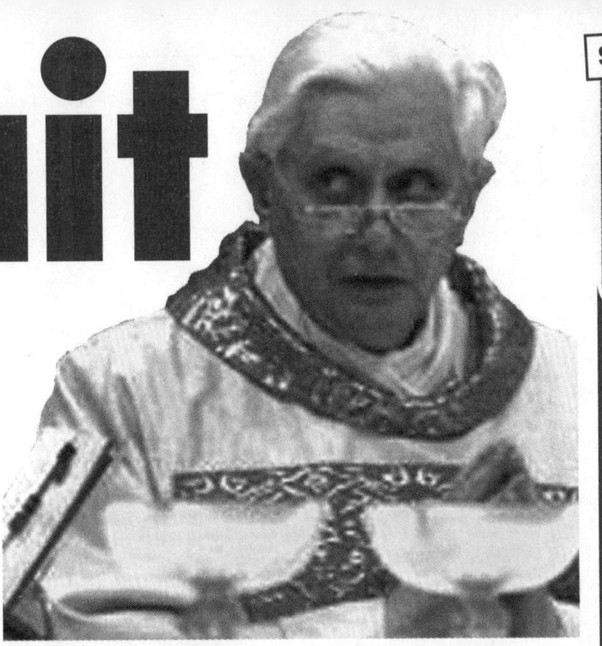

2020 vision of Heaven: *Prog Pope Benedict VI, yesterday (right). Church of England fanny chops Rowan Williams (below left) and evangelical preacher Anal Roberts (below right)*

style makeover for life everlasting. On ITV's Saturday morning *Ministry of Mayhem* programme he hit out at the Pope's plans.

"We must consider the feelings of the older residents of the hereafter," he told viewers. "People like Jesus, the Virgin Mary, the Good Samaritan, the Prodigal Son and Daniel in the Lion's Den have been living up there for the best part of two thousand years and they've got used to the gentle way of life in Heaven.

Nelson Mandela

"I'm very worried that these changes are going to come as a terrible shock to them," the big hairy arsehole added.

Meanwhile in the US, evangelist hellfire preacher Anal Roberts has launched a TV appeal to raise over fifteen million dollars in order to modernise Purgatory.

"It's all very well bringing Heaven into the twenty-first century," he told viewers of Cincinatti's WKRP Christian Channel, "but what really matters is bringing the everlasting torment and suffering of Hades bang up-to-date."

Roberts plans to scrap the lake of fire into which sinners have traditionally been tossed for over two millennia. "I'm going to replace it with an almighty microwave oven," he announced. "We're going to put those damned souls in a non-metallic bowl and 'wave their sorry butts at full power (850W).

"And that little bell ain't never going to ring," he added.

HEY, I'VE GOT INDIGESTION OFF EATING TOO MUCH LOBSTER THERMIDOR.
DON'T TAKE ANY NOTICE OF HIM. HE'S FULL OF SHIT.

SHOWBIZ GOSSIP

GAV
BRITAIN'S HOTTEST SHOWBIZ REPORTER

★ **Gary Lineker** seems to have it all ~ money, a lovely wife, money, great kids, and a lucrative career as Britain's favourite footie presenter. But what would his loyal wife say if she... *actually, does anyone mind if I open a window? It's like the bloody Seychelles in here.*

★★★★★★★★★★★★★★★★★★★★★★★★★★★★★★★

★ In a recent poll **Richard Madeley** & **Judy Finnigan** were named as Britain's favourite married couple. But what would their loyal fans say if they knew that just before they begin broadcasting their chat show on Channel 4 every afternoon Richard likes nothing better than to... *wow! It's blazing today, isn't it? Is the air conditioning actually working? My armpits are sodden.*

★★★★★★★★★★★★★★★★★★★★★★★★★★★★★★★

★ Little **Natasha Bedingfield** looks stunning when she sings about love and sex and boyfriends and that sort of thing but what would her loyal parents say if they found out about what she gets up to with her... ***Jesus!*** *You know it looked cloudy when I set off this morning. I really can't take this heat – sorry, I'm going to have to take my shirt off.*

★★★★★★★★★★★★★★★★★★★★★★★★★★★★★★★

★ Poptastic teen heroes **McFly** have got a shock in store for their loyal female groupies – if they ever reveal what their lead singer likes putting in his mouth when he should be eating his dinner... *Actually, is the work experience around? Send her out for a couple of big bottles of Volvic and a Solero, would you. And one of those little handheld fans. Give her a tenner out of petty cash.*

★★★★★★★★★★★★★★★★★★★★★★★★★★★★★★★

★ Virginal **Katie Holmes** isn't going to be too happy on her wedding night when loyal fiancé **Tom Cruise** shows her how he likes to... is there a legal maximum temperature in offices? ***Fuck a duck**, it's nearly **103°** in here. What's that fact about transporting cattle? I actually can't see, there's so much sweat in my eyes.*

...More celebrity tittle-tattle next week, gossip fans. Phew! Jesus... I think I'm going to faint.

Archbishop of Canterbury Coughs Up Pellet onto Queen's Shoe

By our Religious Affairs Correspondent

LAMBETH Palace moved quickly last night to quash rumours that the Archbishop of Canterbury, Dr Rowan Williams is an owl after it was reported that he coughed up a pellet containing mouse bones onto the Queen's shoe.

The incident is said to have taken place at a banquet following the state opening of Parliament. The Archbishop was talking to the Queen, but then seemed to get distracted.

"I saw him jerk his head a few times," said one horrified onlooker. "Then he rolled his eyes right up into his head and coughed up this disgusting, brown furry thing the size of a grapefruit," he continued.

A spokesman for the General Synod admitted that Dr Williams had coughed up a foreign object onto the Queen's foot, but denied that it contained mouse bones. When asked if it contained the bones of a shrew or vole, he refused to comment further.

TSK. LOOK AT THAT IDIOT. HE'S WEAVING ALL OVER THE ROAD.

The PRINCESS who would be KING

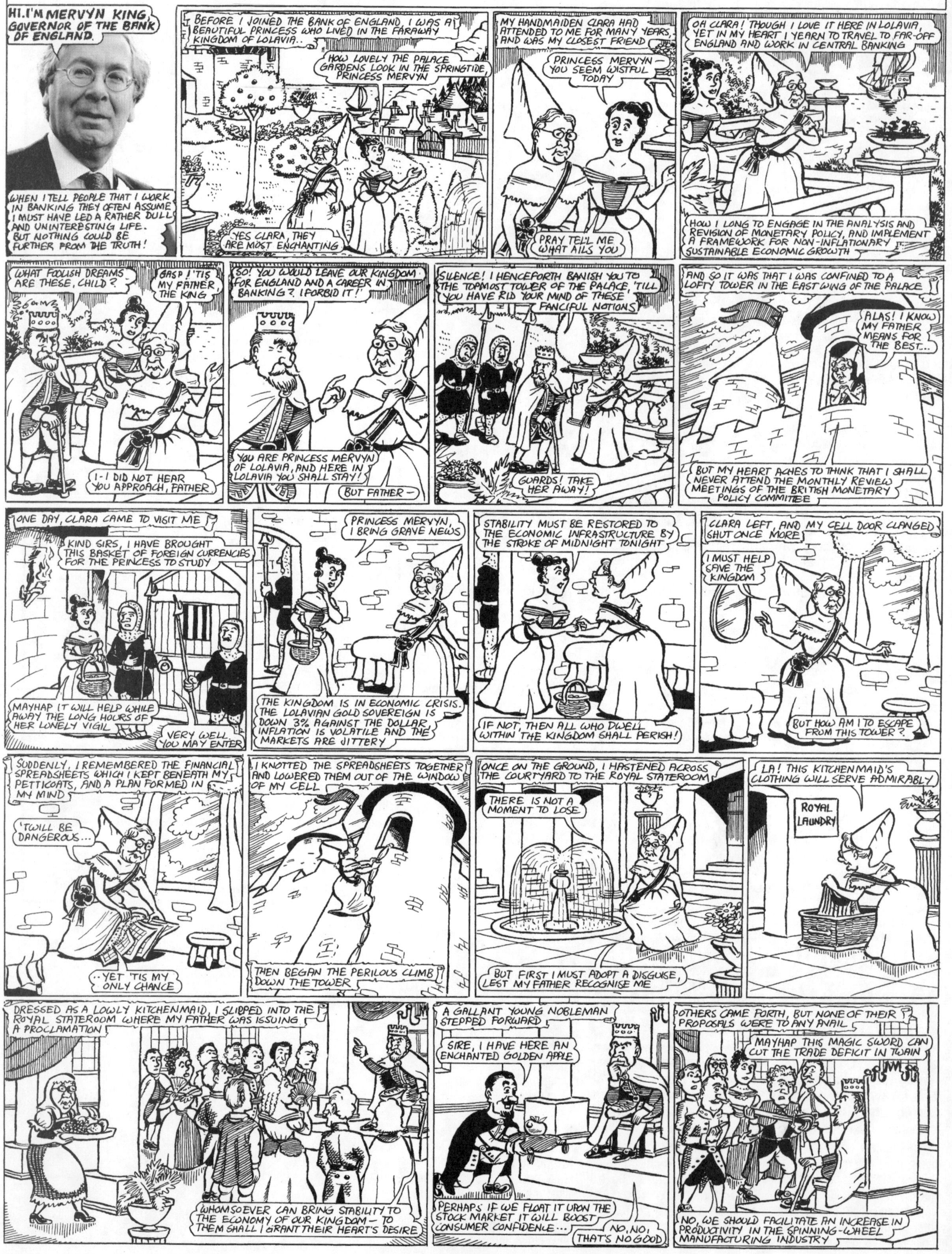

HI. I'M MERVYN KING, GOVERNOR OF THE BANK OF ENGLAND.
WHEN I TELL PEOPLE THAT I WORK IN BANKING THEY OFTEN ASSUME I MUST HAVE LED A RATHER DULL AND UNINTERESTING LIFE. BUT NOTHING COULD BE FURTHER FROM THE TRUTH!
BEFORE I JOINED THE BANK OF ENGLAND, I WAS A BEAUTIFUL PRINCESS WHO LIVED IN THE FARAWAY KINGDOM OF LOLAVIA..
HOW LOVELY THE PALACE GARDENS LOOK IN THE SPRINGTIDE, PRINCESS MERVYN
YES CLARA, THEY ARE MOST ENCHANTING
MY HANDMAIDEN CLARA HAD ATTENDED TO ME FOR MANY YEARS, AND WAS MY CLOSEST FRIEND
PRINCESS MERVYN — YOU SEEM WISTFUL TODAY
PRAY TELL ME WHAT AILS YOU
OH CLARA! THOUGH I LOVE IT HERE IN LOLAVIA, YET IN MY HEART I YEARN TO TRAVEL TO FAR-OFF ENGLAND AND WORK IN CENTRAL BANKING
HOW I LONG TO ENGAGE IN THE ANALYSIS AND REVISION OF MONETARY POLICY, AND IMPLEMENT A FRAMEWORK FOR NON-INFLATIONARY SUSTAINABLE ECONOMIC GROWTH
WHAT FOOLISH DREAMS ARE THESE, CHILD?
GASP! 'TIS MY FATHER THE KING
I-I DID NOT HEAR YOU APPROACH, FATHER
SO! YOU WOULD LEAVE OUR KINGDOM FOR ENGLAND AND A CAREER IN BANKING? I FORBID IT!
YOU ARE PRINCESS MERVYN OF LOLAVIA, AND HERE IN LOLAVIA YOU SHALL STAY!
BUT FATHER—
SILENCE! I HENCEFORTH BANISH YOU TO THE TOPMOST TOWER OF THE PALACE, 'TILL YOU HAVE RID YOUR MIND OF THESE FANCIFUL NOTIONS
GUARDS! TAKE HER AWAY!
AND SO IT WAS THAT I WAS CONFINED TO A LOFTY TOWER IN THE EAST WING OF THE PALACE
ALAS! I KNOW MY FATHER MEANS FOR THE BEST...
BUT MY HEART ACHES TO THINK THAT I SHALL NEVER ATTEND THE MONTHLY REVIEW MEETINGS OF THE BRITISH MONETARY POLICY COMMITTEE
ONE DAY, CLARA CAME TO VISIT ME
KIND SIRS, I HAVE BROUGHT THIS BASKET OF FOREIGN CURRENCIES FOR THE PRINCESS TO STUDY
MAYHAP IT WILL HELP WHILE AWAY THE LONG HOURS OF HER LONELY VIGIL
VERY WELL. YOU MAY ENTER
PRINCESS MERVYN, I BRING GRAVE NEWS
THE KINGDOM IS IN ECONOMIC CRISIS. THE LOLAVIAN GOLD SOVEREIGN IS DOWN 3% AGAINST THE DOLLAR, INFLATION IS VOLATILE AND THE MARKETS ARE JITTERY
STABILITY MUST BE RESTORED TO THE ECONOMIC INFRASTRUCTURE BY THE STROKE OF MIDNIGHT TONIGHT
IF NOT, THEN ALL WHO DWELL WITHIN THE KINGDOM SHALL PERISH!
CLARA LEFT, AND MY CELL DOOR CLANGED SHUT ONCE MORE
I MUST HELP SAVE THE KINGDOM
BUT HOW AM I TO ESCAPE FROM THIS TOWER?
SUDDENLY, I REMEMBERED THE FINANCIAL SPREADSHEETS WHICH I KEPT BENEATH MY PETTICOATS, AND A PLAN FORMED IN MY MIND
'TWILL BE DANGEROUS...
..YET 'TIS MY ONLY CHANCE
I KNOTTED THE SPREADSHEETS TOGETHER AND LOWERED THEM OUT OF THE WINDOW OF MY CELL
THEN BEGAN THE PERILOUS CLIMB DOWN THE TOWER
ONCE ON THE GROUND, I HASTENED ACROSS THE COURTYARD TO THE ROYAL STATEROOM
THERE IS NOT A MOMENT TO LOSE
BUT FIRST I MUST ADOPT A DISGUISE, LEST MY FATHER RECOGNISE ME
LA! THIS KITCHENMAID'S CLOTHING WILL SERVE ADMIRABLY
ROYAL LAUNDRY
DRESSED AS A LOWLY KITCHENMAID, I SLIPPED INTO THE ROYAL STATEROOM WHERE MY FATHER WAS ISSUING A PROCLAMATION
WHOMSOEVER CAN BRING STABILITY TO THE ECONOMY OF OUR KINGDOM — TO THEM SHALL I GRANT THEIR HEART'S DESIRE
A GALLANT YOUNG NOBLEMAN STEPPED FORWARD
SIRE, I HAVE HERE AN ENCHANTED GOLDEN APPLE
PERHAPS IF WE FLOAT IT UPON THE STOCK MARKET IT WILL BOOST CONSUMER CONFIDENCE...
NO, NO, THAT'S NO GOOD
OTHERS CAME FORTH, BUT NONE OF THEIR PROPOSALS WERE TO ANY AVAIL
MAYHAP THIS MAGIC SWORD CAN CUT THE TRADE DEFICIT IN TWAIN
NO, WE SHOULD FACILITATE AN INCREASE IN PRODUCTIVITY IN THE SPINNING-WHEEL MANUFACTURING INDUSTRY

AS THE CLOCK APPROACHED MIDNIGHT, I SPOKE UP FROM THE BACK OF THE HALL
LET THE INTEREST RATE BE SET AT 3.75% — A FALL OF 0.25%
INSTANTLY I UTTERED THOSE WORDS, A MIRACULOUS CHANGE CAME OVER THE KINGDOM
LOOK - IT'S WORKING! INFLATION HAS STOPPED SOARING
EQUILIBRIUM HAS BEEN RESTORED TO THE KINGDOM'S ECONOMIC INFRASTRUCTURE ONCE MORE
COME FORWARD AND IDENTIFY YOURSELF, HUMBLE KITCHENMAID
YOU HAVE SAVED THE KINGDOM AND SO I SHALL GRANT YOU YOUR HEART'S DESIRE
MY ONLY DESIRE IS TO WORK FOR THE BANK OF ENGLAND, FATHER
GASP! 'TIS PRINCESS MERVYN!
MY CHILD, YOU HAVE PROVEN YOURSELF TO BE COURAGEOUS OF HEART, AND MODERATE OF FISCAL POLICY
VERY WELL. TOMORROW MORNING, YOU SHALL SET SAIL FOR ENGLAND.
AND THE NEXT DAY, AS MY SHIP DEPARTED FOR LONDON, I FELT AS THOUGH I WOULD SWOON WITH HAPPINESS.
FAREWELL PRINCESS MERVYN
MY OLD LIFE LAY BEHIND ME NOW. NO LONGER WOULD I BE KNOWN AS PRINCESS MERVYN OF LOLAVIA ~ HENCEFORTH, I WOULD BE MERVYN KING, GOVERNOR OF THE BANK OF ENGLAND!

HEIGHT CONTROL

"If I can do it... anybody can do it!"

says **HeightWatchers**™ **'Shrinker of the Year 2005'**
Bertram Bromley, Kent

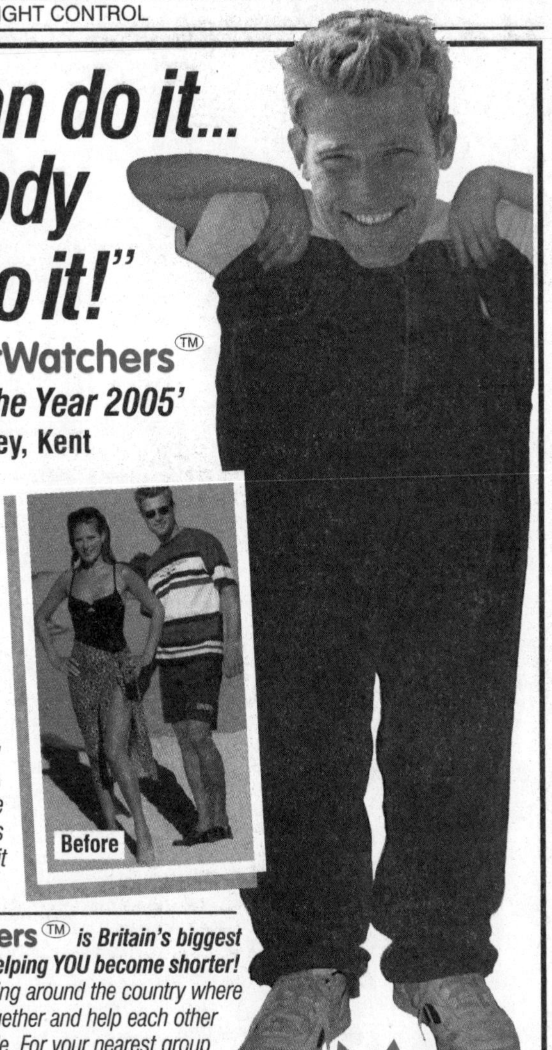
Before

*"It's hard to believe that just 8 months ago I was 6 foot 2 inches tall. I didn't realise just how big I was until I got my holiday snaps back... **I looked like a beached giraffe!** That's when I realised I had to do something about my height. A tiny friend told me about Heightwatchers and I thought I'd give it a go. I'm glad I did."*

HeightWatchers™ ***is Britain's biggest group dedicated to helping YOU become shorter!*** *We hold weekly meeting around the country where tall people can get together and help each other shed unwanted altitude. For your nearest group and for membership details, call today.* ***You have nothing to lose but inches!***

0800 000 022

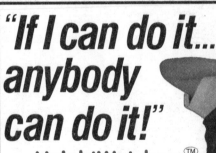

Take the first step to a shorter you!

Boring Bastard

MORNING, READERS!
COUGH!
NOTICE BOARD
COUGH!
AHEM!
SEE YOU NEXT TIME, READERS!

THE ADVENTURES OF
BONO
OUT OF
U2
ONE DAY...
SEE YOU, NAN... I'M OFF, TO BE SURE, TO BE SURE
WHERE ARE YOU GOING, OUR BONO?
I'M GIVING A LECTURE IN THE VILLAGE HALL ABOUT POVERTY, DEBT AND THE ENVIRONMENT AND THAT, SO I AM
WELL, BE BACK FOR TEA...
OKAY, SO, NAN
AND BE CAREFUL CROSSING THE ROAD
SO...
AH, MR. BONO... YOU'RE ON IN FIVE MINUTES
OH, BEJASUS AN' BEGORRAH
WHAT IS IT?
OH, DEAR...
...IF I HAVEN'T ONLY JUST LEFT ME HAT AT ME NANNIES
WHY, I CAN'T GIVE ME LECTURE ON POVERTY, DEBT AND THE ENVIRONMENT WITHOUT ME HAT, NOW, CAN I?
ER... NO, MR BONO
I'D LOOK A ROIGHT FECKIN' EEJIT!
HELLO, NAN... IT'S ME. I'M SENDING SOMEONE ROUND FOR ME HAT. HAVE IT READY AT THE GATE, WILL YOU?
A HAT, Y'SAY?...
...OKAY, OUR BONO
ROIGHT, YOU... CHARTER A PRIVATE BOEING 747 AND HAVE ME HAT FLOWN OVER.
RIGHT AWAY, MR. BONO, SIR
10 MINS LATER...
AH! HERE IT COMES!
VWOOOOOSH!
THE PILOT SAYS YOUR NAN'S GARDEN IS TOO SMALL TO LAND A BOEING 747, MR. BONO...
BEJASUS.
HE SAYS HE'LL HAVE A GO IN A CESSNA, IF YOU LIKE
WHAT!?! A CESSNA?
HAS IT GOT A BAR?... AND AN IN-FLIGHT MOVIE?
ER... NO!
I'M BONO, FOR GOD'S SAKE... YOU CAN'T EXPECT MY HAT TO SLUM IT IN A LIGHT AIRCRAFT...
WHY DON'T I JUST SEND A CAR?
A CAR!?... A FECKIN' CAR!?
WELL... A... A STRETCHED LIMO... ER... OBVIOUSLY...
WITH A JACUZZI, WIDESCREEN DVD, CIRCULAR BED AND TEN PLAYBOY MODELS IN IT.
LISTEN... THAT DEGREE OF LUXURY MIGHT BE ALROIGHT FER STING'S HAT, BUT NOT MOINE
YES, MR. BONO, SIR
NO!.. I WANT IT FETCHED IN A GOLD CARRIAGE, DRAWN BY SIX ELEPHANTS
NO... PANDAS!
SIX ELEPH-ANTS, YES!
SIX ELEPHANTS RIDDEN BY PANDAS... ALBINO PANDAS.
NO! WAIT! FORGET ALL THAT!... I'VE GOT IT!
PING!
I WANT IT SAILED UP THE ROAD TO ME IN A DIAMOND ENCRUSTED GONDOLA... ON A RIVER OF VINTAGE CHAMPAGNE!
SAILED BY PAVAROTTI
YOU GOT IT, MR. BONO...
...OPERATOR! GET ME KRUG CHAMPAGNE...
SHORTLY...
KRUG
KRUG
JUST-A-ONE CORNETTO, GEEF-EET-A TO MEEE
DEE-LEECIOUS ICE-A CREAM OF EE-TA-LEEEEE
DE-DAAAAAAA! DE-DUM DE DEEE!
GEEF ME CORNETTO FROM-A WALL'S ICE CRE-EA-EAM!
ROIGHT, NOW TO GIVE ME LECTURE ON POVERTY, DEBT AN' THE ENVIR-ONMENT AN' THAT!
HOLY MARY MOTHER OF GOD... IF ME NAN HASN'T SENT ONE OF HER OWN FECKIN' HATS, TO BE SURE!
SO...
AND... ERM... SO THAT'S HOW I WOULD SOLVE POVERTY AND DEBT... ER... AND NOW HOW I WOULD SOLVE THE ENVIRONMENT...
WHAT A STUPID LITTLE TWAT!
HA! HA! HA!
SCREAM!
HA! HA!

GILBERT RATCHET
TOOLS
BA-A-A-ARP! THAT LEMONADE WAS DELICIOUS!
LIFTER
BUT NOW I NEED TO GO FOR A WEE.
I'LL NIP INTO THIS PUBLIC BOG
PUBLIC CONVENIENCE
GENTS
AND MY PATENTED "NO-PLOPS™ AUDIO IMPAIRER" WILL PROTECT ME FROM HEARING THE DISTRESSING SOUNDS OF ANYONE HAVING A POO IN ONE OF THE CUBICLES.
AW BOO! THIS LAVVY COSTS 20P TO GET IN
GENTS
20P TRAMP DETERRENT
I SPENT ALL MY MONEY ON THAT FIZZY POP.
I'LL HAVE TO FIND 20P PRETTY QUICKLY
GENTS
HOP HOP HOP
MY NEED FOR A WAZZ IS GETTING URGENT
HULLO - THAT CAR-PARK ATTENDANT LOOKS GLUM
CAR PARK
NCP
SIGH
I'M SO DISAPPOINTED, GILBERT. CRAIG DAVID HAS JUST LEFT HIS CAR IN MY CAR PARK...
..BUT THIS SPRAINED WRIST MEANS THAT I AM UNABLE TO SMEAR DOG SHIT ALL OVER HIS DOOR HANDLES
FOR 20 PENCE I'LL INVENT A DEVICE WHICH WILL COAT CRAIG DAVID'S ENTIRE VEHICLE WITH CANINE FAECES
NCP
NAILS
IT'S A DEAL!
SHORTLY
THERE. THE DOGS DO THEIR BUSINESS ON THE CAR ROOF, WHILST THEIR WAGGING TAILS POWER THE ROLLERS WHICH VIGOROUSLY RUB IT INTO THE BODYWORK
LAXATIVE CHOC DROPS
NCP
WIPE SMEAR
SMASHING!
BY! YOU'VE DONE A GOOD JOB THERE, GILBERT. THIS CAR IS THOROUGHLY BESHITTED
THERE IS HOWEVER ONE LITTLE PROBLEM....
...CRAIG DAVIDS CAR IS THAT ONE OVER THERE. THIS IS MY CAR, YOU CRETIN!
OOPS!
NCP
THAT'S IT, DARLING. SMEAR THE DOGGY-DO ONTO THE WING-MIRROR
YOU'LL GET NO TWENTY PENCE FROM ME!
GOLLY! I'M ABSOLUTELY BURSTING FOR A ROD LIDDLE
IF I DON'T FIND 20P SOON, I'LL WET MY KNICKERS
BUSINESS IS SLACK
DAILY MAIL
EXTRA! EXTRA!
I HAVEN'T SOLD A SINGLE COPY OF THE DAILY MAIL ALL DAY.
IN ORDER TO SELL THE DAILY MAIL, YOU NEED TO FRIGHTEN STUPID MIDDLE-AGED WOMEN
DAILY MAIL
READ ALL ABOUT IT
I'LL CONSTRUCT A MACHINE THAT WILL SCARE THE BEJASUS OUT OF THEM.
THAT SHOULD DO THE TRICK. IT'S A GIANT BATTERY-DRIVEN ABU HAMZA GYPSY PAEDOPHILE IN A HOODIE, WHICH SELLS CARCINOGENIC LUCKY HEATHER TO MIDDLE-CLASS CHILDREN.
RARGH! I WANT YOUR BABIES!
CANCER RAYS
LUCKY HEATHER, DEARIE?
GASP!
EEH! OUR WORST FEARS HAVE BEEN REALISED! I MUST READ THE DAILY MAIL TO FIND COMFORT IN ITS RIGHT-THINKING EDITORIALS
ME NEXT
DAILY MAIL ASYLUM SEEKERS ARE AFTER YOUR AGA
DAILY MAIL
I'LL TAKE TWO COPIES... NO, THREE!
MAKE THAT FOUR
AND SOON
I'VE SOLD OUT! THANKS, GILBERT~ HERE'S A PERCENTAGE OF THE TAKINGS.
£100
YOWZA! A HUNDRED QUID
AAAAH! THAT HUNDRED QUID PAID FOR A WEE IN THE MOST LUXURIOUS PUBLIC TOILET IN TOWN.
POSH CLASSICAL MUSIC
CHANEL No 5
CHANEL No 5
CHANEL No 5
MINK-LINED JOHNNIES
CAVIAR FLAVOUR
QUAIL FLAVOUR
CHAMPAGNE SPEW
SOLID GOLD
EXPENSIVE CUBAN CIGAR BUTTS
SILK
JEEVES! I'M NEARLY READY TO HAVE THE DRIPS SHAKEN OFF MY TASSLE
COMING RIGHT UP, SIR.

I'm a Celebrity Skidm
Get Me Out of Here!

IT'S A JOB WE ALL HATE. Doing the laundry. Modern day washer-driers have made the task a little easier, but it's still a chore. And while it's a chore, people like *Barry Featherstone* will be in work. Because Barry runs his very own laundrette, offering a full service from pre-wash to fluff dry. Seven days a week, he washes other people's dirty clothes. It might seem like a depressing way to make a living, but when you consider that the socks and pants belong to such names as *Leonardo di Caprio*, *Liv Tyler* and *Johnny Depp*, the job takes on a little more sparkle.

In a lather over the stars' smalls: ***Barry Featherstone*** *(left) and some of the famous faces into whose gussets he has had a privileged peek. (below): Diehard man* ***Willis****, (right): Basic Instinct flasher* ***Sharon Stone****, (righter): Mafia crooner* ***Sinatra****, (even righter): Baywatch babe* ***Pamela Anderson*** *and (bottom): trial star* ***OJ Simpson****.*

EXCLUSIVE

Featherstone, 42, began in the laundry business in 1983 when he opened his first shop, The Park Street Lav-o-Mat in Birmingham. But after 20 years he decided to move on, and opened a second shop in the more glamourous Belle Air district of Hollywood. Here he rubbed shoulders with the famous while he rubbed their gussets with Omo. Now, after nine months he's back in Birmingham. And he's about to blow the lid off the stars' shreddies secrets in a new book *Acdo All Areas* (Saucepan Macmillan Books, £9.99). In this extract, Barry gives us a taster of his life at the Hollywood soapface.

"I was known as the Laundry King of Hollywood. Everyone who was anyone used to come to my Belle Air Washetaria for their weekly service wash. They knew I'd do a good job on their smalls, and, just as important, that I'd be discreet. To my customers, privacy was all important. Intimate appareil exposes the secrets of the inner person in startling detail. But they trusted me, and as a professional laundryman I would never dream of revealing what I have found out about the stars whilst examining their scads.

animals

But having said that, some of these celebrities were no better than animals in their habits. I remember one Hollywood star coming into my shop with a week's worth of laundry, and the state of his underpants had to be seen to be believed. My professional ethics prevents me from naming him, but his bowels were Every Which Way including Loose that week, I can tell you. You'd think with all the money he had, he could have bought a roll of toilet paper. Even orang-utans wipe their arses on leaves - this man just didn't bother. I had to put them through the boil was twice. Thankfully, most of my customers practiced good personal hygeine, and their underwear generally just needed a pre-soak and an economy wash."

It may seem that even washing celebrities' undercrackers would quickly become mundane, and Barry admits that most of his work was run of the mill. But every now and then, a bag of laundry would throw up a surprise:

"I remember on one occasion I was doing a bio-wash of **Denzil Washington***'s underpants, when there was a screech of tyres outside the shop. I turned to look and saw a Ferrari had pulled up outside, and* **Sharon Stone** *was getting out carrying a black bin liner. She came into the laundramatte and asked me to do a service wash on her clothes. I told her it would be £5.50, although because it was America I told her the price in dollars. She thought it was a little pricey, but when I told her that included a 40° pre-wash she agreed. I gave her a docket and she left. She may have been one of the most desirable women in the world, but it was just another job it me and I started loading her clothes into the machine. But I was suddenly stopped in my tracks. In my hand was a pair of her knickers, and I recognised them immediately.* ***It was the same pair that she wasn't wearing in the famous leg-crossing scene in Basic Instinct.***

"News travels fast in Tinseltown, and when you have Sharon Stone's knickers in your hand, it travels even faster"

News travels fast in Tinseltown, and when you have Sharon Stone's knickers from Basic Instinct, it appears to travel even faster. Soon the press were swarming around my shop wanting to see them. There was even the chief executive from the Planet Hollyood chain of restaurants. He wanted them for the wall of their New York branch, and he offered me fifty thousand dollars for them on the spot. I showed him the door.

Being in the laundry business is a bit like being a doctor - client confidentiality is paramount, so it's a mystery to this day how the word got around about those famous knickers. I had only told my brother-in-law and his brother, and neither of them would have breathed a word. When Sharon came back for her laundry that afternoon, she had to run the gauntlet of reporters. She was not too pleased, I can tell you, and I'm sorry to say that she didn't come back to my shop again."

Barry may have lost Sharon Stone as a customer, but many of Hollywood's greats came back to him time and time again. One regular face at the Belle Air Washetaria was Die Hard heart-throb **Bruce Willis**:

"Bruce was a very good customer of mine. He was always busy making one film or another, and they always involved him wearing a vest. He'd regularly have to roll around the floor and blow things up and everything, and at the end of a day's shooting his vest would be filthy. Despite his hard-man image, Bruce liked clean clothes,

and every night he'd come into my shop with his soiled singlet and ask for the best wash possible. Money was no object to Willis.

He would pick the vest up the next morning on his way to the studio. The ironic thing was, because of film continuity, he couldn't suddenly appear halfway through a scene in a clean vest. So when he arrived on set, the make up artists would spend the first couple of hours each morning 'dirtying up' the vest I had just laundered! ...only in America!"

Barry saw a lot of things during his nine months as the Hollywood Laundryman to the Stars, and most of it has remained confidential until now. But on one occasion, he was forced to break that confidentiality and go to the police:

"It was a Wednesday lunchtime. I remember it well because I closed half day on Wednesdays and I was just about to lock up. Suddenly, perhaps the most famous face in America

ark! Hollywood Undercracker Cleaner's Wash 'n' Tell Story of the Star's Shreddies

HOLLYWOOD

walked in with a cloth laundry bag. It was **OJ Simpson**. *He asked me to put all his things through the wash and he would pick them up the next day. There wasn't a lot, so I thought I would just put them through the twin tub.*

As I was loading them in, I noticed that everything, pants, vests and socks, were all extremely small - far too small to fit a man the size of OJ. It was definitely the case that this man liked to wear all his clothes too small. A shiver ran down my spine as I thought that this threw new light on the 'tight glove' evidence in his famous murder trial.

I hated breaking a confidence, but I went to the police with his underpants. They were very excited, but pointed out that unfortunately he had already been acquitted of the murder, and that as much as they'd like to, they couldn't try him for the same crime again."

Barry ran a tight ship at the Belle Air Washetaria. Customers orders were always completed on time and to thier satisfaction. But on one occasion, Barry slipped up, and nearly paid for it with his life:

"I'm sure you've heard that **Frank Sinatra** *never wears the same socks or pants twice. Well let me tell you that's not true. And I should know, because I used to wash them. I remember Frank came in one day with a load of his smalls in a pillow case. He said he wanted the same day service, as he had a gig that night with* **Sammy Davis Jnr** *at the Hollywood Bowl and had got nothing clean to wear. I said I'd have them done by 3.30pm. He left the shop, and as I was writing Frank's label, commedian* **Normal Collier** *came in. He was carrying an identical pillow case of underwear. We started chatting about things, and then he suddenly started doing his chicken impression. It was hilarious, and I was laughing so much that I must of put the label on the wrong pillowcase.*

The next day, two big men in dark suits with violin cases under their arms came in and said they wanted to have a word with me about Frank's underpants. You can guess what had happened - I'd given Norman Collier's laundry to Frank Sinatra and vice versa. I knew of Frank's Mafia connections, so I was pretty scared, I can tell you. I called Collier to explain what had happened, but he thought I was joking and kept doing that thing where he pretends the microphone was cutting out. The two Mafia men were furious. One of them grabbed the phone off me and yelled some thinly veiled threat to Collier. They told him to 'stop playing the fucking wise ass', and said they were coming round to fetch Frank's smalls. They let me know in no uncertain terms that if this mistake happened again, it would be the last one I made.

I don't know what happened at Collier's house, but the poor devil

"Two men with violin cases under their arms wanted to have a word with me about Frank Sinatra's underpants"

came back into the Washetaria the next day with a pair of underpants in one hell of a state. They could have walked to there on their own, I can tell you."

Of course it's not just vests, pants and knickers that Barry laundered in his nine months in Tinseltown. The bras of the stars were also given the famous Feather-stone treatment. **Uma Thurman**, **Julia Roberts**, **Marlena Dietrich** - you name 'em, he's washed their bras:

"If I told you who's titpants I'd had in my hands, you would think was making it up. The list reads like a who's who of gorgeous women. Some men may think that this is one of the best parts of the job, but let me tell you, when I'm handling bras, putting them in and out of the washers and driers, it's all kept on a professional level.

I remember this one time, **Pamela Anderson** *came into the Washetaria and asked if I could do her bras. I told her how much a service wash and spin dry would cost and she agreed. She went out to her car and came back with a wicker basket full of her bras. I thought nothing of it and got straight to work. But as I was loading them into the machine, I couldn't help thinking that something wasn't right. On screen, Pam is most famous for her 38FF assets, yet all her bras were size 32A.*

When you wash someone's most intimate cloathing, there's a bond

between you that isn't there for anyone else. So when Pam returned the next day to collect her washing, I felt I could ask about the discrepancy in size. I'll never forget her reaction. She roared with laughter and opened her coat. She was naked from the waist up, and I was treated to a private showing of the tiniest pair of 32A breasts I've ever seen. I was taken aback, but she explained to me that whenever she is on screen, her breasts are computer generated to look massive. I was amazed. Hollywood is certainly the land where appearence can be deceptive. She swore me to secrecy, and of course I agreed. It is a secret I shall carry to my grave. ”

Despite the glitz and glamour, Barry tired of the showbiz life. After nine months of being the King of the Hollywood laundry circuit, he returned to his shop in Birmingham, which his nephew, Paul Featherstone, had been running in his absence. Rumours that Barry had just served a nine months prison sentance were denied by Barry, but confirmed by his nephew, Paul.
"He admitted twelve charges of stealing women's underwear from the Park Lane Lav-o-Mat, and asked for a hundred and forty other cases to be taken into consideration", he told reporters. "It might have been two hundred and forty, I can't remember. It was fucking loads, anyway", he added.

Letterbocks, Viz Comic,
PO Box 656, North Shields NE29 1BT
Email: letters@viz.co.uk

I HAVE a 18-foot tall Leylandii hedge that gives my garden privacy. However, my neighbour always complains that it cuts light out to his garden. This summer I went on holiday to Spain, and when I came back, I discovered that he had cut it down to just six feet high. I was absolutely furious and I decided to get my own back. So the next day when he was at work, I nipped round to his house and murdered his wife and kids.

R Plywood
Wormwood Scrubs

I HAVE to chuckle whenever I hear the expression 'I couldn't give a fig', because I could... *and I do!* You see, I have lots of fig trees in my garden, and I often give the fruit away to friends and neighbours.

W Jumblat
Leeds

WHAT IS it with celebrities falling off horses? First it's Christopher Reeve, now Madonna. You think with all their money they'd be able to stay in the saddle.

Edna Holdfast
Blyth

I WENT to Nice this year for 10 days, and when I got back Robin Cook and Mo Mowlam were dead. I think I'd better stay at home next year.

R Porter
Nottingham

WHILST ON a beach holiday in the south of France this year, I was watching my young son happily digging a hole in the sand. Suddenly, three German children came along, took his spade off him and just stood in the hole he had dug with serious expressions on their faces. Now I know that they were only children, that the war finished 60 years ago and we have to move on, but a leopard really doesn't change its spots, does it?

R Crabtree
Essex

'TOUCH me, touch me, touch me now', sang busty Sam Fox in the 1980s. Funnily enough, she was singing a different tune when I broke into her penthouse apartment the other week. All I got was a sexual assault charge for my efforts. I'll never understand women.

Lee Procter
e-mail

MY friend's mum recently pointed out that I have the same ironing board cover as her. Can anyone think of a more mundane and pointless remark to make than this?

Alun Daniel
e-mail

IF I were one of the doctors at the hospital where Madonna was taken after falling off her horse, I would have made up some story about her injury. I would have told her, using long scientific and medical terminology that breaking her collar bone could have loosened connecting tissue in her breasts and that I would have to have a feel of them to see if everything was alright.

Dr J Wilmslow
Kent

Lame to FAME

THE LAD I used to sit next to at work, his auntie's dog came from the same litter as Cynthia Lennon's dog that she had in the early 80s. I think both dogs are now dead and the auntie is divorced. So in other words, ex-Beatle John Lennon's ex-wife's ex-dog was from the same litter as the ex-dog of the ex-auntie of the lad I used to sit next to at work.

Paul E, Somewhere

** Congratulations, Paul. The Lame to Fame appeal is now closed as we believe the lameness of this claim cannot be beaten.*

Star Letter

I'LL never understand my neighbour. He has recently started wheel-clamping his own caravan when he finds he has inadvertently parked it in his own drive! I wonder if he is a sadist, a masochist or both.

Brian Battenberg-Cake,
Derbyshire

RIP-OFF Britain? No way. There's a cafe in Cleveleys near Blackpool charging just 40p for a single HobNob biscuit. What excellent value. If my letter wins a fiver, I'm going to buy a dozen, and with the 20p change I'll put down a deposit on another.

John Turner
Blackpool

P.S. Do you know that the *Sunday Sport* keeps lifting your letters word for word?

WHILST watching a recent wildlife documentary, my girlfriend came out with the revelation that Tony the Tiger of the breakfast cereal fame must, in fact, be a girl 'because lions are boys and tigers are girls.' And she studies biological sciences at university.

A Firefalcon
e-mail

I HAVE no evidence for this, but I reckon that when failed rock musician Tony Blair was at school, he was the sort of boy who released odious and foul-smelling silent farts during assembly. While those around spluttered and retched, he just stood there with that conceited smile on his smug little face.

Donald Dougelly
Croydon

I'M NOT convinced by all this talk of non-smoking and healthy eating. My dear old grandad ate chips his whole life and smoked 60 fags a day, and he lived to the ripe old age of 42.

Y Name
e-mail

LIKE MANY people, I am concerned about global warming. Could we not break open the backs of old fridges and release whatever it is that makes them cold into the atmosphere? Surely this would help.

Larry
Goa

FOR ALL Sainsbury's employees reading this, no, I don't have a Nectar Card.

Rob Ryan
e-mail

WITH reference to Mr Ryan's letter above, I do have a Nectar Card, but I'm afraid I've left it at home.

J Butterworth
Carshalton

**Don't worry, Mr Butterworth. A spokesman for the woman on the till at Sainsbury's said that if you keep your receipt, the points can be added to your card on your next visit to the store.*

I RECENTLY got into a spot of bother outside a nightclub and ended up spending a night in a police cell. On reflection, if I learned anything from the experience, it is that some things are better left unsaid. "It's a good job they don't have height restrictions in the force any more because you wouldn't stand a cat in hell's chance, you short-arsed cunt," is a prime example. We live and learn.

Hazel Harwood
Solihull

AT A football match recently, my team were winning one-nil, but in the space of five minutes, the other team scored twice. The opposing team's supporters started chanting "You're not singing, You're not singing, You're not singing any more," which I have to say was quite correct as we stopped almost immediately after their second goal.

Marion Shap
e-mail

A BLOKE in the pub told me that the M25 is just a big carpark. But when I parked my car on it some twat in a 32-ton truck smashed me into the middle of next week. That's the last time I use that car park and the last time I listen to anyone in a pub.

C Mundy
e-mail

I WAS watching *Top Cat* the other day when I realised how naive some people are. I mean, if a talking cat approached me I would be extremely wary. I certainly wouldn't sign a con-

TOP TIPS

OLD people. Ensure a good fight at your wake by leaving a valuable antique in your will to a distant relative, whilst promising it to a closer relative verbally before you die.
T Poldark, Cornwall

AMERICANS. Wipe out the Iraqi insurgency by simply joining their side. With your 'friendly fire' tactics, the war should be over in days.
Gaz, e-mail

FINCHLEY parkies. Putting a second 'No Ball games' sign 8 yards (7.32m) to the left of the current one will save us having to use a jumper for a goalpost.
Anthony Reuben, e-mail

MICRA drivers. The little number 5 on your gearstick refers to what is known as 'fifth gear'. This will allow you to reach speeds of over 25 mph.
Rebecca, e-mail

PAUL Daniels. Liven up your routine by actually sawing the 'lovely' Debbie McGee in half on stage.
Rollo Bin Web, White City

Factual Mistake OF THE MONTH

This week's Mistake Spotter of the month is *David Brown* of Camden Road in Wanstead. He wins a Concise Oxford Dictionary, an Encyclopædia Britannica, a pair of thick glasses and a wank mag for spotting this howler...

"Whilst reading Viz 148, I was horrified to see that Fru T. Bunn's wife referred to him as Frubery. Until now, he has always been referred to as Frubert. Is it any wonder that standards are plummeting in our schools when you can't even get basic facts like names right? Do I win £10? If so, please could you donate it to Great Ormond Street like Sir Alan Sugar in the Premium Bond advert?"

We at Viz are constantly striving for perfection, and we need your help. Can you spot any innacuracies in any issue of Viz? It's probably easier than you think. Mark your envelope *'Please Put into the Bin Unopened'* and send it to the usual address.

tract granting me exclusive rights to a virtuoso violin concert performed by its mate (another talking cat) in exchange for $50,000. It's lucky there was a sympathetic police officer at hand to stop things getting completely out of control.
Mr Derek
e-mail

ON holiday a few years back, I took part in a quiz and managed to reach the final only to lose out after what I consider to this day, to be a correct answer. The question asked 'What 'C' would you associate Jeremy Clarkson with?' to which I confidently replied 'cunt'. Not only was I told the answer was incorrect, but I was asked by the holiday rep to leave the premises immediately. Has anyone else experienced such appalling treatment whilst holidaying with one's family?
Noel
Leeds

ON THE evening news last Sunday it was reported that the police were investigating an assault, and that they wished to speak to anyone who might have been at Border's Bookshop in Rundle Mall on Saturday afternoon. Well, I was going to go there to get my mum a birthday present, but I just got her a card from our local shop instead. When I reported this to the police, they weren't in the least bit interested. That's the last time I try to do the right thing.
Olly
e-mail

WHAT with all the extremist preachers being deported this month, can Tony Blair see to it that that cunt in Oxford Street who bangs on about Jesus gets thrown out too, please?
David Goodall
e-mail

I JUST sent you a letter about deporting that preacher in Oxford Street. If you decide to print it, could you replace the word 'cunt' with the phrase 'scouse cunt.' I don't think the former accurately describes my hate for the man.
David Goodall
e-mail

THE OTHER day I spotted celebrity twat Peter Stringfellow as he surreptitiously left his nightclub by the back door to avoid being spotted. Unfortunately for him, he opted to leave during the rush hour, onto Leicester Square, wearing a pristine shiny white suit and covered in bling. Have any of your other readers spotted any D or E listers trying to be recognised to the embarrassment of everyone around them?
Andy Fairhurst
e-mail

WHILST watching the end titles of the latest titty fest that is *Hollyoaks,* I noticed that the girls who play identical twins on the show are actually identical twins in real life too. What are the chances of that?
P Bear
Leeds

THOSE FUNNY FOREIGNERS!

This week's funny foreigner with English as his second language is Lee Chang Ho from Nagarahora, Japan. He writes...

You funny men. Many years ago I am living in London, England UK and I am reading your funny comic. Sometimes you don't keep manners but I much like! But, please, where is Pathetic Shark? I get your Viz recently some times and Pathetic Shark not there. I like many of your people (Fat Slags - them funny man!) and sometimes am not to understand Sid the Sexy. What language is that man? Not in any my dictionary. But my favourite is always Pathetic Shark. To bring back please. I love they stupid fish. Kind regards,
Lee Chang Ho

Are YOU a foreigner with a half decent, yet still rather comical grasp of English? Or can you pretend to be one, as we suspect the writer of this week's letter may have done? Drop us a line in your best English to the usual address. Mark your envelope: 'I am comedy foreigner, please to include my write.'

AFTER watching several television programmes with subtitles and signing for the hard of hearing, I cannot help but notice that some deaf people readily resort to extreme gurning when signing, often entirely inappropriately in my opinion. Why is this, and why do it when it only serves to reinforce the erroneous impression that deaf people are in some way mentally retarded?
Jack's dad
Pembrokeshire

I WAS recently on the internet when I came across a site dedicated to raising funds to buy books for illiterate people. Call me stupid, but wouldn't it be better to buy them videos instead?
PW Cracker
e-mail

IS IT me or is petrol getting worse? I used to get a week's motoring from twenty quid's worth, but now I'm lucky if I make it to Thursday before having to fill up. I reckon it's being watered down by the oil companies.
Jim Ashby
e-mail

ACCORDING to the Ordnance Survey, no place in the UK is more than 72 miles from the sea. Nonsense. I travelled from Sheffield to London by train last week, a distance of 190 miles, and I never saw the sea once. Pull the other one, Ordnance Survey.
Colin Trent
e-mail

I NOTICED on a recent advert for the film *Pride and Prejudice* the warning 'contains very mild innuendo'. Thank goodness I spotted it as I almost took my fourteen year-old daughter to see it.
J Thorn
Hexham

I AM writing to express my disgust at the illiteracy of people from Denmark. At a recent international football match, my sharp eyes noticed a Denmark supporters holding a scarf with 'Danmark' printed on it. I ask you! Don't they have schools over there?
Margaret Sneddon
Gillingham

WHO says George Orwell's book *Animal Farm* is a classic? I've just watched a made for video version, and I fail to see the relevance between a woman being shagged by a sheepdog and communist Russia.
Alun Daniel
e-mail

I AM currently working in Canada, and a work colleague of mine has just uttered 'Ah well, another day, another dollar'. I am feeling very awkward now I realise am am earning nearly 400 times what she is. Should I say something?
J Portelli
e-mail

MY MATE John Stallard is such a legend. He's great looking, has a 10-inch cock and women always orgasm when they have sex with him. Apparently he's going to be down Jumpin' Jak's in Maidstone this Friday.
Jim Stullerd
Madesten

I AM certain that Charlotte Church has had a boob job. She's got massive whackers in her new video. When her first album came out she was virtually flat-chested. I just find it upsetting that celebrities feel the need to tamper with their bodies like this.
Alex Trembath
e-mail

"THERE'S A HOLNESS IN MY POCKET"
YOUNG DANNY DEARLIZADEARLIZA WAS THE LUCKY OWNER OF A MINIATURE 'BLOCKBUSTERS' PRESENTER BOB HOLNESS, WHICH LIVED IN HIS JACKET POCKET
HOLY O'MOLY! I'M GOING TO BE LATE FOR SCHOOL!
BUT DANNY ~ YOU HAVEN'T HAD YOUR BREAKFAST YET.
DON'T WORRY MUM — MY POCKET BOB HOLNESS WILL SEE ME RIGHT
I'LL HAVE A 'T' PLEASE, BOB
AND HEY PRESTO
A LOVELY CUP OF TEA FOR MY BREKKY
>SLURP< BUT NOW I'LL HAVE TO DASH OR I'LL BE IN TROUBLE
HEAVENS TO MURGATROYD! MRS ANAXIMANDER IS ON THE SCHOOL GATE
SCHOOL
SHE'LL GIVE ME A RIGHT EARFUL FOR BEING LATE
BUT I KNOW HOW TO DISTRACT HER
GIVE ME A 'B' PLEASE, BOB
THIS SHOULD DO THE TRICK
BZZZZZ
MRS ANAXIMANDER IS TERRIFIED OF BEES
SHRIEK! I AM MIGHTILY AFEARED OF GETTING STUNG!
CHOO
CHORTLE!
OH DEAR. WE'VE JUST JOINED THE SIXTH FORM GIRLS' ORNITHOLOGY CLUB ~ BUT THERE ARE NO BIRDS AROUND FOR US TO SPOT.
OHO!
MY POCKET-SIZED HOLNESS CAN HELP YOU THERE
I'LL HAVE A 'J' PLEASE, BOB
OH LOOK! A BLUE JAY
I'LL WRITE IT DOWN IN OUR BIRDSPOTTING BOOK.
THANKS DANNY ~ YOUR POCKET BOB HOLNESS IS COOL.
SMOOCH
GAWSH!
DON'T WASTE YOUR TIME WITH THAT PIPSQUEAK, GIRLS. I'VE GOT A MINIATURE 'COUNTDOWN' PRESENTER RICHARD WHITELY IN MY UNDERPANTS.
IT'S BASHER BLOGGS AND HIS Y-FRONTS WHITELY.
HUH! WE'RE NOT IMPRESSED BY THAT WHITELY IN YOUR KNICKERS ~ ALL IT DOES IS SIT THERE MAKING LAME PUNS WITH A SMUG EXPRESSION ON ITS PODGY FACE.
..HO-HO! AND SPEAKING OF FACES... IT'S TIME TO "FACE" OUR NEXT ROUND..
GRRR! I'M GOING TO EXTERNALISE MY NEGATIVE FEELINGS OF ENVY AND HUMILIATION BY GIVING YOU A PROPER DUFFING UP!
OO-ER!
HA-HA! WELL I'M SURE OUR NEXT CONTESTANT WON'T BE GIVING US ANY "DUFF" ANSWERS...
BOSH!
TAKE THAT!
OOYAH! QUICKLY, BOB ~ GIVE ME A 'P' PLEASE
WAH! AN ENORMOUS JET OF PISS
SCOOSH!
HO-HO! I THINK BASHER SHOULD HAVE WATCHED HIS "PEES" AND QS, DON'T YOU AGREE, CAROL?
MEANWHILE
THAT'S A SPLENDID NEW BRASSIERE BRUCIE YOU'VE GOT THERE, HEADMASTER
DON'T TOUCH THE PACK, WE'LL BE RIGHT BACK
YES, THE PLUNGING NECKLINE REALLY SHOWS OFF MY MINIATURE 'PLAY YOUR CARDS RIGHT' PRESENTER BRUCE FORSYTH TO FULL ADVANTAGE
UGH! MY NEW BRA HAS BEEN SOILED BY THIS URINE-SOAKED CHILD!
HA-HA! WELL BASHER, IT LOOKS LIKE "URINE" BIG TROUBLE WITH THE HEADMASTER
DANNY! CAN'T YOU GET YOUR POCKET BOB HOLNESS TO SAVE ME FROM A WHACKING?
HMM, LET ME SEE ~ GIVE ME A 'V' PLEASE, BOB
ARF ARF! DOES THAT ANSWER YOUR QUESTION, BASHER?
YOU GET NOTHING FOR A PAIR – NOT IN THIS GAME!
BAH!
WELL CAROL, YOU'VE GOT A REPUTATION FOR BEING SMART — BUT IT'S BASHER'S BOTTOM THAT IS REALLY "SMARTING" NOW. HO-HO!

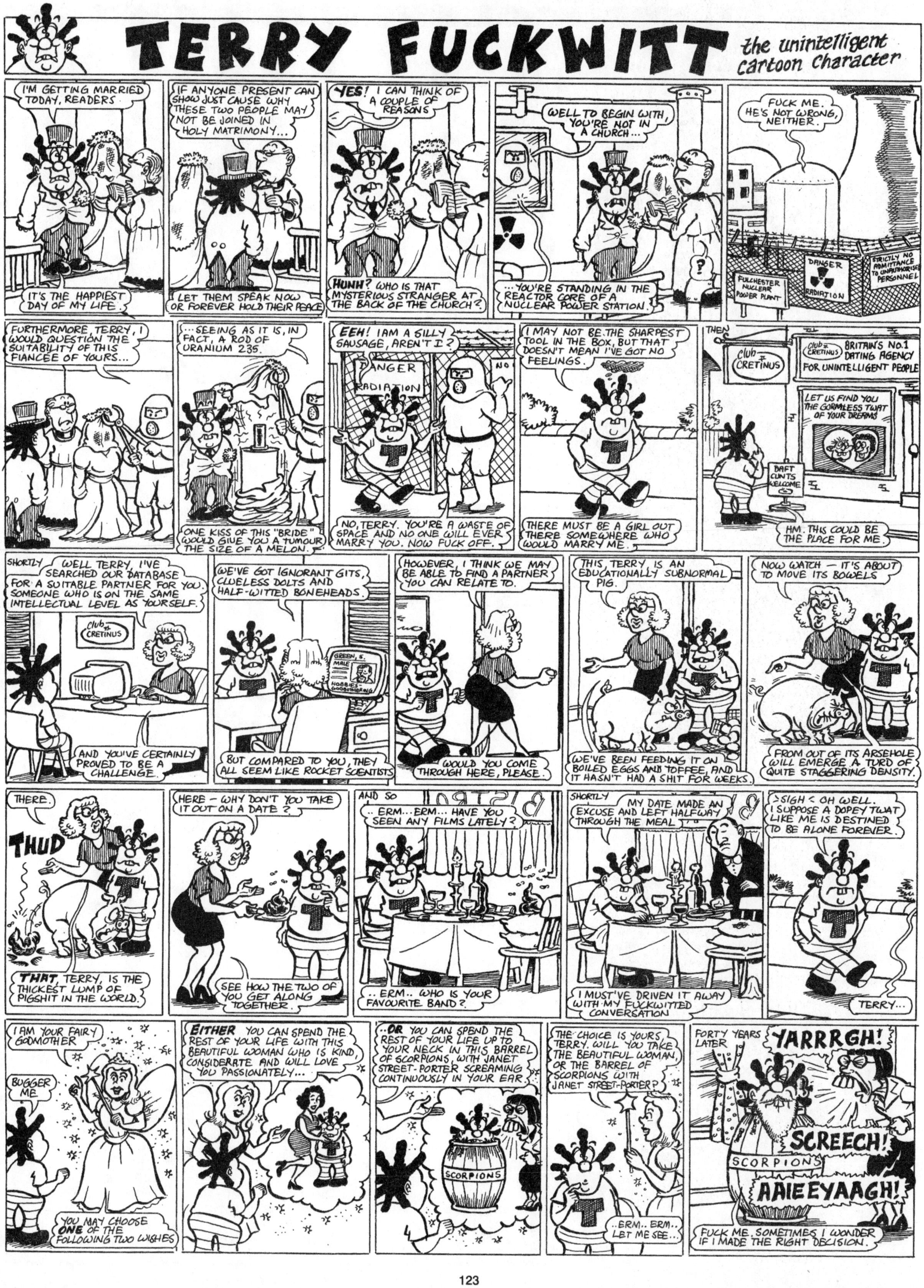
TERRY FUCKWITT
the unintelligent cartoon character
I'M GETTING MARRIED TODAY, READERS
IT'S THE HAPPIEST DAY OF MY LIFE.
IF ANYONE PRESENT CAN SHOW JUST CAUSE WHY THESE TWO PEOPLE MAY NOT BE JOINED IN HOLY MATRIMONY...
LET THEM SPEAK NOW OR FOREVER HOLD THEIR PEACE
YES! I CAN THINK OF A COUPLE OF REASONS
HUNH? WHO IS THAT MYSTERIOUS STRANGER AT THE BACK OF THE CHURCH?
WELL TO BEGIN WITH, YOU'RE NOT IN A CHURCH...
...YOU'RE STANDING IN THE REACTOR CORE OF A NUCLEAR POWER STATION.
FUCK ME. HE'S NOT WRONG, NEITHER.
FULCHESTER NUCLEAR POWER PLANT
DANGER RADIATION
STRICTLY NO ADMITTANCE TO UNAUTHORISED PERSONNEL
FURTHERMORE, TERRY, I WOULD QUESTION THE SUITABILITY OF THIS FIANCÉE OF YOURS...
...SEEING AS IT IS, IN FACT, A ROD OF URANIUM 235.
ONE KISS OF THIS "BRIDE" WOULD GIVE YOU A TUMOUR THE SIZE OF A MELON.
EEH! I AM A SILLY SAUSAGE, AREN'T I?
DANGER RADIATION
NO, TERRY. YOU'RE A WASTE OF SPACE AND NO ONE WILL EVER MARRY YOU. NOW FUCK OFF.
I MAY NOT BE THE SHARPEST TOOL IN THE BOX, BUT THAT DOESN'T MEAN I'VE GOT NO FEELINGS.
THERE MUST BE A GIRL OUT THERE SOMEWHERE WHO WOULD MARRY ME.
THEN
Club CRETINUS
Club CRETINUS BRITAIN'S No.1 DATING AGENCY FOR UNINTELLIGENT PEOPLE
LET US FIND YOU THE GORMLESS TWAT OF YOUR DREAMS
DAFT CUNTS WELCOME
HM. THIS COULD BE THE PLACE FOR ME.
SHORTLY
WELL TERRY, I'VE SEARCHED OUR DATABASE FOR A SUITABLE PARTNER FOR YOU. SOMEONE WHO IS ON THE SAME INTELLECTUAL LEVEL AS YOURSELF.
Club CRETINUS
AND YOU'VE CERTAINLY PROVED TO BE A CHALLENGE.
WE'VE GOT IGNORANT GITS, CLUELESS DOLTS AND HALF-WITTED BONEHEADS.
GREEN, S. MALE HOBBIES: GOBBOTHERING
BUT COMPARED TO YOU, THEY ALL SEEM LIKE ROCKET SCIENTISTS
HOWEVER, I THINK WE MAY BE ABLE TO FIND A PARTNER YOU CAN RELATE TO.
WOULD YOU COME THROUGH HERE, PLEASE.
THIS, TERRY, IS AN EDUCATIONALLY SUBNORMAL PIG.
WE'VE BEEN FEEDING IT ON BOILED EGGS AND TOFFEE, AND IT HASN'T HAD A SHIT FOR WEEKS.
NOW WATCH — IT'S ABOUT TO MOVE ITS BOWELS
FROM OUT OF ITS ARSEHOLE WILL EMERGE A TURD OF QUITE STAGGERING DENSITY.
THERE.
THUD
THAT, TERRY, IS THE THICKEST LUMP OF PIGSHIT IN THE WORLD.
HERE — WHY DON'T YOU TAKE IT OUT ON A DATE?
SEE HOW THE TWO OF YOU GET ALONG TOGETHER.
AND SO
..ERM...ERM... HAVE YOU SEEN ANY FILMS LATELY?
..ERM.. WHO IS YOUR FAVOURITE BAND?
SHORTLY
MY DATE MADE AN EXCUSE AND LEFT HALFWAY THROUGH THE MEAL.
I MUST'VE DRIVEN IT AWAY WITH MY FUCKWITTED CONVERSATION
>SIGH< OH WELL. I SUPPOSE A DOPEY TWAT LIKE ME IS DESTINED TO BE ALONE FOREVER.
TERRY...
I AM YOUR FAIRY GODMOTHER
BUGGER ME
YOU MAY CHOOSE ONE OF THE FOLLOWING TWO WISHES
EITHER YOU CAN SPEND THE REST OF YOUR LIFE WITH THIS BEAUTIFUL WOMAN WHO IS KIND, CONSIDERATE AND WILL LOVE YOU PASSIONATELY...
..OR YOU CAN SPEND THE REST OF YOUR LIFE UP TO YOUR NECK IN THIS BARREL OF SCORPIONS, WITH JANET STREET-PORTER SCREAMING CONTINUOUSLY IN YOUR EAR.
SCORPIONS
THE CHOICE IS YOURS, TERRY. WILL YOU TAKE THE BEAUTIFUL WOMAN, OR THE BARREL OF SCORPIONS WITH JANET STREET-PORTER?
..ERM.. ERM.. LET ME SEE...
FORTY YEARS LATER
YARRRGH!
SCREECH!
SCORPIONS
AAIEEYAAGH!
FUCK ME. SOMETIMES I WONDER IF I MADE THE RIGHT DECISION.

MAY THE CO[U]
WITH YOU

HOLLYWOOD EXCLUSIVE!

FRESH FROM the success of his latest epic sci-fi adventure, billionaire Star Wars creator *George Lucas* may be about to mount the most spectacular fight of his career. But this time his adversary won't be a seven-foot wheezing Sith - *it'll be a 48-year-old mother of nine from the West Midlands.*

And if she has her way, instead of the wide open spaces of an alien galaxy far, far away, the battle could take place in the more mundane surroundings of Redditch Magistrates Court.

For Solihull cinema usherette Maureen Herpes claims that the plots for all six Star Wars films have been lifted directly from her own life story. She told us: "George Lucas has made a fortune, and it's all based on things that have happened to me; the plots, the characters, everything. It's only fair that I should get a cut of the proceeds."

dress

Herpes first noticed similarities between her own life and Star Wars when the first movie was released in 1977. "It was a little bit spooky, to say the least," she told us. "The film's principal character was called Princess Leia and she had black hair and a white dress. Well, my hair was black at that time too, and I'd bought myself a white dress in the BHS sale just a few weeks earlier.

pass port

"At the time I thought it was just a bizarre coincidence and I thought no more about it," she added. But when the second film, *'The Empire Strikes Back'* came out, Maureen's earlier suspicions were confirmed. She told us: "It turned out that Princess Leia and Luke Skywalker were twins. Well, I've got a twin brother too." But the coincidences didn't stop there. "Luke is a space pilot who flies X-wing fighters for the Rebel Alliance, and my brother Alan drives an X-reg van for Allied Carpets. It sent a shiver down my spine when I realised, I can tell you."

Who Leias Wins: *Luke Skywalker (left), Darth Vader (not quite as left), so sad Maureen (above), R2-D2 lookalike Henry Hoover (below right), Chewbacca dog Tyson (same amount right but bit further below), and the real Princess (rightest of all), yesterday.*

What finally clinched it for Maureen was the film's climactic deathbed revelation that arch-villain Darth Vader was the twins' estranged father. "When he took that mask off and I saw his blotchy, purple face gasping for breath, the hairs on the back of my neck stood up," she told us. "It was the spitting image of our dad. He used to drink a bit, and was on eighty un-tipped Woodbine a day."

> *'...Vader was the spitting image of our dad. He used to drink a bit, and was on eighty un-tipped Woodbine a day'*

pass stools

"Just like Luke and Leia, we didn't see a lot of our father when we were growing up," she continued. "He might not have been a Jedi Knight, but he did get into a lot of fights, mainly at closing time. And like Vader, he turned to the dark side at an early age, drinking mainly Guinness and Younger's Scotch Bitter."

pass partout

The day after seeing the movie, Maureen went to her local Police Station to launch an action for copyright theft against the film's director. "I told the duty constable what had happened, and that I wanted to press charges. He told me he was just finishing his shift, but he'd leave a note for the desk sergeant who came on at nine, asking him to telephone the Police Station in Hollywood and have George Lucas arrested.

"As he ushered me out, he assured me they'd have him safely locked up in prison by tea-time," said Herpes.

"However, when I turned on the TV news that night, there was no mention of the case. I can only assume that Lucas had used his wealth and position to get off the charge."

Maureen thought that the movie mogul's brush with the law might have scared him off, but as the Star Wars films continued to come out over the next few years, the catalogue of similarities between them and Herpes' life grew longer and longer. She told us: "For example, the young

DESSERT?
HONESTLY, DARLING. I COULDN'T EAT ANOTHER THING.

RTS BE

Solihull Usherette Maureen set to sue Star Wars Lucas

Luke and Leia are watched over by a kindly uncle figure, Obi Wan-Kenobi, who they refer to as Ben.

Dr Watson

"While we were children, we used to have many uncles who came to stop the night at our house, mainly long distance lorry drivers. I'm almost certain one of them was called Ben."

And the coincidences didn't stop there.

- *Droid R2-D2 looks strikingly similar to Maureen's Henry Hoover.*

- *The light sabres wielded by the Jedi Knights bear more than a passing resemblance to her cinema usherette's torch.*

- *A scene where the Rebel Alliance detroy the Death Star has distinct echoes of an incident from Maureen's life when she had an accident with a microwave oven and a tin of Aldi Noodle Doodles.*

- *Hairy wookiee Chewbacca can stand on his back legs and wears a bullet-belt, just like her dog Tyson.*

Herpes was so angry that she decided to go to the Police again, this time armed with a dossier of evidence. Unfortunately, the duty constable was just coming off his shift again, but he assured Maureen that her complaints were being taken seriously. She told us: "He explained he was going to fly to Hollywood and arrest George Lucas himself, just as soon as he had finished his cup of tea."

However, once again Lucas somehow escaped formal charges. To make matters worse, the bizarre plot parallels continued to appear in further Star Wars films, getting ever more blatant. Maureen told us: "As an usherette I stood through each of these films hundreds of times. On each viewing, more and more similarities became apparent. Names, faces, gadgets, relationships. It was like Lucas was taunting me.

'...Hairy wookiee Chewbacca can stand on his back legs and wears a bullet-belt, just like my dog Tyson.'

Sancho Panza

"In the end, I was so upset by what was happening that I couldn't cope any more and I went to see my doctor," said Maureen. "He prescribed me nerve pills, put me on the panel for three months and had the kids taken into care." In the end, Maureen spent more than six months off work before she felt well enough to return. However, she couldn't have picked a worse time to go back to her job at the cinema.

Henry

"I couldn't believe it. The day I returned, the film that was showing was *'The Phantom Menace',* the one where the Gungans join forces with Obi-Wan Kenobi and Liam Neeson to battle the evil Trade Federation," said Maureen. "And this time, the similarities between the plot and my life were obvious to everyone."

"You see, for the previous 4-months I had had a Gungan lodger from the planet Naboo staying in my spare room. Like in the film, he had been expelled from his own planet, where he lived in a huge bubble at the bottom of the sea. You might dismiss it as a mere coincidence until you hear his name. It was Jam-Jar Binx."

NEXT WEEK..................

Maureen explains how the plot of the final Star Wars film *'Revenge of the Sith'* is based on the time she got pregnant off the cinema projectionist Anikin Skywalker, and then gave birth to herself and her twin brother before being sectioned under the Mental Health Act.

Mrs Brady Old Lady
HOSPITAL
COO-EEE! DOLLY! IT'S ONLY ME - ADA.
HELLO LOVE.
NOW I'LL NOT TAKE ME COAT OFF, DOLLY, BECAUSE I'M NOT STOPPING. HOW ARE YOU AFTER YOUR PROCEDURE..?
WELL I'M NOT TOO GOOD ACTUALLY, ADA... YOU SEE...
...I ONLY ASK BECAUSE I HAD THAT DONE ONCE, YOU KNOW, ONLY THERE WAS COMPLICATION I WAS VERY DRY AND THEY'D N
USED ENOUGH GREASE ON THE PROBE, YOU SEE...
CAN YOU SMELL LILIES?
...WELL, THE CAMERA LEN SNAGGED ON AN ANAL POLYP AND THE WHOLE LINING OF ME RECTUM SLOUGHED OFF IN A SINGLE PIECE.
IT'S... IT'S ALL GOING DARK, ADA...
A SINGLE PIECE! TWO FOOT IT WERE. LOOKED LIKE THE INNER TUBE OFF A BIKE, MR. CHAKRABORTY SAID...
I CAN HEAR A CHOIR...
NOT THAT THEY WAS NONE THE WISER AFTERWARDS. JUST SENT ME HOME, SAID I WERE PROBABLY ALLERGICT TO GLUTEN... YOU KNOW,
SUMMAT IN BREAD.
I'M... I'M IN A TUNNEL, ADA. THERE'S A BRIGHT LIGHT AT THE END.
ALLERGICT TO BREAD - AT MY AGE! I ASK YOU. ME - A BAKER DAUGHTER! I'VE NEVER HEAR OF OUT SO RIDICULOUS.
I CAN SEE SOMEBODY... IT'S ME MAM AND ME DAD... AND ME SISTER ETHEL...!
I SAID TO HIM, MR. CHAKRABORTY, I SAID, WE DIDN'T HAVE TIME TO BE ALLERGICT IN MY DAY, I SAID, WE HAD THE ALLEY TO SCRUB. THAT SHUT HIM UP. MIND, DON'T GET ME WRONG, DOLLY. HE'S A NICE MAN, THOUGH... BLACK, BUT VERY NICE WITH IT.
I'M RUNNING TOWARDS THEM, ADA... THEY'RE WAVING AT ME... HELLO MAM!... HELLO DAD...!
WELL I SAY BLACK, HE'S NOT REALLY BLACK, HE'S COLOURED... YOU KNOW, LIKE DJ PANDIT G OUT OF ASIAN DUB FOUNDATION.
CROAK!
MIND, THEY'RE EVERYWHERE NOW, AREN'T THEY. THE BUS DRIVER WHAT BRUNG ME HERE, THE 42, HE WERE ONE, DOLLY... LOVELY TEETH...
BEEEEEP..!
BEEEEEEEEEEEEEEEEP..!
I MISSED THE NUMBER SIX. WELL I SAY MISSED. I WAS AT THE ST BUT THE DRIVER WOULDN'T LET ME ON. SAID I WERE TOO EARLY FOR ME PASS.
TWO MINUTES TO NINE IT WERE, DOLLY...
TWO MINUTES TO! CAN YOU BELIEVE IT?! THE ROTTEN BLOODY TURK... AN' HE WERE WHITE TOO!
THERE'S NO PULSE, NURSE. I'M GOING TO SHOCK HER.
YES DOCTOR.
DID YOU HEAR ME, DOLLY? I SAYS HE WERE WHITE..!
CLEAR!
WHITE!
BOOMPH!
MIND YOU, I THINK HE MIGHT OF BEEN ONE OF THEM... VERY LONG FINGERS HE HAD. VERY GENTLE.
HER NEXT DOOR BUT TWO, HER ELDEST, WELL, HE'S ONE.
TURNS MY STOMACH, IT DOES. THE THOUGHT OF WHAT HE GETS UP TO, THE FILTHY LITTLE BUGGER.
WE'VE GOT A HEARTBEAT NURSE.
GROAN
VERY CLEAN, THOUGH, APPARENTLY. NOT AFRAID TO PUSH A HOOVER ABOUT. HE WAS VERY GOOD WHEN SHE HAD HER FALL.
SHE STILL CHUCKED HIM OUT, THOUGH, AND I DON'T BLAME HER NEITHER.
MY SIDNEY, GOD REST HIS SOUL, HAD NO TIME FOR 'EM, YOU KNOW. OH NO. DROWN 'EM AT BIRTH, HE SAID.
AND HE KNEW WHAT HE WERE ON ABOUT TOO, 'COS HE'D HAD A COUPLE OF EXPERIMENTS IN THAT DIRECTION WHEN HE WERE IN THE MERCHANT MARINE.
...JUST A BIT OF MUTUAL MASTURBATION WITH A PETTY OFFICER, THE ODD FELTCH... YOU KNOW. BUT IT WASN'T FOR HIM, HE SAID.
HE LIKED RIMMING, THOUGH. WELL, THE WAR WERE ON, WEREN'T IT. YOU HAD TO TAKE YOUR PLEASURES WHERE YOU COULD IN THEM DAYS, DIDN'T YOU?
WELL, YOU DIDN'T KNOW IF YOU WAS EVER GOING TO SEE YOUR HOME AGAIN, DID YOU?
...AGAIN, NO. THAT'S RIGHT, YES.

WELL, I'VE GOT TO GO, DOLLY. I CAN'T SIT HERE LISTENING TO YOU ALL DAY.
NO, WAIT ADA. LISTEN...
I'VE JUST HAD A NEAR DEATH. I'VE BEEN TO THE ASTRAL PLANE!
EEH. WHAT WAS IT LIKE?
VERY CLEAN, ADA.
THEY WAS ALL THERE - ME MAM, ME DAD... ME SISTER ETHEL...
YOUR ETHEL!? SHE'S NOT DEAD, DOLLY. SHE LIVES IN LEEDS.
I KNOW.
EEH. SHE GETS EVERYWHERE, THAT ONE.
SHE DOES, ADA.
IT'S HER NORMAN, YOU SEE. HE WORKED ON THE TRAINS AND SHE KEPT HIS PASS WHEN HE DIED.
ANY ROAD UP, ADA, I'VE GOT TO TELL YOU - WHILE I WERE ON THE OTHER SIDE, I SAW YOUR SIDNEY!
EEH, FANCY! MY SIDNEY! IS HE HAPPY IN HEAVEN?
OOH, YES. HE IS, ADA.
DID HE HAVE A MESSAGE FOR ME, DOLLY.
NO. HE NEVER MENTIONED YOU, ADA. HE'S LIVING OVER THE BRUSH WITH THAT BLONDE PIECE FROM NUMBER EIGHTY-SIX...
WHO!?
YOU KNOW. HER WHO GOT RAN OVER BY THE COAL LORRY DURING THE COD WAR.
EEH. I MIGHT'VE RUDDY KNOWN IT. ALLUS MAKING COW EYES AT MY SIDNEY, SHE WAS. THE SLUT.
WELL, IT'S NOT JUST HER, ADA. IT TAKES TWO TO TANGO, YOU KNOW.
WELL DON'T BLAME MY SIDNEY. HE'S JUST A MAN - AND YOU KNOW WHAT THEY'RE LIKE, DOLLY.
IF SHE'S PUT IT ON A PLATE FOR HIM, HIS SPIRIT'S GOING TO TAKE IT AND SAY THANK-YOU VERY MUCH.
EEH, MEN! TSK! THEY'RE ALL THE SAME, AREN'T THEY..?
THEY ARE, DOLLY. BEASTS.
FUCKING PIGS.
YOUR SIDNEY WAS A BEAST WHEN HE WAS AROUSED, ADA. A STALLION OF A MAN, HE WAS.
I COULDN'T WALK SOMETIMES, WHEN HE'D FINISHED WITH ME.
WHAT!? YOU MEAN YOU'VE HAD CARNIVAL KNOWLEDGE OF MY HUSBAND?
OOH YES, ADA. MANY TIMES.
HE'D COME ROUND EVERY SUNDAY AND WE'D SPOON. THEN HE'D DO ME UP THE GARY GLITTER.
MIND YOU, DON'T TELL ADA, WILL YOU?
NIL BY MOUTH
OOH NO, DOLLY.
YOUR SECRET'S SAFE WITH ME.
THANKS ADA. IT'S BEEN WEIGHING HEAVY ON ME CONSCIENCE ALL ME LIFE, THAT HAS.
WELL, YOU SHOULDN'T BLAME YOURSELF.
IF HIS WIFE HAD BEEN PERFORMING HER MARITAL DUTIES, HE WOULDN'T OF BEEN FORCED TO GO ELSEWHERE TO FULFIL HIS NEEDS.
EEH. THANKS, ADA.
YOU'RE WELCOME, DOLLY.
WELL - THIS WON'T GET BABY A BONNET, WILL IT, ADA? I'D BEST BE OFF.
THANKS FOR COMING TO SEE ME, DOLLY LOVE.
THAT'S ALRIGHT ADA. I'LL POP IN TOMORROW. SEE HOW YOU ARE.
BYE.
...SORRY, LOVE. YOU'RE 2 MINUTES LATE. YOU CAN'T USE YOUR PASS.
BUS STOP
EEH. YOU ROTTEN BLOODY TURK.
...RIGHT THEN MRS...ER... EARNSHAW, LET'S GET YOU READY FOR YOUR PROCEDURE, SHALL WE?
...PROCEDURE, YES. THAT'S RIGHT DOCTOR.
NEXT DAY...
COO-EEE! ADA! IT'S ONLY ME - DOLLY.
HELLO LOVE.
NIL BY MOUTH
NOW I'LL NOT TAKE ME COAT OFF, BECAUSE I'M NOT STOPPING. HOW ARE YOU AFTER YOUR PROCEDURE?
WELL I'M NOT TOO GOOD ACTUALLY, DOLLY... YOU SEE...

Barely Legal Tyres
The best photos of
XXX-ply Tyres
you will EVER SEE!
INSIDE...
*Jailbait Radials!
*Bald Remoulds!
*Tyres with just 1mm of tread!
OUT NOW!

When the going gets tough, the tough get...

Billy Ocean FINANCE

Whether you're wanting to consolidate two halves of a stolen car into one manageable deathtrap or fancy jetting-off on that once (a year) in a lifetime trip to Majorca, contact us today. We won't ask questions, in fact we don't even pick up the phone... *WE JUST SEND THE MONEY!!!*

"My scratchcard-addicted wife constantly nagged me about a holiday abroad. Thanks to an outrageous loan from Billy, she's now my Carribbean Queen"

Mr B, Essex

"Billy's loan got me out of my dreams and into my car, which was repossessed by Billy's bailiffs after two missed payments"

Mr P, Kent

"After I appeared on the TV advertisement for Billy Ocean Finance, people would see me in the street and ask if I was the fat. mudskipper tramp from the telly"

L. Bardswell, Liverpool

Call Billy Today... ☎ **0900 84425 2868**

GNER

Head Trainspotter

£32-40k Ref: H20/33

As part of their Care in the Community scheme, Great North Eastern Railways are looking for a young enthusiastic trainspotter to work the East Coast mainline between York and Newcastle. The sucessful applicant will have:

- ***A notebook and pencil***
- ***An uninspiring personality***
- ***Chronic acne***

He will be a static individual with at least 4 years experience crossing out numbers in a book. A 6-year-old stained anorak and a super pair of binos will be provided.

Apply in writing stating your favourite class 37 locomotive to GNER, York Station, York, YO1 1AB

Are YOUR Trousers 4 inches too short?

A vacancy has arisen at Derby railway station for a

Grade 3 Railway Enthusiast.

28,500 pa (inc sandwiches and flask)

The sucessful applicant will live with his mother, have no social skills and be completely unable to interact with the public on any level. He will be required to stand at the very end of platform 4 in a kagoul with the hood up, squinting at trains.

Send a current CV to The Station Master, Derby Train Station, Derby

Railway Enthusiast, Technical Class 4

£45-48k (inc London weighting)

Based at Euston Station. Duties will include speaking the numbers of trains into a dictaphone in a monotone voice and videoing trains coming into the station and writing the numbers down later on. The sucessfull applicant must be familiar with the use of dictaphones and video cameras and must be able to ignore the accusations of more traditionalist railway enthusiasts that his method is 'not proper spotting'.

Send a long and pedantic cv to: The Station Manager, Euston Station, London

Railway Enthusiast Grade 5

£42-45k

- ***Are you at least four stone overweight?...***
- ***Are your glasses held together with a plaster?...***
- ***Are you on the Sex Offenders register?...***

If you can answer *YES* to all these questions, then you may be the man we are looking for.

West Coast Rail are looking for a middle-aged-bachelor to head a team of social misfits writing down train numbers at Crewe Station. The sucessful candidate will smell of salt and vinegar crisps, and will have a proven track record of getting very excited when a train comes in. A load of limp, margarine sandwiches in a tupperware box would be an advantage.

For an application form, get your mum to call 0900 800 900, and ask her to quote Ref: 27/001

SWR

Senior Spotter

92hr/wk £42k

There are trains coming in and out of the station all day. How many of their numbers can you write down?

Is it 80%?... 90%?... *99%?...*

...Yes?

Don't even fill in the form.

South Western Rail are looking for a socially inept man in his early twenties who is committed to standing hunched on the end of a platform at Tiverton Parkway station. The sucessful candidate must be serious about railway procedure will have thick glasses, a facial tick and Aspergers Syndrome. If you think you've got what it takes to write down train numbers all day in all weathers, then we'd like to hear from you.

Write to: Personnel Officer, South Western Rail, Beeching Street, Tiverton. Please quote ref: 30/00.

99.99% NEED NOT APPLY

- **Are you tired of people who don't know the Flying Scotsman is a scheduled service and not a *TRAIN?***
- **Are you infuriated by idiots who can't tell the difference between a Deltic and a Class 55?**
- **Do morons who don't understand railway procedure make you *SICK?***

Great Western Rail

Principal Train Spotter ***£40k pa***

Great Western Rail are looking for a 52-year-old paedophile to stand with flecks of saliva at the corner of his mouth, masturbating in his trousers whenever a class 47 Deltic comes past. Severe BO and a wonky eye would be an advantage, but full training in not washing will be given.

For an application form call 0898 000 700

...then WE want to hear from YOU

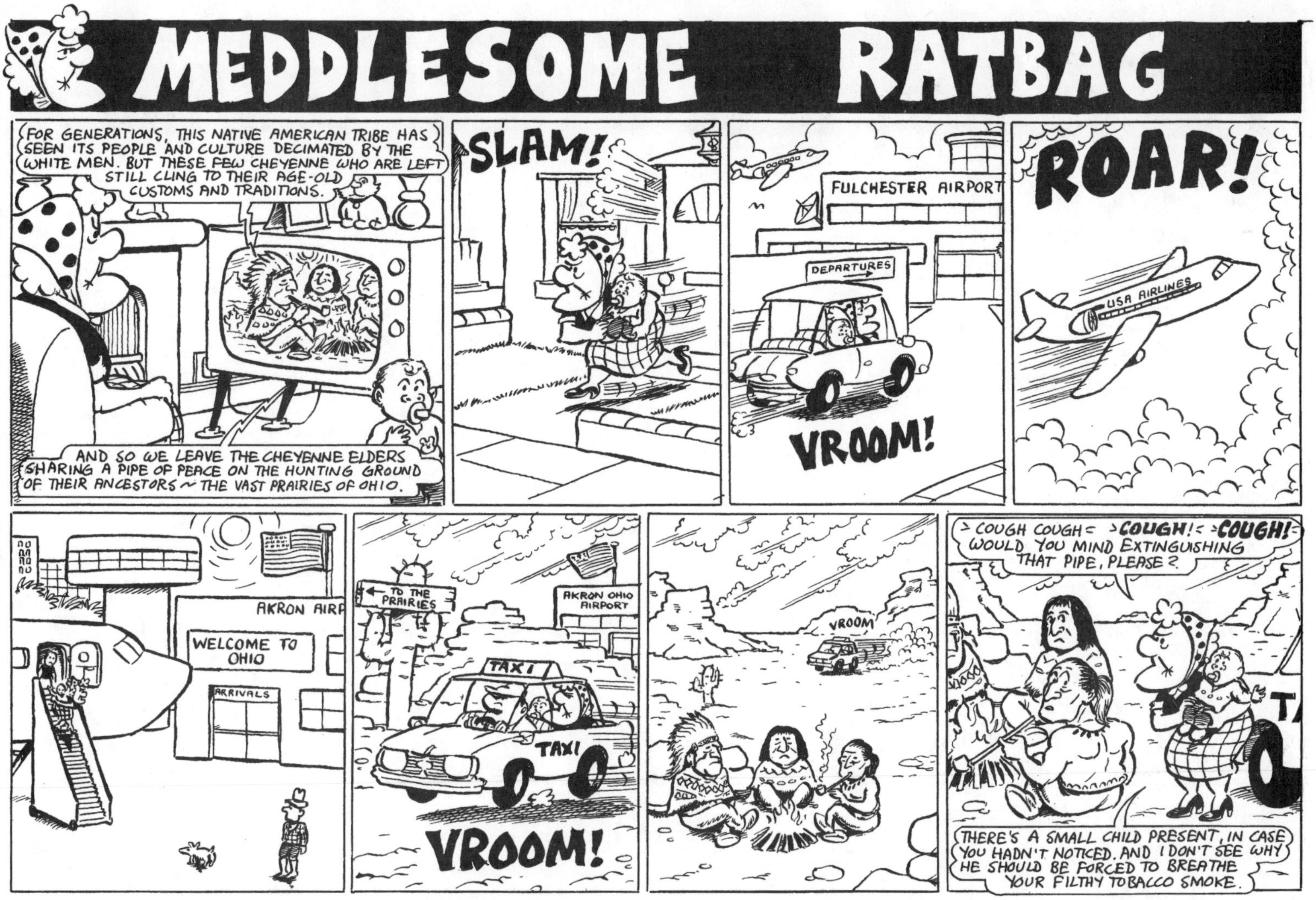
MEDDLESOME RATBAG
FOR GENERATIONS, THIS NATIVE AMERICAN TRIBE HAS SEEN ITS PEOPLE AND CULTURE DECIMATED BY THE WHITE MEN. BUT THESE FEW CHEYENNE WHO ARE LEFT STILL CLING TO THEIR AGE-OLD CUSTOMS AND TRADITIONS.
AND SO WE LEAVE THE CHEYENNE ELDERS SHARING A PIPE OF PEACE ON THE HUNTING GROUND OF THEIR ANCESTORS ~ THE VAST PRAIRIES OF OHIO.
SLAM!
FULCHESTER AIRPORT
DEPARTURES
VROOM!
ROAR!
USA AIRLINES
AKRON AIRP
WELCOME TO OHIO
ARRIVALS
TO THE PRAIRIES
AKRON OHIO AIRPORT
TAXI
TAXI
VROOM!
VROOM
COUGH COUGH COUGH! COUGH!
WOULD YOU MIND EXTINGUISHING THAT PIPE, PLEASE?
THERE'S A SMALL CHILD PRESENT, IN CASE YOU HADN'T NOTICED. AND I DON'T SEE WHY HE SHOULD BE FORCED TO BREATHE YOUR FILTHY TOBACCO SMOKE.

Start an exciting new hobby...

GAMBLING

Cheering your* racehorse first past the post is always a thrilling experience, especially when it's the last two grand of a bank loan that you took out to re-mortgage your house behind the wife's back.

And it was a well known fact that back in the olden days, gambling was the sole preserve of the idle rich and great train robbers. *BUT NOT ANY MORE!*

Because LIFE SAVINGS RACING now make it possible for any debt-ridden buffoon to really let him or herself go with a chronic addiction to gambling. By the time we've finished with you, you won't be able to walk past a bookies or read the back pages without thinking of the odds on a little three-way spread.

The concept is quite simple, join with us and you will receive all the knowledge that you could hope to need in order to spunk away your family's life savings and then money that isn't even yours!

Before you know it you'll be on that downward spiral of debt, home repossession and family break-up!

* the racehorse that you've bet on.

Get Betting NOW!

Have your family hoarded anything of value in your home?

Perhaps your Mother or Grandma has a valuable vase or old piece of furniture?

Turn that unwanted bit of tat into CASH now!

Experience the BUZZ!

Forget about each way bets and Yankies - we'll show you how to lose BIG MONEY in high odds bets!

Should you win, we'll show you how to piss it straight back up the wall in the next race!

It's as simple as losing 3-2-1!

"After only 2 months I'd lost all me money down at the bookies, and me mates had fucked me right off." ***Mr D.D., Sheffield***

Life Savings Racing Ltd, 12 Lester Piggott Way, Monkford Titwank, Somershire, England.

❑ I would like to receive a membership pack (Contains a full list of UK credit card offers and betting shops, plus a ***FREE*** copy of 'How I Won a Million at Ascot' by HRH Sheik Al-Unsheera.)

❑ I would like a representative of your company to visit my invalid mother's house and compile a list of any valuables she has.

Name________________ **Address**________________

________________ **Postcode**________________

❑ Tick here if you do not want your children to receive any presents next Christmas.

*"I'd lost everything after 5 weeks with **LIFE SAVINGS RACING**, and soon there was nothing for it but for my wife to go on the game."* ***Mr. B, Essex.***

the THREE WISE STOOGES in: FOR UNTO NUTS A CHILD IS BORN
CURLSPAR MOECHIOR LARRY THAZAR
COME MARY - THIS HUMBLE STABLE SHALL SHELTER US THIS NIGHT -
BING-DONG!
... EH? WHO'S AT THE DOOR?
WHY HELLO SIR - WE'RE TRAVELLING SALESMAGI, AND WE'VE COME TO INTEREST YOU IN SOME WONDROUS GIFTS!
YEAH! WE'VE GOT GOLD, AND FRANKINCENSE, AND - OH NO! MOE, WE FORGOT THE MYRHH!
TUMBLE!
YEAH? I'LL GIVE YOU SOME MYRHH! HERE - MYRHH-Y CHRISTMAS!
I HEARD THE LADY WAS POORLY, SO I BROUGHT HER SOME GRAPES!
FREEMP!
OOO!!
NEEE!
SHE DOESN'T NEED ANY GRAPES YOU NUMBSKULL - LOOK AT THE SIZE OF HER! SHE'S CHOWED DOWN PLENTY ALREADY!
SAYYY, I'VE HEARD OF HER - HAIL MARY, FULL OF GRAPES!
DOINK!
LISTEN SISTER - IF YOU WANNA LOSE THAT WEIGHT YOU'RE GONNA HAVE TO EXERCISE!
HERE, TRY LIFTING THESE! THEY'RE TERRIFIC FOR YOUR LUMBAR!
BOOMP!
100 LBS
100 LBS
NO KIDDIN' - I'M LUMBERED WITH A PAIR OF DUMBELLS TOO! NOW BACK UP AND GIVE THE FAT LADY SOME ROOM!
NYAA!!
OOO!
KLONK!
100 LBS
NO NO NO - MARY IS GREAT WITH CHILD!
OH, GOOD WITH KIDS HUH? SHE SHOULD BE A TEACHER - OWWW!!
YOU NINCOMPOOP - HE MEANS THE DAME'S GONNA HAVE A BABY! AND SINCE THERE'S NO DOCTOR, WE'LL HAVE TO DELIVER IT OURSELVES!
WAP!
LAAA DE DEEE,,, FORCEPS!
FORCEPS!
FIVECEPS!
FIVECEPS! HOW'S THE PATIENT, DOCTOR?
IN STABLE CONDITION! NYUK NYUK!
OKAY, NOW PUSH! PUSH!!
WELL OKAY MOE, IF YOU SAY SO!
GAAH! NOT YOU, YOU LAMEBRAINS!
SHOVE! KRASH!
POP!
HEY MOE, LOOK WHAT CAME OUT! IT'S A BABY JESUS,,, AND IT'S UPSIDE-DOWN!
IT'S HEAVENLY PAPA MUST BE AUSTRALIAN!
,,, AUSTRALIAN PAPA!!
I'LL POP YOU TO THE LAND DOWN UNDER, KNUCKLEHEAD!
GIMME THAT PRECIOUS LAMB OF GOD!
OWWW! HEYYY, WHAT'S THE BIG IDEA!
GRAB!
SPLAP!
HIT ME WITH THE PRINCE OF PEACE WILL YA! HERE, TRY A PIECE OF THIS!
NYAA! I'VE GOT A MESSIAH IN MY EYE-AH!
WHY I OUGHTA -
SHPLEP!
COME ON MARY - LET'S GO FETCH A POLICEMAN.
OH, WISEGUY HUH?
NYEEEE!!
OOOOO!!
NGA! NGA! NGAAA!!
TOING!
BEP!
WONK!
PANG!
WOO WOO WOO!!
HEY, WAIT A MINUTE - WHERE'S THE CHRIST CHILD?
DON'T WORRY - IT'S SAFE! I PUT IT IN THAT MANGER WITH ALL THE NICE SOFT STRAW!
YOU NITWIT! THAT'S NOT STRAW - THAT'S HAY! NOW THAT DONKEY'S EATEN MAN'S PROMISED REDEEMER!
WE'VE GOT TO REPLACE THAT SAVIOUR BEFORE THEY COME BACK WITH THE COPS!
NOW LISTEN UP - I'VE GOT AN IDEA!
THEY'VE GONE - BUT WHAT'S THAT PRAM?
RH 05
WHA-?!? THREE BABIES?
THAT'S RIGHT TOOTS - YOU HAD HOLY TRIPLETS! I'M JESUS!
AND I'M LESUS!
AND I'M MESUS!
AREN'T THEY ADORABLE! OH JOSEPH, CAN WE KEEP THEM?
OF COURSE, MARY - THEY ARE, ERM, THE BLESSED FRUIT OF YOUR WOMB.
HEY MOE, IT WORKED! WE'RE GONNA BE THE SONS OF GOD!!
YEP!
IT'S EASY STREET FOR US FROM NOW ON, BOYS!
33 YEARS LATER,,,
HEY MOE, LOOK - I'M THE LETTER 'T'!
YEAH - LIKE IN TOTAL IMBECILE!
GONK!
WAP!
BOP!
NYAA!!
NOW MOE, DON'T GET CROSS - OOO!!

Dog in a Million!

One Ron and his dog: Stonybridge with life-saver Bonzo

Every dog owner thinks that their pet is special, but meet Bonzo, the pooch in a million who has just been named 'Bravest Dog In Britain' at the prestigious *Daily Mirror* Animals of Courage awards. And it's a well deserved prize, for Bonzo's owner Ron Stonybridge reckons the heroic hound has saved his life no fewer than *TWENTY TIMES.*

EXCLUSIVE

The six-year-old Lurcher was presented with the 'Golden Bone' award at a glittering ceremony at the Albert Hall yesterday after owner Ron wrote to the newspaper to nominate him.

"Without that dog, I literally would not be here today," he told us. "Bonzo first saved my life a couple of weeks after I got him. I was sitting at home watching the racing on the telly when suddenly I heard an almighty crash from the kitchen. A bloke I owed a bit of money to had sent somebody round with a baseball bat to sort me out, and he had kicked the back door in.

"I'd had a few drinks so I was in no state to defend myself, but luckily Bonzo came to my rescue. He'd had a bit of an upset tummy for a few days, and there was quite a bit of shit in the hall. When this heavy come running through, he slipped in one of Bonzo's turds and went arse over tit, cracking his head on the banister.

"It gave me the few seconds I needed to escape out the window in the front room. If my dog hadn't crapped all over the hall, this bloke might have broke my legs, or even worse."

This incident alone would have been enough to win the award, but barely two weeks later Bonzo was to save Ron's bacon yet again.

"This one night, I'd had quite a skinful and I was fast asleep on the couch downstairs. At about 3am, I was woken up by Bonzo. He was making a terrible racket in the hall, retching something up. I got up to see what was going on, and I found him coughing up a tampon which I'd seen him eat down by the canal earlier that day.

"At the time I was angry that he had woken me up and went over to kick him. But as I did, I heard the letterbox rattling. Then I saw the nozzle of a fuel can come through, and somebody started pouring petrol onto the mat. I opened the door and saw a man I'd borrowed some money off a few weeks earlier. He was trying to light some newspaper with a match, but when he saw me he ran off.

"I chased him for a couple of streets, but eventually I had to give up as I was in my vest and pants and I only had one shoe on. I owe Bonzo my life. If it hadn't been for him waking me up, I doubt I would have been here to tell the tale."

The next occasion that Ron's life was threatened, there seemed no way that his faithful hound could help. But the wonder dog was to come to his master's rescue in a most unexpected way.

"It was just before Christmas, and I was in my flat when there was a knock at the door. When I answered it, there on the step stood two nasty looking blokes. One of them had a shotgun in a carrier bag. At that time I'd run up quite a slate with an unlicensed bookmaker, and he'd been trying to get the money off me for months. Finally he had lost patience and sent a couple of his heavies round to kill me.

"I shouted for Bonzo, but then I remembered I had shut him in the coal house because he'd been barking for his dinner all night. I thought my number was up, but then suddenly a police car pulled up and two coppers got out and came up the path. The two hitmen scarpered.

"I couldn't believe my luck. It turned out that the previous day I had left the gate open and Bonzo had got out into the back lane where he had savaged a toddler. The attack only lasted a couple of minutes and the kid just need a few stitches in his face and throat, but his mum had made a bit of a song and dance about it.

"The coppers had turned up to charge me with failure to keep control of a dangerous dog. Bonzo had done it again. If he hadn't have bitten that kid, the coppers would never have come to my door, and I dread to think what would have happened."

Bonzo left the stage with his tail held high, a golden bone medal and his prize, which included a year's supply of worming powder and a voucher for a free shampoo at a top London dog-grooming parlour.

"They say a man's best friend is his dog," said Ron. "And that's certainly true of me and Bonzo. I may have got him for free off a man in the pub, but after what he's done for me I wouldn't sell him for a hundred pounds!"

"But I will sell the grooming voucher and the worming powder. I need £15 before tomorrow morning, or someone I borrowed a bit of cash off says he's going to break my thumbs with a hammer," he added.

"I owe Bonzo my life. If it hadn't been for him waking me up, I doubt I would have been here to tell the tale."

Top of the Pox

CLAP EXPERTS are predicting that Chlamydia will beat Syphillis to the coveted top spot in this year's Christmas venereal disease charts. The prediction follows a year which has seen a marked drop in cases of more traditional VDs, such as Gonorrhoea, Non-specific Urethritis and Genital Herpes.

"2005 has been a year of record success for Chlamydia," said Dr Frances Discharge of the British Institute of Genito-Urinary Medicine. "It has rarely been out of the Top Ten STDs in the past twelve months, and for the last six weeks it's been firmly ensconced in the number one slot."

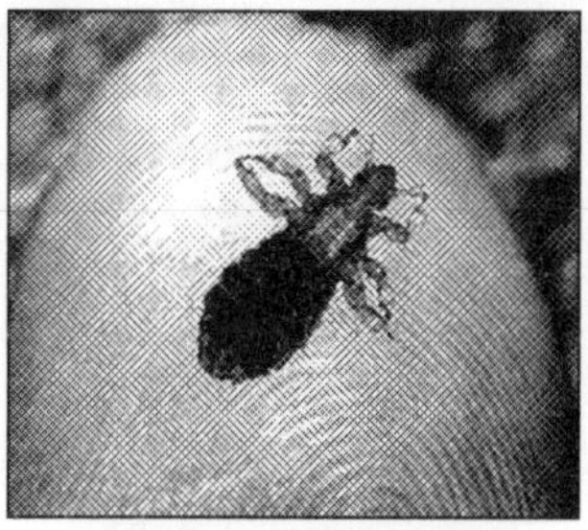

VD nasty: A Chlamydia germ yesterday. *(Picture courtesy of Dame Shirley Bassey)*

And she had this advice for anyone thinking about having a flutter on the Christmas Sexually-Transmitted Disease Charts. "Traditional evergreen infections such as Syphillis, the Peter Pan of Pox, have had their day. There are simply too many new up-and-coming diseases about for dated, old-fashioned claps to dominate the December chart rundown like they used to."

"If I had to bet on the Christmas top position, I know where I'd put my money," she added. "Vaginitis may be bubbling under, but Chlamydia's the infection that's on everyone's lips at the moment."

1	Chlamydia
2	Trichmoniasis
3	Human Papilloma Virus
4	Crabs
5	Gonorrhoea
6	Vaginitis
7	Non-specific Urethritis
8	Syphillis
9	Genital Herpex Simplex 2
10	Molluscum Contagiosum

The December 1st Chart: but which VD will be celebrating on Christmas Day?

40 million dead... 50 million dead

FLU, WHAT A SCORCHER!

MAKE the most of this Christmas, because it will almost certainly be your last. But amazingly, it's not a giant flaming meteorite, a terrorist dirty bomb or catastrophic global warming that's going to finish us all off, it's a few sneezing chickens. That's because experts reckon that 2006 will be the year that bird flu strikes the UK, and when it does we're all going to die.

By our We're All Going to Die Correspondent
CHICKEN LICKEN

Avian influenza, or to give it its correct scientific name *bird flu,* is spreading across Europe like wildfire. Fortunately, it's carried by chickens which can't fly. They can only walk slowly as they have to stop every few steps to peck at grit. But we can take little comfort from this, according to government scientist Professor Jackie Pallo. He told us: "People shouldn't be alarmed about bird flu, but sooner or later a stray hen is going to walk through the Channel Tunnel and cough on someone. And when that happens it will be curtains for the entire UK population within days."

But it's not all doom and gloom. A vaccine has been produced although the supply is very limited. Professor Pallo told us: "The Royal Family have all been inoculated to protect them from the bird flu. The remaining stocks of vaccine will be distributed strictly according to need. Politicians and celebrities from the worlds of entertainment, pop music and reality TV will all receive jabs before Christmas," he added. "Any stocks left over after that will be set aside for the Queen's dogs, horses and servants."

Swings and Roundabouts of Bird Flu

THE forthcoming pandemic may spell doom for everyone in the country, but it is good news for Britain's undertakers. With the prospect of 60 million burials to organise in the next twelve months, 2006 looks set to be a boom year for UK's funeral directors.

"We're very excited about bird flu," says British Embalmers' Society president Len Duxbury. "It's going to be a real shot in the arm for my members. Life expectancy has soared over the last few years, and the average person can now expect to live to a ripe old age. Sadly, as a result, our profits have taken a dive. An unstoppable fatal plague scything through the population will be a great morale booster for the undertakers of Britain."

Also smiling is Ernie Shadrack, spokesman for the Federation of British Boiled Ham Producers. "Sixty million funeral teas means a lot of boiled ham," he laughs. "So my members are looking forward to a bumper year. My advice to anyone expecting to succumb to avian flu this year is; Get your boiled ham in the larder with plenty of time to spare. People are going to be queuing round the block for it once the pandemic hits in earnest."

But the forthcoming plague will spell disaster for another traditional UK business. Birthday card manufacturers estimate that they will see sales plummet by up to more than 98% when bird flu reaches our shores. "The disease typically kills its victims within seven days," says British Birthday Card Trade Association head Billy Waterhouse. "That means that only one person in fifty-two will see their next birthday. With such a marked drop in demand for our products I can foresee widespread redundancies throughout the birthday card industry."

And tap shoe manufacturers are also expecting to find themselves out of pocket. "Bird flu is going to hit the tap shoe industry hard," says Tap Shoe Institute chief Lionel Blair. "When you're dead, the last thing you need is a new pair of taps. It's as simple as that."

60 million dead...

Chicken gravy: A hen in a cemetery yesterday

HOW YOU CAN PROTECT YOURSELF FROM BIRD FLU

Advice from the Government's Chief Medical Officer **Dr LIAM DOUBLEDAY**

1. Avoid large crowds of chickens. Places to steer clear of include chicken shows, battery farms, henhouses and pillow factories.

2. Wear a protective face-mask to stop you breathing in bird flu germs. If you can't find a facemask, a coffee filter secured round your ears with an elastic band is just as effective.

3. Set chicken traps to kill any wild hens that may come near your house. An ordinary rat trap baited with grit should do the trick.

4. Eat more chickens. It may sound like twisted logic, but think about it; the more chickens we eat, the less are left alive to sneeze their deadly germs at us.

5. If you have a bird table you can prevent your garden birds catching flu by mixing up a bit of Lem-Sip powder with their seed, and instead of hanging up a bag of peanuts for them to peck, hang up a bag of Tunes, Lockets or Mentholyptus.

6. If, despite all these precautions, you get bird flu symptoms such as a sore throat, tickly cough or runny nose this winter, write your name and national insurance number on your forehead with a marker pen, climb into a binbag and sit outside your local mortuary until you die.

Miriam

Dr MIRIAM STOPPARD, WHO QUALIFIED AS A DOCTOR SEVERAL DECADES AGO, ANSWERS YOUR QUESTIONS ABOUT BIRD FLU

Dear Miriam...

I HAVE heard a lot about this avian flu that is coming from Thailand. According to the paper, between 50,000 and 2 million britons will die. Should I panic?

Mrs Etherington, Rotherham

Miriam writes...

YES. Tests have shown that running around in small circles with your hair all stuck up whilst screaming at the top of your voice could reduce your susceptibility to H5N1 infection by up to 14%.

Blackpool Gears Up for Avian Flu

"Bring it on" ~ says Lord Mayor

One place that certainly isn't worrying about bird flu is Blackpool. The popular Lancashire resort town already has preparations well underway to deal with the worst that the forthcoming killer superbug can throw at it. And Lord Mayor Ivan Taylor has this message for the 100% fatal virus: "It'll take a bigger germ than H5N1 to stop the fun and games along the Golden Mile."

No matter what happens, councillor Taylor is determined that the north-west seaside town is going to keep smiling through. "The rest of the country might be feeling sick as a parrot," he told us, "but make no mistake, here in Blackpool it's going to be business as usual."

To ensure that the global pandemic affects the town's tourist trade as little as possible, the council has already prepared a 7-point action plan.

- *The Community Health Clinic on Tower Road will suspend its current appointments only system, replacing it with a more flexible 'drop-in' arrangement for people exhibiting symptoms of the fatal virus.*
- *Due to restrictions on the gathering of large crowds, the weekly Glamorous Granny competition at the Winter Gardens will be held behind closed doors, with a council official present to ensure fair play.*
- *Local boy scouts are presently going door to door at weekends and after school, collecting unwanted cotton sheets and shirts. These are going to be washed, cut up and hemmed by the members of Blackpool Women's Institute before being distributed to the population as emergency hankies. The ladies of the Blackpool, Lytham and Fleetwood Embroidery Circle have volunteered to apply personalised initials for a small charge, the proceeds of which will be presented to next year's BBC Children in Need appeal.*
- *Ice cream vans and parlours will be making and selling special Beecham's Hot Lemon ice lollies whilst the killer pandemic is at its height.*
- *The mayor's 11-year-old son has designed a special warning poster featuring a chicken with a thermometer sticking out of its beak, and the slogan 'Cluck Out! Bird Flu's About!' The poster is now on display in the foyer of the Town Hall on Corporation Street.*
- *The municipal dog catcher Mr Nicely will be issued with a smaller hoop, suitable for catching chickens.*
- *When the first case of bird flu is identified on the UK mainland the 15th, 16th, 17th and 18th holes of Reach Golf Course, between Normoss, Staining and Great Marton, will be closed to enable the excavation of a vast lime-lined pit capable of accommodating up to 250,000 corpses.*

"Blackpool holidaymakers are a hardy bunch," insisted councillor Taylor. "They're not going to let a worldwide fatal plague spoil their fortnight on the beach, that's for certain. Avian influenza may have a 100% mortality rate, but Blackpool's got a 110% fun rate, and that's not to be sneezed at," he added.

LETTERBOCKS

Viz Comic, PO Box 656
North Shields NE26 1BT
e-mail: letters@viz.

RORY the Tiger certainly looked like he was having more than just fun at Caister last week. Do I win £5?

Bob Forsyth
email

THE OTHER day when boarding a number 83 bus, I noticed that the driver was a *woman*. Now I'm all for interesting sociological experiments, but I draw the line at risking people's lives. Come on London Transport, get your priorities straight.

Chris Stink
e-mail

IT REALLY annoys me to see these suicide bombers blowing up people as well as themselves. In my day, suicide was done in a more dignified way, such as slicing your wrists in the bath, or hanging yourself from a door with a belt.

Paul Mulraney
Belfast

WHILST watching an ad for Royal Navy careers, I couldn't help noticing that it was rather selective in its content, mainly showing people jumping out of helicopters and firing missiles out of massive cannons. Perhaps they should have included some of the more mundane tasks of a seaman, such as noshing off, and being bummed by, higher-ranking crew members.

H Fisty
HMS Tentpole

FOR A supposed comic genius, Ronnie Barker checked out in seriously unfunny circumstances. Contrast this with Rod Hull. Although unamusing during his entire career, he checked out in hilarious fashion. Come on, comedians, let's have a bit more thought about how you exit this world.

Roy Elliff
e-mail

IT'S A shame Fred West is dead. He would have made a cracking Mungo Jerry on *Stars In Their Eyes.*

Fish Kid
e-mail

CONSIDERING that the Chinese can't pronounce the letter L, how do they say Lawrence Llewellyn Bowen? They probably just say 'that cunt with the floppy cuffs' like everyone else.

Pingu
e-mail

I SPOTTED this van in Portobello, Edinburgh. Surely it deserves an award for its outstanding collection of empty tab packets, apple cores, Ginsters pasty wrappers and other 'dashboard dross'. Can any of your readers beat that?

Simon
Edinburgh

Star Letter

★ **YESTERDAY** I found a copy of your magazine in the airport in London. I was shocked to see how you disrespect your creator. Perhaps you don't believe that God has created you, but that doesn't change the fact that He did. Your comic reminds me of Goliath who defied his Creator. God dealt with him severely through a human being. I'm not a Muslim fundamentalist who might want to stop you by violence, rather I'm a follower of Jesus who has been commanded to love you. Therefore I urge you to repent from making this comic. You'll bear eternal consequences if you don't. Having read this one comic you evidently have some knowledge of the Bible and are aware of God's judgement on those who reject Him. On the other hand, His grace is still available to you as much as for the murderer next to Jesus on the cross who... *(the rest of this letter has been deleted because it just goes on and on and on.)*

Kees van Dieren, e-mail

I'VE JUST seen a car with show dogs in the back and a big rosette on display which read 7th. Beat that.

Jaffa
e-mail

I WAS out walking with my granddaughter the other day when we spotted a lovely thatched cottage. "Look at that house, Granny," she said. "It's wearing a wig!" How I laughed.

Edna Turpentine
Leeds

I HAVE to write to tell you about Edna Turpentine, the writer of the above letter. The fact is her granddaughter lives in Australia. Her son left in 1992 and she's never actually seen her granddaughter other than in photographs. She just walks about the streets having pretend conversations with her. It's tragic, really.

June Cockroach
Leeds

IN RESPONSE to A Firefalcon's letter *(page 120)* about his girlfriend saying that lions are boys and tigers are girls. I can beat that - my housemate Lucy once claimed that ducks and geese aren't birds. Honestly, if women want equality they'd better start being a bit smarter.

Lord Mitz
e-mail

WHY IS IT radio DJs always say "back in a minute" before a commercial break, suggesting that they are going somewhere? Then afterwards they say "welcome back" as though I've been somewhere. I wish they'd stop it, as I'm starting to be unsure as to whether I'm coming or going.

Lee Gartland
e-mail

INSTEAD of punishing people for driving offences, I think the world would be a happier place if the police gave presents to people who obeyed the rules of the road. I for one would check my mirror before indicating if I thought a policeman might appear and give me a box of chocolates or a bunch of daffs.

Hilda
Solihul

WHY IS IT that pubs won't serve me if I'm drunk, but McDonald's continue serving them fat fuckers? It's hardly fair.

Christina Martin
e-mail

Spot a Shaven Star
...and pocket £1 million

★★★

MANY STARS are more famous for their moustaches than their faces. But could YOU recognise a moustacheoed celebrity by their face alone? We've hidden the taches of three famous faces. See if you can guess who they are. There's a cool *ONE MILLION POUNDS* to the lucky millionth reader to send in the correct answers.

This semi-ventriloquist would be 'spit'-ing mad if you shaved his tache off. That's because it was the only thing that stopped you seeing his lips move on Tiswas, 25 years ago.

This is surely the king of moustaches – or rather it's the Queen. And you are the champions if you spot the wearer of this pomp rock homosexual hairy handlebar.

If this ex-Watchdog presenter has a weak link, it's certainly not in the moustache department. Her facial fuzz wins top marks in every round.

*Send your answers to **Viz Comic, PO Box 656, North Shields, NE29 1BT**. Competition is not open to employees of Fulchester industries, Dennis Publishing or their friends and families or any readers of Viz Comic.*

UP THE ARSE CORNER

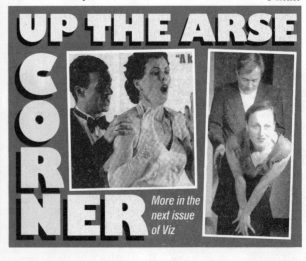

More in the next issue of Viz

I THOUGHT you might like to see this pornographic photo I found on the *'Dear Dierdre'* page of *the Sun.* Now is that a steering wheel in his hand, or is he extremely pleased to see her?

Jeff Dugdale
Lancashire

NEVER MIND a pretend knob, this *'Dear Dierdre'* has got a real fanny in it, I reckon.

J Thorn
Hexham

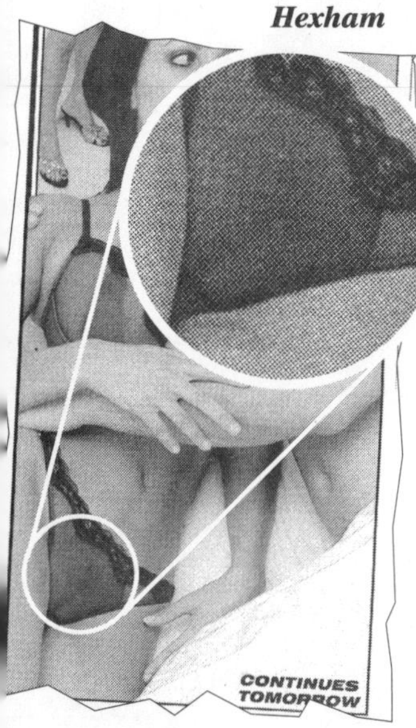

CONTINUES TOMORROW

PETER Andre might look smug all the time, but I'd just like to remind him that, as a *Playboy* reader, I have seen his wife's minge. He hasn't seen my wife's, so who's had the last laugh?

P Lorimer
Leeds

WITH REFERENCE to Mr Lorimer's letter *(above).* It is a very good point, but one which I am unable to claim, since Mr Andre may well have read the *Readers' Wives* section of the May 1993 edition of *Razzle.*

T Plywood
Luton

I RECENTLY saw a young fellow wearing a hat with *Nike* written on the front. Impressed with his interest in Greek Mythology, I attempted to start a conversation on the subject, and was impressed to discover he also had an encyclopaedic knowledge of Anglo-Saxon swearwords. Well done today's teachers, I say.

Lee McGinn
e-mail

CAN YOU JUST TAKE A BIT OFF THE TOP?
BARBERS

THAT'S SAUSAGES!

BRITAIN'S *LIVELIEST* SAUSAGE DEBATE

MY HUSBAND loves sausages. He eats so many, I sometimes think he'll turn into one.

Mavis Nonentity, Croydon

I LOVE *sausages, but I never felt happy eating them because you never know what's in them. So now I buy sausage meat from the butchers and make my own.*

Ada Simpleton, Wessex

"THESE sausages aren't cooked," roared my husband one breakfast. "I know," I replied. "That's because they are still in the packet in the fridge and I haven't started cooking them yet." How silly he felt.

Dolly Dishmop, Staines

MY DAUGHTER *doesn't eat meat, yet the other day I saw her eating sausages. "They're vegetarian sausages," she told me when I questioned her. Vegetarian sausages indeed! Perhaps I should start eating meat potatoes.*

Ron Ironic, Burton on Trent

NUTRITIONISTS say that eating sausages is bad for you. But I love them. Live for today, I say. You may get hit by a bus tomorrow.

T Dreadnaught, Pudsey

I USED *to be a mechanic at a second hand car lot, so I used to restore old bangers for a living. However, I was recently made redundant, but I very quickly found another job - restoring the exhibits at a sausage museum! So I still restore old bangers.*

Fred Lampray, Wales

DURING the Second World War sausages were on ration, but in the army we were allowed one sausage a day. I never ate mine, but saved them to take them back to my family. When I took my leave twice a year, I always went home with twelve dozen sausages. They were completely rancid, but there was a war on and we ate like kings.

Horace Turtle, Rhyll

HOW *Jews can say they don't like sausages is a mystery to me. If they tried them, they might actually like them. Still it's their loss, and it simply means more yummy bangers for the rest of us.*

Dr Rowan Williams
Canterbury

NUTRITIONISTS don't know what they are talking about when they say sausages are bad for you. My grandad ate sixty a day, and he lived until he was ninety.

Arthur Wellington, Croydon

I'M A *widow and I have been seeing a gentleman for several months. We have had some lovely times going for walks and tea dances. Last Sunday he asked me if I'd like to go back to his house saying he had a lovely blood sausage for me. As I love sausages I went. I don't think I shall be seeing him again.*

Audrey Pumpkin,
Cheedle

I LOVE sausages, and when I went on holiday abroad I was looking forward to having them every morning for breakfast. Imagine my disappointment when I found foreign sausages were all the wrong shape and had garlic in them. I was glad to get home.

Stan Tortoise, Burnley

MY *grandad ate sixty sausages a day, and he was run over by a bus when he was ninety - whilst going for a packet of cigarettes!*

Mavis Fibreboard,
Surrey

I AM a widow, and I've been seeing a gentleman for several weeks. We have had some lovely times going to the theatre and the park. Last time we went out, he asked if he could come back to my house for a sausage sandwich. Since I was peckish I readily agreed. Men really are beasts.

Audrey Pumpkin
Cheedle

SAUSAGE TIPS

PRICK your sausages with a fork before frying. That way your bangers won't go *BANG!* For cocktail sausages use a smaller fork.

D. Blackpudding, Blackpool

MAKING a sausage sandwich is much easier if you cut the sausage in two lengthways with a sharp knife, and lay the two halves flat side down on the bread.

M. Cundall, Middlesbrough

Call my SAUSAGE Bluff...

This week's mystery word:

BRADWORST

Is it...

a) A woodworking tool
b) A coniferous tree
c) A German sausage

Last week's Call My Sausage Bluff:
CHIPOLATA
Ans. b) A small sausage.

Ask Doctor SOZIDGE

Dear Dr Sozidge
Why are sausages called bangers?
Mavis Trumpton, Wells

THE WORD banger derives from BHANGA, the Indian word for a small cylindrical roll of fried meat. During the days of the Raj, serving soldiers would eat bhangas for breakfast, and on returning to england, they would refer to their sausages as bhangas, which eventually became bangers.

Heinz Sozidge is Professor of Sausages at Brunel University.

TOP TIPS

DRUNKEN drivers. When making your way home put 'L' plates on your car to convince police that any careless driving is the result of inexperience rather than drink. How you explain a 3am driving lesson is up to you.

Captain Fuck, Derrington

EPILEPTICS. Next time you have a seizure, check yourself in the toilet mirror afterwards to make sure your best friends haven't drawn glasses on your face with a marker pen to the amusement of the rest of the nightclub.

J Roo, e-mail

POLICE. Save money on expensive sirens by putting a police dog on the roof of your patrol car and shutting the door on its tail before attending a 999 call.

Andy Bradshaw, e-mail

SUDOKU lovers. Solve your puzzles in seconds by logging on to *http://sudoku.sourceforge.net/*, typing the clues into the grid and clicking the 'solve' button. This will save hours, leaving you plenty of time to do something worthwhile.

T Wensleydale, Cheshire

PUBLIC ANNOUNCEMENTS

Fulchester District Council Planning Applications

Ref. No. 463/882 B 22.6.05
Field adjacent to Fulchester Convalescent Home for the Nervous. (Plans available to view at council offices) An application has been received from Amalgamated Foghorns and Monster Trucks Ltd., to change the use of the current Convalescent Home Garden of Meditation into a 24-hour foghorn and monster truck testing station.

Ref. No. 146/371B 23.2.05
33b Lower Hotspur Terrace, Bartlepool. An application has been received from Amalgamated Fishing Baits Ltd., to convert a flat above a cake shop into a commercial maggot farm. Full 24-hour access will be required through the front of the cake shop for the delivery of pig carcasses, abattoir waste and bluebottle eggs.

Objections in writing must be received at the Planning Office before Nov. 8th.

Feather-weight o

WHO'S B
BEST P

AS THE country gears up for the Royal Wedding of the millennium, the only one question on everyone's lips... Why will Her Majesty the Qu not be attending? And did Prince Charles really get caught bumming of his butlers? So that's two. But something else everyone wants to kno just who is Britain's best Prince... Naseem Hamed, or of Wales?**

In the blue corner is Charles Philip Arthur George Windsor, the Prince of Wales. Own Cornwall and the scourge of modern arechitecture, bonny Prince Charlie has been the nat right Royal darling for the past 57 years. Whether he's talking to plants, enjoying

OF WALES

Thanks to his mother and father being cousins, Charles' incestuous genes have landed him with a whopping pair of ears. Whilst this has its advantages (at Gordonstoun school, the young Prince discovered he was able use echo location to navigate his way round the dormitory after lights out, emitting a series of shrieks too high to be heard by staff or other boys) it also leaves him open to cruel jibes from other crowned heads of Europe. Consequently, Charles gets off to a poor start in the first round.

1

ROUND
1

Prince of Waleses throughout history have been noted for their dapper elegance. Edward VII swept the ladies off their feet in his top hat, cummerbund and spats, whilst Edward VIII set Mrs Simpson's heart a-flutter with his fashionable plus fours, flamboyantly checked blazers and trademark wide tie knot. However dull Charles, with his drab grey suits, sensible brown shoes and boring jumpers, has bucked this trend.

6 STYLE

Despite being a real life Prince, Duke of Cornwall, Earl of Rothesay and having over 100 lordships under his belt, Charles has never worn a crown in his life! And, if Royal boffins are correct, it'll be a long time yet before he gets the chance. That's because if the Queen lives as long as her mother did, Charles will be be a doddery 82-years old before he gets the chance to slip the Crown of England onto his balding bonce.

5

ROUND
3

It wasn't long after Charles married his first wife, the late Lady Di, that the country rejoiced at the birth of an heir - Prince William. William has since grown up into a shy and sensitive young man who studied art history at University, which is frankly not the most manly subject in the world. Diana also produced Prince Harry, who has followed his father's example by joining the army.

6 HEIRS

Charles doesn't have a full time job and is forced to rely on money from the Civil List, a sort of extremely posh dole. However, with a county, a principality, several houses, a mistress and a large entourage of bumlickers to support, the Prince is so hard up he has to supplement his meagre income by selling needlessly expensive biscuits from his Duchy of Cornwall estate.

7

ROUND
5

It is a well known fact that the Prince of Wales is forbidden by constitutional law from performing menial tasks. Opening doors, putting toothpaste on his brush and having sex with his first wife are all tasks that Charles preferred to delegate. Similarly, tying his shoelaces is the responsibility of Captain Sandy Tibbs-Urquhart, knotter of the lace equerry pursuivant to the Duchy of Cornwall. Never having looked at, let alone tied his own shoelaces, Charles is completely unable to perform this simple task, and consequently trips up in this round.

4 LACE TYING

Despite strutting about with a chestful of medals on his military uniforms, Charles has never actually fired a shot, nor indeed thrown a punch, in anger. Always happier talking to a windowbox of pansies or sitting in a skirt on a Scottish hillside painting a shit watercolour, it's frankly doubtful that the Prince of Wales could handle himself in a pagga. However, since he's an unknown quantity he gets the benefit of the doubt in this round, earning a respectable, if unspectacular, middle-of-the-range score.

7

ROUND
7

Charles was educated at posh public schools like Gordonstoun and Cambridge, where his life was one long round of luxury and privilege. Each day was spent eating caviar and drinking champagne in a top hat before, after a ten course evening meal of swans, the young Charles would roast a naked fag on a roaring log fire in the prefects' dorm. Despite his expensive education, since leaving university in 1969 Charles has not found work easy to come by. Instead he has taken a series of odd jobs such as patron of the British Pteridological Society and cadre of the Royal Thames Yacht Club.

6 EDUCATIO

In 1937 the then former Prince of Wales King Edward VIII spoke straight to the nation's heart in a moving broadcast from Buckingham Palace. Speaking directly to his subjects, the King explained that he could not live without the love of Mrs Simpson, and so was regretfully giving up the British throne. Fifty years later his successor, Prince Charles, touched his subjects in a similar radio address about his own love for Mrs Parker-Bowles. In the broadcast, Charles declared his wish to become Camilla's Tampax, absorbing the blood of his mistress's menstrual discharge before swirling round in her toilet bowl forever. Charles's heartfelt jamrag ambitions mean that he soaks up full marks in this final round, swelling his overall score impressively.

10

ROUND
9

The Winner, and undisputed King of the Princes is Charles of Wales. Despite being on the ropes throughout the majority of the contest, the big-lugged toff battled royally to defeat the pretender to his crown in the dying seconds. He may not always play by the Queensbury rules, but when it comes to attending galas, waving from Rolls Royces and opening hospital wings, Charles is a true superheavyweight!

52

TOTAL
POINTS

eather-crested?

RITAIN'S RINCE?

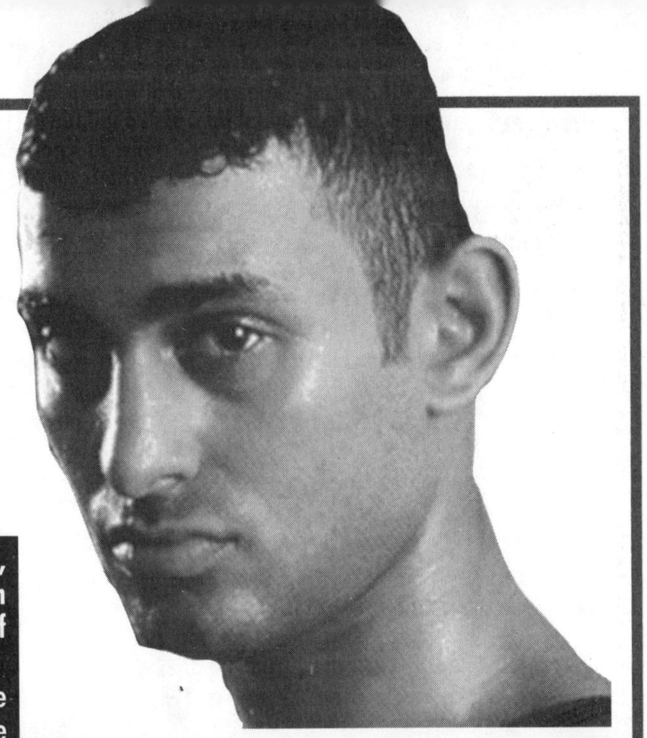

h one of The Three Degrees, or chastising his alleged son for dressing up as a nazi, has seldom been out of the media spotlight. Meanwhile, in the red corner is Naseem med, the Prince of pugilism. Weighing in at just 5 foot 3 inches, this Sheffield man of el packs a knockout punch that belies his short-arsed stature.

The question is simple. Who is the better Prince? In this 9 round match, we compare eir princely attributes and come to a points decision before awarding one of them the e Undisputed King of the Princes.

So, take a ringside seat because *it's seconds out...*

NASEEM

SMALLNESS OF EARS	**2**	Boxers' ears traditionally take a pounding in the ring, often turning into cauliflowers, and Naseem's prominent lobes must have presented his opponents with a tempting pair of targets. However his lightning reflexes enabled the Sheffield Hammer to dodge the blows with ease and as a result, his lugholes are as pristine now as the day they were born over 30 years ago. However, with the best will in the world Naseem's ears could not be described as small, so even though he beats of Wales in this round, it's by the narrowest of margins.
 ROUND 2	**8**	**Prince Naseem has often rightly been called the Naomi Campbell of the boxing ring. Never seen without his flashy silk kimono-style dressing gown, his trademark leopardskin shorts or his trendy leather boxing gloves, he turns every blood-soaked, concussion-filled bout into a fashion show fit for the catwalks of Paris or Milan. He's a worthy winner of this second round.**
CROWNS	**6**	When it comes to having crowns, this feisty featherweight professional boxer makes Charles look like a rank amateur, easily knocking the big-eared Royal into the middle of next week. At the tender age of 21, Naseem's flying fists had already notched him up an incredible tally of over 8 world boxing crowns, including Olympic golds, the 1988 WBA Flyweight championship, and the WBC Bantamweight and Rizlaweight titles. Naseem's sitting room, where he displays his glittering collection on a series of polysterene wig stands, is said to make the Crown Jewels room at the Tower of London look like Cilla Black's jewellery box.
 ROUND 4	**7**	**The stocky Yorkshire Hurricane is well known for punching above his weight in the boxing ring, and he's just as effective when it comes to impregnating his wife between the sheets. The hugely fecund 30-year-old featherweight has sired a pair of strapping sons who possibly already show signs of following their illustrious father into the sporting spotlight.**
WEALTH	**8**	The Don Valley Dynamo may have begun life in much humbler circumstances than his Royal namesake, but he has made up for it since. Over his thirty-eight professional fights, he has amassed purses well in excess of many millions of pounds. And assuming he has invested it wisely, that money will now be worth a king's ransom to the Prince of pugilism.
 ROUND 6	**5**	**Anyone who has seen Prince Naseem fight, couldn't fail to spot the enormous amount of laces on his boxing boots. Although easily rich enough to hire someone to tie them for him, the Dales Sledgehammer prefers to keep in touch with his roots and tie them himself before every fight. However, a perfect score of 10 in this round is spoilt by the fact that he cannot tie the laces on the last boxing glove he puts on, and has to rely on his trainer Brendan Ingle to do the honours.**
FIGHTING	**8**	Hamed has rightly been nicknamed 'The Featherweight Anaesthetist' because of the number of victims he has knocked out who have later woken up in hospital with stitches. In 34 professional fights, the South Riding thunderbolt left an incredible 30 opponents out cold on the canvas, ample proof that he's pretty tasty with his fists. Indeed, despite his diminutive stature, terrier-like Naseem would undoubtedly prove more than a match for any drunk in any boozer the length and breadth of the country. Consequently he wins this round by two falls, a submission and a knockout.
 ROUND 8	**7**	**After leaving Sheffield's tough Wincobank Comprehensive School at the age of sixteen, the Steel City slayer started studying at the University of Life. Three years later he graduated with first class joint honours in hard knocks and common sense. And Naseem certainly didn't put his degree to waste in the ring where he was just as well known for fighting with his wits as with his fists. Indeed, boxing fans nicknamed him 'Professor Punch', because of the intelligent way he used psychology to outfox his less clever opponents before hitting them really hard on the side of the head.**
SANITARY TOWEL AMBITION	**0**	Prince Naseem Hamed has proved over and over again that he's a man who gets what he wants, whether it's boxing championships, fancy cars with probably personalised numberplates like NAZ KO or leopardskin shorts. With the not far from Rotherham bulldog's track record it's a safe bet that if wanted to do something, nothing would get in his way. Since he is not a ladies' sanitary product, it can only be concluded that he has never had any ambitions to be one. As a result, he is forced to throw in the towel and suffers a heavy loss in the final round.
 TOTAL POINTS	**51**	**Ladies and gentlemen, please show your appreciation for the gallant loser, Naseem Hamed. He put up a spirited fight, but in the final analysis this working class lad was thoroughly outclassed by his first class upper class opponent. He may be able to hack it in the safety of a boxing ring but when the gloves came off in this battle of the Princes, Naseem was shown up as the spindly featherweight he really is.**

OH, LORDY... IT'S THE FAT SLAGS
YAWN!
PLAP! PLAP!...GOOD MORNIN', SAN.
IS IT?
EH!? WOT'S UP WI' YOU?
IT'S BAZ... I DON'T THINK HE LOVES ME ANYMORE
OH?
SKRIT! SKRIT! SKRIT!
WHY D' Y' SAY THAT?
WELL, I OFFERED 'IM A BIT OF BACK DOOR ACTION LAST NIGHT... AN' HE TURNED ME DOWN
WELL, THAT DUN'T MEAN OWT, SAN
IT'S NOT EVERY BLOKES CUP O' TEA, ANAL... SOME LIKE IT, SOME DON'T
AYE! BUT IT IS BAZ'S CUP O' TEA, TRAY. Y'VE ONLY GOT T' LOOK AT 'IS VIDEO COLLECTION T' SEE THAT
HMM!
ANAL LUST
MIND, Y'SEE, THESE PORN STARS 'AVE ALL GOT NICE, CLEAN, PINK NIPSIES, SAN
DIRTBOX FUN
WELL, 'OW COME? I WIPE MINE PROPER, BUT IT'S STILL BROWN
AYE! WELL YER NATURAL ARSEHOLE IS BROWN. BUT THIS LOT 'AVE ALL 'AD ANAL BLEACHES
DIRTBOX FUN
ANAL BLEACHES?
AYE... THEY DID ONE ON THAT COSMETIC SURGERY LIVE!
EEH! WOT DID THEY DO?
WELL, THEY GOT A PEROXIDE PASTE AN' PAINTED IT ON THIS WOMAN'S ARSE. AN' WHEN THEY CHIPPED IT OFF, ER FRECKLE WERE NIPPIN' CLEAN...
Y'COULD OF ATE YER DINNER OFF IT!
SO WHERE DO Y' GET 'EM DONE?
'OLLYWOOD, MAINLY... MIND YOU...
THAT STRIPPER AT THE DOG AN' HAMMER DID 'ER OWN WI' SOME READY BREK AN' DOMESTOS, AN' 'ERS WERE LOVELY.
COME T' THINK OF IT, IT MUST OF WORKED, COZ BAZ DID 'ER UP THE SHITTER ONCE, DIDN'T HE?
AYE! HE DID...
...AT HIS DAD'S FUNERAL DO
SHORTLY...
THERE Y'GO... NICE AN' SMOOTH
RIGHT... PAINT IT ON, TRAY. THERE'S A PASTRY BRUSH IN THE DRAWER
DOMES
BEST GIVE IT A COUPLE OF COATS
OOH! OUCH! 'OW LONG DOES IT 'AVE TO STAY ON?
DUNNO... TILL IT DRIES, I SUPPOSE
OW!
FIZZ!
2 HOURS LATER...
OOH JESUS!... OOH, NO! I CAN'T STAND IT NO MORE, TRAY... CHIP IT OFF!
POP! FIZZ! POP! CRACKLE!
DOME
CHIP! CHIP! CHIPPITY CHIP!
OUCH!
AIYAH!
'OW DOES IT LOOK, TRAY? IS IT ALL NICE AND PINK?
WELL, IT'S... SORT OF... WELL IT'S NOT BROWN ANY MORE, PUT IT THAT WAY... I'LL TELL BETTER WHEN THE BLISTERS GO
A WEEK LATER...
HEY, TRAY... I'VE 'AD A LOOK AT IT IN THE MIRROR AN' IT'S AS PINK AS A PUPPY'S NOSE
THAT'S SMASHIN'
BAZ IS GOIN' T' LOVE IT!
COME ON! LET'S GO OUT AN' CELEBRATE
AYE!
SHORTLY...
CURRY CAPITAL
WELCOME TO THE CURRY CAPITAL PROP. ABDUL LATIF
WORLD'S HOTTEST CURRY
TAXI
NEXT DAY...
A BOX OF READY BREK, PLEASE, AND A CAN OF MR. MUSCLE OVEN CLEANER
CRISPS

STONE MASON
THE GRANITE CENTRE FORWARD OF BARNCHESTER ROVERS
TOMMY MASON WAS THE BEST CENTRE FORWARD BARNCHESTER HAD EVER SEEN UNTIL HE FELL VICTIM TO A CURSE, AFTER CHEEKING A FAIRGROUND GYPSY. TURNED TO SOLID GRANITE, IT LOOKED LIKE HIS CAREER WAS OVER. BUT BRAVELY HE FOUGHT BACK FROM HIS MISFORTUNE...
...AND EVENTUALLY REGAINED HIS PLACE IN THE ROVERS FRONT LINE.
AFTER A HARD TRAINING SESSION, THE BARNCHESTER PLAYERS WERE GOING HOME FOR A WELL-EARNED REST BEFORE THE FOLLOWING DAY'S FA CUP FINAL.
SIGN THIS PLEASE, MISTER.
ALRIGHT, SONNY, BUT THEN IT'S HOME FOR SOME KIP BEFORE OUR TRIP TO WEMBLEY.
YOU WANT US TO BEAT LIVERFORD, DON'T YOU?
NOT 'ALF!
COR! LOOK EVERYONE!
WOW! IT'S TOMMY MASON!
WILL YOU SIGN MY PROGRAMME PLEASE, TOMMY?
YOU WERE GREAT AGAINST GRESLEY SPARTANS ON SATURDAY. WHAT A HAT TRICK!
NOW STAND BACK, LADS. LEAVE MR MASON ALONE. MRS MASON'LL HAVE HIS TEA ON THE TABLE, AND WE DON'T WANT IT GETTING COLD, DO WE?
DON'T LET US DOWN.
BRING US BACK THE CUP, TOMMY.
AT HOME.
NOT HUNGRY, LOVE?
YOU MUST BE EXCITED ABOUT THE MATCH, EH?
I'M NOT SUPRISED. TOMORROW IS THE MOST IMPORTANT MATCH OF YOUR CAREER.
I CAN'T WAIT TO TAKE MY PLACE IN THE STANDS AND CHEER YOU ON.
WHY DON'T YOU GET AN EARLY NIGHT?
THE COACH TO WEMBLEY LEAVES FIRST THING TOMORROW. YOU DON'T WANT TO BE LATE.
THE NEXT MORNING, THE SQUAD WERE IN GOOD SPIRITS AS THEY SPED THEIR WAY TO LONDON.
WE'RE GOING TO WIN THE CUP, WE'RE GOING TO WIN THE CUP, E...I...ADDIO, WE'RE GOING TO WIN THE CUP!
BARNCHESTER FA CUP TEAM
THREE O'CLOCK AND THE MATCH KICKED OFF.
PHEEP!
AND HIGH IN THE STANDS BEHIND THE GOAL, ONE VOICE WAS SHOUTING LOUDER THAN THE REST.
COME ON, TOMMY!
UP THE ROVERS
RIGHT FROM THE WHISTLE, BARNCHESTER TOOK THE GAME TO LIVERFORD. TIME AND AGAIN MASON'S SHOTS TESTED THE KEEPER, FORCING HIM TO MAKE SAVE...
OOH, MASON'S HIT THAT LIKE A BULLET!
GOOD SAVE!
...AFTER SAVE...
WHAT A DAISYCUTTER!
YES BUT THE GOALIE MANAGED TO GET A FINGER TO IT.

...AFTER SAVE.
A PILE DRIVER SHOT!
YES, MASON'S GOT HIS SHOOTING BOOTS ON TODAY.
THERE'S THE HALF-TIME WHISTLE. IT'S NIL NIL.
PHEEP!
I CAN'T SEE THE LIVERFORD KEEPER SOAKING UP MASON'S PRESSURE FOR ANOTHER 45 MINUTES.
IT'S ONLY A MATTER OF TIME BEFORE TOMMY STARTS TO FIND THE ONION BAG.
WHEN HE GETS ONE, HE GETS A HATFUL.
THIS MATCH IS OURS FOR THE TAKING, LADS. LIVERFORD DON'T KNOW WHAT DAY IT IS.
ALF...STAN, KEEP PASSING IT ABOUT. DON'T GET CAUGHT IN POSSESSION
YES, BOSS.
SID AND BILL. YOU TWO KEEP IT TIGHT IN MIDFIELD. PLAY IT WIDE AND SQUARE. OPEN UP THE GAME.
YOU CAN COUNT ON US, BOSS.
AND TOMMY, DON'T WORRY...
...IT'LL COME.
NOW LET'S GET BACK OUT THERE AND WIN THAT CUP!
I'LL BE BACK IN A MINUTE WITH THE SACK BARROW FOR YOU, TOMMY.
PRIVATE KNOCK BEFORE ENTERING
LEFT ON HIS OWN IN THE DRESSING ROOM, TOMMY 'STONE' MASON SUDDENLY BECAME AWARE OF A SINISTER FIGURE SNEAKING IN THROUGH THE DOOR.
TOMMY MASON. WELL I NEVER.
YOU'RE HAVING A GOOD GAME, TOMMY. THE WAY YOU'RE PLAYING YOU'RE BOUND TO GET YOUR NAME ON THE SCORE SHEET IN THE SECOND HALF....
...WHICH WOULD BE A SHAME.
YOU SEE, I'VE BET FIFTY POUNDS ON A NO SCORE DRAW.
AND I DON'T LIKE LOSING, MR MASON.
SO IF YOU COULD SEE YOUR WAY CLEAR TO MISSING THE GOAL FOR THE NEXT FORTY-FIVE MINUTES,
...I'D BE EXTREMELY GRATEFUL...
...AND SO WOULD YOUR WIFE! HA! HA! HA!
AS TOMMY MADE HIS WAY ONTO THE PITCH...
...HIS WORST FEARS WERE REALISED.
UP THE ROVER
P-P-PLEASE...DON'T HURT ME!

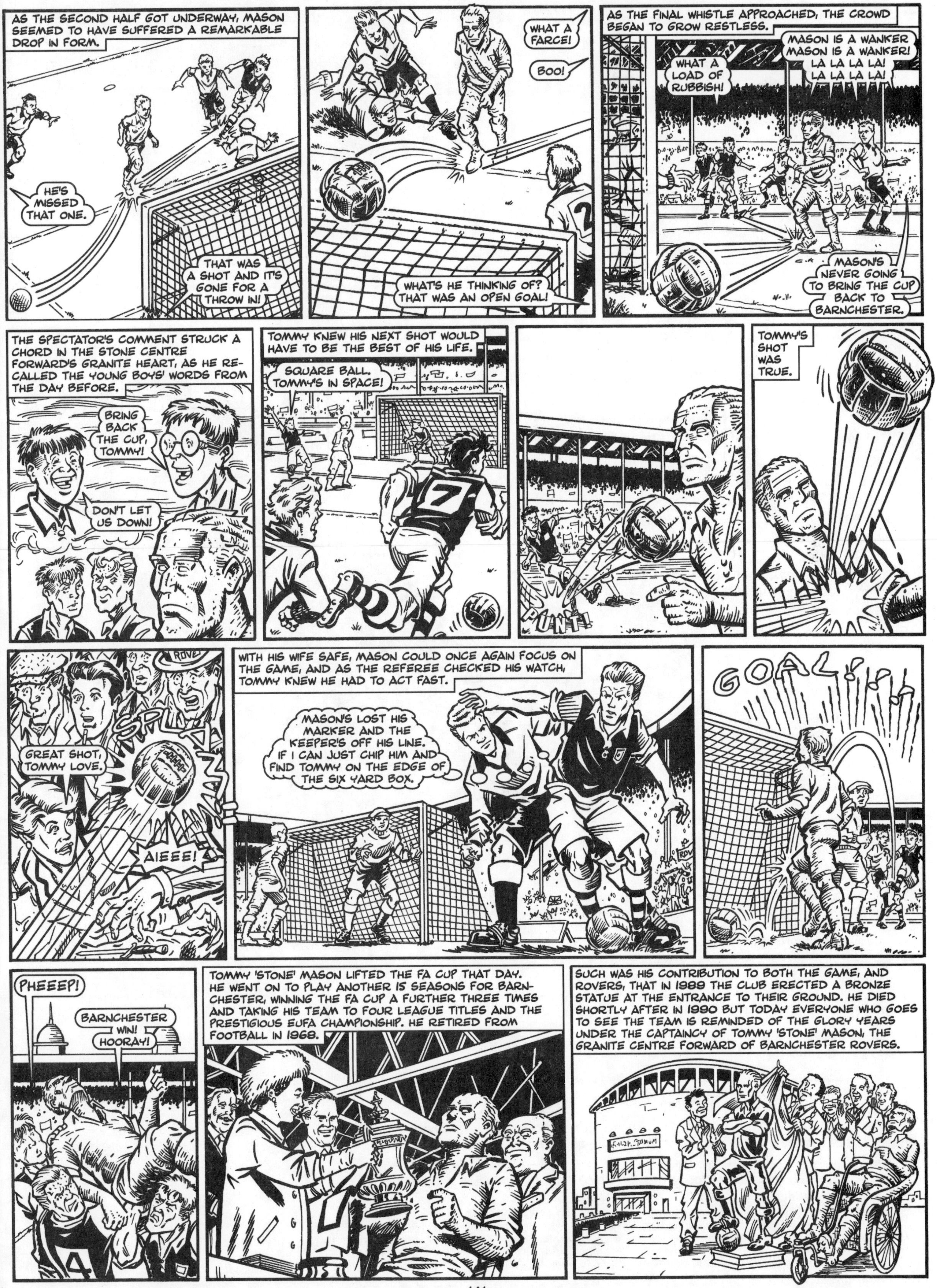
AS THE SECOND HALF GOT UNDERWAY, MASON SEEMED TO HAVE SUFFERED A REMARKABLE DROP IN FORM.
HE'S MISSED THAT ONE.
THAT WAS A SHOT AND IT'S GONE FOR A THROW IN!
WHAT A FARCE!
BOO!
WHAT'S HE THINKING OF? THAT WAS AN OPEN GOAL!
AS THE FINAL WHISTLE APPROACHED, THE CROWD BEGAN TO GROW RESTLESS.
WHAT A LOAD OF RUBBISH!
MASON IS A WANKER MASON IS A WANKER! LA LA LA LA! LA LA LA LA!
MASON'S NEVER GOING TO BRING THE CUP BACK TO BARNCHESTER.
THE SPECTATOR'S COMMENT STRUCK A CHORD IN THE STONE CENTRE FORWARD'S GRANITE HEART, AS HE RE-CALLED THE YOUNG BOYS' WORDS FROM THE DAY BEFORE.
BRING BACK THE CUP, TOMMY!
DON'T LET US DOWN!
TOMMY KNEW HIS NEXT SHOT WOULD HAVE TO BE THE BEST OF HIS LIFE.
SQUARE BALL. TOMMY'S IN SPACE!
PUNT!
TOMMY'S SHOT WAS TRUE.
GREAT SHOT, TOMMY LOVE.
SPLAM!
AIEEE!
WITH HIS WIFE SAFE, MASON COULD ONCE AGAIN FOCUS ON THE GAME, AND AS THE REFEREE CHECKED HIS WATCH, TOMMY KNEW HE HAD TO ACT FAST.
MASON'S LOST HIS MARKER AND THE KEEPER'S OFF HIS LINE. IF I CAN JUST CHIP HIM AND FIND TOMMY ON THE EDGE OF THE SIX YARD BOX.
GOAL!!!!
PHEEEP!
BARNCHESTER WIN! HOORAY!
TOMMY 'STONE' MASON LIFTED THE FA CUP THAT DAY. HE WENT ON TO PLAY ANOTHER 15 SEASONS FOR BARN-CHESTER, WINNING THE FA CUP A FURTHER THREE TIMES AND TAKING HIS TEAM TO FOUR LEAGUE TITLES AND THE PRESTIGIOUS EUFA CHAMPIONSHIP. HE RETIRED FROM FOOTBALL IN 1968.
SUCH WAS HIS CONTRIBUTION TO BOTH THE GAME, AND ROVERS, THAT IN 1989 THE CLUB ERECTED A BRONZE STATUE AT THE ENTRANCE TO THEIR GROUND. HE DIED SHORTLY AFTER IN 1990 BUT TODAY EVERYONE WHO GOES TO SEE THE TEAM IS REMINDED OF THE GLORY YEARS UNDER THE CAPTAINCY OF TOMMY 'STONE' MASON, THE GRANITE CENTRE FORWARD OF BARNCHESTER ROVERS.

Reflect on a miraculous life of selfless devotion whilst enjoying the cool flavour of a pipe

The Compost and Shitehouse Mint proudly presents the

Pope John Paul II

Papal Pipe

ON SATURDAY ***2nd April 2005, the entire population of the Earth wept like babies as Pope John Paul II passed from this life and took his place at God's right hand. Serenely succumbing to a massive infection of the urinary tract, septic shock and a couple of heart attacks, he slipped peacefully away to a well-earned retirement in the hereafter.***

And all our lives will never be the same again. Seldom in the history of Popes has a single man made such a difference to the world as did John Paul II. This was the man who literally tore down the Berlin Wall, took on the forces of Communism in the Polish shipyards and enveloped the world in a cloud of his love. Regardless of their religion, colour or creed, he was a man who loved everyone, except the queers and people who used rubber johnnies.

ONLY
£9.99†
(Includes a Free Ounce of Tobacco)

But there was another side to the Pope. Despite being the spiritual leader of over a billion souls, he was modest beyond measure, and was humble enough to kiss the tarmac wherever his private jet touched down in a foreign country.

Throughout history, the Popes have employed the world's greatest painters to decorate the ceilings of their Cistine Chapels - artists such as Michelangelo, Leonardo da Vinci and Ludwig van Beethoven. And following in this tradition, the Compost and Shitehouse Mint have employed world renowed pipe artist Fernando Gastroenteritis to create the John Paul II Pope Pipe. This finest quality smoking instrument is hand crafted in genuine briarinique* by pipesmiths, and will stand as a testament to the Pope's life and **YOUR** good taste for ever. Demand is sure to be high for this unique and uncompromising pipe, so order early to avoid disappointment.

** Briarinique is an authentic 100% ebony-type hardwood effect pipe material which combines the lightness of brown, injection-moulded plastic with the brown-ness of light, injection-moulded plastic.*

JOHN PAUL II POPE PIPE RESERVATION CERTIFICATE

Please reserve me ____ John Paul II Pope Pipe(s) ***(remember, the more pipes you buy, the more you loved John Paul II)***

Name ____________________ **Address** ____________________

Post Code __________ **Bank Branch** ____________________

Sort Code __________ **Account Number** ____________________

† I hereby give the Compost and Shitehouse Mint permission to withdraw any amount of money from my account at any time as they see fit.

Signed ____________________

Send to: ***Compost and Shitehouse c/o Joe Smoke's Cut Price Pipe Warehouse, PO Box 8, Leeds.***

We occasionally pass on intimate personal details of our customers to Lord God Almighty who uses it when deciding who to allow into the kingdom of Heaven and who to cast into the Lake of Fire for all eternity. Tick this box if you want to double your chance of getting into Heaven by doubling the number of pipes you order. Further Pope Pipes will be sent for all 264 previous Popes at a rate of one or two per week. You are under no obligation to be able to return them for a full refund at any time. Your, your children's, and your children's children's place in Heaven is at risk if you do not keep up payments on your Pope Pipes.

HOLY SMOKE! JUST LOOK AT THESE FEATURES!

- Generous sized bowl will accomodate 28g of baccy - that's 1g for every year of his papal pontificate
- Easy-grip mouthpiece allowing smoke to fill your lungs the way his boundless love filled up our hearts
- Wide bore flue on stem provides ease of lighting up, the way his cheeky smile lit up the lives of every living being
- Reinforced rim, allowing dottle to be safely tapped out, the way his ministry was tapped out by multiple organ failure

Thermos O'Flask
THERMOS... YOUR DAD'S HAVING ANOTHER HEART ATTACK, AND HE'S RUN OUT OF HIS PILLS...
OOER!
HNNG!
NIP TO THE CHEMIST TO GET SOME, THERE'S A LOVE... HERE'S A TENNER AND HIS PRESCRIPTION
OKAY, MUM
QUICK AS YOU CAN, THERMOS. AND THAT MONEY IS FOR YOUR DAD'S HEART PILLS... DON'T GO SPENDING IT ON PROSTITUTES
I WON'T
SHORTLY...
HMM... LOOKS LIKE IT'S SHUT...
...AND THERE'S A NOTE ON THE DOOR...
CHEMIST
OH, DEAR!
CLOSED
CLOSED DUE TO BEREAVEMENT
NEAREST CHEMIST ON FULCHESTER HIGH STREET. (NEXT DOOR TO THE FANNY GALORE BROTHEL)
SHORTLY...
RIGHT... YOU'VE GOT ANOTHER TENNER, NOW GO AND GET THOSE PILLS... AND FOR HEAVEN'S SAKE, SHOW A LITTLE SELF CONTROL, THERMOS
YES, MUM. SORRY, MUM
HNNNG!
SELF CONTROL!. JESUS, THAT'S A LAUGH... I'M AS WEAK AS A KITTEN WHEN IT COMES TO SPENDING ON WHORES.
THERE IT IS... BUT I KNOW WHAT'LL HAPPEN IF I GO ANYWHERE NEAR THAT BROTHEL AGAIN...
PHARMACY
FANNY GAL
GIRLS
XXX FANN GALOR BROTH
I KNOW, I'LL ASK SOMEONE TO GO INTO THE CHEMISTS FOR ME... AH! THAT LADY MIGHT HELP...
EXCUSE ME, MISS, I WONDER IF YOU COULD GIVE ME A HAND...
A HAND!?
...OF COURSE, LOVE.. BEHIND THIS SKIP...
...TEN POUND
WANKSCREEN SKIP HIRE
SHORTLY AGAIN...
FOR GOD'S SAKE, LEAVE THOSE PROS ALONE AND GET YOUR DAD'S PILLS
YES, MUM... SORRY, MUM
THE MAN'S LIPS ARE GOING BLUE!
RIGHT! I'M GOING TO BE REALLY STRONG THIS TIME... I'LL GO TO THE CHEMIST BY THE FOOTBALL GROUND TO KEEP WELL AWAY FROM THAT RUDDY BROTHEL
GOSH! IT'S WAYNE ROONEY... AND DAD'S A MASSIVE MAN U. FAN ...I'LL FOLLOW HIM AND GET HIS AUTOGRAPH
IT'LL CHEER DAD UP NO END
MR. ROONEY!.. MR. ROONEY!..
GOSTAMON
MR. ROONEY!..
...MR. ROONEY!... MR. ROO...
EH!?
THE VELVET PUSSY KNOCKING SHOP
THE VELVET PUSSY KNOCKING SHOP
...OH, BUGGER!
SHORTLY ONCE MORE...
SORRY, MUM... I DIDN'T GET DAD'S PILLS, BUT I DID GET HIM WAYNE ROONEY'S AUTOGRAPH
SHAME
I'M AFRAID THAT'S NO GOOD TO HIM, THERMOS
...YOUR DAD'S DEAD!
CRUMBS!
HERE'S A THOUSAND POUNDS... TAKE HIM TO THE UNDERTAKERS AND GET HIM BURIED, WILL YOU?
YES, MUM
SO...
POOR DAD... DEAD BECAUSE HE DIDN'T HAVE ANY HEART ATTACK PILLS... AND I CAN'T HELP FEELING PARTLY RESPONSIBLE
STILL, WITH £1000, AT LEAST HE'LL GET A DECENT BURIAL
SQUEEK! SQUEEK!
HERE WE ARE... OH!.. LOOKS LIKE THEY'RE SHUT!
SHADRACK & DUXBURY FUNERAL DIRECTORS
SHADRACK & DUXBURY
FUNERAL DIRECTORS
SQUEEK! SQUEEK!
BUGGER! BUGGER! BUGGER!
CLOSED DUE TO BEREAVEMENT
NEAREST FUNERAL PARLOUR IS IN CHETWYN RD. (NEXT DOOR TO FANNY AKIMBO'S RUB-A-TUG SHOP)

!?
... HAVE YOU HAD A FALL IN THE PAST 3 YEARS THAT WASN'T YOUR FAULT? YOU COULD BE ENTITLED TO COMPENSATION...
TELLY SHOP
...MR EIGER OF FULCHESTER RECEIVED ONE POUND FORTY-NINE AFTER HE TRIPPED ON AN UNEVEN PAVING SLAB. REMEMBER, IT'S NO WIN-NO FEE, SO WHY NOT CALL IN AND SEE US TODAY?
COMPENSION DIRECT
SHORTLY...
COMPENSION DIRECT
A'D LIKE TER 'AVE A FALL THAT'S NOT MY F-FF-FF-FFFUCKIN' F-FF-FFF-F-FFAULT...
WELL YOU'VE COME TO THE RIGHT PLACE. DO YOU HAVE A PARTICULAR FIGURE IN MIND?
ERM...
£10,000
NEW
ONE FORTEH NINE.
ONE FORTY NINE... ONE FORTY-NINE... AH, YES, HERE WE ARE...
COMPENSION RATES
£1.49... THAT'S SMASHED TEETH TRIPPING ON AN UNEVEN PAVING SLAB.
...IF YOU'D CARE TO FOLLOW ME INTO THE BACK LANE...
SO...
NOW HERE'S THE OFFENDING SLAB, MR. ACE. JUST WALK ROUND THE CORNER, MINDING YOUR OWN BUSINESS, TRIP UP, HAVE A NASTY FALL, THEN WE CAN GO INSIDE AND SORT OUT THE PAPERWORK.
CHAMPION.
THAT'S IT, MR. ACE. KEEP GOING...
ERM... YOU'VE MISSED IT, MR. ACE. TELL YOU WHAT, CARRY ON ROUND THE BLOCK AND GET IT NEXT TIME.
F-FF-FFUCKIN' REYT YER ARE, PAL.
I'LL LEVER IT UP A BIT, MAKE IT A LITTLE EASIER FOR YOU, EH?
AH. YOU SEEM TO HAVE MISSED IT AGAIN, MR. ACE.
BBOLLOCKS. A CAN F-FF-FFUCKIN' SEE IT... A JUSSS CAN'T TRIP OVER'T CUNT.
I'LL LIFT IT A BIT MORE.
BUT...
AH... FUCKITT.
AND...
B-BASTOD!
SEVERAL CIRCUITS LATER...
...NOW CONCENTRATE, MR. ACE. THINK OF THAT £1.49. THIS IS YOUR LAST CHANCE.
I CAN'T GET THE SLAB ANY MORE UNEVEN THAN THIS.
SMECK!
THAT WILL DO NICELY. JUST SIGN HERE, PLEASE.
F-FF-FF... GROAN.
A WEEK LATER...
EIGHT! EIGHT!
FUCKIN' WEK UP!
WORRISSIT, LUV?
YER COMPENSION'S CUM THROO, EIGHT. IT MUN BE YER CHEQUE, LOOK.
F-FFUCKIN' GREAT.
A TELL YOO F-FFUCKIN' WOT, LUV... THIS MUNNEH'S GOIN' TER BE SPENT ON YOO AN' THEM F-FFUCKIN' B-BB-BBAIRNSES... NOT ME.
'OD ON... ME FFUCKIN' SOLICITEH'S TOOK AALL ME F-FFUCKIN' WINNINS.
COMPENSION DIRECT
36a. Bollocks St. Fulchester
Client: Mr. O. ACE 13 SHIT ST. FULCHESTER
COMPENSION FOR ACCIDENT........ £1.49
LESS LEGAL EXPENSES, DISBURSEMENTS, STAMPS, TELEPHONE CALLS & PHOTOCOPYING.... £1.49
TOTAL PAYABLE £0.00
Pay Mr. O. Ace £0-00
Fuck all & nowt
EIGHT ACE.
FAIRY SNOW
DAZ

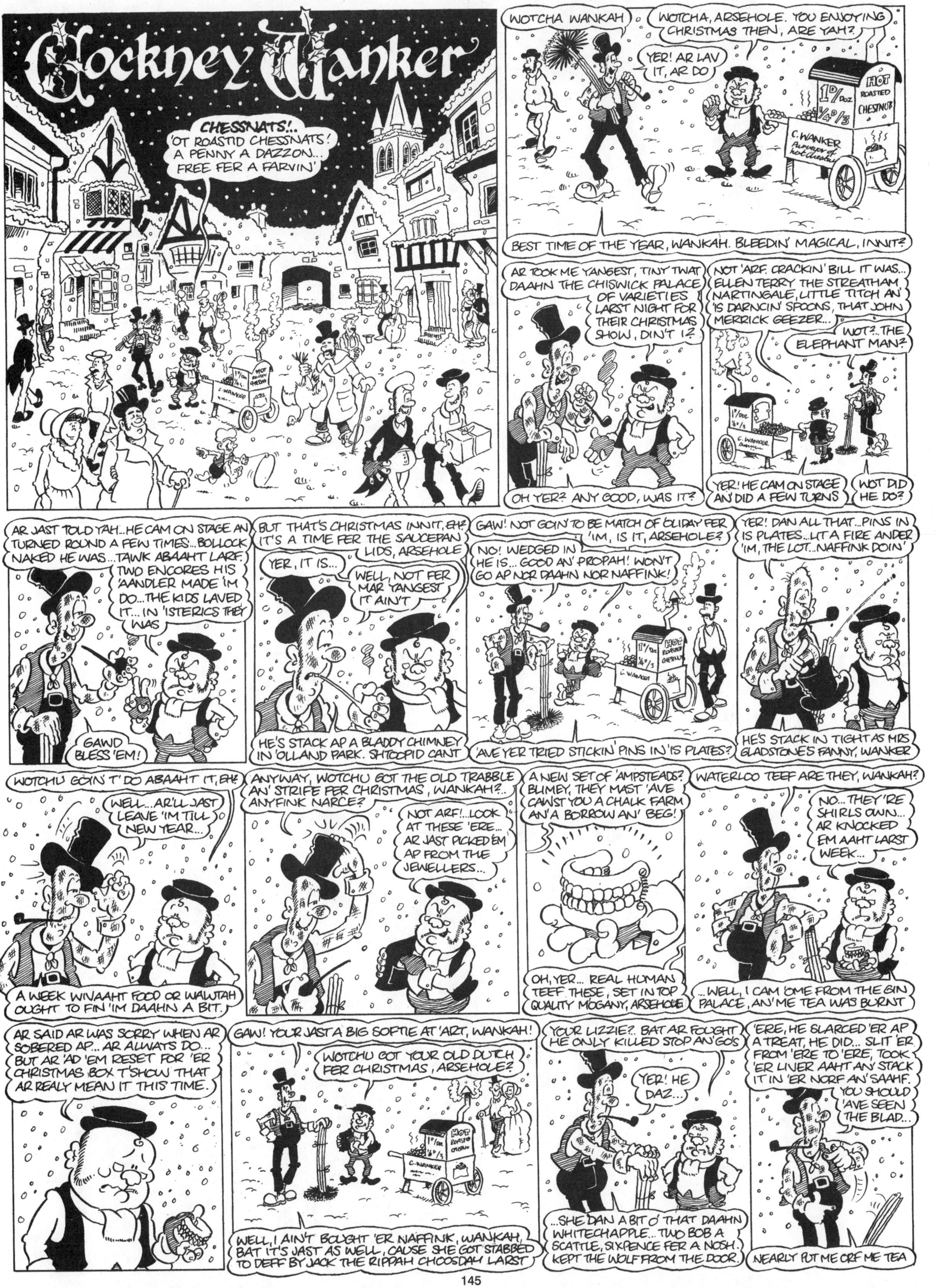
Cockney Wanker
CHESSNATS!.. 'OT ROASTID CHESSNATS! A PENNY A DAZZON... FREE FER A FARVIN'
HOT ROASTED CHESSNUTS
C. WANKER
WOTCHA WANKAH
WOTCHA, ARSEHOLE. YOU ENJOYING CHRISTMAS THEN, ARE YAH?
YER! AR LAV IT, AR DO
BEST TIME OF THE YEAR, WANKAH. BLEEDIN' MAGICAL, INNIT?
AR TOOK ME YANGEST, TINY TWAT DAAHN THE CHISWICK PALACE OF VARIETIES LARST NIGHT FOR THEIR CHRISTMAS SHOW, DIN'T I?
OH YER? ANY GOOD, WAS IT?
NOT 'ARF. CRACKIN' BILL IT WAS... ELLEN TERRY THE STREATHAM NARTINGALE, LITTLE TITCH AN' 'IS DARNCIN' SPOONS, THAT JOHN MERRICK GEEZER...
WOT?.. THE ELEPHANT MAN?
YER! HE CAM ON STAGE AN' DID A FEW TURNS
WOT DID HE DO?
AR JAST TOLD YAH... HE CAM ON STAGE AN TURNED ROUND A FEW TIMES... BOLLOCK NAKED HE WAS... TAWK ABAAHT LARF.
TWO ENCORES HIS 'AANDLER MADE 'IM DO... THE KIDS LAVED IT... IN 'ISTERICS THEY WAS
GAWD BLESS 'EM!
BUT THAT'S CHRISTMAS INNIT, EH? IT'S A TIME FER THE SAUCEPAN LIDS, ARSEHOLE
YER, IT IS...
WELL, NOT FER MAR YANGEST IT AIN'T
HE'S STACK AP A BLADDY CHIMNEY IN 'OLLAND PARK. SHTOOPID CANT
GAW! NOT GOIN' TO BE MATCH OF 'OLIDAY FER 'IM, IS IT, ARSEHOLE?
NO! WEDGED IN HE IS... GOOD AN' PROPAH! WON'T GO AP NOR DAAHN NOR NAFFINK!
'AVE YER TRIED STICKIN' PINS IN 'IS PLATES?
YER! DAN ALL THAT... PINS IN 'IS PLATES... LIT A FIRE ANDER 'IM, THE LOT... NAFFINK DOIN'
HE'S STACK IN TIGHT AS MRS GLADSTONE'S FANNY, WANKER
WOTCHU GOIN' T' DO ABAAHT IT, EH?
WELL... AR'LL JAST LEAVE 'IM TILL NEW YEAR...
A WEEK WIVAAHT FOOD OR WAWTAH OUGHT TO FIN 'IM DAAHN A BIT.
ANYWAY, WOTCHU GOT THE OLD TRABBLE AN' STRIFE FER CHRISTMAS, WANKAH?.. ANYFINK NARCE?
NOT ARF!... LOOK AT THESE 'ERE... AR JAST PICKED 'EM AP FROM THE JEWELLERS...
A NEW SET OF 'AMPSTEADS? BLIMEY, THEY MAST 'AVE CAWST YOU A CHALK FARM AN' A BORROW AN' BEG!
OH, YER... REAL HUMAN TEEF THESE, SET IN TOP QUALITY MOGANY, ARSEHOLE
WATERLOO TEEF ARE THEY, WANKAH?
NO... THEY'RE SHIRLS OWN... AR KNOCKED 'EM AAHT LARST WEEK...
...WELL, I CAM 'OME FROM THE GIN PALACE, AN' ME TEA WAS BURNT
AR SAID AR WAS SORRY WHEN AR SOBERED AP... AR ALWAYS DO... BUT AR 'AD 'EM RESET FOR 'ER CHRISTMAS BOX T'SHOW THAT AR REALY MEAN IT THIS TIME.
GAW! YOUR JAST A BIG SOFTIE AT 'ART, WANKAH!
WOTCHU GOT YOUR OLD DUTCH FER CHRISTMAS, ARSEHOLE?
WELL, I AIN'T BOUGHT 'ER NAFFINK, WANKAH, BAT IT'S JAST AS WELL, CAUSE SHE GOT STABBED TO DEFF BY JACK THE RIPPAH CHOOSDAH LARST
YOUR LIZZIE?.. BAT AR FOUGHT HE ONLY KILLED STOP AN' GO'S
YER! HE DAZ...
...SHE DAN A BIT O' THAT DAAHN WHITECHAPPLE... TWO BOB A SCATTLE, SIXPENCE FER A NOSH. KEPT THE WOLF FROM THE DOOR.
'ERE, HE SLARCED 'ER AP A TREAT, HE DID... SLIT 'ER FROM 'ERE TO 'ERE, TOOK 'ER LIVER AAHT AN' STACK IT IN 'ER NORF AN' SAAHF.
YOU SHOULD 'AVE SEEN THE BLAD...
NEARLY PUT ME ORF ME TEA

JACK THE RIPPAH, EH!?.. HE'S A REAL EAST END CHARACTER, INNEE?
WELL, AR DUNNO...
HOT ROASTED CHESTNUTS
C. WANKER
NOBODY KNOWS 'OO THE BARSTAD IS, DO THEY?
'ERE! WOTCHIT, ARSEHOLE. AR WON'T 'AVE A WORD SAID AGAINST THE OLD RIPPAH! BELIEVE YOU ME, HE'S A FACKIN' DIAMOND GEEZER
TAKES 'IS OLD MAWAH A BANCH OF FLAAHS EVERY DAY, HE DAZ
'OWJOO KNOW?
MAR BRAVVAH TOLD ME...
...HE 'AD 'IM IN THE BACK OF 'IS 'ANSOM CAB LARST WEEK
STRAIGHT AP... CAWERED IN BLAD HE WAS. WON'T MEET A NARCER FELLER, MAR BRAVVER SEZ... A PROPAH GENT. AN' YER WON'T GUESS 'OO IT TURNS AAHT HE IS...
WELL AR RECKON IT'S A CHINEE, AR DO, WANKER.
AR DUNNO... THEY CAM OVER 'ERE, KILLIN' ALL AR TOMS.
NAH, ARSEHOLE, NOT A CHINEE... IT'S ONLY THE BLEEDIN' DUKE O' CLARENCE, INNIT?.. EDWARD.
WOT?.. 'ER MAJESTY'S ELDEST?
C. WANKER
THE VERY SAME, AS AR LIVE AN' BREAVE
BLADDY 'ELL, WANKAH... MY LIZZIE, SLARCED AP BY ROYALTY... GAW! THAT'S BROUGHT A LAMP TO ME FROAT, THAT 'AS.
SWELL!
AR'M AS PRAAHD AS A PEACOCK.
Y'KNOW, WHEN AR FINK BACK, SHE WAS RIPPED AP PROPAH CLARSEY... MAJESTIC, IT WAS.
YER...
WELL, THEY DO A MARVELOUS JOB, ARSEHOLE, THE ROYALS...
C. WANKER
...DON'T DO NAFFINK BY ARVS, THEY DON'T
YER! WELL AR FEEL PRIVILAGED TO 'AV 'AD ME BALL AN' CHAIN BUTCHERED BY THE FUTURE KING OF ENGLAND
YOU'RE A LACKY GEEZER, ARSEHOLE
ANYWAY, AR CAN'T STAND 'ERE BACON AN' PORKIN' ALL CHRISTMAS DAY. AR'U GOT T' GET 'OME AN' GIVE MAR SHIRL 'ER PRESSIE
RIGHTCHOO ARE, WANKAH. SEE YOU BAKED POTATAH!
FIVE MINUTES BAKED POTATAH...
ORWIGHT, WANKAH. MERRY CHRISTMAS, LAV. CAM IN AN SHAT THE ROGER MOORE
MERRY CHRISTMAS, SHIRL... AN' MERRY CHRISTMAS TO YOU AN' ALL, TINY TWAT
GAWD BLESSUS, EVERY ONE!
'ERE, SHIRL... AR GOT YOU A LITTLE PRESENT FER CHRISTMAS...
OH, WANKAH!... FANKS! THEY'RE LAVERLY!
GO ON, THEN, PUT 'EM IN, SEE IF THEY FITCHAH!
GAW! THEY FIT A TREAT... THEY'RE JAST AS NARCE AS THEY WAS BEFORE YOU SMASHED 'EM OUT
THEY LOOK TOP NOTCH!

LISTEN, YOU SIT DAAHN, LAV, AN' AR'LL GETCHOO A GLARSE O' STOUT BEFORE YER SAINT AN' SINNER
LAVERLY! WOT ARE WE 'AVIN?
A PROPAH CHRISTMAS FEAST... 'ANGMANS NOOSE WIV ROAST SPADS AN' ALL THE TRIMMINS. IT'LL BE READY IN ARF AN' OUR.
ARF AN' OUR!?.. LAVERLY! AR'V JAST GOT TIME FOR A SWIFT LILY THE PINK DAAHN THE GIN SHOP
WELL, ORWIGHT, WANKAH, BAT JAST REMEMBAH- ARF AN 'OUR!...
...AN' NOT A MINUTE BAKED POTATAH!
ORWIGHT, DARLIN'
SIX HOURS BAKED POTATAH...
OH, JINGLE 'EAVEN AN' 'ELLS, JINGLE 'EAVEN AN' 'ELLS,
JINGLE ALL THE STRAW AN' HAY!
OH WHAT CURRENT BUN IT IS TO SLIP AN' SLIDE, ON A ONE SEMAPHORE AN' MORSE OPEN CHINA CLAY,
HEY!
MERRY ≡HIC!≡ CHRISTMAM..MAR LAV... MERR ≡HIC≡ FACKIN' CHRISM.
WELL, SHIRL...≡HIC≡ AR'M 'ANK MARVIN, 'AR AM... AR'M READY FOR MAR MICHAEL ≡HIC≡ WINNER
AR BETCHOO BLEEDIN' ARE
THEN AR'LL 'AVE A NARCE LITTLE SNOOZE
'ERE YER GO MERRY FACKIN' CHRISTMAS.
FACKIN' 'ELL!! WOTCHOO FACKIN' DAN TO THE BLEEDIN' 'ANGMANS NOOSE?.. IT'S BURNT TO A FACKIN' QUENTIN
IT AIN'T MAR FAULT...
...ARV BEEN TRYIN' T' KEEP THE BLADDY FING WARM IN THE OVEN FER SIX EIFFEL TOWERS AIN'T I?
DONTCHOO ARNSWER ME BACK, MAR GAL... ARV 'AD ENNAFF O' YOUR RATTLE!
OH, SHAT YOUR BLADDY NORF AN SAAHF!
WOT!? WOT DID YOU JAST SAY?
YOU CHEEKY FACKIN' CAAAH!
'ERE, WANKAH! CALM DAHN A BIT!
BOXING DAY...
AR'D LIKE THESE MADE AP INTO A SET OF DENTURES FOR 'ER INDOORS...
FEZZIWIG & SON JEWELLER
JEWELLER
SAME MEASUREMENTS AS LAST TIME, SIR?
YER! AR FINK SHE MIGHT 'AVE SWALLOWED A FEW, BAT I'LL BRING 'EM IN TOMORRER!
ANY CHARNCE OF GEDDIN' 'EM DAN IN TIME FOR 'ER BIRFDAY NEXT WEEK, SQUIRE?

LETTERBOCKS

Viz Comic, PO Box 656, North Shields, NE29 1BT
e-mail: letters@viz.co.uk

Star Letter

★ I JUST bought a new car and when I insured it, the broker informed me I wasn't covered for acts of God. Imagine my anger when I looked out of my bedroom window in the early hours and saw the Lord scratching it up the side with a key. *Christina Martin, e-mail*

I HAVEN'T heard much about HRH Anne, the Princess Royal for a while now. Nevertheless, I'm sure she still does a marvellous job and she does it with a grace and majesty which the rest of the world can only envy.

Emlyn Flange
Widnes

I WOULD like to take this opportunity to apologise to any members of Bournemouth East Conservative Club who may have been upset recently after I vomited all over their doors and windows. Unfortunately, it is unlikely that this will be an isolated incident as I have just moved in three doors down.

G Ayling
Bournemouth

I AM annoyed by those massive brown signs at the sides of motorways, pointing to places like Blenheim Palace and Chatsworth House. Why, in this supposedly classless society, should massively wealthy aristocrats enjoy greater ease in finding their junctions, all paid for out of our taxes? It makes my blood boil, it really does.

H Sifty
Email

I RECENTLY bought my wife a dress for her birthday and I was a little uncertain about the size. So imagine my delight when she tried it on and said it 'fitted like a glove'. Imagine my subsequent disappointment when I realised she was referring to the black leather glove that OJ Simpson wasn't wearing when he didn't kill his wife, and had to take it back for a bigger size.

P Norton
Rhyll

AS A window cleaner, it really annoys me when I hear George Formby singing his famous song about my profession. How would he like it if I cleaned a window about being a buck-toothed, dead ukulele player? Not much I bet.

Les Convey
Gateshead

HOW about a nice picture of a pelican to brighten my day?

Dr G Hough
Halifax

I RECENTLY saw a lady tramp wearing a mobile phone hands-free headset. Do any readers have any idea what she could have been doing which meant she was too busy to take a call?

Dave Roberts
Fawdon

I RECENTLY took my children to the zoo and was appalled to find that, thanks to the politically correct lobby, the animals are now treated humanely and kept in enclosures approximating their natural habitats. Well I for one am not interested in seeing a sleeping tapir under a bush a hundred yards away. I want to see eight chimpanzees in nappies fighting over a teapot, a tiger going for a walk on a lead and a keeper washing an elephant with a hosepipe and a yardbrush while it shits everywhere. Come on British zoos, sort yourselves out before it's too late.

Mrs Edna Ashworth
Tiverton

MY faithful 14 year old dog recently developed a large tumour. The vet said it was inoperable, and as he would be in great pain the kindest thing to do would be to have him put down. I didn't want to do this as we'd had some wonderful times and I would miss him terribly. But I could not bear to see him suffer, and when he looked at me it was as if he was begging me to release him from his pain. It was the hardest decision I have

TOP TIPS

TO MAKE a pot of supermarket coleslaw go further, simply grate a carrot, some cabbage and an onion into the tub, then add some mayonnaise.

SA, Derby

SAVE 20p when using the swimming pool changing rooms at Butlins, Skegness. Lockers 113, 655 and 670 can be locked fully by turning the key without having to deposit a coin beforehand.

C Frank, Billingham

REMOVE lice cheaply and easily by putting onion juice on your head. Wait a few moments until the lice rub their eyes and simply fall off your head.

S Hughes, Email

WOULD-BE criminals. Before you commit a crime, get a foretaste of what the world would look like from inside a prison by holding a fork up close to your eye.

R Simple, Email

SALAD lovers. A clever way to store lettuce, cabbage and the like is to individually punch holes in the leaves and place them in a ringbinder in the fridge. File cos under 'C', iceberg under 'I' and so on. Simple!

A Stepney, Turniptop

MAKE your own cherry tomatoes by watering beefsteak tomato plants with bonsai feed.

Mounty Don, Email

SHOE bombers. Increase your payload by becoming a clown.

Mark Johnson, Email

OWNERS of mouse circuses. A Toblerone bar makes an ideal bike rack for your display team's motorcycles when they are not in use.

Horst Farqhar, Warwick

JOHN Wayne. Never show any pain when receiving the beating of a lifetime, but wince when having your wounds tended by a woman.

Oggerina, Email

TIMMY TIMPSON IS SPOILT BASTARD
CHRISTMAS MORNING...
GOSH, TIMMY... LOOK AT ALL THESE PRESENTS. I'M SURE YOU GET MORE AND MORE EACH YEAR
YES I DO
BIG TRUCK
AND YOU BETTER MAKE SURE IT STAYS THAT WAY.
THAT ONE'S FROM AUNTY PAT... SHE ALWAYS GETS YOU SOMETHING UNUSUAL... WHAT IS IT, MY POPPET?
I HAVEN'T A RUDDY CLUE. SOMETHING TO DO WITH GOATS.
OH, TIMMY, IT'S AN 'ETHICAL GIFT'. SHE'S BOUGHT A GOAT IN YOUR NAME FOR AN AFRICAN VILLAGE. THIS IS YOUR CERTIFICATE
CERTIFICATE
ONE GOAT
AAH! HOW NICE TO THINK YOU HAVE A GOAT LIVING IN AFRICA, PROVIDING A FAMILY WITH MILK
A WEEK LATER...
COME ON, MOTHER. TO THE AIRPORT.

ver had to make. Luckily it as made easier by the vet ying he wanted £37.25 to o it. Thirty seven quid for ne needle in a dog's neck? only paid a fiver for him in e first place.

B Jackson
Wales

AM married to a Taiwanese dy, and people often ask me she was a mail-order bride. find this very insensitive. he Royal Mail loose around million letters and parcels ach year, and to suggest that would trust the delivery of y wife to them is insulting in e extreme. She was sent by HL next day delivery.

L Palmer
London

VITH reference to Mr almer's letter *(above)*. I am lso married to a Taiwanese dy, but nobody ever asks e if she is a mail order ride. But perhaps that's ecause I am also Taiwanese. nd we live in Taiwan.

Lo Chi Chang
Taipei

CONSUMER GRIPES

***I RECENTLY** bought a bottle of brown sauce which carried the warning 'Do not use if seal is broken'. As soon as I opened it the seal broke, immediately rendering it unusable. I wonder how many other innocent shoppers, especially pensioners, have fallen for this evil scam.*

Drew Peacock, e-mail

***ACCORDING** to the manufacturers of Walker's Crisps, the reason their bags often appear to be empty is that the contents often settle in transit. However, in an experiment I recently carried out at work, I managed to get the contents of three bags of smokey bacon crisps into a single empty packet and still got it closed. I then re-enacted the settling phenomenon by violently walking and jumping up and down the corridor for several minutes. When I had finished, there were still just as many crisps in the bag.*

John Rostron, e-mail

***YESTERDAY,** whilst visiting my local Tesco, I saw a sign which read 'Mum of the Year 2006. Enter Your Mum Now!' I was so disgusted I vomited. Come on Tesco, clean up your act or get out of town.*

Ian Bemail, e-mail

PS. Would this have been better with a photo of the sign?

***HAS ANYONE** managed to open a Rustlers microwave food packet without the corner coming off in your hand? If they have, then they are a better man than me, which isn't saying much.*

Jimmy Graham, e-mail

Not Time, Gentlemen, Please!

24-hour pub opening spells last orders for last orders.

TONY Blair's recent decision to legalise round-the-clock pub opening has been greeted with mixed reactions from all sides of society. Whilst people who live close to pubs and the police have slammed the plans, homeless alcoholics, fruit machine manufacturers and binge drinkers have welcomed them. But who is right, and who is lying? We went on the streets and found the public's opinion divided.

...I'M A bus driver and 24-hour drinking will suit me down to the ground. If I can stay in the pub until the early hours, my hangover won't kick in till the following afternoon, well after I've finished my morning shift.

Reg Varnish, Chester

...THANKS to the ban on smoking and the new 24-hour opening hours, I'll be able to stay in the pub drinking all night without being forced to breathe in a load of unhealthy cigarette smoke.

Mrs Potatoes, Cheshunt

...THE NEW opening hours are a farce. I'm a designated driver, so when I go to the pub with my mates I usually make a pint of beer last all evening. With bars open round the clock, it looks like I might potentially have to make a single pint last for the rest of my life.

Terry Sperm, Chessington

...PEOPLE who say that relaxing the licensing laws will lead to an increase in violence should look at the figures. The present opening hours were introduced in 1914, and were followed by four years of fighting in which millions of people were killed.

Audrey Potter, Chelmsford

...TONY Blair has no right to change the law until he proves that he can drink round the clock. When he shows himself capable of spending a solid 24-hours sinking pints, then and only then will I listen to him when he tells me how long I must drink for.

Joe Philpott, Chelsea

...THE NEW opening hours are ridiculous. Each night after closing time at my local, we have a lock-in till 3am. Now that the landlord has applied for a licence to stay open till 4am, I'm not going to get home till breakfast time. Just when does Mr Blair expect me to get some sleep?

Horace Guyzance, Chertsey

...WHAT sort of saddo feels the need to drink in a pub 24 hours a day? What's wrong with a carrier bag full of cans and a bench in the town centre?

Jimmy Jackson, Cheltenham

...NOW that my local is open 24-7, I have no need to ever go home again. I'm going to sell my house and spend the money on lager and peanuts.

Karl Lauder, Chesterfield

...HEAVY drinking never did anyone any harm. My grandfather drank 80 pints a day from the age of twelve, and he was killed on his hundredth birthday when he was trampled to death by a Salvation Army Temperance band.

Phoebe Booth, Cheddar

...IRELAND and Scotland already have round-the-clock drinking, and you don't see drunk people on the streets there.

Marjorie Kerbishley, Cheadle Hulme

...AS usual, the moaning minnies say they are concerned about the effects of all day boozing. But they should bear in mind that just because a pub is open round the clock, its customers won't necessarily be drinking 24-hours-a-day. They'll have to go out for a piss or a fight occasionally, or to lean out of the door and vomit into the street.

Frank Phonebook, Cheam

...IT'S all very well having 24-hour drinking, but what happens when the clocks go back in the Autumn and there's a 25-hour day? Do the police propose to arrest everyone who's in the pub at 2am? As usual, the government really hasn't thought this through.

Percy Tarrant, Cheng-Tu-Fu

Pretty Clever

THE proportion of attractive teenage girls pictured receiving A-Level results in news reports has reached 96%, the highest level since records began.

A-Level Results

Despite a flurry of television and newspaper images of jubilant pupils checking wall charts and hugging their classmates, only a tiny handful showed pockmarked pasty boys with bad glasses, or fat girls with frizzy hair, and these were mainly kept at a safe distance from the camera, mercifully obscured by a willowy blonde waving an envelope.

FOREHEAD

The increasing proportion of photogenic female A-Level students in news reports has drawn some criticism from educational groups concerned that standards are falling.

"You need to be studious and bespectacled, often with bad posture and pale skin, to do a hard subject like Maths or Chemistry," says Dr Lauren Sue-Ellen Bowen of the Bossert Institute who has a big forehead. "But any flaxen haired bimbo can get an A-Level in media studies and be seen smiling winningly on the Six O Clock News."

FORESKIN

"Clever people are supposed to be a bit wonky in the face. This is dumbing down, pure and simple."

Despite these concerns, education chiefs and picture editors are predicting that the trend will continue.

"Next year, I guarantee it," says *Daily Express* picture editor Ron Dribble. "The A Level results spread will look like sodding Hollyoaks. Get in."

SUE-DO-KU SOLUTION

SU-DOC-WHO SOLUTION

STEW-DO-KU SOLUTION

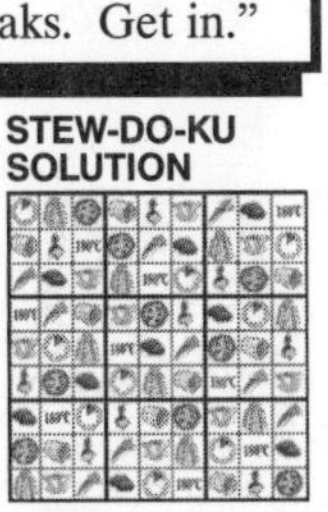

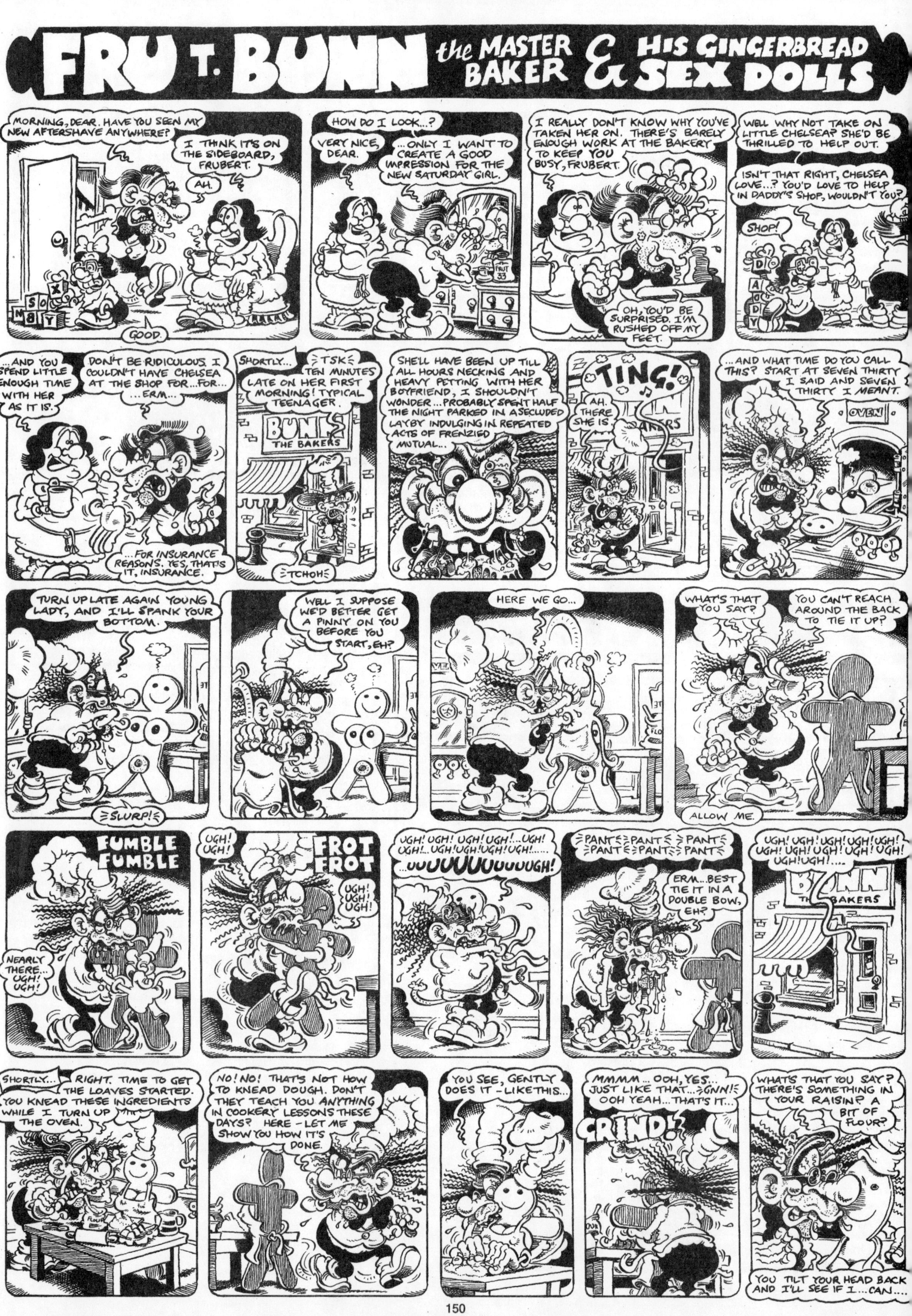
FRU T. BUNN the MASTER BAKER & HIS GINGERBREAD SEX DOLLS
MORNING, DEAR. HAVE YOU SEEN MY NEW AFTERSHAVE ANYWHERE?
I THINK IT'S ON THE SIDEBOARD, FRUBERT.
AH.
GOOD.
HOW DO I LOOK...?
VERY NICE, DEAR.
...ONLY I WANT TO CREATE A GOOD IMPRESSION FOR THE NEW SATURDAY GIRL.
FRUT 33
I REALLY DON'T KNOW WHY YOU'VE TAKEN HER ON. THERE'S BARELY ENOUGH WORK AT THE BAKERY TO KEEP YOU BUSY, FRUBERT.
OH, YOU'D BE SURPRISED. I'M RUSHED OFF MY FEET.
WELL WHY NOT TAKE ON LITTLE CHELSEA? SHE'D BE THRILLED TO HELP OUT.
ISN'T THAT RIGHT, CHELSEA LOVE...? YOU'D LOVE TO HELP IN DADDY'S SHOP, WOULDN'T YOU?
SHOP!
...AND YOU SPEND LITTLE ENOUGH TIME WITH HER AS IT IS.
DON'T BE RIDICULOUS. I COULDN'T HAVE CHELSEA AT THE SHOP FOR...FOR... ...ERM...
...FOR INSURANCE REASONS. YES, THAT'S IT, INSURANCE.
SHORTLY...
TSK TEN MINUTES LATE ON HER FIRST MORNING! TYPICAL TEENAGER.
BUNN THE BAKERS
TCHOH
SHE'LL HAVE BEEN UP TILL ALL HOURS NECKING AND HEAVY PETTING WITH HER BOYFRIEND, I SHOULDN'T WONDER...PROBABLY SPENT HALF THE NIGHT PARKED IN A SECLUDED LAYBY INDULGING IN REPEATED ACTS OF FRENZIED MUTUAL...
TING!
AH. THERE SHE IS.
...AND WHAT TIME DO YOU CALL THIS? START AT SEVEN THIRTY I SAID AND SEVEN THIRTY I MEANT.
OVEN
TURN UP LATE AGAIN YOUNG LADY, AND I'LL SPANK YOUR BOTTOM.
SLURP!
WELL I SUPPOSE WE'D BETTER GET A PINNY ON YOU BEFORE YOU START, EH?
HERE WE GO...
WHAT'S THAT YOU SAY?
YOU CAN'T REACH AROUND THE BACK TO TIE IT UP?
ALLOW ME.
FUMBLE FUMBLE
NEARLY THERE... UGH! UGH!
UGH! UGH!
FROT FROT
UGH! UGH! UGH!
UGH! UGH! UGH! UGH!...UGH! UGH!...UGH! UGH! UGH! UGH!......
...UUUUUUUUUUUGH!
PANT PANT PANT PANT PANT PANT
ERM...BEST TIE IT IN A DOUBLE BOW, EH?
UGH! UGH! UGH! UGH! UGH! UGH! UGH! UGH! UGH! UGH! UGH! UGH!....
BUNN THE BAKERS
SHORTLY...
RIGHT. TIME TO GET THE LOAVES STARTED. YOU KNEAD THESE INGREDIENTS WHILE I TURN UP THE OVEN.
FLOUR
NO! NO! THAT'S NOT HOW TO KNEAD DOUGH. DON'T THEY TEACH YOU ANYTHING IN COOKERY LESSONS THESE DAYS? HERE - LET ME SHOW YOU HOW IT'S DONE.
YOU SEE, GENTLY DOES IT - LIKE THIS...
MMMM...OOH, YES... JUST LIKE THAT...GNN! OOH YEAH...THAT'S IT...
GRIND!
WHAT'S THAT YOU SAY? THERE'S SOMETHING IN YOUR RAISIN? A BIT OF FLOUR?
YOU TILT YOUR HEAD BACK AND I'LL SEE IF I...CAN....

....JUST....
LUNGE!
NG!NG! NNG!!
NG!NG! NG!
SLOBBER NNNNG! PANT
SLAP!
YOU LITTLE BITCH! WHAT THE HELL WAS THAT FOR?
SEXUAL HARRASSMENT!? YOU LIAR! YOU KNOW YOU WANTED IT AS MUCH AS I DID.
YOU WERE GAGGING FOR IT, YOU DIRTY LITTLE SL.... WHAT'S THAT!?
THE POLICE!?... NO... NO... NOW LET'S NOT DO ANYTHING HASTY...
NO! PLEASE... THINK ABOUT MY FAMILY. A SCANDAL LIKE THIS WOULD DESTROY THEM.
MY WIFE WOULD LEAVE ME AND TAKE LITTLE CHELSEA.
...SHE'S ALL I'VE GOT. SHE'S GOT A LAZY EYE AND A BUILT-UP SHOE... PLEASE DON'T REPORT ME!... NO! PLEASE!
DON'T GO TO THE AUTHORITIES... I... I... I'VE BEEN UNDER A LOT OF STRAIN LATELY... YOU DON'T UNDERSTAND...
OPEN
LATER...
DRING! DRING! DRING!
HELLO?... YES,... FRUBERT - WHAT IS IT?... WHERE ARE YOU?... IT'S GONE EIGHT O'CLOCK. I'VE BEEN WORRIED SICK.
ERM... YES. SORRY ABOUT THAT, DEAR, ONLY SOMETHING'S COME UP AT WORK AND I'M GOING TO BE A LITTLE LATE GETTING HOME.
WHAT IS IT, FRUBERT?
OH... IT'S SOMETHING AND NOTHING, DEAR. DON'T TROUBLE YOURSELF. I'M SURE IT WILL SORT ITSELF OUT...
NONCE
BAKERS
CASTRATE THE SEX BEAST
KILL THE PERV
PRESS
POLICE
DO NOT CROSS
POLICE LINE

GILBERT RATCHET
I'D LOVE A BAG OF CHIPS
FISH 'n' C
CHIPS PEAS BURGERS ETC
BUT AS MY "AUTOMATIC SKINTNESS DEMONSTRATOR" SHOWS, I HAVEN'T GOT ANY MONEY.
TELL YOU WHAT, GILBERT. BUSINESS HAS BEEN ROTTEN LATELY.
JOE'S CHIPPY
FISH 'n' CHIPS
IF YOU CAN DRUM UP SOME CUSTOMERS FOR ME, I'LL GIVE YOU A FREE PORTION OF CHIPS
BROWN'S
HM. THAT LADY LOOKS LIKE SHE COULD PUT AWAY A CHIP OR TWO
BUT HOW DO WE PERSUADE HER THAT SHE'S FEELING PECKISH?
I KNOW!
I'LL INVENT A DEVICE THAT WILL MAKE HER FEEL MISERABLE. THEN SHE'LL WANT TO "COMFORT-EAT" LOADS OF JUNK FOOD IN ORDER TO CHEER HERSELF UP.
THERE. MY "AUDIOSHIT-O-MATIC" WILL FOLLOW HER AROUND AND CONTINUOUSLY BROADCAST A TAPE-RECORDING OF NIGEL REES'S RADIO 4 QUIZ PROGRAMME "QUOTE, UNQUOTE"
IF THIS DOESN'T SEND HER INTO A BINGE-EATING DEPRESSION, I DON'T KNOW WHAT WILL
IT'S WORKING! HER SPIRITS ARE VISIBLY DROPPING
RUTH, CAN YOU TELL ME THE ORIGIN OF THE PHRASE "LIFE'S RICH TAPESTRY"?
HM. SOUNDS LIKE IT COULD BE SHAKESPEAREAN, NIGEL...
SHE'LL SOON TURN TO YOUR CHIP SHOP IN A FUTILE ATTEMPT TO PERK HERSELF UP
OH MY!
...NOW I ASKED THE PANEL TO BRING ALONG THEIR FAVOURITE QUOTES ABOUT WASPS...
SHE'S TURNED TO THE NOOSE, IN A WHOLLY SUCCESSFUL ATTEMPT TO PERK HERSELF DOWN, INSTEAD.
I HARDLY THINK THAT LADY'S CORPSE HANGING OUTSIDE MY SHOP IS GOING TO GET THE CUSTOMERS FLOCKING IN
GET RID OF IT, GILBERT, AND THEN PISS OFF!
THEN
EXCUSE ME, SON
MAY I BORROW THAT CONTRAPTION OFF YOU?
I OWN A HARDWARE SHOP, AND I CAN EARN A FORTUNE SELLING LENGTHS OF ROPE TO "QUOTE, UNQUOTE" LISTENERS WANTING TO END THEIR MISERY
ROPES £5
HARDWARE
KITCHEN GOODS
ELECTRICAL ITEMS
SO, PERHAPS YOU CAN TELL US WHEN AND WHERE THE EXPRESSION "A PLAGUE ON BOTH YOUR HOUSES" WAS FIRST USED
THAT SHOPKEEPER GAVE ME A SMASHING NEW DEEP-FAT FRYER AS A REWARD
ACME DEEP FAT FRYER
NOW I CAN MAKE MY OWN CHIPS AT HOME
BUT OH NO! DUE TO A FACTORY ERROR, I'VE BEEN GIVEN A "DEEP FAT FRIAR" INSTEAD.
ACME DEEP FAT FRYER
IF BY ETERNITY IS UNDERSTOOD NOT ENDLESS TEMPORAL DURATION BUT TIMELESSNESS, THEN HE LIVES ETERNALLY WHO LIVES IN THE PRESENT.

MAJOR MISUNDERSTANDING
GETCHER ORANGES. THREE FORRA POUND.
OUTSPAN
FINE SPUDS
M&S
GET OFF THE STREETS! THERE'S A MAN-EATING TIGER ESCAPED FROM THE ZOO!
ZOO
CHRIST!
DIDN'T YOU HEAR WHAT HE SAID? THERE'S A DANGEROUS TIGER LOOSE!
WE'D BETTER GET OFF THE STREETS, MATE.
THERE'S NO POINT TELLING ME IN KILOS. I DON'T UNDERSTAND ANY OF IT, AND NEITHER DO I WANT TO.
ALL MY LIFE I HAVE BOUGHT FRUIT AND VEGETABLES WEIGHED IN POUNDS AND OUNCES. AND I INTEND TO CONTINUE DOING SO.
YES, AND I'LL BUY MY BEER IN PINTS, TOO. PINTS, MARK YOU.
NOT LITRES, OR KILOMETRES, OR WHATEVER IT IS THAT THE BRUSSELS MANDARINS DICTATE.
I SUPPOSE YOU WON'T ACCEPT BRITISH BANKNOTES, EITHER.
I SUPPOSE YOU WANT ME TO PAY YOU IN "EUROS" WHICH HAVE GOT A PICTURE OF THE EIFFEL BLOODY TOWER ON THEM.
WELL I WISH TO BUY A POUND OF CARROTS, AND PAY FOR THEM WITH COINS OF HER MAJESTY QUEEN ELIZABETH'S REALM
AND IF THATS AGAINST YOUR PRECIOUS EUROPEAN LAW, THEN YOU'D BETTER HAVE ME ARRESTED.
GO AHEAD AND FETCH A POLICEMAN.
I'M NOT AFRAID TO STAND MY GROUND

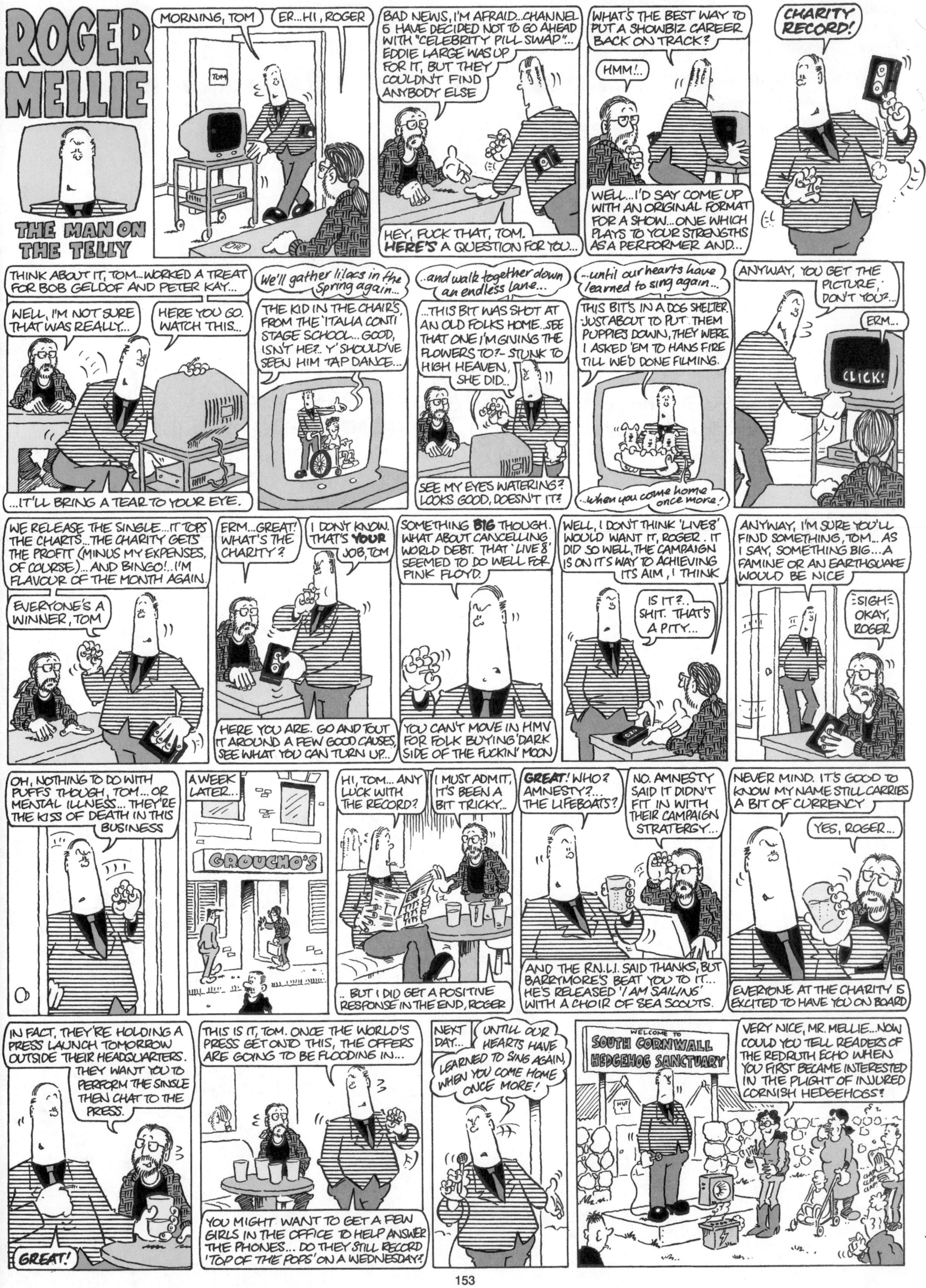
ROGER MELLIE
THE MAN ON THE TELLY
MORNING, TOM
ER...HI, ROGER
BAD NEWS, I'M AFRAID...CHANNEL 6 HAVE DECIDED NOT TO GO AHEAD WITH "CELEBRITY PILL SWAP"... EDDIE LARGE WAS UP FOR IT, BUT THEY COULDN'T FIND ANYBODY ELSE
HEY, FUCK THAT, TOM. HERE'S A QUESTION FOR YOU...
WHAT'S THE BEST WAY TO PUT A SHOWBIZ CAREER BACK ON TRACK?
HMM!..
WELL...I'D SAY COME UP WITH AN ORIGINAL FORMAT FOR A SHOW...ONE WHICH PLAYS TO YOUR STRENGTHS AS A PERFORMER AND...
CHARITY RECORD!
THINK ABOUT IT, TOM...WORKED A TREAT FOR BOB GELDOF AND PETER KAY...
WELL, I'M NOT SURE THAT WAS REALLY...
HERE YOU GO. WATCH THIS...
...IT'LL BRING A TEAR TO YOUR EYE.
We'll gather lilacs in the Spring again...
THE KID IN THE CHAIR'S FROM THE 'ITALIA CONTI' STAGE SCHOOL...GOOD, ISN'T HE?.. Y' SHOULD'VE SEEN HIM TAP DANCE...
...and walk together down an endless lane...
...THIS BIT WAS SHOT AT AN OLD FOLKS HOME...SEE THAT ONE I'M GIVING THE FLOWERS TO?- STUNK TO HIGH HEAVEN, SHE DID..
SEE MY EYES WATERING? LOOKS GOOD, DOESN'T IT?
...until our hearts have learned to sing again...
THIS BIT'S IN A DOG SHELTER. JUST ABOUT TO PUT THEM PUPPIES DOWN, THEY WERE. I ASKED 'EM TO HANG FIRE TILL WE'D DONE FILMING.
...when you come home once more!
ANYWAY, YOU GET THE PICTURE, DON'T YOU?..
ERM...
CLICK!
WE RELEASE THE SINGLE...IT TOPS THE CHARTS...THE CHARITY GETS THE PROFIT (MINUS MY EXPENSES, OF COURSE)...AND BINGO!..I'M FLAVOUR OF THE MONTH AGAIN.
EVERYONE'S A WINNER, TOM
ERM...GREAT! WHAT'S THE CHARITY?
I DON'T KNOW. THAT'S YOUR JOB, TOM
HERE YOU ARE. GO AND TOUT IT AROUND A FEW GOOD CAUSES, SEE WHAT YOU CAN TURN UP...
SOMETHING BIG THOUGH. WHAT ABOUT CANCELLING WORLD DEBT. THAT 'LIVE 8' SEEMED TO DO WELL FOR PINK FLOYD.
YOU CAN'T MOVE IN HMV FOR FOLK BUYING 'DARK SIDE OF THE FUCKIN' MOON
WELL, I DON'T THINK 'LIVE 8' WOULD WANT IT, ROGER. IT DID SO WELL, THE CAMPAIGN IS ON IT'S WAY TO ACHIEVING ITS AIM, I THINK
IS IT?.. SHIT. THAT'S A PITY...
ANYWAY, I'M SURE YOU'LL FIND SOMETHING, TOM...AS I SAY, SOMETHING BIG...A FAMINE OR AN EARTHQUAKE WOULD BE NICE
SIGH OKAY, ROGER
OH, NOTHING TO DO WITH PUFFS THOUGH, TOM...OR MENTAL ILLNESS...THEY'RE THE KISS OF DEATH IN THIS BUSINESS
A WEEK LATER...
GROUCHO'S
HI, TOM...ANY LUCK WITH THE RECORD?
I MUST ADMIT, IT'S BEEN A BIT TRICKY...
.. BUT I DID GET A POSITIVE RESPONSE IN THE END, ROGER
GREAT! WHO? AMNESTY?... THE LIFEBOATS?
NO. AMNESTY SAID IT DIDN'T FIT IN WITH THEIR CAMPAIGN STRATERGY...
AND THE R.N.L.I. SAID THANKS, BUT BARRYMORE'S BEAT YOU TO IT... HE'S RELEASED 'I AM SAILING' WITH A CHOIR OF SEA SCOUTS.
NEVER MIND. IT'S GOOD TO KNOW MY NAME STILL CARRIES A BIT OF CURRENCY
YES, ROGER...
EVERYONE AT THE CHARITY IS EXCITED TO HAVE YOU ON BOARD
IN FACT, THEY'RE HOLDING A PRESS LAUNCH TOMORROW OUTSIDE THEIR HEADQUARTERS. THEY WANT YOU TO PERFORM THE SINGLE THEN CHAT TO THE PRESS.
GREAT!
THIS IS IT, TOM. ONCE THE WORLD'S PRESS GET ONTO THIS, THE OFFERS ARE GOING TO BE FLOODING IN...
YOU MIGHT WANT TO GET A FEW GIRLS IN THE OFFICE TO HELP ANSWER THE PHONES... DO THEY STILL RECORD 'TOP OF THE POPS' ON A WEDNESDAY?
NEXT DAY...
UNTIL OUR HEARTS HAVE LEARNED TO SING AGAIN, WHEN YOU COME HOME ONCE MORE!
WELCOME TO SOUTH CORNWALL HEDGEHOG SANCTUARY
VERY NICE, MR. MELLIE...NOW COULD YOU TELL READERS OF THE REDRUTH ECHO WHEN YOU FIRST BECAME INTERESTED IN THE PLIGHT OF INJURED CORNISH HEDGEHOGS?
CLAP CLAP

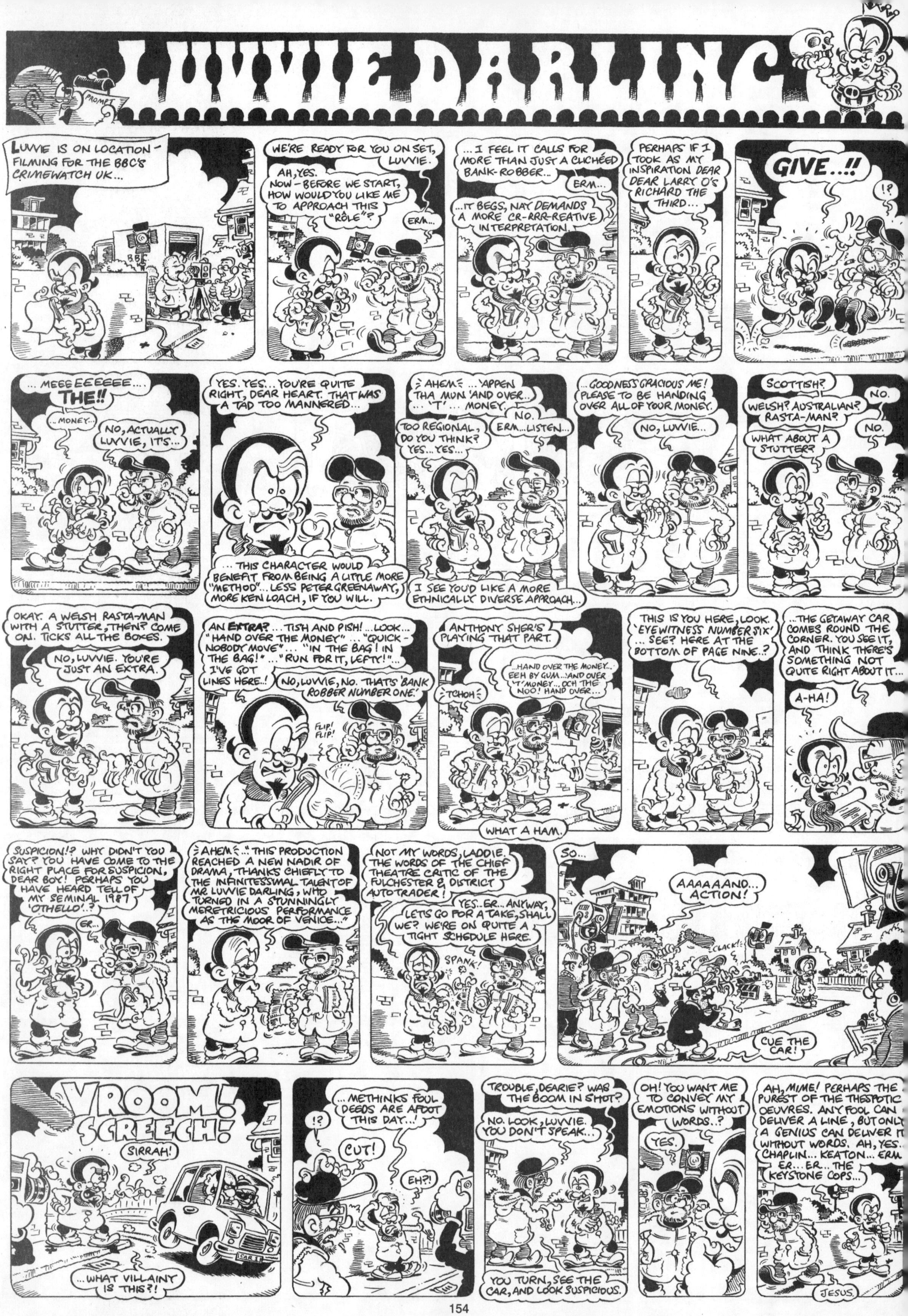
LUVVIE DARLING
PROMPT
LUVVIE IS ON LOCATION - FILMING FOR THE BBC'S CRIMEWATCH UK...
BBC
WE'RE READY FOR YOU ON SET, LUVVIE.
AH, YES. NOW - BEFORE WE START, HOW WOULD YOU LIKE ME TO APPROACH THIS "RÔLE"?
ERM...
...I FEEL IT CALLS FOR MORE THAN JUST A CLICHÉED BANK-ROBBER...
ERM...
...IT BEGS, NAY DEMANDS A MORE CR-RRR-REATIVE INTERPRETATION.
PERHAPS IF I TOOK AS MY INSPIRATION DEAR DEAR LARRY O'S RICHARD THE THIRD...
GIVE...!!
!?
...MEEEEEEEE.... THE!!
...MONEY...
NO, ACTUALLY LUVVIE, IT'S...
YES. YES... YOU'RE QUITE RIGHT, DEAR HEART. THAT WAS A TAD TOO MANNERED...
...THIS CHARACTER WOULD BENEFIT FROM BEING A LITTLE MORE "METHOD"... LESS PETER GREENAWAY, MORE KEN LOACH, IF YOU WILL.
AHEM ...'APPEN THA MUN 'AND OVER... ...'T'... MONEY.
NO.
TOO REGIONAL, DO YOU THINK? YES... YES...
ERM... LISTEN...
I SEE YOU'D LIKE A MORE ETHNICALLY DIVERSE APPROACH...
...GOODNESS GRACIOUS ME! PLEASE TO BE HANDING OVER ALL OF YOUR MONEY.
NO, LUVVIE...
SCOTTISH?
NO.
WELSH? AUSTRALIAN? RASTA-MAN?
NO.
WHAT ABOUT A STUTTER?
OKAY. A WELSH RASTA-MAN WITH A STUTTER, THEN? COME ON. TICKS ALL THE BOXES.
NO, LUVVIE. YOU'RE JUST AN EXTRA.
AN EXTRA?... TISH AND PISH!... LOOK... "HAND OVER THE MONEY"... "QUICK - NOBODY MOVE"... "IN THE BAG! IN THE BAG!"... "RUN FOR IT, LEFTY!"... I'VE GOT LINES HERE..!
NO, LUVVIE, NO. THAT'S 'BANK ROBBER NUMBER ONE.'
FLIP! FLIP!
ANTHONY SHER'S PLAYING THAT PART.
...HAND OVER THE MONEY... EEH BY GUM... AND OVER 'T' MONEY... OCH THE NOO! HAND OVER...
TCHOH
WHAT A HAM.
THIS IS YOU HERE, LOOK. 'EYEWITNESS NUMBER SIX' ... SEE? HERE AT THE BOTTOM OF PAGE NINE..?
...THE GETAWAY CAR COMES ROUND THE CORNER. YOU SEE IT, AND THINK THERE'S SOMETHING NOT QUITE RIGHT ABOUT IT...
A-HA!
SUSPICION!? WHY DIDN'T YOU SAY? YOU HAVE COME TO THE RIGHT PLACE FOR SUSPICION, DEAR BOY! PERHAPS YOU HAVE HEARD TELL OF MY SEMINAL 1987 'OTHELLO'..?
ER...
AHEM ..."THIS PRODUCTION REACHED A NEW NADIR OF DRAMA, THANKS CHIEFLY TO THE INFINITESSIMAL TALENT OF MR. LUVVIE DARLING, WHO TURNED IN A STUNNINGLY MERETRICIOUS PERFORMANCE AS THE MOOR OF VENICE..."
NOT MY WORDS, LADDIE. THE WORDS OF THE CHIEF THEATRE CRITIC OF THE FULCHESTER & DISTRICT AUTOTRADER!
YES.. ER... ANYWAY, LET'S GO FOR A TAKE, SHALL WE? WE'RE ON QUITE A TIGHT SCHEDULE HERE.
SPANK!
SO...
AAAAAAND... ACTION!
CLACK!
CUE THE CAR!
VROOM! SCREECH!
SIRRAH!
...WHAT VILLAINY IS THIS?!
...METHINKS FOUL DEEDS ARE AFOOT THIS DAY...!
!?
CUT!
EH?!
TROUBLE, DEARIE? WAS THE BOOM IN SHOT?
NO. LOOK, LUVVIE. YOU DON'T SPEAK...
YOU TURN, SEE THE CAR, AND LOOK SUSPICIOUS.
OH! YOU WANT ME TO CONVEY MY EMOTIONS WITHOUT WORDS..?
YES.
AH, MIME! PERHAPS THE PUREST OF THE THESPOTIC OEUVRES. ANY FOOL CAN DELIVER A LINE, BUT ONLY A GENIUS CAN DELIVER IT WITHOUT WORDS. AH, YES. CHAPLIN... KEATON... ERM. ER... ER... THE KEYSTONE COPS...
JESUS.

SCENE SEVEN... TAKE TWO... ...AND... ACTION!
CUE THE GETAWAY CAR!
VROOM! SCREECH!
OH, FOR CHRIST'S SAKE.. ...CUT!
DON'T TELL ME, LOVE. A HAIR IN THE GATE?
NO, LUVVIE. IT'S... IT'S... IT'S YOU. WHAT WAS ALL THAT ABOUT?
IT WAS SUSPICION.... ...PORTRAYED AS A METAPHOR.
COME AGAIN.
YOU SEE, WHEN I SAW THE CAR I WAS TRAPPED IN THE GLASS BOX OF SUSPICION, ONLY TO BREAK OUT AND IMMEDIATELY BE BUFFETED BY THE STRONG WINDS OF ... ER... ERM...
SUSPICION?
THAT'S IT. SUSPICION.
LOOK- THIS IS THE FINAL SHOT AND THE LIGHT'S GOING. THAT CAR'S GOING TO COME ROUND THE CORNER ONE LAST TIME, SO FURROW YOUR BROW... SCRATCH YOUR CHIN... THEN WE CAN ALL FUCK OFF HOME - ALRIGHT?
OKAY... LAST TAKE... AND... ACTION!!
VROOM! SCREECH!
.. CUT! PERFECT. IT'S A WRAP.
ERM... I THINK I RATHER FLUFFED IT THERE, DEAR HEART. SCRATCHED THE BROW AND FURROWED THE OLD CHIN...
IT WAS FINE, LUVVIE.
ONE FOR OLD DENNY-DEN NORDENNY-WORDENNY TO HAVE A CHUCKLE AT, I EXPECT!
NO, IT WAS OKAY, LUVVIE. IT'LL DO.
OH, DEAR ME. NO, NO, NO AND THRICE NO! THERE'S AN OLD THEATRICAL EXPRESSION... "IT'LL DO... WILL NOT DO!"
WE'LL GO FOR IT AGAIN.
IF YOU CAN JUST GIVE ME A FEW MINUTES TO GET MYSELF FULLY INTO...
SLAM!
FLAP FLAP FLAP
B-B-BRUMMMM!
...CHARACTER.
B.B.C.
OI! COME BACK! WHAT ABOUT MY LIFT HOME!? I HAVEN'T EVEN GOT ENOUGH FOR MY BUS FARE!
THE FOLLOWING WEDNESDAY...
... NOW CAST YOUR MIND BACK TO JANUARY 10th. WERE YOU ANYWHERE NEAR FULCHESTER HIGH STREET AROUND ABOUT 1 pm..?
THIS IS IT, DEAR! WATCH!
... BECAUSE IF YOU WERE, YOU MAY HAVE INFORMATION THAT COULD BRING TWO VIOLENT BANK ROBBERS TO JUSTICE...
I'M ON AFTER THIS BIT.
..H-HEE-HER-H-HAND OVER THE M-MEE-MER-M-MONEY, LOOK YOU BACH, AN' T-TEE-TER-T-TING...
TSK! HE'S SUCH A HACK.
BANG! DINGALINGALING! VROOM!
IT'S COMING UP NOW! GET READY!
VROOM! SCREECH!
THIS IS ME!
THIS IS ME!
THIS IS MY BIT!
THERE!
WHAT DID YOU THINK, DEAR?
WELL... IT WAS...
BE BRUTAL! BE BRUTAL! BECAUSE GOD KNOWS, THE BROADSHEET SCRIBES WILL TAKE NO PRISONERS IN THE MORNING!
IT WAS WONDERFUL, LUVVIE! YOU WERE A TRIUMPH!!
THANK-YOU, THANK-YOU... SNIFF! ...I GAVE THAT RÔLE MY HEART, MY SOUL, MY EVERYTHING. MY MUSE IS SPENT.
OOH, LOOK LUVVIE! YOU'RE ON AGAIN!
WHAT!?
... AND BARNTONSHIRE POLICE WOULD LIKE TO SPEAK TO THIS MAN, WHO WAS CAUGHT ON CCTV PERFORMING AN ACT OF GROSS INDECENCY IN THE GENTLEMEN'S LAVATORY AT FULCHESTER BUS STATION LAST MONDAY...
... IF YOU THINK YOU CAN IDENTIFY HIM, PLEASE CALL THE INCIDENT DESK.
... SO PLEASE - DON'T HAVE NIGHTMARES. DO SLEEP WELL.

UNLUCKY FRANK
OH NO! I'VE JUST FOUND OUT FROM THE DOCTOR THAT I AM ACTUALLY A WOMAN WHO WAS BORN INTO A MAN'S BODY!
HOW UNLUCKY CAN I GET?
SHORTLY
WELL THAT COST A FORTUNE, BUT I DO FEEL BETTER IN MYSELF
GENDER REALIGNMENT SURGEON
FROM NOW ON, I WANT TO BE CALLED 'UNLUCKY FRANCESCA'.
PARDON ME, MISS. MY EMPLOYER IS A BIG NAME IN THE ENTERTAINMENT INDUSTRY AND WANTS TO GO OUT ON A DATE WITH YOU.
DRIVER
HEY WOW! PERHAPS MY LUCK HAS CHANGED
BUT
PHIL SPECTOR
DRAT.
DEAD
NOT AGAIN.

Professor Piehead
OKAY JOE. ALL READY TO TEST MY NEW INVENTION - A JUSTIN LEE COLLINS - PROOF TV SET!
RIGHT. LET'S SWITCH IT ON AND SEE IF IT STOPS THE UNFUNNY ARSEHOLE'S FAT FACE APPEARING ON THE SCREEN...
CLICK!
HMM...
ANOTHER PARTIAL SUCCESS.

BIFFA BACON
ONE DAY..
HOO, BIFFA!.. WOT THE FUCK 'AVE Y' DONE T'ME FRIGGIN' GARDEN
EH!?
WHERE'S THE BORNT OOT WASHA... AN' THE KNACKAD FRIDGE... AN' THE MATRASS?
ER...
Y'VE TORNED IT INTO A FUCKIN' PUFF'S GARDEN
LOOK AT YER... GROWIN' FLOOAHS LIKE A BIG FUCKIN' HEEMASEX
THESE ISN'T FLOOAHS, FATHA, MAN... THESE IS AALL FUCKIN' VEG!
BEANS...PEAS...SPUDS... FUCKIN' COLLIES...CARRATS
CARRATS!
Y'DINVEN'T WANT T' GRUB CARRATS, SON... THEY'RE BAD F'YER TEETH!
BAD F'YER TEETH!?!
GAN AN' SHITE!
IT'S TRUE, SON. LOOK
FUCK!
SMACK!
OH, AN' I THINK THEY'RE BA F'YER BAALLS AN' AALL, SO

ANNE WIDDECOMBE and her HIGH CHURCH MICE
IT'S ELEVEN O'CLOCK
TIME FOR MORNING SERVICE IN MY PORTABLE MOUSE CHURCH.
HANG ON – WHAT'S THIS BEHIND THE FONT?
DRUGS
EMPTY
A GREAT BIG BAG OF DRUGS ~ AND IT'S EMPTY!
MY MOUSE PARISHONERS HAVE CONSUMED THE ENTIRE STASH...
THESE MICE ARE UNBELIEVABLY HIGH!
I'VE NEVER SEEN MY MOUSE CONGREGATION AS BAKED AS THIS. THEY'RE TOTALLY ZONED OUT.
PARK
I'LL TAKE THEM FOR A GENTLE STROLL IN THE PARK WHERE THEY CAN JUST CHILL AND FIND THEIR NEUTRAL SPACE.
AH, ANNE. THE VERY PERSON I WANTED TO SEE.
GOOD MORNING, BISHOP.
I WONDER IF YOUR MOUSE CHURCH WOULD ASSIST ME?
A GUST OF WIND HAS BLOWN MY BISHOP'S HAT INTO THE BRANCHES OF THIS TREE.
PERHAPS YOUR RODENT CHURCHGOERS COULD SCAMPER UP THERE AND FETCH IT DOWN FOR ME
SORRY BISHOP, NO CAN DO. THESE MICE ARE RIPPED TO THE FUCKING TITS ON DRUGS.
WELL, REALLY!
THEY COULDN'T GET THEIR SHIT TOGETHER TO GO TO THE SHOP FOR A PACKET OF RIZLAS, LET ALONE RETRIEVE SOME FREAKY-LOOKING HAT FROM UP A TREE.
OH NO! HERE COMES A COPPER ~ WE'D BETTER SCARPER
IF MY MOUSE PARISHONERS GET BUSTED BY THE PIGS, IT WOULD REALLY BUM THEIR TRIP.
QUICKLY MICE, FLUSH YOUR GEAR DOWN THE VESTRY TOILET ~ IT'S A RAID!
CHIP CHIP
PARK SCULPTOR
ATLAS HOLDING UP THE WORLD WITH ONE FINGER
TRUNDLE
YOW!
CHOP
I'VE BEEN JABBED IN THE ARSE BY A PASSING STEEPLE!
MY MOUSE CHURCH!
CRUNCH
HO HO! LOOKS LIKE ANNE'S MICE ARE REALLY "STONED" NOW...
ALL SQURSHED
...IN THE SENSE THAT THEY'VE BEEN CRUSHED TO DEATH BY A LARGE PIECE OF STONE.
BAH!

7x8 Crisis Deepens

THE GOVERNMENT is preparing to make sweeping changes to the national mathematics curriculum after a poll revealed that 75% of the country think that seven eights are 62.

by our 8x Times Table Correspondent
Octavia McTable

Within hours of the report's publication, commissioned by the University of Leicester's Ignorance Department, cross-party pressure was growing for swift action to reflect public concerns on the issue.

The government was quick to respond to the poll's findings. "If a sufficient number of people strongly believe that seven eights are 62, then we must ensure their views are represented in our schools," said Thunderbird-faced Education Secretary Ruth Kelly last night. "It's not enough to teach from the top down, we need to listen to what the public wants from education, and deliver appropriately."

In a draft syllabus presented to reporters on the back of a Palace Of Westminster Speedo Pizza leaflet, Kelly showed how 75% of the school year could in future be spent teaching that seven eights are 62, while remaining lessons might reflect the scientific establishment's consensus of 56. A special two-week course unit would cover minority views such as nine and a million.

This isn't the first time that the eight times table has come under fire recently. The poll follows President Bush's controversial remarks last week that "the jury is out on 7x8."

"There's no proof there's an eight times table," said little Bush. "If a eight times table had ever existed, they'd have dug one up by now."

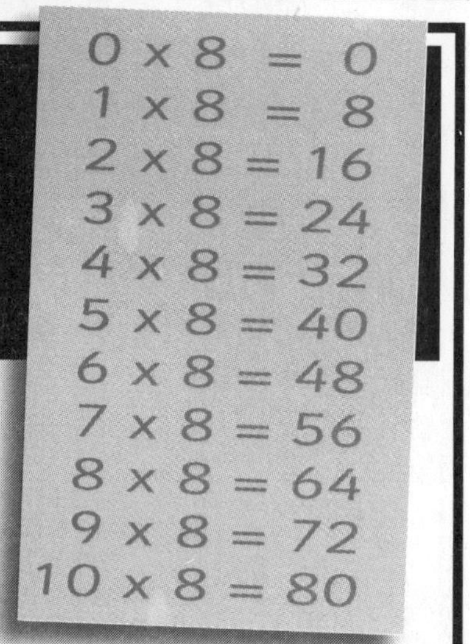
0 x 8 = 0
1 x 8 = 8
2 x 8 = 16
3 x 8 = 24
4 x 8 = 32
5 x 8 = 40
6 x 8 = 48
7 x 8 = 56
8 x 8 = 64
9 x 8 = 72
10 x 8 = 80

(left) ***Ruth Kelly:*** *face like Virgil out of Thunderbird 2, and (above)* ***8:*** *the times table at the centre of the storm, yesterday*

Pressure is mounting from pro-mathematics groups for the government to mount a hasty defence of the popular table. "This is a very disturbing finding," said Derren Goodenough from 7x8.com. "Clearly the Department of Education needs to do more to support the eight times table."

However, in a statement issued last night, a spokesman restated the government's position, insisting that it was "committed to delivering best practice in improving accessibility standards for customers of the eight times table" or something.

SPOILT BASTARD
...AND FLINTOFF RUNS UP... ROUND THE WICKET... THE BALL PITCHES ON MIDDLE OFF AND PONTING STEPS FORWARD...
CLACK!
...JUST NUDGES IT FORWARD THERE... NO RUN SO AUSTRALIA REMAIN 42 FOR NO WICKET...
TIMMY!...
I'M WATCHING THIS
...AS A BUS MAKES ITS WAY... IT'S MAJESTIC WAY... UP TO THE TRAFFIC LIGHTS ON RADCLIFFE ROAD... AN OMINOUS CLOUD THERE...
TIMMY, DARLING... GUESS WHAT MUMMY'S GOT
SAGGY LILS AND BAD BREATH
NO, MY POPPET... I'VE GOT YOU...
...THIS! A FOOTBALL SIGNED BY THE ENGLAND SQUAD
WOW! THAT'S JUST WHAT I WANTED!
OH, WONDERFUL... LOOK, IT'S GOT MICHAEL OWEN AND DAVID BECKHAM AND...
AND...
RIGHT, I'M IN... YOU'RE BOWLING, WOMAN, AND I'M GOING TO KNOCK YOU FOR SIX
OKAY, TIMMY, HERE WE GO!
SWOOSH!
TOSS
TONK!
NO BALL! THAT'S ONE RUN TO ME.
BOWL AGAIN
SWISH!
TONK!
ANOTHER NO BALL! ANOTHER RUN TO ME! GOD, YOU'RE USELESS
WHOOPS! BUTTER-FINGERS!
HA! YOU CAN'T CATCH FOR TOFFEE... AND IT'S IN THE NETTLES... AND IN THE NETTLES IS SIX!
ANOTHER HOUR LATER...
GOSH, TIMMY... I'M SO TIRED. DO YOU THINK WE COULD...
TONK!
NO BALL!
ANOTHER RUN TO ME
RIGHT! THAT'S 300 RUNS TO ME, NOT OUT. I'M GOING TO DECLARE. MY TURN TO BOWL, WOMAN...
RIGHT, MY LOVE
...BUT I WARN YOU, I'M A FAST BOWLER AND I'M NOT GOING TO GO EASY ON YOU JUST BECAUSE YOU'RE OLD.
FLICK!
TRUNDLE! TRUNDLE!
TONK!
YES! YOU HIT IT IN THE NETTLES! YOU'RE OUT!
OUT?.. BUT I THOUGHT IN THE NETTLES WAS SIX
NO! IT'S OUT!... AND DON'T YOU DARE QUESTION THE UMPIRE AGAIN, OR YOU'RE DOUBLE OUT!
HONESTLY, YOUR SPORTSMANSHIP IS DREADFUL... JUST GET THE BALL!
OUCH! OOOH! OUCH!
SO...
PUFF!.. PANT!..
...IF I CAN ...JUST...
HURRY UP... WE'RE LOSING THE LIGHT.
...NEARLY... OOF!... IN...
GASP!
THUNK!!
FLASH! FLASH!
WEEE-OOO! WEEE-OOO! WEEE-OOO! WEEE-OOO! WEEE-OOO! WEEE-OOO!
WEEE-OOO! WEEE-OOO! WEEE-OOO! WEEE-OOO! WEEE-OOO! WEEE-OOO!
TUT!
2 HOURS LATER...
POLICE